The International Library of Sociology

THE MENDE OF SIERRA LEONE

Founded by KARL MANNHEIM

The International Library of Sociology

THE SOCIOLOGY OF DEVELOPMENT
In 18 Volumes

I	Caste and Kinship in Central India	*Mayer*
II	Economics of Development in Village India	*Haswell*
III	Education and Social Change in Ghana	*Foster*
	(The above title is not available through Routledge in North America)	
IV	Growing up in an Egyptian Village	*Ammar*
V	India's Changing Villages	*Dube*
VI	Indian Village	*Dube*
VII	Malay Fishermen	*Firth*
VIII	The Mende of Sierra Leone	*Little*
IX	The Negro Family in British Guiana	*Smith*
X	Peasants in the Pacific	*Mayer*
XI	Population and Society in the Arab East	*Baer*
XII	The Revolution in Anthropology	*Jarvie*
XIII	Settlement Schemes in Tropical Africa	*Chambers*
XIV	Shivapur: A South Indian Village	*Ishwaran*
XV	Social Control in an African Society	*Gulliver*
XVI	State and Economics in the Middle East	*Bonne*
XVII	Tradition and Economy in Village India	*Ishwaran*
XVIII	Transformation Scene	*Hogbin*

THE MENDE OF SIERRA LEONE

West African People in Transition

by
KENNETH LITTLE

First published in 1951
by Routledge

Reprinted in 1998, 2000, 2002
by Routledge
2 Park Square, Milton Park, Abingdon, Oxon, OX14 4RN
or
270 Madison Avenue, New York, NY 10016

First issued in paperback 2010

Routledge is an imprint of the Taylor & Francis Group

© 1967 Kenneth Little

All rights reserved. No part of this book may be reprinted or reproduced
or utilized in any form or by any electronic, mechanical, or other means,
now known or hereafter invented, including photocopying
and recording, or in any information storage or retrieval system, without
permission in writing from the publishers.

The publishers have made every effort to contact authors/copyright holders
of the works reprinted in *The International Library of Sociology*.
This has not been possible in every case, however, and we would
welcome correspondence from those individuals/companies
we have been unable to trace.

British Library Cataloguing in Publication Data
A CIP catalogue record for this book
is available from the British Library

The Mende of Sierra Leone
ISBN 978-0-415-17575-3 (hbk)
ISBN 978-0-415-60550-2 (pbk)
The Sociology of Development: 18 Volumes
ISBN 978-0-415-17822-8
The International Library of Sociology: 274 Volumes
ISBN 978-0-415-17838-9

Publisher's Note
The publisher has gone to great lengths to ensure the quality
of this reprint but points out that some imperfections
in the original may be apparent

PREFACE

By Raymond Firth

PEOPLE in Britain know very little about people in West Africa. Yet now that one West African colony, the Gold Coast, is well set on the road to self-government and others may follow, it behoves the outside world to pay more attention to what manner of men they are who live there. This book about the Mende helps to fill a need. For, backward as Sierra Leone may have been since the philanthropic impulses which established Freetown as a home for liberated slaves in the early nineteenth century spent themselves, its people are sharing in the social and political awakening of West Africa. The Mende of the Sierra Leone Protectorate are a numerous and proud people, likely to make themselves felt with increasing force in the affairs of the region. The fact, too, that they share a common culture with their neighbours across the Liberian border may come to be of significance if their group consciousness should take the form of a political nationalism.

This book does not really need a preface. Dr. Little is no novice who has to have an introduction to his public. Already he is the Head of a University Department of Anthropology, and is widely known as the author of an important and authoritative work, *Negroes in Britain*, based largely on his own field study of the coloured community in Cardiff nearly ten years ago. He has asked me to write these few opening words here, I take it, mainly as a gesture of friendship—especially recalling, perhaps, that for a few days I shared with him his field experiences in the heart of Mendeland. There I was witness to his amicable relations with the people, to his wide knowledge of their affairs, and to the enthusiasm and care with which he was collecting his data. Under his guidance I visited chiefs' compounds, mosques, mission schools, administrators' offices and traders' stores. I saw African soap being made

PREFACE

from palm oil and wood ash, and marvelled at the virtues of cleansing clothes and giving smoothness to the skin said to be possessed by the resulting black round balls. Doubtless a psychoanalyst could explain how soap even in this guise can stimulate lyrical advertisement! He also showed me men weaving on the narrow loom, making strips of cotton fabric no more than six inches wide, and helped me to bargain for some of the Mende 'country cloth'. I took down samples of the curious Vai script, and tested its value for communication. I was taken inside Mende households, and was shown from the outside a round Njayei cult building, with its speckling of red and blue dots on a white wall. As we went round together on foot and by motor-lorry on this ethnographic Cook's tour, I was given a glimpse beneath the surface into current social and economic problems: attempts to prevent soil erosion in upland agriculture; improvement of methods of tax collection; the burden of peasant indebtedness to the Syrian trader; rôle of girl's initiation rites; promotion of Mende literacy; relations between Muslim, Christian and Pagan; efficiency of administration in the chiefdoms. But in particular I could appreciate the magnitude and complexity of the field task that Dr. Little had set himself, and the success with which he was grappling with it.

Dr. Little had his headquarters for much of the time at Bo, the principal town of the Mende country. When Mr. Graham Greene set off for Liberia on his *Journey without Maps*, he stopped a night at Bo. In his account, he says he was happy there, despite the usual tough dry tasteless chicken of the rest-house, the lack of medical equipment and of any mosquito rods for his bed, the presence of a large cockroach in the bathroom, and of a 'native' standing and complaining about something outside all night with folded hands. In similar circumstances, an anthropologist would have taken less notice of the cockroach and more of the 'native'. But Mr. Greene was happy because he had at last left behind something he distrusted—the Protectorate was different from the Colony of Sierra Leone, he felt; he was with the real African at last.

This is the feeling that many Europeans have. I had it too, as the little train got away from Freetown, and went up past places with attractive names, like Moyamba, Rotifunk, and Mano, before arriving at Bo. Partly, it was due to the mere leaving of a comparatively large town and seaport, with its numerous stores,

PREFACE

Government offices and busy traffic. Partly, it was the reduction in contrast. The unpaved badly eroded back streets and slums of Freetown in 1945 were a grim background to the complex administrative organization, the developed commercial atmosphere, and the urbane European life of the bungalows. In the Protectorate the difference of standards was much less, the contrast less glaring. Again, one was in the midst of an African tribal culture, with a coherence and a value system that, while more alien, tended to evoke that respect which one is always inclined to accord to what one believes to be an integrated way of life.

But the change to the Protectorate is not to be expressed simply as the discovery of the 'real African'. As Dr. Little shows in this book, between the Creole of the Colony and the Mende of the Protectorate there is friction, jealousy, suspicion, due in part to the competition for jobs and in part to clash over social status. But he shows also how far Creole and European standards have penetrated. Literacy rather than geographic origin is the main distinguishing social criterion. The literate Mende of the Protectorate is as close in many ways to the Colony Creole as he is to his non-literate local cousin. Moreover, there are many Creoles in the Protectorate. Yet all literate Mende and many Creoles have wives or kin who are not in the literate stratum and who are a vital link between the literates and the unlettered tribal society. The 'real African' nowadays is well aware of Western values. Superficially at least he has absorbed many of them. In the economic field his activities are ultimately geared to the Western market system, and politically he has a sensitivity—deeper than is often suspected—to changes that are taking place in relations between Africans and Europeans elsewhere.

For the anthropologist here is a society of West African Negro type with a strong consciousness of solidarity, but split into a large number of relatively small and variant political units. What are the indices of the society? What are chief modes of activity of its members? What are the forces in common action?

The analysis Dr. Little gives in this book and his answers to these and other questions are unpretentious. The author is not concerned to invent new terms, to finesse with precise definitions, or to try and put forward original theories of social action. His aim is to give a straightforward ethnographical account of Mende society in a fairly comprehensive way. No such account has previously been given. It is sometimes deplored that of recent years

PREFACE

the fashion in anthropology has been to write extensive monographs about a single institution or facet of culture and to ignore the claims for general ethnographic description of all the major aspects of the society in one volume. From this point of view Dr. Little has made a contribution to general African studies. He examines the traditional account of the shaping of Mende society and the outstanding part which warfare seems to have played in that process. He examines also the history of the Mende Rising against the imposition of house tax and the legacy which that has left in the Mende political system. (It has entered even into Mende art. I have an interesting memento of this, a series of water colours for school instruction painted by a headmaster and depicting in crude but vivid style the various stages in the Rising from the time the District Commissioner leaves the Chiefs' Council amid jeering and laughter while the warriors display their swords in defiance until the leaders of the rebellion meet their fate on the gallows and the District Commissioner receives payment of house tax in palm wine and other commodities. And then the epilogue: 'What we get in return for house tax'—schools, motor roads, dispensaries, letters by post, railways, and—perhaps with unconscious irony—'native administrations, district commissioners and court messengers'.)

The analysis goes on to deal with rice farming and with its social and religious implications as a major preoccupation of Mende life; with the principles of local grouping, kinship grouping and social stratification; with the system of authority; the rôle of women in social affairs; the general process of socialization of a Mende individual; the system of religious and magical beliefs and practices; the part played by Islam in modern Mende life; and the multiple functions of the secret societies.

In all this there is material of theoretical as well as ethnographic interest. Examination of the rôle of the *mawè* shows an extended family system in a projection of gross household type in which a core of agnatic kin is augmented by other cognatic and even affinal kin. All the members of this body in varying degree share in this management, especially in its farming operations. Here is a type of unit, primarily on a kinship basis, which can be set alongside analogous units among Central African and other peoples who do not confine themselves to using a unilineal principle in their corporate kin groups. That the structure of the kin group is a function of the social services the group performs is

PREFACE

an arguable proposition. But in such argument Dr. Little's material should be taken into consideration.

One asks how a set of chiefdoms with the major units independent and the chief as a purely secular figure lacking ritual sanctions could enter into effective co-operative action. This question is illuminated by the author's analysis of the rôle of the Poro society. It is shown how no person can hope to occupy a position of authority in the chiefdom without being a Poro member and receiving Poro support. Even nowadays the Poro seems to play an important rôle in the election of a chief. The primary function of the Poro is to equip every Mende man for his life as a member of the community. But because its net is so wide the society also has been able to serve as an important regulating force in Mende life and to provide social and ritual ties which cross the boundaries of chiefdoms for political functions.

These two examples are an indication of some of the important problems raised. Some years ago it was said by Dr. E. B. Worthington that research on African cultures as they are today in a state of transition was perhaps the most important need in African anthropological studies. This book is a definite contribution to such research.

RAYMOND FIRTH

AUTHOR'S NOTE

The material for this study of the Mende people was gathered 'in the field' during my stay in the then Sierra Leone Protectorate throughout 1945, and again in the latter half of 1946. My main aim in undertaking the investigation was to provide a general description of Mende culture, with particular regard to the changes which were coming about in Mende institutions. Respecting the latter, in an article published in 1955 I examined the role of the emergent educated class of Protectorate-born person and endeavoured to show how achieved forms of status were tending to multiply.[1] This, however, was before Independence and in the meantime even greater changes, sociological as well as technological, have come about in Mendeland. This second edition of my book does not take them into account, but records what I found twenty years ago.

The Mende, as I shall indicate in the text, form the largest single cultural group in Sierra Leone, and their culture is shared to a considerable extent by peoples living in a wide region around them. Despite this there was, when I wrote, no comprehensive study of Mende life. The only ethnographic material available was scattered in numerous periodicals and in a number of books by travellers and visitors to the area. A good deal of this was out of date by modern standards, though there were important exceptions. For example, Dr. S. Hofstra, who worked in Mendeland in the nineteen-thirties under the auspices of the International Institute of African Languages and Culture had written several papers of great value to the student.[2]

The nature of my own enquiries necessitated a good deal of travel in the country, although I spent quite a large part of the time at Bo. Bo was the administrative headquarters of the then Protectorate and (as it is now) the largest town in Mendeland,

[1] 'Structural Change in the Sierra Leone Protectorate', *Africa*, XXV, No. 3, 1955.
[2] See later citations and Bibliography.

AUTHOR'S NOTE

although 'cosmopolitan' by local standards. Methodologically, there were two sets of difficulties to overcome. At the start, I was regarded by the people, literate and non-literate alike, as an official of the Government. This had certain advantages in affording an easy perhaps too easy, access to notable members of Mende society. It also had a number of obvious disadvantages which were greatly accentuated by the circumstances of the recent war. It was only too clear that certain war-time measures, like the quota of rice required from every able-bodied male person in the Protectorate, had aroused a good deal of resentment against the 'Government' and its officials. There were complaints about the black market in foodstuffs and other commodities, and the 'Government' was alleged to be giving special favours to the European firms and Lebanese traders over the Africans. The prejudice arising out of these attitudes and complaints had to be obviated, as well as the more conventional difficulties, with which every field worker is confronted, of establishing *rapport*.

Most, if not all, non-literate people are suspicious of the European outsider, and the Mende are certainly no exception to the rule. In the present case, perhaps, the difficulty was also increased slightly by the fact that 'secrecy' itself is of institutional significance in Mende life. A large part of their culture is controlled by societies and cults whose more important rites are intentionally concealed from the wider community. As I shall explain in the text, there is also a special political and economic value attached to information of certain kinds. For example, in certain circumstances, it is both 'treasonable' and bad politics to disclose the genealogical history of a 'ruling house'. One of the greatest sins a Mende man can commit is to 'give away' the 'secrets' of the country. I had personal experience of this when an African stranger to Mendeland, known to be a friend of mine, accidentally touched on one or two matters of local and controversial importance in the course of addressing a gathering of chiefs. It was said—and in my rôle of investigator I took the suggestion as a back-handed compliment—that the only way he could have come by the information was through me!

The secret societies, and the Poro in particular, play a very large part in the regulation of life throughout most of Sierra Leone and Liberia. It is virtually impossible to provide an adequate description and analysis of Mende culture without dealing at some length with their organization and social function. At the

AUTHOR'S NOTE

same time, certain ethical as well as methodological questions are involved. The affairs of non-literate peoples used to be of interest to very few besides the social anthropologist, administrator, and missionary. But today these peoples are entering rapidly into the world community and they naturally expect the same regard for their susceptibilities that western nations extend to each other. More positively, the implication is that the social scientist should be bound by the same considerations of restraint in writing about the affairs of these present non-literate communities as he would in studies nearer to home. The anthropologist is bound to consider everything that comes within view as proper grist for his mill; but he has also an obligation to the people studied, if he is to deserve their confidence. This meant, for me, that a number of the things that I saw and heard myself cannot be reported.

To the Mende, a good deal of their traditional lore is sacred as well as secret and cannot, in any circumstances, be imparted to an outsider, whether African or European. Each new initiate in the secret societies takes an oath never to disclose what he learns, and from this there is no future release. Naturally, such an oath would be as binding upon an anthropologist as anyone else, and so I purposely declined more than one invitation to the membership offered me. I was, also, I must admit, somewhat diffident about the requisite surgical operations!

I wish, therefore, to make plain that all the information I gained regarding the activities of secret societies was as a non-member. In view of the implications of the matter, I would also like to add that I purposely refrained from putting specific questions to society members. Instead, the method I adopted was this. I drafted an account of the activities in which I was interested, basing it on already available material and on my own indirect observations. This account I checked with informants, asking them merely to indicate what in their opinion was incorrect. By gradually revising and reconstructing it I was able to gain sufficient understanding of the institutions concerned without embarrassing anyone. In fact, I doubt very much if any Sierra Leonean who has been brought up in a traditional home will find much that is new in this book. In addition, I have deliberately omitted certain particulars from these present writings which do, in fact, include the question of secret signs and symbols. I regret doing so, because the material concerned includes a store of proverbs richly illustrative of important patterns of culture. How-

AUTHOR'S NOTE

ever, from the Mende point of view it is essentially private and so I am regarding it as such.

This description of my difficulties is sufficient introduction to the more general problem—that I will now discuss—that of establishing contact with the people studied. The ordinary Mende man is not attracted by the idea that one is writing a book to let the outside world know about him. The Mende are proud, and justly so, of their culture, but unlike most of their contemporaries among western nations they are in no hurry to advertise it.

I found, in the long run, that one of the best methods of approach was through the educated members of their society—chiefs as well as commoners. It is quite untrue, as some members of the European official class in West Africa proclaim, that the educated African, merely because he happens to be educated, is necessarily out of touch with his non-literate fellows. Quite often, it is the reverse, and it is the educated man—the local teacher or catechist—to whom the people pay more attention than to the local headman. Once persuaded of the sincerity of one's intentions many members of this group did a great deal to allay traditional suspicions on my account and a number went out of their way to seek out fresh channels for me even at the cost, in some instances, of laying themselves open, also, to the charge of 'betraying the country'. A further group of people who rendered invaluable aid were the missionaries who, too, are apt to be maligned. I, personally, do not always see eye to eye with certain evangelical methods, but I confess most readily that in the Sierra Leone Protectorate I found individual missionaries with a rare knowledge of and sympathy with the people whom they are endeavouring to serve.

Once the initial and psychological barriers had been broken down the task was less difficult. Despite their strong trait of secretiveness, the Mende are a friendly people with a sly sense of irony which they are as ready to turn against themselves as others. They appreciate an outsider's willingness, particularly if he is a European, to respect their customary etiquettes. They are even prepared, if they like him and provided it can be done without public ostentation, to talk quite freely about themselves and their way of life. They are ready, nearly always, to discuss their farms and the technicalities of farming; and topical matters, like 'woman palaver', usually evoke an interested response. The tabooed subject, as already stated, was the one which had to do in any way

AUTHOR'S NOTE

with secret societies, more particularly the Poro. Genealogies were essentially a matter for private conversation and the question of land tenure was also delicate, but sufficiently topical and controversial to be introduced without fear of resentment. The reaction to religious matters I found vague and even apathetic, though more specific references to 'medicine' could usually be relied upon to arouse a considerable and rather self-conscious degree of curiosity.

Obviously, therefore, one's technique had to vary a great deal with the circumstances. It was never possible to hurry things. Certain data required a lengthy and deliberate skirting of the subject. Other material which, as mentioned above, included farming matters, could generally be obtained by direct questioning, through working on the farm, and by ordinary observation.

There are a few further matters to mention before concluding this preface. The first is to apologize for certain omissions because I have written very little about the technical side of Mende culture, such as arts and crafts. Readers interested in these matters should consult Dr. Hofstra's article, 'The Social Significance of the Oil Palm in the Life of the Mendi', *Internationales Archiv für Ethnographie*, Band XXXIV, 5-6, 1937, and Dr. M. C. F. Easmon's pamphlet on 'Sierra Leone Native Cloths'. There are also many shorter articles in past numbers of the *Sierra Leone Studies*, previously published by the Sierra Leone Government and now by the Sierra Leone Society, Freetown.

Also, lack of space unfortunately only permitted my providing data on the social aspects of farming. Particulars of its economics and ritual, however, will be found in two papers entitled 'The Mende Rice Farm and its Cost' that I published in *Zaire* (Louvain), March and April, 1951.

In particular, I should like to draw the reader's attention to the more recent works of other authors, including a short note on Mende names for the months of the year by Mr. J. Bockhari.[1] More extensively, on the historical side, Dr. A. P. Kup has written about the antecedents of the Mende[2] and a number of geographers as well as historians have thrown fresh light upon the earlier trading and political relations between Mendeland and the Sierra

---

[1] 'The Derivation of Mende Names for the Months of the Year', *Sierra Leone Studies*, New Series, No. 4, 1955.
[2] *A History of Sierra Leone, 1400–1787*. Cambridge, 1961.

AUTHOR'S NOTE

Leone Colony during the nineteenth century.[1] Of particular value in this regard is the detailed documentation and information provided in two books by Mr. Christopher Fyfe.[2]

A number of articles by the Rev. Professor Harry Sawyerr and the late Rev. W. T. Harris have thrown additional and more detailed light upon religious belief and ritual. For example, ancestral rites are classified by Professor Sawyerr in terms of goodwill, thanks, propitiatory and mediatory offerings. Both of these writers also clarify the distinction to be made between several categories of ancestors. In addition to four main varieties, Professor Sawyerr lists an amorphous group who when alive were of migratory tendencies and never really belonged to the family hearth or to the village or town. He also explains that the Mende talk of the *kɛkɛni*, the fathers, whose memories are relatively fresh, and the *ndeblaa*, the forebears, who are virtually forgotten but are nevertheless a moral force in their communities.[3] Mr. Harris makes a similar point, and he also shows that the 'prayer-leader' (*hɛmɔi*) plays his part in the nature cults as well as in ancestor veneration.[4] He gives an example of the former ritual, illuminates the place of the Supreme Being in Mende cosmology, and traces the derivation of the two names by which 'God' is known. His explanation demonstrates how these names—ŋgewɔ and Leve—are used in conventional sayings to rationalize various social institutions and to regulate social behaviour.[5] Further examples are provided by Professor Sawyerr in an earlier article dealing with the Mende belief in God within the wider context of African religion.[6]

In a somewhat similar connection the Rev. Isaac Ndanewa

---

[1] See, *inter alia*, P. K. Mitchell, 'Trade Routes of the Early Sierra Leone Protectorate', *Sierra Leone Studies*, New Series, No. 16, June 1962, and J. D. Hargreaves, 'The Establishment of the Sierra Leone Protectorate', *Cambridge Historical Journal*, No. 1, Vol. 2. 1956.

[2] *A History of Sierra Leone*, 1962. Oxford, and *Sierra Leone Inheritance*, 1964. London.

[3] 'Ancestor Worship—The Mechanics', *Sierra Leone Bulletin of Religion*, Vol. 6, No. 2, 1964.

[4] 'Ceremonies and Stories connected with Trees, Rivers and Hills in the Protectorate of Sierra Leone', *Sierra Leone Studies*, New Series, No. 2, June 1954, and 'How the Mende People first started to pray to ŋgewɔ', *Sierra Leone Bulletin of Religion*, Vol. 5, No. 2, 1963.

[5] 'ŋgewɔ and Leve', *Sierra Leone Bulletin of Religion*, Vol. 5, Nos. 1 & 2, 1963.

[6] 'Do Africans believe in God?', *Sierra Leone Studies*, New Series, No. 15, 1961.

AUTHOR'S NOTE

has explained how *ŋgewɔ* is involved in the ritual of the 'swear' (*sondu*) when an offended person invokes a curse on someone who has offended him. The medicine on which the curse is pronounced is said to release a spirit which goes out hunting for the culprit and others associated with him and when it finds them duly punishes them. Mr. Ndanewa's account also shows that elaborate preparations are required in order to make this procedure legal. They include payment of a nominal fee to the local authority, securing the services of a medicine man, public announcement of the prospective ceremony, and an explanation on the spot of the reason for the swear and why a particular medicine is being used.[1]

The implications of the 'swear' and of other supernatural sanctions for social psychiatry have been examined in a paper by Dr. John Dawson. He points out that personal misfortune and mental or physical illness are often attributed to the infraction of an important taboo. Specifically, the culprit is said to have contravened the rules of certain secret societies which possess powerful medicines. These societies, such as the Humoi and the N'jayei, also possess the means to deal with the effects of his anti-social behaviour and Dr. Dawson shows that treatment involves a species of group therapy. It is not just a 'doctor-patient relationship', but a form of social re-integration. The methods used are designed to counteract the supernatural powers that have been activated by the 'patient's'' misdemeanour as well as the effects of the disaster he has suffered. The practitioner deals, Dr. Dawson argues, with the complete man as a total entity treating physical, psychological and social symptoms.[2]

Closely related to religion is folklore. Our knowledge of the latter and its implications for Mende social life has been increased by scholarly articles from the pen of Gordon Innes. He distinguishes two broad categories of oral literature in terms o traditional narrative and fictional tales. Of the latter the most common are animal trickster stories centering on the Spider and the Royal Antelope. The Spider is always selfish, ruthless and callous, apparently devoid of all fine feelings. The Royal Antelope is likeable, gentle and yet shrewd. There is a very rich store of these and other folktales which frequently reflect, as Mr. Innes shows, the

[1] 'The Rationale of Mende "Swears"', *Sierra Leone Bulletin of Religion*, Vol. 6, No. 2, 1964.

[2] 'Therapeutic Functions of Social Groups in Sierra Leone', *Bulletin of British Psychological Society*, 17, 56, 1964.

AUTHOR'S NOTE

tensions and conflicts within Mende society. Jealousy between co-wives, for example, is a frequent theme. He also illustrates the different ways in which songs are used within the narrative. Sometimes they serve as magical formulae, giving power over wild animals or spirits of the bush. Sometimes, songs comprise mostly the utterances of spirits (usually of the dead) and of birds. Such utterances are in nearly all cases messages. The main point of the song, however, is at climactic points or at crises in the narrative. It is most often uttered by a character in a tale who is under severe stress, either physical or mental.[1]

Mrs. Marion D. de B. Kilson, too, has analysed social interactions through the stories related by Mende people, mainly by men. Her hypotheses are that the relationships reflected will be those about which there is the greatest anxiety in daily life, and that the sex of the narrator will be a significant variable in determining the types of the relationships projected. A major anxiety reflected was the impermanence of friendship between men. Nearly all the stories about the relationship between spouses reflected a general lack of trust of the wife. On the other hand, the consanguineal tie between parents and children appeared to be less fraught with anxiety than those between non-consanguinially related persons. The ideal for affective harmony in interaction between co-wives was also stressed in the stories. In summing up, Mrs. Kilson found that men tend to be concerned about the harmonies of extra-familial relationships as well as those within the family, while women emphasize solely intra-familial ones.[2]

Continuing with social organization, we have an account of the growth of Moyamba to its present position as one of the largest urban centres in the provinces,[3] and a short description of a nearby village.[4] Another important Mende town recently studied is Kenema where the effects of urbanization on family life and structure have been analysed and compared with social changes

---

[1] 'Some Features of Theme and Style in Mende Folktales', *Sierra Leone Language Review*, No. 3, 1964, and 'The Function of the Song in Mende Folktales', *Sierra Leone Language Review*, No. 4, 1965.

[2] 'Social Relationships in Mende Dɔmɛisia', *Sierra Leone Studies*, New Series, No. 15, 1961.

[3] Harry Ranson, 'The Growth of Moyamba', *The Bulletin (Journal of the Sierra Leone Geographical Association)*, No. 9, 1965.

[4] William H. Fitzjohn, 'A Village in Sierra Leone', *Sierra Leone Studies*, New Series, No. 7, 1956.

AUTHOR'S NOTE

of a similar kind in Temne country.[1] The role of the Mende as town dwellers has also been reviewed outside Mendeland itself. According to Professor Michael Banton's report the Mende who move to Freetown make a more individual kind of adaptation to city-life than other tribal migrants who rely extensively on voluntary associations for mutual benefit as well as recreation.[2]

Finally, there are recent publications which deal with political institutions, modern as well as ancient. For example, in *Political Parties and National Integration in Tropical Africa*,[3] Dr. Martin Kilson has considered and analysed the part played by Mende politicians and their supporters in the formation of national political parties. His article shows that a particularly significant factor of the Sierra Leone People's Party's recruitment has been the prominent role of traditional leaders. Paramount and other chiefs are important at various levels of the party organization. He also traces the part played by kinship and points out that the pre-eminence of the S.L.P.P. in post-war politics stems partly from the educational advantages enjoyed by the Mende.

On the traditional side, using mainly historical data, a recent article of my own has attempted to reconstruct the relation of the Poro to indigenous government in pre-colonial times. I have tried to show similarities with methods of administration found in other regions of West Africa.[4]

The above list does not include everything that has been written about the Mende since the 1940's. It is large enough, however, to indicate that the hope expressed in the first edition of this book is gradually being realized. Research has gone on and there is no doubt that extra stimulus will come from such important events as the recent establishment of a University College (Njala) in Mendeland itself, as well as the creation at Fourah Bay College (now the University College of Sierra Leone) of an Institute of African Studies.

There is, indeed, need for haste before the traditional way of life is lost and before modern development and change have bitten too

---

[1] David Gamble, 'Family Organization in New Towns in Sierra Leone', in *Urbanization in African Social Change*, Centre of African Studies, Edinburgh University, 1963.

[2] Michael Banton, *West African City*, 1957. London.

[3] (eds.) James S. Colman and Carl G. Rosberg, Berkeley and Los Angeles, 1964.

[4] Kenneth Little, 'The Political Function of the Poro', *Africa*, XXXV, No. 4, 1965, and XXXVI, No. 1, 1966.

AUTHOR'S NOTE

deeply into the cake of custom. Moreover, the fact that Sierra Leone is now one country makes it all the more essential that adequate records should be made not only of the Mende but of the other peoples and cultures. All of them have their own special characteristics and traits which in several respects are the unique social heritage of the Guinea coast. Here, therefore, is a challenge, particularly to Sierra Leonean scholars and researchers themselves.

Whatever the quest, it will be amply repaid in personal experience alone. No doubt every anthropologist gains a regard and affection for the people he studies. In connection with my own fieldwork, there comes to mind the hot humid air, which oppressed one almost as soon as the sun had arisen; the delays and the seemingly endless 'palavers'. But one also recalls the bush pathways, the gleaming rivers, the tiny forest-hidden villages, the red laterite and myriad colours. Above all, I remember the general laughter and friendliness, and the almost daylight clear nights when the drums beat, and all of us—chiefs, elders, men, women and children—went dancing under the shining moon.

Edinburgh, June 1966.

ACKNOWLEDGEMENTS

This study of the Mende people was made possible through the award of the William Wyse Studentship in Social Anthropology by Trinity College, Cambridge, and with the help of a further grant from the Colonial Social Science Research Council. My sincere thanks are due, therefore, both to the Council of Trinity College and to the Colonial Office. I have also to thank the Sierra Leone Government for providing me with rail and lorry facilities and with the use of rest-houses during my stay in the Protectorate.

I should also like to take this opportunity of thanking many officers of the Government of Sierra Leone, who rendered me hospitality, assistance, and advice; and in particular, Sir Hubert Stevenson, K.C.M.G., O.B.E., M.C., sometime Governor of Sierra Leone; Mr. R. O. Ramage, C.M.G., sometime Colonial Secretary; Mr. J. S. Fenton, C.M.G., O.B.E., sometime Secretary for Protectorate Affairs; and the late Mr. L. W. Wilson, O.B.E., sometime Chief Commissioner for the Protectorate. I have also to thank the various Christian missions and, in particular, the late Reverend W. T. Harris and the Reverend Stanley Brown of the Methodist Mission; and the Reverend Father Coleman and the Reverend Father Jackson of the Holy Ghost Mission.

To my Assistant, Mr. A. R. Wurie, I am specially in debt. He was with me throughout my two stays in the Protectorate, and I owe a very great deal to him for his sympathetic understanding of traditional society and his never failing tact and constant interest in the work we did together. His help in gathering material was invaluable.

It is impossible to mention by name all the other Mende people—paramount chiefs and commoners—from whom I received courtesy and assistance. May I therefore take this opportunity of thanking them as a group for all that they did for me in their towns and villages?

ACKNOWLEDGEMENTS

I should also like to thank Dr. Arthur Phillips, now Professor of English Law at the University of Southampton, and Dr. James Littlejohn, Senior Lecturer in Social Anthropology, University of Edinburgh, for reading proofs.

Portions of this book have already appeared in slightly different form in *Africa* (International Institute of African Languages and Culture); the *American Journal of Sociology; African Studies*; the *American Anthropologist*; the *Sociological Review*; and *African Affairs*.

CONTENTS

PREFACE BY PROFESSOR RAYMOND FIRTH	page 1
AUTHOR'S NOTE	7
ACKNOWLEDGEMENTS	17

I. TRADITIONAL CULTURE AND WARFARE   23
1. Some Nineteenth-Century Ideas of the Mende. 2. Early Mende Origins. 3. Methods of Settlement. 4. The Coming of the Warriors. 5. Warfare as a Cultural Pattern. 6. Kabba Sei, the War Chief. 7. Military Organization and Tactics. 8. Slavery. 9. The Freeborn. 10. Judicial Methods.

II. POST-MORTEM ON THE MENDE RISING   43
1. First Political Contacts with Mendeland. 2. Provisions of the Protectorate Proclamation. 3. The Origin of the Rising. 4. The Campaign. 5. Lack of British Military Prestige before the Rising. 6. The Treaties of Friendship. 7. Misapplication of Administrative Methods.

III. MODERN MENDELAND AND ITS PEOPLE   60
1. The Locale. 2. Demography. 3. The Material Background. 4. Mende National Consciousness

IV. RICE-FARMING AND LAND TENURE   77
1. General Significance of Rice. 2. Upland v. Swamp Rice. 3. Cultural Significance of the Rice Farm. 4. Social Incentives and Methods of Rice Farming. 5. The Basis of Land Tenure. 6. 'Ownership' and 'Holding' of Land. 7. Rights in Land and its Inheritance. 8. Religious Implications of Land Ownership. 9. Rôle of the Head of the Kin Group in relation to Land. 10. The Position of the Chief. 11. Settlement as a Method of obtaining Land. 12. Pledging of Land. 13. Leasing of Land.

V. SOCIAL ORGANIZATION AND KINSHIP   96
1. The Mawɛ as a Social Unit. 2. Domestic and Agricultural Organization of the Mawɛ. 3. The Local Group. 4. The Rôle

CONTENTS

of the 'Kuloko'. 5. Interrelationship of Town and Country. 6. Subordination of the Village. 7. Implications of Kinship Terminology. 8. Kinship Duties and Obligations.

VI. THE SOCIAL CYCLE AND INITIATION   page 113

1. Infancy. 2. Childhood. 3. Puberty. 4. Initiation and the Bush School: (a) Preparation of the Poro camp; (b) Entry into the school; (c) The marking ceremony; (d) The training; (e) The Initiation Rites; (f) Completion of the Poro school. 5. Initiation into the Sande. 6. Social Implications of Adult Life. 7. Manhood and Womanhood. 8. Improvements in Status. 9. Widowhood. 10. Old Age and Ancestorhood.

VII. MARRIAGE AND 'FRIENDSHIP'   140

1. Social Significance of Marriage. 2. Prerequisites to Marriage. 3. Prohibited Relationships. 4. The Humui and Sexual Behaviour. 5. The Legal Conditions of Marriage. 6. The Implications of 'Woman Damage'. 7. Ways of making a Marriage. 8. Marital Obligations. 9. The Dissolution of Marriage. 10. Re-Claim of Bridewealth.

VIII. THE POSITION OF WOMEN   163

1. Women's Position a Paradox. 2. Tensions between the Sexes. 3. 'Husbandless Women'. 4. Difficulties of the 'Literate' or 'Educated' Woman.

IX. THE CHIEF AND HIS CHIEFDOM   175

1. Basis of Political Authority. 2. Political Confusion following British Protection. 3. Partition of the Mando Chiefdom. 4. Succession to the Chieftainship. 5. Duties and Perquisites of the Chief. 6. Councils. 7. The Rôle of the Poro Society. 8. The Chief's Court and Court Procedure. 9. Social Insignia of Chieftainship. 10. Women as Chiefs. 11. Other Political Figures: (a) The Speaker; (b) The Sub-chiefs; (c) Town Chiefs, Village Headman, etc.

X. MODERN METHODS OF GOVERNMENT   199

1. Modern Methods of appointing the Chief. 2. Introduction of the Native Authority System. 3. Later Developments in Administrative Organization. 4. Some Anomalies of the Administrative Situation. 5. The Present Political Trend and its Possibilities.

XI. RELIGION AND MEDICINE   216

1. Introduction. 2. The Supreme God. 3. Ancestral Spirits. 4. The 'Dyinyinga', or Genii. 5. 'Nameless' and Mischievous

CONTENTS

Spirits. 6. Spirits of the Secret Societies. 7. The Nature of 'Hale' or 'Medicine'. 8. Practitioners in 'Hale'. 9. 'Bad' Medicine Men and Witchcraft. 10. The 'Bɔfima'. 11. Practical Uses of Medicine and other Medical Paraphernalia.

XII. CULTURAL RÔLE OF THE PORO AND OTHER SOCIETIES   *page* 240

1. The Secret Societies as Cultural Arbiters. 2. Traditional Explanation of the Poro. 3. Structure of the Poro. 4. Women as Poro Members. 5. Poro Spirits. 6. The Sacred Bush of the Society. 7. Secret Society Operation of Medical and other Services. 8. Entertainment and Recreation.

XIII. THE MODERN SOCIAL TREND   254

1. Factors Promoting Social Change. 2. The Significance of Literacy. 3. Some Features of the New Society. 4. Sources of Social Ambition. 5. The Creole as a Cultural Medium. 6. The Effect on Group Relations. 7. A Structural Analysis of the Situation: (a) The 'European' class; (b) The 'Creole' Class; (c) The 'Literate Native' class; (d) The 'Non-Literate' class. 8. Conclusion.

APPENDICES

I.	THE PART OF ISLAM IN MENDE LIFE	273
II.	THE *BONGA*-TRADERS	281
III.	THE COST OF A COUNTRY CLOTH	289
	BIBLIOGRAPHY	292
	INDEX	296

MAPS AND DIAGRAMS

	facing page
Map of Sierra Leone and Mendeland	62
Plan of Mobai	68
Plan of Moyamba sections and villages	107
Chart of the Lineage of Mando Ruling House	180
Drawing of a Paramount Chief's Compound	191
Map of Coastal Fishing Grounds, etc.	282
Plan of Serabu	end of Book

CHAPTER I

TRADITIONAL CULTURE AND WARFARE

1. *Some Nineteenth-Century Ideas of the Mende*

THE term 'indigenous culture' is conventionally taken to denote native institutions before a tribe has had significant contact with Western civilization. This omits consideration, for the sake of convenience, of prior changes in the organization of native society.

Any re-construction of Mende culture, as it existed before the impact of European and British influence, must necessarily be based very largely upon traditional accounts handed down to the present generation. In addition, there is a certain amount of information recorded by European missionaries and travellers who lived in, or visited, Mende country before the British took over. Most of these writings concern the latter years of the nineteenth century and they indicated that the main institutional features of 'indigenous' Mende life, such as the secret societies, domestic slavery, warfare, etc., were still in full swing. Perhaps the earliest account of any significance is that of an American missionary, George Thompson, who paid several visits in the middle of the century to the Mendi Mission, recently extended up country in the neighbourhood of Tikonko, from its original foundation in Sherbro. Thompson describes a number of customary etiquettes and provides an interesting account of his efforts to secure peace between the people of Bumpe and Tikonko.[1]

By the latter part of the century, a Mende population of several thousands was resident in the Colony. It consisted very largely of

[1] *Thompson in Africa*, New York, 1852. *An Account of the Missionary Labours, etc., of George Thompson in Western Africa at the Mendi Mission.*

refugees from the 'tribal' wars, of former domestic slaves and their descendants, and of petty traders. Most of the two former categories found employment as agricultural labourers, hammock-bearers, boatmen, etc. Few of them rose above manual and menial occupations. Mende traders appear to have been attracted by the market in Freetown relatively early in the history of the Colony. The standard of life, however, of this immigrant Mende community was very low by European and the best Creole[1] criteria and created a very unfavourable impression of their tribal compatriots. The general conception gained of the up-country Mende was of an entirely 'barbarous' people, lacking in morals and 'civilized' qualities.

Though a similar attitude colours contemporary accounts of Mende life as actually observed in the hinterland, it was by no means exclusive or unqualified. This is evident from the remarks of Travelling Commissioner Alldridge, who concluded a large number of treaties with the up-country chiefs prior to the proclamation of the Protectorate.[2] The first comprehensive description is contained in a communication by the Reverend William Vivian, one time Superintendent of the Methodist Free Church Missions. While condemning certain features as repulsive, he admits that there is also another side to the picture, and that amongst the Mende are 'many things that are quite idyllic and patriarchal in simplicity and attractiveness'. He also takes Governor Cardew to task for characterizing the Mende as 'lazy'.

'The moral temper and character of these Mendes combines various elements. They have long been known as fierce, brutal, and war-loving people; and would, in all probability, quickly return to the exercise of these qualities if British influence were withdrawn from their country. But they are not simply a brutal people by any means. . . . I met people in the country who were repulsive in their condition, and despicable in themselves; but I met others who in demeanour, presence, and character called up to my mind pictures I have seen of the Old Testament times.'[3]

[1] The term 'Creole' was applied originally to the children, born in the Colony, of the original settlers of Sierra Leone. It came at a later date to refer to all persons born in the Colony. See later sections and, in particular, Chapter XIII.
[2] T. J. Alldridge, *The Sherbro and its Hinterland*.
[3] William Vivian, 'A Visit to Mendeland', *Journ. Man. Geog. Soc.*, 1896.

TRADITIONAL CULTURE AND WARFARE

Another writer, Colonel Trotter, was a member of the topographical expedition which marked out the boundary between French Guinea and the British Protectorate. His experience of the Mende was confined to employing them as carriers, and he did not visit Mendeland itself.

'The Mende . . . are all pagans, intensely ignorant and superstitious and very low in the scale of civilization. They are strong powerful men, hard workers, willing, and capable of severe exertion under great privations. Their good qualities are most apparent when circumstances are most adverse; prosperity only brings out their vices. When half starved they will work without complaint till they drop, and they have no notion of giving in. . . .

'At the same time, though valuable and courageous workers, the Mende are no value for fighting purposes, nor are they to be dreaded as enemies. There is amongst them no discipline, cohesion, or binding motive to give them power of carrying out a common purpose. They have the greatest dread of white men, and are ready to obey them like slaves do their masters'.[1]

2. *Early Mende Origins*

There are indications that by the 1890's, European influence was affecting Mende country, with the result that more attention was given to agricultural than to war-like pursuits. Though the disturbed nature of the hinterland was apparent from the earliest date of British contact, a traditional view is that the original settlement of Mendeland was on peaceful lines.[2] It is said that the arts of war were either brought to, or forced on, previous settlers by invaders from the north during a period relatively recent in history. Such a suggestion is not incompatible with what is known of the historical movement of peoples in the region of the western Sudan. One factor was the establishment and expansion of powerful kingdoms, such as Mali and Songhay, in the late Middle Ages. There was also the westward drive of the conquering Fulani towards their present habitat in northern Nigeria and the neighbourhood of Lake Chad. It is assumed that this had the effect of

[1] Lt.-Col. J. K. Trotter, *The Niger Sources*, 1896.
[2] If this view is correct, it is probable that the original settlement was on rather sparse and temporary lines (as would probably be the case with hunters), since most present-day Mende towns claim foundation by a warrior (see also later paragraphs).

forcing the indigenous peoples, who lay in their way, further into the coastal rain-forests. The latter areas were covered so densely that resettlement in large groups was impossible. A living had to be gained mainly by hunting the wild animals, such as the elephant, bush cow, etc., which were in plentiful supply.

A further suggestion, which would be in keeping with the idea of a forced migration of peoples, is that the ancestors of the present-day Mende emanated from the same ancestral stock as Mande-speaking people of French Guinea. Possibly, they arrived in what is now Sierra Leone at least four hundred years ago, as small bands of hunters, little larger in size than the immediate family. These initial settlers set a pattern of life which was suited to the natural environment and which is still followed in various parts of the Protectorate, including Mendeland, where trapping game and wild animals, and fishing in the inland swamps and rivers, is a less laborious way of getting a living than cultivation. The almost impenetrable forest made outside communication impossible even over short distances, except by river; while the continual movement of the chase militated further against permanent habitation on the part of large groups of people. On the other hand, larger animals, like the elephant, once killed could not be moved from the spot, so at least a temporary shelter had to be erected.

3. *Methods of Settlement*

This helps to explain why one particular locality rather than another gradually developed into a permanent site. It is significant that very many accounts relating to the founding of present towns describe how they originated out of the killing of an elephant by a hunter and his party.[1] There, whilst skinning the animal and consuming its flesh, they would erect a few temporary huts[2] and clear

---

[1] Elephants figure quite often in Mende folk-lore and particularly in the founding of early towns and villages. It is possible that they were looked upon, in a sense, as the original owners of the country. The traditional account of the foundation of Serabu in the Bumpe chiefdom, relates how its founder, a Mandingo '*mori*-man', was out prospecting in new country one day, when he met a Banta hunter. The latter gave him charge of the new country, after they had made friends, and it turned out that this Banta man was an elephant, 'because in those days, elephants had the power of changing themselves into human beings'.

[2] A common place name, 'Mattru', is derived from the Mende term for 'buffalo', which is *taewui*.

enough, perhaps, of the surrounding virgin forest to grow a few grains of supplementary food. The reputation of the kill would attract outsiders, more huts would be set up, and the settlement grew into a large village under the leadership of the original pioneer and his kin. As the size of the habitation increased, so did the need for fresh sources of food, and expansion was favoured by the occupational circumstances of hunting. The younger and more active men would venture off on their own and find fresh sites within the vicinity. But they retained their connection with the parent village, visiting it from time to time to pay homage.

Thus, the picture emerges of a number of villages, each with its out-lying hamlets, subsisting on a combination of hunting and primitive agriculture. On the river banks, the situation was repeated. Fishermen seeking fresh and more profitable grounds would naturally settle where they found the fish most plentiful, and in the same way, the more skilful and successful communities would attract other settlers to them. Grains found growing wild on the banks, or in marshy places, provided them with a staple food.

If we can trust traditional accounts further, this process of gradual settlement and opening out of the country not only preceded, but made possible the secondary and more militant phase of Mende culture. To the north of present-day Mendeland, the movement of people from the western Sudan towards the coast was less impeded by forests and a number of rivers facilitated communication with it. This fact accounts, possibly, for the eventual arrival of the Temne who, according to Butt-Thompson, were originally a fighting legion[1] of the Baiga in Futa-Jallon, French Guinea.[2] He suggests that, settling and moving down the Sierra Leone River, they reached the coast itself in the sixteenth century.[3] He also thinks that the Temne consolidated themselves in the area north and north-west of Mendeland in the face of opposition from the Mende. If this is correct, the Mende themselves must have already become a warlike people. It is just possible, therefore, that

[1] The Mende term for Temne is *Tei-la-lei-mui*—'one who opens the town', i.e. generally a warrior.

[2] F. W. Butt-Thompson, *Sierra Leone in History and Tradition* and *Secret Societies of West Africa*.

[3] According to F. A. J. Utting, *The Story of Sierra Leone*, a Portuguese religious settlement, established at what is now Kroo Bay in the Sierra Leone Colony, was in touch with the Temne at the beginning of the sixteenth century.

the invasion of Mende country by conquering peoples from the north, related in traditional Mende lore, had taken place before the sixteenth century. Such a conquest would require that a good deal of virgin forest had already been cleared and that the invaders were able to live on the settlements they overran.

4. *The Coming of the Warriors*

How far such invaders were culturally or racially alien to the original 'Mende', if the latter may be so called, can only be surmised. There are various divergent features in existing Mende culture, not only in language, but in the existence of both patrilineal and matrilineal forms of inheritance, which would support the idea of cultural admixture. It is also noteworthy that, according to Migeod, the modern Mende population contains two fairly distinctive racial types.[1]

Migeod, who based his conclusions on an anthropometric examination of some seven hundred subjects, describes one type as well but slightly built with a long head and vertical forehead; the other is short, sturdy in build, with a round head and prominent frontal 'bosses'. He associates the former type with the Mandingo from French Guinea, and suggests that the latter type is more 'indigenous' to the forest regions.[2] Migeod, unfortunately, does not differentiate between the social origins of his subjects, but the assumption of mixed elements is not unreasonable in view of the general circumstances. A number of present-day Mende 'ruling houses' are avowedly of Mandingo origin, and it is possible, therefore, that the taller and more long-headed type represents the strain brought by newcomers to Mendeland.

Whatever may have been their culture and racial affinities, all tradition agrees that these invaders forced their way into the country and waged war against anyone opposing their right to settle there. They killed any of the local rulers whom they captured and made slaves of the younger men and women, or put them to work on their farms. Their leaders set themselves up as chiefs; but difficulties over boundaries brought them into constant conflict with each other, as well as with any of the original rulers who were able to withstand them. This helped to establish warfare as the principal form of activity and institution.

[1] F. W. H. Migeod, *A View of Sierra Leone*, 1926.   [2] ibid.

TRADITIONAL CULTURE AND WARFARE

5. *Warfare as a Cultural Pattern*

The original hunting, fishing, and agricultural settlements were now transformed into primitive fortresses. Each parent village or small town with any strategic value for military or administrative purposes was strongly stockaded on lines described in the next chapter. Sometimes, too, outlying villages were similarly stockaded to serve as outposts. Within the town lodged the local chieftain and his company of warriors, or 'war-boys', who acted as his bodyguard and private army in the event of a dispute with his neighbours.[1] A chief derived his power and authority from his own prowess and that of his followers and warriors. The latter served him almost entirely in the capacity of mercenaries, and were rewarded by a share of the booty, mainly slaves that could be gained by raids and forays in the neighbourhood. Successful warrior chiefs attracted a larger number of mercenaries and young men who came to them for military training, and they were able, thereby, to overawe a stretch of territory far beyond their own principal town.

Consequently, it appears as if relatively large hegemonies or confederacies, grew up in certain regions. These were under the general leadership and control of a single chief, or 'high chief', whom the local rulers acknowledged as their overlord. Fealty was displayed in the shape of customary presents and, sometimes, of periodical tribute, and the arbitration of the high chief was accepted in local disputes. Fealty might also involve the provision of military assistance if the head chief were attacked. He, in return, would go to the aid of chiefs whose towns lay within his sphere of influence, when war threatened them.

This kind of paramount rôle seems to have been played by the chiefs of such towns as Panguma, Bumpe, Mongheri, and Tikonko, and it probably secured conditions under which a little ordinary trade and industry could be carried on. It is probable, however, that both individual suzerainty and local 'policing' depended to a varying degree on the offices of the Poro society. It is likely that Poro sanctions regulated general behaviour among the earliest settlers and that they were adapted to the newer political situation. Chiefs who could count on the backing of the Poro were able

[1] In addition to this 'standing army', every male person practised bush fighting in peace time. Groups of boys fought each other with sticks. At the outbreak of war, every able-bodied man was mobilized.

to use its quasi-religious symbols to control a territory more effectively, and even without the continuous exercise of military force. As explained in greater detail in Chapter IX, the Poro also functioned on its own account as a powerful arbitrator in local feuds, and in other ways.

The political picture thus emerges as one in which a number of individual head or paramount chiefs exercise regional control of varying degrees of importance over a large number of petty chiefs. Local administration was centred in a large number of small towns surrounded by outlying villages which, mainly for military purposes, were in charge of the chief's principal lieutenants. Though the main object of war was plunder and not, directly, the acquisition of fresh territory, it was the custom, sometimes, of the chief to leave one of his warriors in charge of a captured town. More often, however, a town was simply burned after it had been sacked, and its rebuilding and resettlement was left to those of its inhabitants who had escaped into the bush.

6. *Kabba Sei, the War Chief*

The following is a part-historical, part-traditional account of the activities of some of these earlier warrior chiefs and the towns they founded. (Incidentally, the main characters, Kabba Sei and Kai Lundo, were visited by Alldridge in the course of his travels in eastern Mendeland.)

'Kabba Sei is the first chief (of the Mando chiefdom) about whom there is any detailed information. He was born at Potolu and was a son of Kpana, the eldest son of Mondor, who were the two previous chiefs. His mother's name was Bayeh Bia. About the latter part of the *Kpove* War in 1880, he rebuilt Potolu and some other towns and villages. He ruled from this time until 1890 as the sole administrator who could pass sentence of death on any person found guilty of murder. He signed the Treaty with the British Government on behalf of Mando, Dia, and Guma chiefdoms.

'While rebuilding the country in 1880, he started a society... *Tukpay*, meaning "push forward". When the four chiefdoms, Mando, Dia, Malema, and Guma, became united at Woloma, it was said that Chief Yaku of Dia refused to join the society on the grounds that Kabba Sei was carrying on the organization without his knowledge. Kabba Sei tendered an apology with one head of money (i.e. one slave), a goat, and some rice. Shortly afterwards,

TRADITIONAL CULTURE AND WARFARE

Yaku, who was an old man, gave his powers to Kabba Sei. The object of this society was to combine under the leadership of Kabba Sei in order to repel enemies invading any of the four chiefdoms and to collect annual tributes.

'In the next year, Mbawulomeh (lit. "rice—little eat") and several war-boys came from Ndawa ("mouth-big") of Wende and settled at Giehun Tomago in Guma chiefdom. He was disrespectful to the Chief and refused to answer his call. His attitude culminated in a war between him and Chief Foreka of Bomaru in Guma in which the latter was massacred and the former's belongings destroyed.

'To carry out the objectives of the Tukpei society the chiefdoms concerned, under their leader Kabba Sei, planned to carry war against Mbawulomeh, and invited their allies and his enemies, Mendigla of Gowra and Kai Lundo of Luawa, to join in the feud. The confederacy built stockades, fought and bested Mbawulomeh by burning his town at Giehun Tomago. He took flight and sought refuge with Fobaywulo of Gbandi. The allies, however, gave him no rest and pursued him under the leadership of Kai Lundo. Kabba Sei and Mendigla were left to maintain the fort in their absence. Gbandi was burned and Fobawulo killed. Mbawulomeh continued his flight and sought refuge in the Belleh country where cannibalism is practised by the men. Having shown their superiority in this way, the allies gave up the pursuit, consolidated their position, and returned home.

'Kabba Sei was a war chief and acted as one in his early days, but when he became rich he turned his attention to peace making. He settled enmity between Mendigla and Kai Lundo by inviting them to meet amicably at Potolu. While this conference was being held, word reached Kai Lundo that Kai Woni of Pendembu had seized his head wife, Golei, and several of his young wives with their belongings, while they were on their way to join him at Potolu. The military inferiority of Kai Woni and the pacific attitude of their host detracted from Kai Lundo's determination to take immediate and forceful steps against him. They learned in the meantime that Kai Woni was supported by Nyagua of Panguma, and therefore any action they took would require preparation. But just when war seemed inevitable, the captives were released and arrived at Potolu. Subsequently, Chief Nyagua showed that he disowned this action of Kai Woni.

'The efforts of the Tukpei society had been sufficient to banish

Mbawulomeh from their territory, but owing to the methods of appeasement adopted by Kabba Sei, he was not subjugated. A feud between him and Kai Lundo still existed as the result of the death of one of the old warriors of Kai Lundo at the hands of Mbawulomeh. Kai Lundo died before Kabba Sei had an opportunity to make peace between them.

'Kabba Sei was now old and weak and so the Belleh fugitive, who was a hardy warrior, took his opportunity. He seized Vahun and compelled its inhabitants to do him homage. Encouraged by this success, he extended his raid to Kpombali in Luawa, where he burned a town called Limeiyama and caused the chief of Bonduwolo to be murdered. Mbawulomeh's action at Vahun was displeasing to Kabba Sei, but he had no desire for war. Moreover, having no jurisdiction over Mbawulomeh, he could not restrain him from Luawa. Unfortunately, the report which Fabunde, the Chief of Luawa, made to Nyagua regarding Mbawulomeh's action was distorted to the extent of placing the responsibility on Kabba Sei. When he heard about this, Kabba Sei sent one of his "big men", Sipo, together with his dancers and singers to attest his innocence to the people of Luawa and to make plain that he too had been injured by Mbawulomeh's action. Before this could be done, the Major (Fairtlough, of the British Frontier Police) and Nyagua joined together with Fabunde to oust Mbawulomeh from Vahun, intending afterwards to move against Kabba Sei's town, Gohun. Kabba Sei, not wishing to embroil himself in war with the white man, took to flight and went westward to Freetown. His town was destroyed, and all the cattle taken away. The pursuit was continued and the fugitive decided to give himself up to Gevao of Malema. He was taken to Freetown and released after two years, when the facts had become known.

'Six days after his return, most of the Mendes rebelled against the Government. He was asked to join them, but he refused and along with Fabunde, assisted the Captain of Panguma Barracks. . . .'[1]

7. *Military Organization and Tactics*

The fact that personal prestige and affluence, as well as safety,

[1] From an account of the history of the Mando chiefdom, compiled by the late Hon. Paramount Chief Bai Comber, and loaned to the writer by Paramount Chief Sei Comber, the present chief.

TRADITIONAL CULTURE AND WARFARE

depended almost entirely on success in war led to quite an elaborate military technique, which can be recorded in some detail. The presence of so much thick bush made open fighting a rare occurrence, and rendered the movements of an opponent difficult to detect. This meant that both sides found it convenient to concentrate their principal goods and main defence inside the kind of strongly stockaded town which was the only means of warding off a surprise attack. To make the sudden approach of an enemy difficult, all paths leading to the town were left as narrow and as overgrown as possible, so that progress along them could only be made in single file. Only a single road led into the town itself, and it was so constructed as to be easily blocked, if necessary. The actual gate into the town was so narrow that it would barely admit a man.[1] Inside the town itself, the houses were deliberately built close to each other, so as to constitute a veritable maze and make it difficult for attacking warriors to find their way about.

The town itself, as described also in the next chapter, was encircled and guarded by fences, usually three in number. There was also, as a rule, a further outer fence consisting of a light breastwork of material, piled up between convenient cotton trees and along a bank. This was not regularly defended, and its object was merely to provide a temporary brake on the attack. The next two fences were regularly guarded and defended by war-boys, stationed at intervals behind each one. There was a shed, or guard-house—*golohg boie*—at each point on either fence where the road passed into the town, and four warriors were posted there at night-time. In charge of them was an 'officer'—*Kɔtulei-mui* (one who passes the stone)—whose duty it was to see that an efficient watch was maintained. A stone was handed to one of the warriors on duty in the guard-house, and he carried it along to the next post, whence it was relayed completely round the fence back to the original point. It was then handed to the second man and completed a further circuit. Its return to the third man marked the changing of the guard, and the second two warriors, who had been resting in the meantime, took over from their comrades.

The warriors did two days' duty at a time and during it they

---

[1] Alldridge (op. cit.) describes the difficulty he had in getting his loads through such gates. He also mentions that salt, transported across the country, was packed into cylindrical bundles of palm leaf about three feet long by only three inches in diameter. Possibly, this was a convenient shape for handling in such circumstances.

TRADITIONAL CULTURE AND WARFARE

cooked food for themselves, because no women were allowed between the war fences.

On campaign, only the principal warriors were allowed to take women with them. Every effort was made to effect a surprise attack, and generally one or two individuals were sent on ahead to spy out the way.[1] If possible, they would insinuate themselves inside the town itself, or gain what news and information they could by listening in the nearby bush to women's gossip on the farm, or at water places. On the strength of this intelligence the attackers decided on which part of the war-fence to make their assault. The whole body then crept up as stealthily as possible; and, provided the outer fences were reached, the following tactics were then followed.

The primary responsibility rested on a number of special warriors called respectively the *Miji* (the 'needle', or 'jumper down'); the *Fande* ('thread');[2] the *Kanye* ('wax'); and the *Hakahoumoi* (holder of the ladder). These acted as leaders in the assault, and before it was undertaken the ordinary warriors (*Kugbangaa*) arranged themselves in parties behind each one. There does not appear to have been any definite number to each leader, but perhaps the average would be about twenty, depending of course on the size of the force. If the *Miji* thought he had insufficient men to follow him, he might choose from those left. If, as usually was the case, the attack was to be made in the dark, two Mende proper names, such as Vandi and Kanga, were used as watchwords. If two men met and one said 'Vandi', the other would reply 'Kanga'.[3]

Led by the *Miji*, the various parties then swarmed as best they could over the outer fences. If any of the fences proved unsurmountable, the *Hakahoumoi*, or ladder bearer, rushed forward with his ladder to help the *Miji's* ascent. It was the custom to hand the latter a bottle of very strong palm wine, before he made his leap, to give him extra courage. It was the duty of the *Miji* and his party to overcome all opposition as quickly and as silently as possible between the fences. At the final stockade, the *Miji* was expected to call out his name as he jumped into the town itself.

---

[1] The Mende term for a spy is *nenɛjia-mui*.

[2] The rôle of the *Fande* was to link up the *Miji's* assaults with the rest of the battle.

[3] cf. W. R. E. Clarke, *The Foundation of the Luawa chiefdom*; also, J. M. Malcolm, 'Mende Warfare'. *Sierra Leone Studies*, No. 21, 1939.

TRADITIONAL CULTURE AND WARFARE

He was followed, in due order, by the *Fande* and the *Kanye* and their men, and then by four warriors known as *kokoyagbla* (drivers from the fence), who immediately split into two couples. The latter went around the inside of the fence killing all they met and preventing anyone from escaping. It was impossible, of course, for all the warriors to use the same ladder, and the remainder swarmed over the fence by means of poles, once a footing inside had been gained. This more general part of the attack was carried out by two further categories known as *ngo-mbuhubla* (men in the midst of the battle), and *gbamai* (ordinary men), who served in reserve. There were also, *kɔ-sokilisia* ('war-sparrows'), who were young recruits and served as carriers, and might be called upon to fight. The Chief himself, who bore the military title of *Kɔ-mahei*, left everything in the hands of his *Miji* and did not enter the actual fighting, unless the day seemed to be going against his men.[1]

Once the inner fence had been forced, the capture of the town was almost certain and any further resistance was soon overcome. Fugitives, who escaped by the back gate, sometimes scattered ants behind them on the bush path to put their pursuers off the trail. Women and children were shut up in the women's houses during the fighting, and the first warriors to enter the town were allowed to slash the outer walls of these houses with their swords, or leave some other token, such as a sheath, on them. This was a sign that they claimed the inmates as their captives. The remaining warriors were expected to continue the fight until they heard the *Miji* call out twice, '*A-wa-o*' ('All come!'), which was the sign of victory. Then they could join the others in marking houses and securing booty.[2]

Once the assault had been started no quarter was given. The actual combat was practically all hand to hand, with swords and spears as the main equipment, and a species of shield called *kafa-lowoi* (fork of the kafa-tree), which was of very hard wood. Strips of iron were placed across the fork, and the whole was used to ward off blows of a sword or to deflect the flight of a spear.[3] Dane guns and muskets were also used, but were of little value after the first volley, as it took too long to re-load them. For success, as well as protection, the warrior also relied on numerous charms, mainly procured from '*Mori*-men', which he wore all over the body.

[1] ibid.
[2] ibid.
[3] ibid.

TRADITIONAL CULTURE AND WARFARE

These were supposed to be proof against even a shot from a gun. Before his departure to war, the warrior's family also made offerings on his behalf to their ancestors, and his uncles prayed for him.

When approaching an adversary in the fight, the warrior would call out the name of his own war-chief, and his opponent would reply in the same way. When the town was entered, the unsuccessful defenders might escape detection by climbing into the eaves of the houses, or by some secret path out of the town. Warriors captured in the fight were brought forward as a group, and those who had resisted most strongly were put to death. Before executing them, the victors danced round the town. The captives were led out and stabbed as they passed through the fences. Their bodies were covered with leaves and left in the bush. For members of the victors' side who had been killed in the fight, the usual funeral ceremonies were performed at a fork of the road. The captured women and children, and the plunder, were then brought before the head warrior for division. Out of every four captives, two went as slaves to the chief himself; one to the head warrior; and one to the man who had made the capture.[1]

If the people inside a town knew that an attack was imminent, their chief's decision as to whether to resist or sue for peace depended mainly on the forecast of his Moslem adviser, as well as on the prestige of individual warriors among the opposing forces. The presence before a town of a well-known fighter, such as Ndawa, is said to have been enough in itself to compel surrender. If the besieged chief decided to call for a truce, he would send a woman of light-coloured skin as his ambassador, with a white country cloth, a gun, and some salt. She would probably be his daughter, or one of the most valued women he had, and she automatically became the wife of the conqueror. Alternatively, he might appeal for help from neighbouring chiefs by sending them gifts of country cloths and a gown.[2] In the event of it being decided to make a stand, the *morale* of the defenders would be strengthened by sacrifices carried out by the chief's Moslems, and by war-dancing. A warrior might be stationed at the only exit from the town to cut down any would-be deserters.

[1] The soles of a slave's feet were washed in water to prevent his escaping. The same water was used to cook rice which the slave was made to eat. Having eaten the rice he could be trusted to go anywhere and would always come back.

[2] cf. Clarke and Malcolm, op. cit.

TRADITIONAL CULTURE AND WARFARE

8. *Slavery*

Though predatory warfare of this kind was carried on partly for the purpose of enhancing prestige, the main incentive was slaves. Slaves constituted the principal form of wealth, and were bartered and exchanged for goods, notably for salt from the coast. They also served as currency in a large variety of transactions. They provided the basis, in fact, of the social system, and upon their labours as domestics depended, very largely, whatever agriculture the Mende possessed. It was they who felled and cleared the high virgin forest in preparation for the rice crop, and they were also responsible for the collection and cracking of palm kernels and extraction of oil. Palm kernels were the main commodity supplied to traders from the Colony during the nineteenth century.

Most other forms of trading, except in slaves, were of a purely local character and consisted of bartering one kind of native produce for another. The passage across country of cattle and salt depended on prevailing conditions along certain well-travelled routes and the payment of local tolls and dues on the way.[1] Native-made cloths and bars of iron were used, in addition to slaves, as standards of value, and it is reported in 1834, when coastal traders and travellers were beginning to find their way up-country, that a 'bar' was an indefinite quantity, ranging in value according to the district concerned. It could be reckoned in a number of different commodities. A bar of tobacco was equivalent to forty leaves of tobacco; a bar of soap to 2 lb.; a bar of rum as one bottle; and a bar of blue cotton as two yards.[2]

Slaves were exchanged at the coast for bags of salt, and up-country for cattle. A single slave was worth from three to six cows, and a man, woman, or child were all considered as one 'head' of money. This was equivalent, later in the century, i.e. 1890, to £3.[3] Slaves also formed an invariable and important part of bridewealth, and were deposited as security in the case of debt or any kind of dispute. It is also possible that the availability of slave labour established rice-growing over any other kind of

---

[1] The total journey across Mende country, say from Yengema in the north-east to Sumbuya in the south-west, is said to have taken about a month.

[2] F. H. Rankin, *The White Man's Grave*, Vol. I, 1836.

[3] cf. Alldridge, op. cit. By this time such trading was, of course, considerably diminished.

economic activity as the predominant form of agricultural industry. The concentration and coercion of relatively large bodies of men and women, as slaves, enabled land to be cultivated on a far larger scale than was likely, or possible, by smaller groups of freemen whose needs could be satisfied by less arduous methods. The practice of cultivation was encouraged further by allotting small plots of land for the slaves' own use, and by allowing them to retain the proceeds.

For the sake of convenience the slaves were housed as close as possible to the fresh tracts of land they cleared on behalf of their masters, and this gave rise to new villages inhabited entirely by populations of slaves. Another feature which added to the general process was the allocation of sites to prominent warriors and war leaders as a reward for their services. In this way, fresh sections inhabited by their followers and slaves were added to already existing towns. In some cases, the warriors founded new towns for themselves, and built up a kind of sub-chiefdom which grew strong enough, sometimes, to challenge the authority of the existing chief.

Slaves settled on the land and employed as domestics were considered members of the households of their owners. As such, they enjoyed certain limited rights, and it was not customary to sell them except for some serious offence, such as adultery with the wife of a freeman. At a later period, there was an improvement in status, especially in the case of descendants of slaves, i.e. 'slaves of the house', as they were termed, and of bought slaves. A slave not only had security of tenure on certain land, but it was recognized that so long as he met his master's requirements, he was entitled to work for himself and to keep the profit of his labour.[1] It was possible by these means for a slave to come to own another slave. It was thought wrong to separate a slave from the land on which he had been born and brought up. Not infrequently, slaves married into the family of their master and rose to positions of

---

[1] cf. *Sessional Paper, No. 5 of 1926, Sierra Leone Govt.*, 'Despatches relating to Domestic Slavery in Sierra Leone'. Among the Mandingo, it was a common practice for slaves to work a number of days a week for their master, and to be entitled to work for themselves on the remaining days. Governor Cardew states this arrangement more specifically and says that five days out of seven were worked for the master.

In a recent visit to the Gambia, the present writer found a similar type of arrangement still in force among Mandingo communities there.

TRADITIONAL CULTURE AND WARFARE

trust; and there are examples of a slave taking charge of a chiefdom during the minority of the actual heir to it.

Probably the growing importance of agriculture in place of warfare itself helped to improve the slave's position by providing him with an economic rôle. By the time the British took over it seems that slaves of the fourth generation were practically indistinguishable from freemen, and there was little difference in their lot from that of the family whose fortunes they shared. A slave who acquired property, while in his master's service, was entitled to redeem himself, if he wished, but could not take away with him any such property. This principle prevented a slave disposing of land that had been allotted to him for cultivation. A slave could also be redeemed by another slave. If a freeman lived with a female slave belonging to someone else, he was required to redeem her and pay bridewealth to her mother. She was then considered his wife. If a freeman lived with his own slave, she was held to be free and any children born to her were free, as were children born to a freewoman by a slave man. In the latter case they belonged, of course, to the family of the woman.[1]

9. *The Freeborn*

Freeborn members of the household, including the younger brothers of the head of the group and the latter's own sons and daughters, had duties in accordance with their status. The men supervised the slaves; the women spun and dyed thread, which the men wove into cloth.[2] All of them were strictly under patriarchal control, but the more senior men were allowed to make farms of their own with the help of their wives and slaves provided by the head of the group. Anything a young man possessed was regarded as the property of his father or the head of the compound. He was also referred to as the 'slave' of his uncle, i.e. mother's brother, and could be offered as a pawn by the latter. In some respects, the position of the younger men and women, like that of their father's wives, differed but little from the status

[1] ibid. According to this Sessional Paper, some 15 per cent of the population of the Protectorate was in servitude as late as 1921, including the same proportion of the Mende population. This estimate is also exclusive of slaves of the fourth generation.

[2] It is said that the mark of a free woman was that her hands were always black with dye.

of the slaves. On the other hand, they were entitled to share in family property, including land, and could not, of course, be sold in any legitimate way. Moreover, their standing increased with age, or could be improved by a successful career as a warrior and freebooter, with its reward of slaves, grants of land and political position.

The kind of general picture of the social structure of pre-Protectorate Mendeland, then, that we obtain, is of two broad social classes, slaves and freemen; these latter had also an 'upper' or ruling stratum. Membership of the class of freemen depended on the factor of birth and ceased if the freeman was taken prisoner. Enslavement was a fate which might befall most freemen and once taken away as captives they could rarely expect any better status than that of the existing slaves of their owner. Nevertheless, both within the respective classes and between them, there was a certain amount of social mobility. Within the free class there was scope for advancement to the rank of 'chief', or of 'war leader'; and the slave's status could be altered, either through redemption or in the course of one or two further generations.

10. *Judicial Methods*

It may be assumed that in this society, law and order was maintained in this way, i.e. either by force of arms or through the supernatural authority of the Poro society. Sanctions on behaviour, in general, probably derived mainly from the secret societies and took the form of traditional usages and practices learned largely under their auspices.[1] Quarrels and disputes were settled as far as possible by the local elders, but if the principals were persons of consequence the case was taken to the chief for arbitration. If either party was still dissatisfied, he might appeal further to the overlord of the local chief, or ask a neighbouring chief to intercede on his behalf. An old Mende man gave the following account of the judicial procedure in use in this respect prior to the present century:

'In the old days, if your wife went to stay with her father's people and became pregnant, you called on them for satisfaction (i.e. "woman damage"). If they did not meet you, you sent a "shake hand" (customary present) to some big man in the town,

---

[1] For elucidation on this point, see further Chapters IV and XII.

asking him to take the matter up in the Chief's court. The Chief sent his messenger to summon you and the defendant, and the case was heard in his *barri*. Each morning you and the defendant would "awaken" the Court with presents to the courtiers. You, as plaintiff, would be asked to state your case, and to swear on your opponent's medicine. Then the defendant stated his case and was sworn on your medicine. The Chief would ask how much damages you were claiming, and you were required to deposit the amount in a nearby house. It might be forty country cloths and a number of slaves. The defendant was called upon to do likewise, and a kind of "betting match" ensued. If you did not own any slaves, you might offer your sister's son or daughter as a pawn, but not your own son, because you had no right to pawn him. If after pledging your nephew, you lost the case, you had to redeem him. The father and mother of the pawn also had to work to redeem him.

'After the cases of both the plaintiff and the defendant had been heard, the Chief called upon them to name their witnesses. The witnesses were sent for, and would ask the Chief to "introduce them" to the parties concerned, i.e. they required a "shake-hand" from both suitors. The witnesses then gave their version of the matter, after being duly sworn, and were asked to withdraw and "hang heads" on it. Providing their verdict was unanimous, the Chief pronounced judgement accordingly. If it was not unanimous the witnesses were fined, and it was left to the Court to bring in a verdict. The plaintiff and defendant were asked to make a further statement, and the courtiers retired and "hanged heads". On their return, the Chief asked each one on whose side he stood and the courtiers arranged themselves accordingly. The Chief then gave his verdict according to the majority of opinion.'

A customary method of summoning the court was for the plaintiff to send a quantity of palm wine to the elders. The defendant was expected to do likewise if he wished to contest the claim. Failure to do this was equivalent to an admission of guilt, hence the question which the elders would put to him, *Mba ndoe la hwei lɔ?*—Will you cross the summons? There was (and still is) a great variety in methods of administering the oath. It might take the form of tapping together two pieces of iron, of stirring a mixture of chopped kola, salt, and water, etc. If the medicine used had to be drunk, the party supplying it had to taste it first himself.

TRADITIONAL CULTURE AND WARFARE

The witnesses gave evidence in each others' hearing, and this had the effect of producing closer collaboration, particularly if they had been approached beforehand by either party. The courtiers, including the chief's Speaker (his deputy), might also be bribed, and the latter might intercede on the side in which he was interested by indicating, by movements of his switch, the appropriate answers to questions put by the court. The Court members indicated their own allegiance to either of the parties concerned by wearing their caps in a distinctive way. The suitors themselves were permitted to cross-examine each other 'on the bridge'. This meant that they stood directly opposite each other at a close distance, and the one questioned the other with the object of pressing him to admit a certain point. The chief, alone, was supposed to be immune from bribery, as this was one of the specific obligations undertaken at his 'crowning'.

CHAPTER II

POST-MORTEM ON THE MENDE RISING[1]

1. *First Political Contacts with Mendeland*

ALTHOUGH the Sierra Leone settlement was taken over as a Crown colony in 1806, the British appear to have made little or no political contact with the Mende until quite well on in the latter half of the century. This was largely because policy, as in the other British settlements in West Africa, was uncertain about the wisdom of taking over the interior. As late as 1865,[2] it looked as if the British would be content to remain on the coast; and not until 1876 was a vigorous attitude adopted towards the hinterland.

In any case, communications inland were difficult and precarious. They consisted mainly of a number of rivers and creeks on the northern side of the Colony which could be navigated by small naval craft. These were used with some regularity in the early days for punitive expeditions in the Scarcies area;[3] and to overawe recalcitrant Timne and other warring chiefs, and drive away Susu invaders of friendly territory. For example, in 1858 a naval force burned down Kambia and returned shortly afterwards to turn out some Susu marauders.

Expeditions of this kind were not only to maintain the frontiers

[1] The Mende Rising, 'House Tax War', was one of the last armed rebellions to occur in British territories in Africa. In the present context, it is important not only as an outstanding event in colonial history, but for the considerable light it throws on the earlier and political background of British contacts with the Mende.

[2] In that year, a Parliamentary Committee recommended a gradual withdrawal from British obligations assumed in West Africa, with the possible exception of the Colony of Sierra Leone.

[3] In the north-west area of the present-day Protectorate.

of the Colony from attack, but to secure conditions sufficiently peaceable in the adjoining territories for inland trade. Further south, the Sherbro river was used for a similar purpose, as well as to check the export overseas of slaves from the adjacent coastal areas whence, it was estimated about 1840, some 15,000 were shipped annually to America. Along this coastal strip, inhabited by the Gallinas and now named Turners Peninsula, there were numerous Spanish factories as well as on the small islands dotting the creeks and adjacent waters.[1]

Overland, British territorial expansion from the original area of settlement was gradual, but slow. In 1825, they took over sovereignty of the Lokko country by treaty with the Temne; and further territory from present day Waterloo to the Ribbi river was ceded in 1861. This was followed by further annexations in the adjacent Quiah country and Sherbro areas in the next year. The latter made possible a closer control over the inland creeks and enabled a check to be maintained over the slave routes from Ribbi, Sherbro and Cockbrough rivers into Susu country to the north.

This extension of British influence over the greater part of Sherbro country removed the frontier between the British and the people of the interior, and it led to the first active collision with the Mende. Hitherto, the Sherbro had acted as a buffer. The clash came in 1875, when the Mende raided the neighbourhood of the Bagru river and carried off plunder and captives from villages now under British jurisdiction. A small British punitive force of nineteen armed police and about a hundred friendly Sherbro was repulsed; but a further expedition, consisting of detachments of the 1st West India Regiments under Governor Rowe, was more successful. It pushed up-country, and treaties were signed with the Mende and Sherbro chiefs at Senehun and Shenge. It was stipulated that the country should be 'de-militarized' by removal of war-fences from the towns, and that, in future, all local disputes should be referred to British arbitration. Roads should also be kept open for trade and all rights to collect dues on the seaboard should be ceded to the British.

The agreement, however, was not sufficient to abate neigh-

[1] Some Mende slaves formed part of the cargo of a Spanish ship which left Sherbro in 1839. They mutineed on the voyage and forced the Spaniards to steer the ship, which eventually reached Long Island, near New York. Their arrival in the United States led to the work of American Missions in Sierra Leone.

bouring disturbances, and so further treaties of friendship were made with the Mende chiefs at Tikonko, Lugbu, and Bumpe, in 1879. In the following year, Mr. Laborde was sent to promote peace further up-country in Mendeland, where the trouble mainly lay. He travelled eastward through Quiah, Senehun, and western Tikonko to Taiama, and returned through the Bumpe, Lugbu, and Boom country. His tour was followed, in the next year, by a meeting between Governor Havelock and Mende and other native chiefs at Bonthe to re-affirm existing arrangements and to seek ways of preventing trouble in the interior. Nothing effective, however, was done about the latter question; though on the Governor's instructions, Mr. Garrett went up as far as the Wende chiefdom, and burned thirteen towns and villages belonging to the notable Mende freebooter, Ndawa.

Despite all this, Mende war-boys continued to lend their services in local quarrels and other people's disputes, and were hired by both sides when a further conflict broke out in Gallinas country in 1884. This was followed by a more serious attack on the Mende themselves when, in 1887, the Yonni Temne assailed Senehun and other towns in Kpaa Mende, which belonged to Madame Yoko. This area was already under British jurisdiction and covered the main trading approaches to the Colony. A military expedition under Sir F. de Winton was sent to drive back the Yonnies. Its commander recommended the establishment of a regular force of Frontier Police and of advanced posts beyond the border-line of the Colony, as the only means of ensuring peace and tranquillity along the frontiers.

In the meantime, the French were approaching in the north and threatened to interfere with the inland markets of the Colony in the same way as they had already 'hemmed off' the Gambia. The only way of remedying this was to take the whole hinterland under British protection as speedily as possible. To do this peacefully, a large amount of new and little known territory, partly in Mendeland, had either to be secured by treaty or overawed by military force. As a preliminary step, therefore, Mr. Alldridge was sent off, as Government Travelling Commissioner, to the more remote Mende chiefdoms, where he concluded a number of treaties of friendship. At the same time, Governor Hay toured Mendeland chiefdoms nearer the Colony with an armed force and made further peace treaties. He was followed, in 1893, by Governor Fleming. Finally, in 1894, and again in '95 and '96, Governor

POST-MORTEM ON THE MENDE RISING

Cardew toured the whole hinterland with the object of informing the chiefs of the terms and conditions under which it was proposed to bring the country under British protection. It was explained that the purpose of this was to save them from absorption by the French.

2. *Provisions of the Protectorate Proclamation*

On Cardew's return to Freetown, it was proclaimed on August 31st, 1896, that Her Majesty had assumed a Protectorate over the whole of the hinterland. This was to be divided up into five administrative districts, namely, Karene, Koinadugu, Bandajuma, Panguma, and Ronietta, each to be under the jurisdiction of a District Commissioner. The three latter districts were inhabited wholly or largely by Mende people. Three separate courts of law were to be established in each district. In the first, jurisdiction was left entirely to the chiefs with authority over all cases arising exclusively between native persons, but with the exception of offences such as murder, homicide, slave-dealing, etc., and cases involving title to land. In the second, the District Commissioners, with chiefs as assessors, had jurisdiction in criminal matters, i.e. murder, homicide, rape, cannibalism, etc. In the third, the District Commissioners enjoyed sole jurisdiction over cases in which natives were not involved, in cases between natives and non-natives, and in all cases involving title to land. Cases of witchcraft and slave-dealing also came under their jurisdiction.[1]

The 1896 Ordinance which defined these administrative powers also enacted that slave-dealing was unlawful and that slaves might purchase their freedom for a fixed sum. Tax was to be paid on every house in the Protectorate at the rate of 10s. and 5s., according to the number of rooms. In return for collecting this tax, the chiefs were to be allowed a rebate of 5 per cent, and the amount was to be paid over in coin, unless this was impossible.[2]

Finally, certain further powers were vested in the Governor, including the right to dispose of 'waste or uninhabited lands', as defined by the District Commissioners.[3] The last provision, however, was revised (though after its proclamation), by the Home Government on the grounds that it might seem to vest the lands of the Protectorate in the Crown.

[1] *Sierra Leone Protectorate Ordinance* (No. 20 of 1896).
[2] ibid. [3] ibid.

POST-MORTEM ON THE MENDE RISING

3. *The Origin of the Rising*

The general events which followed the Protectorate Ordinance and which culminated in the Mende Rising, or House Tax War, of 1898 have been described in several places.[1] The outbreak in Mende country resolved itself as a general revolt against British rule, but the first direct clash was with the Timne. It began with the alleged refusal of a Timne sub-chief, Bai Bureh, to pay the Tax. A force of Frontier Police, sent to collect it and arrest Bai Bureh, came into armed conflict with the people supporting him. In the meantime, the report from District Commissioners in Mende country was also that the majority of the Mende chiefs were not disposed to pay. The Frontier Police were put in charge of the matter and proceeded to arrest refractory chiefs on quite a large scale. When persuasion failed, goods were distrained in a number of instances, and the captive chiefs were subjected to various indignities including, in one case, a sentence of twelve months' hard labour and thirty-six lashes. The latter penalty, however, was afterwards remitted.

Popular resentment, which had shown itself hitherto only in passive form, changed to angry demonstration. There was an attempt by force to release some of the principal chiefs imprisoned at Bandajuma. The latter were then freed on agreeing to pay £5 in a lump sum for each of their towns. But afterwards the houses were counted and they were asked for more.

Possibly, the successful resistance of Bai Bureh in the north was the decisive factor in prompting the Mende to open revolt. Hitherto, many of them had been willing to accommodate, even to House Tax, thinking it foolish to resist the British. At any rate, matters came finally to a head in Mende country on the 26th April when attacks were made simultaneously on all Government posts up-country. Within less than a week nearly every male British subject[2] had been put to death in the areas of Bandajuma, Kwellu, and Sulima. A number of women were also murdered, but the remainder were treated as captured slaves. The victims included European missionaries as well as any African who spoke English and who, like the Creole trader and catechist, was regarded in the

[1] The most complete account is contained in the evidence gathered by the Royal Commission which sat in Freetown immediately after the suppression of the rebellion. See *Parliamentary Papers*, 1899, LX, Pts. I and II. See also C. B. Wallis, *The Advance of our West African Empire*.

[2] i.e. mainly colony-born Africans, or 'Creoles'.

same light as the white man. The most notable massacre took place at Rotifunk, where several American women missionaries were the victims. The Methodist missionary, a Mr. Goodman, further up-country at Tikonko, was spared after an old woman had pleaded with the Bumpe chief for his life.

Beginning mainly in the Bumpe country, the rising soon enveloped almost the entire Mende area, with the exception of a number of Kpaa Mende chiefdoms under Madame Yoko, who remained co-operative with the British throughout the fighting. Elsewhere, all property belonging to British subjects was plundered, except at Bonthe and York Island which were saved by the timely arrival of troops and marines.

It is probable that the rising was carefully engineered for a moment when the available British force was busy elsewhere, in destructive but abortive chase of the elusive Bai Bureh in the north. Its simultaneous nature is accounted for, possibly, in the suggestion that those responsible took away with them from their last meeting an equal number of small stones. One of these was thrown away each day, and on the day on which the last one was disposed of, the plan to kill every English speaking person on whom hands could be laid was set in motion. It is also likely that the Poro secret society was the main instrument, and that the Poro war-sign—a burned palm-leaf—was despatched from town to town and from country to country to call out the war-boys.

4. *The Campaign*

Though the rising started in such concerted fashion, it appears soon to have degenerated into rioting on a large scale, and it met with little success in the face of armed opposition. Attacks on the police stations at Bandajuma and Kwellu were easily repelled, even before military assistance arrived, and hostile activity mainly took the form of marauding. Once the Government in Freetown had recovered from the initial shock, it took prompt measures. Two military expeditions, consisting of companies of the West India Regiment and of armed Frontier Police, were sent up-country. The first, under the command of Colonel Woodgate, left Freetown a fortnight after the outbreak and was transported by sea to Bonthe, and thence by creek to Mattru on the left bank of the Jong river. The second, under Colonel Cunningham, started overland from Freetown on the 31st May. Their progress up-country to the relief of a number of posts, which were still under siege, involved a series of small actions on the way.

The difficulties of the British lay in the long lines of communication they were obliged to maintain, and in the Mende method of fighting, which was mainly in ambuscade. Once the rivers were left behind, paths and tracks were rarely wide enough to permit men moving in anything but single file. Much of the country traversed was unknown even to the friendly warriors who served as guides and fought as auxiliaries. The enemy lay concealed behind stockades, and behind trees in the adjoining thicket, in which he could move on bush paths of his own. Often, the first sign of his presence was a shot at the advance guard, and even when the stockade was reached there was still a network of paths behind it by which his escape could be made good. Supplies of ammunition and hospital hammocks required continuous escort from the base; and officers and men were always in danger during the daytime from snipers, whom it was hopeless to pursue or to attempt to track. Under these conditions, Captain Braithwaite Wallis, who took part in the fighting, estimates that anything between fifty and two hundred rounds were required to pick off a single member of the enemy.[1]

Another favourite tactic of the Mende was to creep into the British camp between the hours of one and four o'clock in the morning and kill anyone they could take unawares. On the other hand, it was possible to bring them to open fight, once a stockaded town which they considered they had some hope of defending was reached. At a number of such places the British met with fierce resistance, despite the overwhelming advantage of light artillery over swords, spears, old muskets, and dane guns. Probably, it was in their war-medicines, as well as in the stout palisades encircling the town, that the Mende warriors placed their faith. So strong and well built were some of these out-works that even 24-pounder rockets and field guns found them difficult to penetrate. The following is a description of the war-fences at Talliah, in the Great Bum country, by an officer who took part in the operations:

'... This town may be taken as a type of the stockaded towns which the natives erect ... (it is) surrounded by the war-fences,

[1] cf. C. B. Wallis, *The Advance of our West African Empire*; see also 'The Sierra Leone Protectorate Expedition'. *Jour. Royal United Services Inst.*, Vol. XLIII, 1899.

POST-MORTEM ON THE MENDE RISING

usually three in number, the inner being made of a double row of logs 14 or 15 feet high, as thick as a man's thigh, and planted some 4 feet deep in a well-rammed clayey earth. It is palisaded with logs 6 feet high of the same size, but split so as to fit together and present a tolerably even surface, and pierced with a double row of loop-holes for musketry. The whole is strongly bound together with powerful withes from 1 to 3 inches thick. The middle fence is distant 7 to 9 feet from the inner and exactly similar to it, except for the addition of a chevaux-de-frise of strong pliable boughs about 7 feet long and firmly interlaced. These are bent outwards, and not being strong enough to support a man's weight without bending downwards, they form an exceedingly difficult obstacle which can only be passed by cutting through, a long process during which the assailants are exposed to the fire of the defenders, who are also provided with long poles armed at the end with large fish hooks to stab the people climbing over. The outermost fence is about 15 feet from the middle one, and is built of a treble row of longer logs than the two others, but not so closely planted, so that it is easy to fire through this fence. This fence is very strongly bound together diagonally by numerous binders, and is surmounted by a double chevaux-de-frise, the lower being about 4 feet from the top. No one who has not seen these fences can realize the immense strength of them. The outer fence at Hahu I measured in several places, and found it to be from 2 to 3 feet thick, and most of the logs, or rather trees, of which it was formed, had taken root and were throwing out leaves and shoots.'[1]

This writer notes that it would take an elongated projectile to pierce the lower part of the fences; round shot or a shell from a field gun to go through two at most; while even the large 24-pounder rockets would not penetrate more than a single fence, unless they struck above the lines of palisades. At frequent intervals between the fences were also strongly palisaded traverses and guard houses.[2]

Previous experience of European methods of warfare had taught the Mende to remove as much inflammable material as possible out of reach of shells; and it was customary, therefore, to take down the thatched roofing of houses when an assault was

[1] Lt. R. P. M. Davis. *History of the Sierra Leone Battalion of the Royal West African Frontier Force*.
[2] ibid.

expected. Realizing, also, that the British preferred to make their attack in the daylight rather than in the darkness, as was the usual native practice, the Mende cleared the bush for several hundred yards in front of the outer fence. This, by denying the ordinary cover of the forest to the attackers, kept their superior firing power at a safer distance and made it more difficult for the British to employ their favourite tactic of rushing the stockade after the rocket bombardment. Once, however, the guns had effectively done their work the capture of the town was a relatively simple matter. The following description of such an attack, a few years earlier than the Mende Rising itself, is taken from the *African Standard*:

'The order to advance was given, and by a succession of rushes our men were taken to within sixty yards of the stockade, and poured in a most telling fire. The allies on the flanks behaved with the utmost gallantry, clambering up the stockades, only to be repulsed by the fire and spear thrusts of the enemy. Three times they obtained a footing inside, to be ruthlessly driven back, maimed and wounded.

'The scene was a vivid and picturesque one—an African stockade under the blazing sun, the gay uniform of the soldiers, intermingled with the red fezzes of the police, and the almost naked bodies of our allies, the flash and rattle of the rifle, and the fiery tails of the rockets as they work their sinuous way into the enemy's lines; the fierce war-cries of our allies as, with swords in their mouths, they again and again endeavour to escalade the fence. But no enemy with inferior weapons, and crowded into a small space, such as were Gbow's people, could stand against the shells that, with such precision, were falling in the midst, and at length a footing inside is gained, the fence is forced outwards in many places, and our allies pour in.'[1]

The Mende opposing Colonel Cunningham's force were not content, however, to remain entirely on the defensive. He reached Mafwie (by present day Sumbuya) on the 17th May to find the town a complete charnel house, with the mutilated bodies of many Creole traders among the ruins. Two days later, he was attacked in determined fashion by a force of about a thousand war-boys

[1] Quoted by G. A. Lethbury Banbury, *Sierra Leone, or The White Man's Grave*, 1888.

from Bumpe.[1] They were driven off after fierce fighting, and the next day the British force pushed on to Bumpe itself, and successfully stormed the town despite the strong resistance of its defenders.

The capture and burning of this warlike place broke the heart of most further opposition.[2] Panguma, where Major Fairtlough and 75 Frontier Police had held out for two months, despite shortages of food and ammunition, was then relieved, and communication was established with Bandajuma. In the meantime, several neighbouring chiefs had sued for peace, and remaining resistance quickly petered out. At the conclusion of the operations, several columns of troops, including artillery, were marched by different routes through the Protectorate to overawe opposition to British rule.

5. *Lack of British Military Prestige before the Rising*

Later in the same year (i.e. 1896), a Royal Commission of inquiry into the causes of the Rising was held in Freetown, and the report of the Commissioner, Sir David Chalmers, is very illuminating. The light thrown on the political background of the matter is of especial interest, and a significant point to emerge is the question of British military prestige. Virtually up to the time of the Rising itself, the greater part of Mendeland had little or no experience of the real power of the British. Nor, prior to the latter part of the century, was any attempt made to show it. As a writer commenting in the *Fortnightly Review*, in 1898, on the Rising points out:

'... provided the tribes outside the defined area of British "jurisdiction" among whose chiefs about £2,000 a year was distributed in pensions, neither quarrelled too much with one another nor broke the terms on which they had accepted "protection" ... they were rarely meddled with. ....'[3]

War was the major industry of the Mende, and their estimation of another people's worth was based largely on the latter's prowess in conducting it. Such skirmishes as they had with the British were

---

[1] On account of its military significance it was decreed that Bumpe should never be rebuilt. Later, however, the Government acceded to the petition of its inhabitants on religious grounds and on condition of their remitting tax.

[2] cf. Wallis, op. cit.

[3] H. R. Fox Bourne, 'The Sierra Leone Troubles', *Fortnightly Review*, 1898.

confined to chiefdoms on the south-western edge of Mende country; the British forces employed were small and the results, though temporarily impressive, were not consistently unfavourable to the Mende. Further up-country, British penetration was entirely peaceful and was confined almost exclusively to Creole traders and a few European and Creole missionaries.[1] The Mende chiefs accepted both traders and missionaries as settlers rather on sufferance and largely because they found them useful. From the trader they obtained gunpowder and arms for their wars, as well as rum, tobacco, and gin. The missionary they considered eccentric, but harmless. The modicum of European education he provided helped to negotiate a better bargain with the trader and the occasional British official, who came seeking favours. European customs were regarded as alien and inferior, and as worthy of emulation only in ways materially pleasurable, such as drinking and smoking and sometimes in headgear. It was strictly against etiquette for a chief to speak, or to use, English before his people.[2]

6. *The Treaties of Friendship*

Far from winning prestige for him, the Creole's western habits simply stamped him as a foreigner—a 'white man'—despised the more because his actual colour was the same as that of the Mende themselves; the missionary's rôle earned him the status of a woman.[3] Their safety was generally secured, however, by treaties of friendship between the chiefs in whose territories they resided and the Colony government. Under the terms of these, the chiefs received an annual stipend and undertook, in return, to keep the roads open, to refer internal quarrels to the Governor for arbitration and to put a stop to slave-dealing, etc. Sometimes, as, for example, in Treaty No. 81 concluded with the Lugbu country in 1875, there was a proviso that traders must establish themselves at such places as the chiefs thought fit. They must not go inland

[1] The first missionaries arrived in Mende country about 1850.

[2] cf. *Parl. Papers*, op. cit.

[3] Note the Bumpe chief's words in sparing the life of the Missionary, Mr. Goodman, as recorded by Davis (op. cit.). 'The King says you are his friend. You have come to this country to do good and show the God-palaver. You are not a Government man; you are not a trader; you are not a soldier. He says you stand like our women who know nothing about war; you do not fight; you teach the children book; you learn the young ones sense. You are kind to all women; you mend people who are sick.'

without the latters' permission. In other treaties, British subjects are granted certain 'extra-territorial' rights. For example, in Treaty No. 96, with the chiefs of Tikonko and Lugbu country in 1879, 'no porro or country law or tax of any kind may be enforced against the subjects of Her Majesty'. If British subjects wrong or injure subjects of the chiefs, the Governor of the Colony will be informed and the chiefs will be satisfied with whatever decision he will come to. The chiefs will permit ministers of religion to exercise their calling and guarantee their free protection.

What is particularly noteworthy about these agreements is the fact, as Chalmers points out in his report, that

'in all treaties from the foundation of the Colony in 1795 to the present day, the characters of chiefs as owners and sovereigns and as independent contracting powers is unequivocally and universally recognized. Only in a few of the later treaties is there provision for the English crown assuming sovereignty and full control in the event of chiefs not fulfilling treaty engagements.'[1]

It is also evident, from Travelling Commissioner Alldridge's account of his negotiations with up-country chiefs, that there was very little notion of political dependence on the British.[2] The chiefs' attitude towards a representative of the Government was friendly and accommodative, but not subservient. Alldridge approaches them as one seeking favours rather than granting them. This was only a few years before the proclamation of the Protectorate itself. He is as convinced as any other European traveller and writer of his day of the advantages, and even moral necessity, of bringing these tribal people under British control. But he is none the less impressed by the dignity of those with whom he must deal and is at pains to preserve it. Of Kai Lundo, the chief of Luawa, he writes:

'Kailundo was a man of small stature, but large intelligence, beloved by his people for miles around, who used to speak of him . . . as their father. He was every inch a chief with immense power and influence in the country. . . . He had a very great objection to any ostentatious display either on himself or on any of his numerous wives. . . . It was splendid to see him get into his hammock, which was simply country cloth tied at both ends to a pole

[1] cf. *Parl. Papers*, op. cit.
[2] cf. Alldridge. The Sherbro and its Hinterland, op. cit.

in which he was closely covered over by a coloured cloth. He was surrounded by a lot of his boys, who were very fresh and in the best possible humour, and who raced along the path with him, all of them seemingly exceedingly proud of their chief, as well they might be. Men, women, girls, boys, all followed in the wake, running, laughing, dancing, joking as they went along under the beautiful tropical vegetation and brilliant sunshine. . . .'[1]

Alldridge is therefore at great pains to create a favourable impression and he makes every concession to local etiquette, and even to some of the foibles of his hosts. For example, on more than one occasion, he allows crowds of sightseers, to whom a white man is a complete curiosity, into his hut to sit and gape at him for several hours, simply to please the chief. Later, when arranging a meeting between the chiefs and Governor Cardew, he stresses the need for tact equally upon the latter. These points and their implications are exemplified very clearly in Alldridge's description of a typical interview with local Mende rulers:

'When everything was in readiness and the chiefs, sub-chiefs, and headmen were seated inside, I, escorted by five or six police, left my hut, entered the *barri*, bowed to all the people, and then took my place at a table covered with a rug or country cloth. My police escort, fully equipped with rifles and side arms, were drawn up at the back of me. I then stood up and removing my helmet, in the name of the Queen, the Governor of Sierra Leone and in my own name, gave all the chiefs and people present a hearty welcome. I then resumed my seat, explaining that I was a high officer of the Government sent into their country to see it and to report on it, and to extend to the paramount chiefs the privilege of making a friendly treaty with the great English Queen.

'But before bringing forward the conditions of the treaty, the custom of the country demands that the paramount chief should be asked what news he had in his country. That is always the first question to be put at a great meeting. By this question, it is intended not only to obtain the information, but to show respect to the chief before his people. . . . I, then, as at Bandasuma, addressed them on the nature of the treaty in the way already described. As at Bandasuma, the chiefs withdrew for consultation, and after a while returned to the *barri*. The old chief then came forward and said they had "looked their heads" . . . and that on

[1] ibid.

behalf of his country, he was ready to accept the responsibilities and was perfectly ready to sign the treaty. I was always extremely particular that the obligations should be clearly understood, and I was satisfied, in going through the country afterwards, that every chief thoroughly knew exactly what these obligations were from the remarks that they made to me. . . .'[1]

Probably, it is largely in the light of considerations of this kind that the many reasons and causes adduced for the Mende Rising should be viewed. The Mende chiefs, who had signed treaties, apparently did not fully realize that the proclamation of the Protectorate altered their relationship with the British crown to any undue extent. In accepting, as in some of these treaties, the Governor's arbitration in their local disputes, they acknowledged the paternal interest of a powerful neighbour, but without subordination. They knew of only one precedent by which one people could claim the right to dominate and regulate the affairs of another—by military conquest.[2]

7. *Misapplication of Administrative Methods*

In the circumstances, it was possibly the general policy followed by the Government rather than the specific imposition of the Hut Tax which underlay the trouble. Transition from the previous state of affairs to the one inaugurated by the Protectorate Ordinance, in which the Government's District Commissioners assumed almost dictatorial powers, was too rapid. The District Commissioners had authority 'subject the approval of the Governor', 'to banish and forcibly deport from their districts any persons— even kings or chiefs—whose presence is thought undesirable'. At the same time, the practical side of administration was left almost entirely in the hands of the recently created force of Frontier Police. The latter were largely recruited from war-refugees and men who were ex-slaves from the very districts of which they were put in charge. Backed by British authority, they speedily won a name for

---

[1] Alldridge, op. cit.
[2] This is also the conclusion of a writer who took part in the British military expedition. 'The rising was bound to come sooner or later, the reasons given for its inception are immaterial, and other and equally powerful reasons could always have been manufactured.' cf. 'The Sierra Leone Protectorate Expedition', *Journ. Unit. Serv. Inst.*, op. cit.

terrorism and petty tyranny which, according to the Freetown press in 1894, was worse than the people had ever experienced before, 'even in their own tribal disputes'.[1] In short, as a missionary commentator points out, the administrative and other provisions of the Ordinance were tantamount to an attempt on the part of the Government to effect a revolution in native life.[2]

For taxation itself, there was some precedent in the native system, if the exaction of tribute by the conqueror from the conquered is taken into account. Broadly speaking, it was an assertion of sovereignty, and its payment an acknowledgement on the part of the conquered of their submission. It also indicated the right of the conqueror to a part, if not the whole, of his vassal's property, if he so desired. But, for payment or exaction of tribute without any demonstration of military superiority there was no precedent, and the idea, in the European sense, of taxation for administrative purposes was quite unknown.

It appears, moreover, that in Governor Cardew's first two tours, in '94 and '95, the official discussions were connected with and confined to the subject of slavery. This was a matter on which the attitude and policy of the British was already well known, and which had entered widely into previous arrangements. Only during Cardew's last tour in 1896 were the provisions of the Protectorate Ordinance, including the need for taxation, explained. On this occasion, the number of chiefs he met was by no means

---

[1] cf. H. R. Fox Bourne, op. cit.

[2] cf. W. Vivian, 'The Missionary in West Africa'. *J.A.S.*, Vol. 3, 100-3. This latter point is also admitted, to some extent, by Cardew himself, though he lays greater stress, perhaps, on the cultural than on the political side of the matter. In his despatch to the Secretary of State (28th May, 1898) he wrote: 'the true causes (of the Rising) ... lie far deeper down; and they are the desire for independence and for a reversion to the older order of things, such as fetish customs, and slave-dealing and raiding. (The chiefs) see the old order of things passing away, the fear and reverence paid to their fetish customs and superstitions diminishing, their slaves asserting their independence, their children being taught by the missionaries a purer religion and the methods of civilization.'

In fact, it is doubtful if missionary influence was felt at all deeply before the Rising, and there is little reason to believe that the teaching of Christianity was regarded as anything like a challenge to existing beliefs and customs. One missionary witness himself informed the Commissioner, Sir David Chalmers, that he was allowed to break down 'devil-houses' without opposition in Mende country. The missionaries suffered severely during the Rising, primarily because they were regarded as representatives of the alien power, not because they were missionaries. cf. *Parl. Papers*, op. cit.

representative of general opinion, and the response was, at best, guarded and ambiguous. The remaining chiefs were left to infer what they liked from those who had met the Governor, or from second or even third hand accounts of the matter: and the initial proclamation, with its clauses about the disposal of 'waste' lands, probably confirmed the growing suspicion that the ultimate intention of the Government was to take complete control of everything in the country, including property.[1]

In any case, it is a consideration of some moment as to how far the various provisions of the proposed Ordinance were properly comprehended even by the chiefs whom Cardew met. There would be very special difficulties of interpretation to overcome, necessitating re-translation in a number of instances. In such circumstances, the attempt to convey novel and culturally alien ideas has often resulted in considerable confusion and misunderstanding, even under modern administrative conditions. It is not improbable, therefore, that many of the chiefs were quite unconscious of the obligations which their agreement to Cardew's plan imposed upon them, particularly so far as the paying of Hut Tax in cash was concerned. Money was, as yet, little employed, and there was no native precedent for its use in that manner.

No doubt, as various witnesses testified before the Commission, there were other reasons, too.[2] It is probable, for example, that British interference with certain native practices, such as slave dealing, in particular, had already aroused a good deal of resentment among the chiefs, whose source of income and prestige was largely bound up with the commerce. There were times, also, when persons like Creole traders and missionaries under British protection strained the patience of the native authorities. The Poro Ordinance, specially enacted in 1897, was a further check on the privileges of particular chiefs, and the limitation of their judicial powers was an additional consideration. On the other hand, it has to be remembered that prior to the Ordinance itself, British authority and influence was effective only in a comparatively small part of Mende country, and the period between the enactment of this wider legislation and the Rising itself was hardly sufficient for the practical requirements of the new laws to be extensively felt.

What is most evident is that the method of collecting the Tax brought already existing resentment to the boiling-point. The

[1] *Parl. Papers*, op. cit.   [2] ibid.

POST-MORTEM ON THE MENDE RISING

officials appointed seemed to have acted nearly everywhere in the most high-handed and arbitrary manner, both in approaching the people and in levying payments. Chiefs were treated as common criminals in a large number of instances and were subjected to considerable indignities if they refused, or even appeared unwilling, to pay. The Frontier Police were given almost a free hand at intimidation, and in some appear to have appropriated a good deal of private property for their own use. Though the evidential basis of some of his criticism is open to question, Chalmers' own conclusion in this connection is that much of the action taken by Government officers, as well as their subordinates, was a gross abuse of the authority vested in them and quite illegal and contrary to all principles laid down by the Government.[1]

What is quite certain from the Royal Commission evidence is that the violent methods adopted were a complete departure from previous peaceful overtures and were backed by insufficient military force. This, as was admitted by Governor Cardew himself, was because the Government considerably underestimated the strength of opposition to the tax. Only in certain areas near the Colony was it paid with any show of readiness, and only three chiefs of any note, Madam Yoko of Kpaa Mende, Nancy Tucker of Bagru, and Caulker of Shenge, were actively loyal during the revolt, though a number of powerful chiefs up-country changed sides or waived their neutrality, when the Government showed its real strength. Its show of force, previously, as Chalmers points out, was merely large enough to cause annoyance: it was not enough to overawe the rebellious and to convince those in two minds that a rising would be unsuccessful.[2]

Chalmers' final commentary contains a number of points which are as relevant to present day administration as to 1900. He raises the general question as to whether methods of 'direct' or 'indirect' rule are most applicable to the circumstances, and indicates the fundamental implications of either system. His reference to the rôle of native authorities and to the attitude of the controlling power in regard to indigenous law and custom provide a fitting prelude to the later chapters of this book.[3]

[1] ibid.   [2] ibid.   [3] ibid.

CHAPTER III

MODERN MENDELAND AND ITS PEOPLE

1. *The Locale*

THE Mende inhabit a fairly compact area of nearly 12,000 square miles in the central and eastern part of the Sierra Leone Protectorate which itself is some 26,000 square miles in extent. Mende country proper also includes the adjacent western corner of Liberia, so that a number of Mende people are outside British administration.

Originally, a very large part of the whole of this geographical region, including Mendeland, was covered by tropical rain forest. The forest, today, is confined to a limited number of local areas, such as parts of the Gola forest close to the Liberian border. There is still, however, a certain amount of forest designated technically as 'high bush', i.e. trees which are not less than twelve years old and twenty-five feet high; but most of the vegetation is 'low bush', or 'orchard bush'.[1]

Three great rivers, the Jong, the Sewa, and the Moa, intersect the western, central, and eastern parts of Mendeland, and run through it roughly from north to south. Up-country, they are navigable for appreciable distances only during the rainy season; the amount of flood water is then very considerable and spreads over the surrounding country for several miles. There are also numerous patches of swamp land. Mende country contains no mountains, but nearly everywhere it is very hilly, with a number of conspicuous ranges, notably the Kambui Hills, north of Kenema.

There are two main seasons, the wet and the dry. The rains

[1] cf. F. J. Martin, *A Preliminary Study of the Vegetation of Sierra Leone.* Published by the Government Printer, Freetown, 1938.

begin early in April and ease off in October. They are very heavy in some parts of the country. The change of season is accompanied by a short period of tornado and marked by a cool dry wind, the Harmattan, which blows from the Sahara Desert during December and January. The climate is hot and very humid throughout the year, except in the middle of the rainy season, but there is some variation according to district and altitude.

The only 'natural' communications with Mendeland from the coast are a number of large creeks which run up from the south and one or two large rivers, such as the Jong and the Sewa which passes by the town of Sumbuya on its way to the Bum Kittam creek. Modern communications, in the shape of the Sierra Leone Railway, connect Mendeland with Freetown and the Colony, the border of which is about thirty miles by rail from the nearest point in western Mende country. There is also a motor road from Freetown which passes through the towns of Port Lokko and Makeni in Timne country before turning south to Bo, in the centre of Mendeland. A further road, connecting Bo more directly with Freetown, has recently been opened. The railway line continues through the heart of Mende country almost up to the French Guinea border, and further roads from Bo help to link the eastern and southern districts (see attached map of Sierra Leone and Mendeland).

2. *Demography*

Demographic data in Sierra Leone, as in other colonial territories in Africa, must be regarded as very tentative. No attempt has yet been made to obtain a complete count of every individual person living in the country, and the available figures represent an estimated population, which is based on sample enquiries carried out locally in the various administrative districts.[1]

There can be no doubt, however, that the Mende constitute the largest single cultural or 'tribal' group in the Protectorate. According to the Sierra Leone official census, they numbered 557,674 in 1921. The 1931 census places them at 572,678, exclusive of some 10,000 resident in the Colony. This was out of a total Protectorate population of 1,672,058. In other words, the Mende comprise rather more than one-third of the inhabitants of the Protectorate. The 1931 census estimates their nearest numerical rivals,

[1] cf. *Sierra Leone Government Census*, 1931.

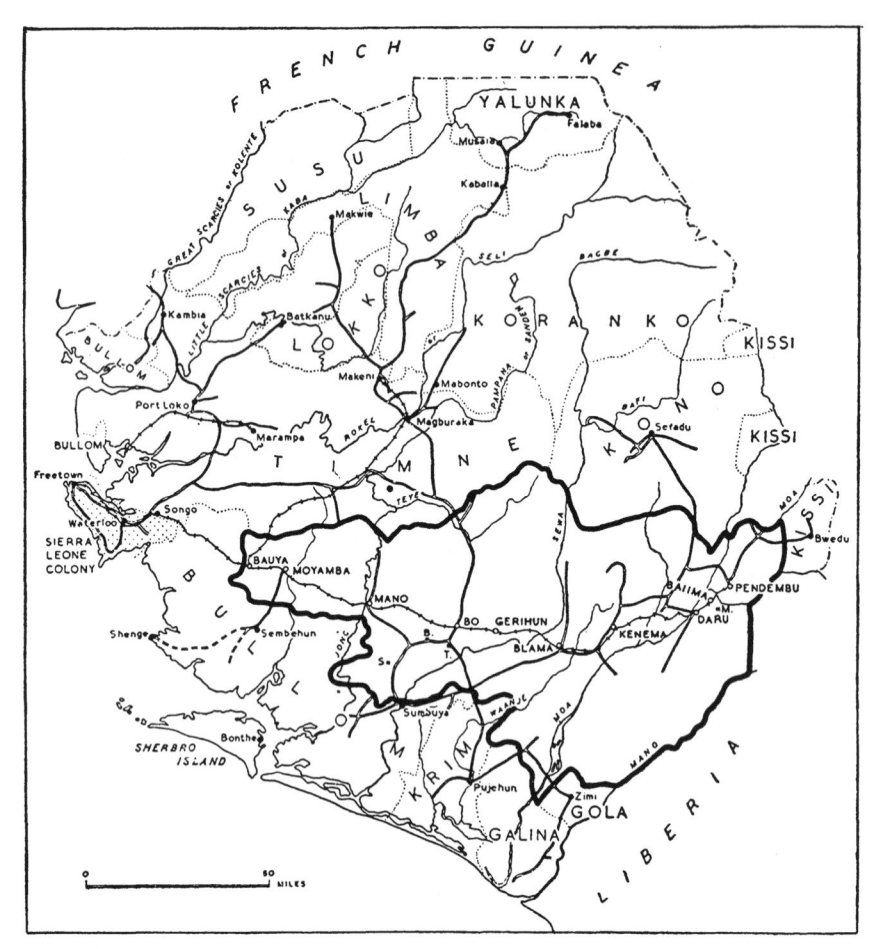

MAP OF SIERRA LEONE AND MENDELAND

the Timne, at 476,970, so that Mende and Timne together make up rather more than three-fifths of the total population of the Protectorate. A more recent estimate of the total population of the Protectorate is 1,733,618.[1]

The Mende claim about seventy out of the two hundred odd chiefdoms of the Protectorate, but a number of these Mende chiefdoms overlap with the 'tribal' groups bordering Mende country. One obvious example of this is the large Luawa chiefdom[2] whose 'capital' town, Kailahun, contains about equal proportions of Mende and Kissi people. The same applies to Timne in the Kpaa Mende chiefdoms to the west; and Mende chiefdoms in the Pujehun area of the south contain a fairly large number of Kissi, Gallinas, and Gola. The presence of non-Mende elements, however, is perhaps most significant in the main towns on the railway line where, in places like Moyamba, Mano, Bo, and Kenema, 'non-natives', such as Creoles from the Colony and Syrian settlers, have also to be taken into account. Bo offers the most extreme case here; nearly half its population is non-Mende in origin, although the town is almost in the geographical centre of Mende country. Other smaller, but widely distributed non-Mende groups include Mandingo, Fula, Limba, and Susu people. Excluding the railway line towns and the frontier area, however, it is probable that the remainder of Mendeland, including the more 'rural' towns, is relatively 'pure'.

The writer obtained a detailed census of Serabu, a fairly representative Section town in the Bumpe chiefdom in Middle Mende country, and out of the town's some 850 inhabitants some 800 were classified as Mende. There were 13 Sherbros, 14 Susus, 8 Fulas, and 5 Kissis, and one or two Timnes, Konos, Mandingoes, etc. The nature of this census is shown in some detail on the map at end of book. A number of features, such as a Mission church, 'shops', 'family houses', farms and plantations, to which reference is made later in the present chapter and in subsequent chapters, are also included (see, in particular, Chapters V and IX).

The official 1931 census suggests that, demographically speaking, the Mende are a progressive population, i.e. that the propor-

[1] *Sierra Leone Census*, 1948.

[2] Luawa is the largest chiefdom in the Protectorate with a population estimated at over 26,000 (1941). The range in the numerical size of Mende chiefdoms is very wide indeed, and some of the smaller ones have probably no more than 5,000 inhabitants.

tion of individuals at a child-bearing age is relatively high. A more recent official estimate (1940) places the total Protectorate population at some two millions, and so it is possible that, today, the Mende population as a whole numbers close on a million, including the Liberian section.

The following demographic particulars, mainly abstracted from the 1931 census, are relevant. Mende masculinity, i.e. the number of males per 1,000 of the population, is 461. This compares with an estimated masculinity of 476 for the Protectorate as a whole. In 1931, some 31 per cent of the Mende population was below the age of fourteen; some 60 per cent between the ages of fourteen and fifty-nine; and some 8 per cent over the age of fifty-nine. This census also records that the average number of children born to a sample of 235 Mende women during the total child-bearing period was five; but approximately half this number died before the age of puberty.

From detailed enquiries made officially in 1943 in a number of Upper Mende chiefdoms, the percentage proportion of adult males in the population was 30; that of adult females, 33; and that of 'children', i.e. males and females approximately below the age of sixteen, 33.[1] From much smaller samples, which the writer himself obtained in the Tikonko chiefdom, in Middle Mende, the proportion of adults to 'children' in Tikonko town was as 64 to 36; in a number of smaller towns, as 70 to 30; and in villages, as 74 to 26. The larger proportion of children in the towns is probably to be associated with the corresponding presence there of a relatively larger number of women. In Tikonko town, the proportion of women to men was as 160 to 100; in the smaller towns, as 120 to 100; and in the villages, as 110 to 100.

It seems evident, also, that generally speaking the larger and the more important the town, the greater is the proportion of married women to married men. In the Tikonko sample, there was an average of 2·5 wives per married man; in the smaller towns, an average of 1·8 wives per married man; and an average of 1·4 wives per married man in the villages.

In further regard to marital status, the consensus of both evidence and opinion is that a relatively large proportion of the

[1] Abstracted from a report on housing compiled by Mr. J. D. W. Hughes of the Sierra Leone Government. Acknowledgement is due both to Mr. Hughes and the Sierra Leone Government for the use of these figures and the report in general.

MODERN MENDELAND AND ITS PEOPLE

women are shared as wives among a relatively small number of husbands. A detailed survey of the Yawei chiefdom, which was officially conducted, found that nearly half the men lacked wives. Of the married men, the average number per husband was about two. Of the adult male population, 'bachelors' constituted about 37 per cent, and 'widowers' about 10 per cent. Of the adult female population, 'widows' constituted about 19 per cent, and 'spinsters' about 4 per cent.[1] A census in Upper Mende country was also made by K. H. Crosby in twenty towns and villages, and from his figures it would appear that of 842 married men, 411 were monogamists, and the remainder had on the average 3·6 wives each. There were 673 other men, unmarried, of marriageable age; and only 84 other women, unmarried, of marriageable age. This would mean that married men constitute about 24 per cent of the total adult population; unmarried men about 19 per cent, married women about 55 per cent, and unmarried women about 2 per cent.[2]

The density of the Mende population appears to vary somewhat from district to district. In the Moyamba district, the 1948 census estimates that there are 80 persons to the square mile; in the Bo district 92·7 persons to the square mile; and in the Kailahun district (which includes part of Kissi country), 85 persons to the square mile. The density per square mile in the Protectorate as a whole is estimated as 62·7.[3]

A very rough estimate from the previous (1931) census is that there were nearly forty towns with a population in each case of more than 1,000 inhabitants. In most of these the population probably did not exceed that figure by more than a few hundreds. The three largest towns are given as Kailahun with 2,545 inhabitants, and Bo and Bumpe (Middle Mende), each with 2,200. Obviously, since 1931 many towns on the railway line, such as Bo and Moyamba, have grown quite considerably. The present writer estimates that modern Bo has at least 10,000 inhabitants.

Data regarding the density of specific localities and towns are limited, but figures are available for three Upper Mende chiefdoms. In Upper Bambara chiefdom, with an area of 86 square miles, the estimate is 110 persons to the square mile; in Jawei chiefdom, with an area of 148 square miles, 87 persons to the

[1] ibid.
[2] K. H. Crosby, 'Polygamy in Mende Country', *Africa*, Vol. X, 1937.
[3] *Sierra Leone Census*, 1948.

MODERN MENDELAND AND ITS PEOPLE

square mile; in Jaluahun chiefdom, with an area of 119 square miles, 87 persons.[1] In Serabu town, Bumpe chiefdom, the present writer estimates that some 850 persons were occupying an area of some 13 acres, which is equivalent to about 4,250 persons to the square mile. In Mobai, the chief's town of the Mando chiefdom, it was estimated that some 17 acres were occupied by some 650 persons, i.e. about 2,500 persons to the square mile.

Finally, a detailed survey carried out officially in four chiefdoms in the eastern part of the country estimated that some 550 houses were occupied by an average of 5·4 persons to a house. Individual averages for the four chiefdoms concerned were 6·6; 4·6; 4·8; and 5·0.[2] The writer's own enquiry in Serabu covered 107 houses and showed an average of 8 persons to a house. A further 80 houses in 13 villages of the same chiefdom showed an average of 5·8 persons to a house. A sample taken from 25 houses in Tikonko town gave an average of 8·4 persons to a house; a further sample of 50 houses in a number of smaller Tikonko towns gave an average of 8·0 persons to a house; and in 82 houses in a number of Tikonko villages, there was an average of 5·3 persons to a house.

It seems clear then that the average house in a town accommodates more persons than the average house in a village. This is due, however, only in part to the fact that 'urban' houses are larger, on the whole, than 'rural' ones. It is also a function of the town's superior position in political and social terms,[3] and of its rôle as a trading place and centre of communications.

3. *The Material Background*

The Mende live in small towns and villages which are divided up into political units, known as chiefdoms. A Mende town is regarded as 'large' if it contains 200 or more houses, which means a population of between 1,200 and 2,000. The ordinary 'town', however, is about the same size in population as an English village, and the ordinary village about the size of an English hamlet. The Mende area occupied is probably less in both cases.

The houses themselves are generally built of wattle and mud daub, with a roof of palm thatch, and are well and stoutly con-

---
[1] Hughes, op. cit. [2] ibid.
[3] See Chapter V for a further note on this point.

MODERN MENDELAND AND ITS PEOPLE

structed. They are invariably either round (in Mende *kikii*), or rectangular (*Kpaekpaei*) in shape, the former type having, as a rule, a veranda and two or three rooms. They are all, of course, of one storey. The main room, or 'parlour', is frequently used as a kitchen during the wet season. In houses of more recent design the kitchen is usually constructed as a separate building.

Every Mende town has a number of official buildings and public meeting places. These include the compound of the chief, or of some other 'big man'; the town *barri*, which is used, sometimes, as a small market; the houses in which more important 'medicines', like those of the Humui and Njayei societies, are kept; the Mosque, etc. Every chiefdom 'capital', or chief's town, also contains the offices of the Native Administration, where it exists; and the chief's court. Outside the town is a section of high forest, which contains the sacred bush of the Poro society, and a further portion usually reserved for use of the Sande (women's society).

Most of these features and a number of domestic amenities are depicted on the attached map of Mobai, the chief's town of the Mando chiefdom in Upper Mende country. It will be noted from this that the town is divided into four 'Sections', i.e. Gorn, Manduwo, Hotala, and Tolobu.[1] The significance of these is explained in Chapter V.

Nowadays, it is necessary to re-classify Mende towns as of two kinds. The first comprises what might reasonably be termed the 'new' towns. These are new in the sense that their position on the railway line, or on a main motor road, has caused their partial rebuilding and the addition of fresh areas to house an expanded population. The second kind comprises the 'old' towns in the 'bush', which have scarcely changed. In the 'new' towns, a large number of the houses stand in regular lines and are spaced out. In the 'old' towns, there are no regular 'streets', and the houses tend to stand together in irregular and closely packed clumps. The ordinary village consists merely of a dozen, or perhaps two dozen, houses which surround a small open space or compound. There are no public buildings and the houses themselves are of poorer quality and structure.

As the result of their position on the railway line and the main roads, the new towns are the principal centres both for native and modern trade and commerce. They all contain stores and 'shops'

[1] cf. Chapter V.

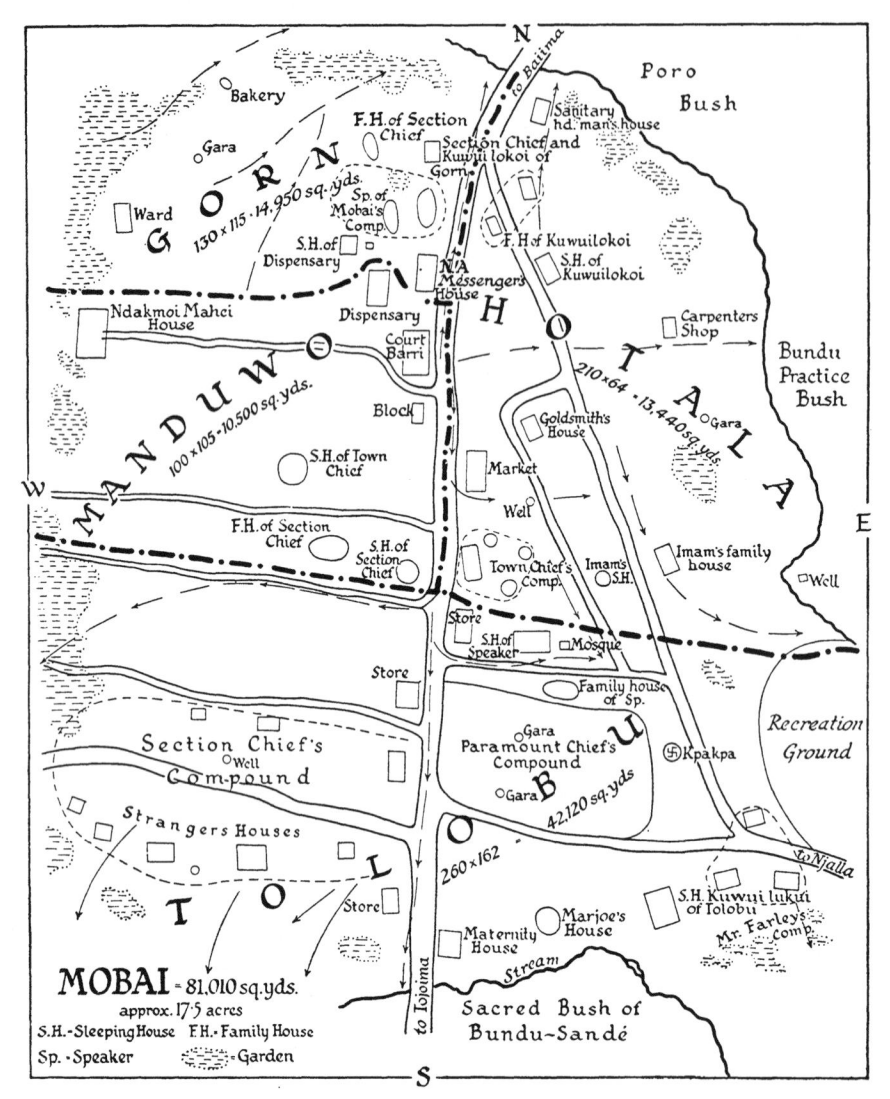

PLAN OF MOBAI

operated by European firms and Syrian and Creole merchants and traders, who are responsible, directly or indirectly, for buying most of the native produce—palm kernels, groundnut, ginger, etc., which finds its way down to Freetown and eventually is shipped abroad. These stores and 'shops' sell mainly cotton goods and a very wide assortment of miscellaneous articles, from enamel ware to cigarettes and sun-helmets. In the large towns of this kind, the public market is under the control of the Native Administration. Quite a large local trade is done there in dried fish, mainly *bonga*, which has been brought up from places like Bonthe and Shenge on the coast.[1] Many varieties of native vegetables as well as palm oil are also sold in large quantities. Bo is typical in these respects, but not in others, for it is disproportionately large in size and the main Government offices outside Freetown are situated there. Bo also has a number of mission churches and schools, including the only secondary school for boys in the Protectorate.

Though there are some Mende traders of wealth and importance, most of the business carried on indigenously is on a small scale and is handled very largely by women. Many of these are 'strangers' to Mendeland and come from all parts of the country. The principal occupation for both sexes, however, is rice farming, with the palm kernel and palm oil industry a good second. A certain amount of time is also spent on the raising of smaller, 'commercial' crops, such as cocoa, ginger, groundnuts, etc. Fishing, among the Mende, is carried on largely by women in the inland swamps, rivers, creeks, and pools. The men specialize in weaving and blacksmithing; the women in dyeing and spinning cotton, and to a smaller extent, in pottery. Work in gold is a man's job and is done more by outsiders, such as the Mandingo. Hunting, nowadays mainly of small animals, is, of course, also a man's occupation. It is carried on with the aid of dogs and nets, and sometimes with the help of an old musket or modern shotgun.

Few Mende have permanent western type jobs. The principal manual occupations are provided by the Public Works Department of the Government, which carries on a certain amount of road-building and repairing, etc., and by the mines. These, however, employ less than 20,000 workers in the whole of the Protectorate, and the principal workings are situated outside Mendeland, in Kono and Temne country. There are also a number of

[1] For a description of this trade in dried fish see Appendix II, 'The *Bonga*-Traders'.

MODERN MENDELAND AND ITS PEOPLE

'white collar' jobs, which occupy a number of Mende men and a smaller number of the women. These include teaching in Government and Mission schools; Native Administration; clerical work in Government offices and in the stores and shops of the European firms and larger Syrian traders; and nursing and dispensing. Posts of this kind are also filled by Creole men and women from the colony.

As already mentioned, the non-Mende population of Mendeland is largest in the railway line towns and it consists mainly of petty traders of whom many are women. In a place like Bo, where there are representative numbers of every cultural group in the Protectorate, the general effect is quite cosmopolitan, particularly as the dress of each 'tribe' has some special features. Temne men, for example, may be recognized by their large 'full buttoned' gowns, their fez or white cap, and their forceful way of walking. Their womenfolk fasten their head-ties in a distinctive way, wear a smock with a *lappa*[1] wrapped round the waist as if it were a belt; they wear bracelets, canvas shoes, and walk with their shoulders straight. Fula men are frequently seen in charge of cattle. They wear a long gown, usually white in colour, and baggy canvas trousers; they have a tall cap of cloth and walk with a 'springy' step. Their womenfolk, if well to do, wear gold rings suspended from their hair instead of the ears, have long gowns and expensive *lappas*, wear embroidered slippers and walk 'majestically'. The Mandingo are usually tall in stature, they wear long black gowns of cotton which have very large pockets, their trousers are baggy, they often carry a chewing stick and wear a sun-helmet, and their walk is very upright and slow. The Mandingo women are very like the Fula. Susu men also wear a 'full buttoned' gown, a fez cap, and slippers. There are not many Kru men; the women wear a black short smock and black *lappa* wound round the waist, and a black or red head-tie; some wear canvas shoes. They make much use of white cream and powder on the face, and sometimes have 'tribal' marks on the side of the face by the eye. The Kissi men wear their gowns up to the neck, and have shorts of native woven or imported khaki cloth. They have 'tribal' marks on the cheek and walk with a 'mountain' gait. The Kono men, who are mostly labourers in the town, wear European shorts and shirt outside the trousers. Their womenfolk wear bright coloured *lappas*, and the

[1] A *lappa* is a length of cotton or silk cloth, usually worn round the waist as a skirt.

wealthier ones, a smock.[1] The Limba wear gowns of native cloth and tight shorts of the same material.

The Mende themselves have two or three small marks high on the cheek bone. They lean forwards slightly when they are walking. The men wear an embroidered jacket, or a cotton gown dyed blue by 'garra'. They also wear shorts of country cloth, or 'small-bottomed' trousers of the same material. Mende women, in the town, tend to copy the Temne in their style of dress; those who are well to do wear a *lappa* and a black woollen smock. Outside the town, on the farms, they very often wear nothing above the *lappa*, which is wrapped round the waist and worn as a skirt.

Creole men invariably wear European clothes, e.g. short trousers and shirt during the daytime, and on more formal occasions, if they can afford it, a tropical or cloth suit. The women wear print and cotton frocks for ordinary use and, usually, a kerchief tied round the head. They wear their hair in European fashion instead of plaiting the hair, as is the native custom. Lebanese also wear European clothes, but usually of a poorer quality and of white calico. Their womenfolk are distinguished sartorially by the white silk shawl which many of them wear over the head, Arab fashion.

The remaining inhabitants of Mendeland consist of the officials and technicians of the British administration; European missionaries; and a few mining engineers. Different parts of Mendeland come under specific Administrative districts which are in the charge of Commissioners and District Commissioners, as the senior political officers are termed. The Protestant Missions have a similar scheme to avoid redundancy and overlapping.

4. *Mende National Consciousness*

'Mende' is a fairly recent word, and possibly a European one. According to Migeod, the name was first used by Koelle in his *Polygatta* in 1834.[2] A previous vocabulary, published by the Society

---

[1] It is hardly necessary to add that there are frequent fluctuations in the type of smock and the colour and design of head-tie which are popular among the women. At the time of the present investigation, there was a tendency to favour 'darker' colours. The fashion is set partly by the more notable women, as well as by Creoles. A Syrian trader informed the writer that he sometimes 'dashed' the Chief's head wife head ties, etc., when he wished to dispose of a certain line of goods.

[2] cf. F. W. H. Migeod, op. cit.

MODERN MENDELAND AND ITS PEOPLE

of Friends in 1828, referred to them as *Kossa*, and a similar term seems to have been applied to the Mende nearly up to the middle of the last century. For example, Robert Clarke, who published a book about the Sierra Leone Colony in 1843, whilst Senior Assistant Surgeon there, writes of them as *Kussoh*.[1] The latter term, like *Kossa*, appears, however, to be Creole in origin, and has derogatory implications. It does not occur in Mende itself.

It is just possible that in their earlier days, the Mende possessed either as a whole, or in separate bands, some form of political organization sufficiently centralized to justify their anthropological description as a tribe. There is some indication of this in traditional lore and in the very scanty historical material of the latter part of the nineteenth century. But considering the Mende as a whole and as we know them today, it is best to think primarily of their cultural and linguistic characteristics. These mark them off as a separate group from any other people in the Protectorate. Omitting, also, the question of a unified 'state', they may be regarded, in the widest sense of the term, as a nation. They inhabit a fairly well-defined territory of their own, and possess a definite consciousness of themselves as a single people.

This national consciousness is the result of their historical contacts with neighbouring peoples, and it is supported by general tradition, including myth, legend, and folk lore. It is exemplified, moreover, by the Mende attitude towards their contemporary neighbours, which is based on the war-like experiences, real as well as imagined, of pre-Protectorate days when the Mende accounted themselves a great warrior people. Even today, it is a matter of pride on the part of a Mende man to lay claim to some 'big warrior' as an ancestor. Stories of the exploits, part historical and part fictional, of famous Mende fighters and chiefs, like Ndawa and Kai Lundo, the founder of the Kissi-Mende chiefdom of Luawa, are the common heritage of the present generation of Mende children.[2]

[1] Robert Clarke, *A Description of the Manners and Customs of the Liberated Africans*, 1843.

[2] It is believed that lions roar when a warrior dies. Special ceremonies are performed in connection with the funeral. The corpse is hidden from the view of everyone who has not handled a sword. All previous warriors in the nearby towns and villages attend the burial, bringing their sword well sharpened. They ask the dead man's relatives for a number of cows proportionate to the number of people he killed when alive. The morning after the burial, the warriors take their swords, don battle dress and engage in mock fighting, killing all the

MODERN MENDELAND AND ITS PEOPLE

Towards the peoples around them, therefore, the Mende have a varying set of attitudes. In particular, they look down on the Kissi and Kono people who occupy the country to the north-east. The Mende claim that they used to capture Kono men and women and sell them as slaves in order 'to provide head ties for their mothers'—*mu nja ne ti wumba gba ya*. The Kissi live in 'backward places', and their customs, such as filing the front teeth, are regarded as particularly degenerate. The Sherbro, inhabiting the country to the south-west, are considered fools. 'If a Sherbro man finds any money, he gives it to a European', and the story is told of a Sherbro who found the sum of £200 and two bales of cotton at the railway station and took them to the District Commissioner. A Mende man would have buried his find until some later and appropriate time. The Fula, who enter Mende country to trade cattle, are regarded as thieves, and as 'flea-ridden', because of their connection with cows. The Lokkos are spoken of disparagingly as 'potato-eaters', as poverty-stricken and backward. Peoples more distant from Mendeland are characterized as *kuhaa-bla*, i.e. people from afar. Especially in Kpaa Mende country there has always been close contact and a good deal of warfare and general rivalry with the neighbouring Temne who are spoken of, sometimes, as thieves. But there is some respect for the Temne on account of their well-known fighting qualities in the past. The Mende speak of the Creole people from the Colony as *pu-bla*, i.e. white men, on account of their European ways. They are sometimes termed 'rogues', 'ungrateful', and are called 'foo-foo eaters', because of the Creole predilection for this particular diet of grated cassadu. They are also described as 'dirty'; their women 'don't wash'; and the Creole is 'landless' and the 'son of a slave'. Lebanese are often regarded as cheats, and as dirty, and are said to eat their meat raw.

On the other hand, the Mende express admiration for some peoples. The Mandingo are described as aristocrats and as clean. The Gallinas are also looked up to as aristocratic, but are regarded as lazy. The cleverness of the Europeans is greatly admired, and they are spoken of, sometimes, as 'genii'. The Europeans have extra prestige because they took the country from the Mende. They hardly ever break a promise. Both Europeans and Syrians, however, are looked upon in a somewhat different way from the

animals. The people around have to calm their frenzy the best way they can. In the old days, the deceased man's relatives had to 'redeem' his body from the warriors.

African groups; and on account of their different racial characteristics and culture are regarded as outside the orbit of native society.

The natural concomitant of these attitudes and feelings of group consciousness is the pride which a Mende person has in his own 'nationality' and institutions. There are specific traits, such as open-handed generosity combined with extreme secrecy over personal affairs, which are considered peculiarly 'Mende' and which frequently earn approbation in some saying, like 'He's a proper Mende man'. This general approval of generosity is typified most strikingly in the native custom of 'begging' a person. Whatever hardship or wrong a Mende man has suffered at the hand of another; whatever concession to personal honour or interest he is required to make, it is expected that a suitable gift will restore his injured feelings and pride. Indeed, this readiness to overlook even custom and precedent in favour of those who are 'kind' to them is one of the reasons why it is impossible to conceive of many institutional aspects of Mende life in a rigid way. Even in respect of some of the more deep-seated items of their culture, the Mende give the impression of being eclectic, both in their way of looking at things and in their actual behaviour.

It is evident, too, that the Mende approve boisterous and friendly behaviour and are suspicious and ill at ease with the individual who is neither open-hearted nor open-handed. As one informant put it: 'Mende people expect you to rejoice with them, and if you dance and mix with them, they will "see with you". If you are reserved, they are afraid of you.' The Mende also respect feats of hardihood and *nonchalance* in the face of difficulty or danger. But the conduct they particularly admire is strongly tinged with bravado, and boastfulness is generally condoned. A person, even an adventurer, may be courted and flattered so long as his success lasts; but, once unfortunate, he is likely to be reviled or forgotten, whatever past service he has rendered. This latter point applies, sometimes, even to relations within the kinship unit. There is little sentiment wasted over fair dealing for its own sake. The natural way to deal with a personal injustice is to seek retribution. It seems to be an especial point of honour that a Mende man should get the better of his opponent, however he may do it. Likewise, Mende women are expected to drive a hard bargain, whether in trading, or in relations with their husbands or lovers.

The various stories of the warrior, Ndawa, serve to illustrate

MODERN MENDELAND AND ITS PEOPLE

some of the qualities which are most admired, and exemplify the contribution of the culture hero to the anatomy of Mende national consciousness.

'Ndawa was born at Majoru (in the present district of Kenema). There, he was initiated into Poro. Many things happened to him which distinguish him from other heroes of his day. Ndawa was of middle height, brown skinned, thickly built, had powerful arms, and a scar on his forehead. He was handsome and very lively in spirit.

'It happened on one occasion that Ndawa "befriended" a wife of Chief Ganglia who, in his anger, sold him as a slave to one, Sellu Tifa. Ndawa vowed that he would do no farm work for this man and made up his mind to be a warrior. He was flogged and punished many times, but remained true to his oath. Seeing that he could do no good with the lad, Sellu Tifa sold him to Chief Macavoreh of Tikonko in exchange for a sword. This provided Ndawa with his opportunity, for Macavoreh was continuously engaged in war. With Macavoreh, Ndawa obtained the training he needed and soon proved himself in many fierce raids.

'About this time, Macavoreh was strongly threatened by Benya, the Chief of Blama. Ndawa undertook to drive him away, and invited the warrior Kai Lundo to help him in his task. Thus began the Kpove War, so called on account of the custom of stowing the heads of cowardly warriors in a large pot. They forced Benya out of Mendeland and he retreated into the Kono hills. Ndawa was then given his freedom by Macavoreh.

'One day, Ndawa crossed the river Sewa to a town called Majeihu. He sat down to play a game of *warri* with the people of the town and won his first game, but was cheated over the second and third games. His anger grew so great at this that he burned down the whole town while the people slept. To spare Ndawa being executed for this, Macavoreh agreed to rebuild the town.

'Ndawa continued to win fame and with a company of young warriors, laid the country waste as far as the border of Liberia. Returning, he built the town of Wende for himself. Then he waged war as far as Pendembu, but his progress into the Luawa chiefdom was barred by his erstwhile comrade, Kai Lundo.

'Ndawa had many enemies as a result of his exploits, and one day a man, Jami Lenge, and some of his friends laid an ambush for him. In trying to beat them off, Ndawa was wounded. He got as far as the river and lay down on its bank, too weak to move or to use the sword which had saved him for so many years. A certain young boy rushed at him and would have killed him, but Ndawa cried out saying, "Come, Jami Lenge. Come and finish me. Let people not say that a small boy killed Ndawa." Thus, died the great Ndawa who had been the terror of all around him. The news of his death went far and wide and many people came to see for themselves if it was true. His left arm was cut off to inform the people of Nongowa, and his head was sent to Benya at Palima and the Kpove warriors met there. His body was burned and the ashes scattered in the river.'

The general Mende consciousness and appreciation of a common way of life is varied, however, by differences in local dialect, social custom, and tradition. Nor, in view of the widely distributed nature of the Mende population and its antecedents, is this surprising. The main distinction is in respect of the Kpaa Mende who inhabit some sixteen chiefdoms in the western corner of the country. The Kpaa Mende have particularly strong military traditions supported by one or two institutions, such as the Wunde society, which are not shared by the rest of the country. In pre-British days the Kpaa Mende bore most of the brunt of the fighting with the Temne. As a result of these experiences, gained sometimes in the service of Temne war-chiefs themselves, Kpaa Mende warriors had a high reputation throughout Mendeland. Further up country, Kpaa Mende people are spoken of, sometimes, as part-Temne, and their distinctive speech may mark them out for unpopularity. Numerically, the Kpaa Mende comprise, perhaps, some 20 per cent of the total Mende population in Sierra Leone.[1]

The inhabitants of 'Middle' Mende country, or Sewa Mende, as they are called, sometimes, on account of their proximity to the Sewa River, regard themselves as somewhat different from the Kpaa Mende as well as from those born in the eastern part of the country. They consider that the latter speak in the Mende language 'like children', and their own speech is 'real Mende'. The eastern Mende, again, have been adulterated culturally and linguistically by Kissis and other eastern peoples. Very roughly, the Sewa Mende comprise some 35 per cent of the Mende population, leaving to the Upper Mende the balance of some 45 per cent.[2]

[1] Estimated by the present writer from figures supplied in the 1931 *Sierra Leone Census*. [2] ibid.

CHAPTER IV

RICE-FARMING AND LAND TENURE

1. *General Significance of Rice*

Essentially, the Mende are an agricultural people whose staple crop and food is rice. Rice, supplemented with oil pressed out of the kernel of the palm fruit and made into a 'soup' or 'sauce' with vegetables, pepper and, sometimes, with meat or dried fish, is their principal form of diet. Generally, two main meals are taken, i.e. 'breakfast' at noon, and an evening meal at about 7 o'clock in the evening. Unless rice has formed part of the menu, the ordinary Mende person will say that he is not satisfied. Individual Mende men who were asked to say what their normal food requirements would be, assuming rice were available every day, estimated at least one bushel per month. In fact, however, except in the more wealthy households, rice is available very rarely in certain months of the year, particularly July and August, which are termed the 'hungry season'. Its place is taken by yams and cassada.[1] The usual method of preparation, after the rice has been thoroughly cleaned by rinsing with water and removing any pieces of grit which may be adhering to it, is by boiling it in water and allowing it to steam off. It is then served in a fairly stiff cake which is solid enough to break up into lumps, when manipulated by the fingers or a spoon. 'Red rice', as rice which has been soaked in palm oil is called, is an essential part of any sacrifice which is made to the ancestors or the spirits. Rice has also a certain ceremonial value in entertaining strangers or an important guest.

[1] Cassada, though not fully grown, can be eaten by August; hence the saying, *Tangei nbei ma baunga*—"The cassada saved the rice'.

2. *Upland v. Swamp Rice*

By far the greater part of the rice grown in Mendeland, as well as in the Sierra Leone Protectorate as a whole, is cultivated on 'uplands', i.e. on ground from which the rain water drains or evaporates soon after it has fallen. The cultivation of rice in swamps or in 'moistlands' (i.e. generally hollows or depressions in the ground which remain partly or wholly under water throughout the season) is a comparative innovation, and its extension as a regular practice is due very largely to the encouragement of the Government's Agricultural Department. There can be no doubt that far more swamp rice ought to be grown. Land suitable for upland crops is becoming more scarce every year owing to erosion. Afforestation, and the reservation of special areas in order to preserve valuable kinds of timber, have also reduced available space, and have added to the general tendency of cropping land to an extent beyond which its fertility can be renewed.

Swamp cultivation yields a very much larger crop than upland rice, but it is not nearly so popular. The conditions of working, which often necessitate wading knee-deep in water, are unpleasant, and some of the usual operations, such as 'brushing', require a harder and more intensive effort. There is the further disadvantage that various subsidiary and important crops, such as cassada, cotton, benniseed, etc., which the farmer plants in his rice-field, or sows alongside the rice itself on an upland farm, cannot be grown in the swamp. There is also a fairly general prejudice against swamp rice as food. It is said to be less 'sweet' than upland rice, more 'watery', and less satisfying. Probably on account of its novelty, swamp rice is not used in any kind of ritual ceremony or offering.[1]

3. *Cultural Significance of the Rice Farm*

Farming, as it is understood in Mende country, means primarily, then, the making of rice farms. The cultivation of other

---

[1] From figures supplied by the Agricultural Department in respect of twenty chiefdoms in eastern Mendeland, it would appear that only between one-seventh and one-eighth as much swamp rice as upland rice is planted per taxpayer. This is inclusive of swamp rice grown under the auspices of Native Administrations. The most general practice appears to be for upland farmers to cultivate a small swamp in addition to their main farm. There are some farmers, however, who grow only swamp rice.

crops, such as cassada, yams, guinea corn, benniseed, or of fruit trees, such as kola, and even the economically very important harvesting of palm fruit, are regarded as supplementary activities. Even the increasing attention paid to purely 'economic' crops, like coffee and cacao, particularly in certain areas, has not diminished the significance of rice as the traditional crop. It still remains the main focus of the Mende man's agricultural interest, and of most of the social life of the people. Many townspeople as well as villagers spend the greater part of the year actually on the farm. From January to October, they set out nearly every morning between 6.30 and 7 o'clock and return home about 6 o'clock in the evening. Between October and January, they may go out as early as 6 a.m. and return about 7.30 p.m.

During the latter part of the year the remainder of the harvest is taken in, the young people are initiated in the secret societies, and many of the evenings are spent in dancing, particularly when the moon is full, until late into the night. With the exception of the clerical and trading communities in the towns and of a few specialized occupations, such as blacksmithing, goldsmithing, etc., most Mende men, from the chief downwards, either have their own farm, work on someone else's farm, or have some more or less direct connection with a farm. In short, farming activity based on rice production, supports virtually the entire economic life of town and country, from the trader to the medicine man. A further number of subsidiary occupations, like the spinning and weaving of cotton, mat and basket making, etc., are hardly to be disassociated from the farming life itself, since they depend upon farm-grown products.

The influence of farming and of rice growing, in particular, is especially significant in a psychological sense. Various ceremonies carried out on the farm are connected with the successful production of rice. They are performed communally, for the most part, and have the effect of bringing the people together emotionally in a way which is complementary to the effect of mutual participation in the farming operations themselves. As a result, the continuous and co-operative union of household and family groups is enhanced, and reciprocal services and obligations are discharged more readily.

It would appear, also, as if a very large part of the aesthetic aspects of Mende life were derived directly from the nature and function of specific kinds of work on the farm. There is a very close and striking similarity between the rhythm and movements of the Mende dancer, and the movements of a woman treading out and threshing rice. In the latter operation, the worker supports the weight of her body by holding on to a cross-piece of the barn and treads with each foot in turn, in a pressing and swaying movement of the body, on the heap of rice-stalks beneath her. The same trampling movement, with arms bent at the elbow and held rigidly to the sides, and with the body inclined to the same position, is seen in the dance itself. The pressing out of palm oil by the women is carried on in the same kind of trampling style. Again, there is a close similarity, both in rhythm and muscular movement, between the clapping with which women accompany a dance or a song, and the movements of women pounding rice in a mortar. In the latter case, the pestle is thrown upwards, caught, and brought down into the mortar by both hands seizing and pressing it downwards to the accompaniment of a definite forward jerk of the body. The similarity is even more striking when, as is sometimes the case, the woman actually claps her hands together, before catching the pestle.

Finally, though the connection is not quite so obvious, there is some similarity between the use of the *segbullei*—a calabash with beads or dried seeds threaded round it—and the winnowing of rice in the large, flat basket employed for the latter purpose. The position of the hands, and particularly the rhythm and arm movements, sometimes fast, sometimes slow, correspond to the handling of the *segbullei*.

4. *Social Incentives and Methods of Rice Farming*

It follows from these general considerations that social incentives for making a rice farm are very great. Its immediate purpose is to provide the household with food. It also affords a large part of the means by which the farmer secures cash needed for House Tax on behalf of himself and other adult members of his group, and often ekes out a bridewealth payment. Rice-farming, moreover, is the main way in which a person, particularly a younger man, rises in social status and establishes himself in the eyes of the community. A large-sized household, including wives, who always constitute a mark of prestige, and the making of a farm go together.

There is a general recognition that to obtain wives and to maintain a family requires both initiative and hard work. These qualities must be displayed, in the first instance, in working for someone else; but they are the test of a man's ability to farm on his own account. He can win additional credit by the way he makes his farm, firstly by the manner in which he tackles the problem of 'brushing' high forest. The really keen and efficient farmer is the one who is always on his land, who begins every operation himself, and sets the pace on all of them for his workmen. The rice on his farm grows with the ears clustering closely together and he always has rice to sell. It will be found stored in his barn long after the harvest. His farm is carefully and closely weeded and is fenced against wild animals. He starts work early in the morning and leaves off late at night. Ultimately, however, having regard to the numerous and arduous operations which the making of a rice farm requires, his success depends on a plentiful supply of labour.

The last point may be appreciated best by considering more specifically the various tasks which are involved. These have to follow the seasons. The first thing is to select a suitable site for the farm, taking care to choose a spot where the bush is reasonably mature. Then begins the work of chopping and lopping off the branches of the taller trees—this is termed 'brushing'—and of felling the larger trees with an axe. The débris is then piled together in heaps and, when it is quite dry, burnt. After this, the ground is harrowed by hoes and seed scattered over it. After the seed has germinated and is growing, the crop is weeded carefully by hand, and care is taken to scare off marauding birds. Finally, it is harvested by means of bamboo or iron knives, and stored away in newly built barns.

The greater part of this work is performed by the farming household, or *màwɛ*. The operations are arduous and not without some danger, in the earlier stages of felling and burning, to the labourers themselves. It also requires a considerable amount of skill and a good deal of agricultural experience on the part of the farmer, or person directing the work. The farming household is helped over the major operations, as a rule, by relatives and friends. There are also various institutional arrangements and forms of communal help, for example, there is the *bɛmbɛ*, a company of young men who hire out their services for the hoeing. In the case of *tewe yenge*, 'by turn labour', individual households, or even whole villages, work on each other's farms in turn. In Upper Mende country, there is also the institution known as *kugbe*, meaning 'strength' (i.e. war strength). The young men and women assemble at brushing, hoeing, and harvest time at each other's farms in the district in turn. Modern commercial practices also exist, sometimes alongside the indigenous ones, and men and women are hired individually as workers and are paid in cash for their services. Communal help is 'free', but the farmer is required to feed every one who comes to his aid. Relatives and friends are usually remunerated with a small token gift, such as tobacco. At the harvest, it is the custom to reward all the helpers with rice.[1]

5. *The Basis of Land Tenure*

Access to land and rights to its occupation and use for purposes of farming, derive from membership of certain families or descent groups, who claim to have made the first settlement in the country. Perhaps, as already explained in Chapter I, a hunter and his family put up a few temporary houses at the spot where his party made their kill. In the course of time they would be joined by other hunters, and the settlement grew under the leadership of the hunter, or his successor. In other and later cases, a warrior chief wishing to found a new town as an outpost would settle a number of his warriors on the spot chosen and allot portions of the bush to them. Allocation of virgin bush was a general method of rewarding services rendered in war and of attracting supporters to one's aid in case of attack by neighbouring chiefs.[2] Slaves captured in war were also set down to work the land, and the virgin bush they cleared passed into the permanent possession of their masters. The accepted rule was that the individual who first brought a piece of land into cultivation gained the right to use

---

[1] For a more detailed description of farming practices, see K. L. Little, 'The Mende Farming Household', *Sociological Review*, Vol. XL, 1948, Sect. 4.

[2] Thus we are told that Madam Nyawoe came from Dama in Upper Mende to Bo with 300 warriors, 100 hampers of salt, 6 kegs of gunpowder, 2 kegs of flints, 12 boxes of caps, and 2 cases of Dane guns, and a number of *mori*-men to work medicine on behalf of the town, when it was besieged. She also presented a large number of sheep to the big men of the town, and for her kindness was given extensive lands outside, which are still occupied by her descendants.

It was the general rule for newcomers of this kind to 'sit down' near previous immigrants from the same district as themselves. They would take along a 'thanking present' to the Chief until such time as they were looked upon as members of the town, and no longer as strangers.

RICE-FARMING AND LAND TENURE

and occupy it so long as he lived. His heirs inherited that right when he died. Land brought under cultivation further afield by the efforts and initiative of younger members of the group was vested in the name of their father, or of its head. Subsequent settlers, who were allotted land which had previously been brought under cultivation, were considered under the protection of their landlord. Their right to occupy and use such land grew progressively greater, the longer they remained with him. It was unlikely that they would be disturbed; but in the meantime, they were dependent upon his good will in vouching for them and in not contesting their usufruct of his soil.[1]

The same kind of rights were acquired by all those who were held as domestic slaves until 1926. Long before that date, slaves were allocated land to cultivate on their own account and for their maintenance.[2] It was recognized that their tenure, i.e. their right to use a part of their master's land, was secure so long as they satisfied his requirements. Legally speaking, the slaves could be described as 'tenant settlers'. So long as they fulfilled their obligations, they were not disturbed and were permitted to keep for themselves any profit made from the cultivation of the ground they occupied.

6. 'Ownership' and 'Holding' of Land

Broadly speaking, therefore, Mende society has two classes of person in relation to land and two forms of land tenure. The first class comprises the descendants of the hunters, warrior chiefs, and warriors, who first settled the country. It consists, in the main,

---

[1] This is not mere theory. The writer heard it argued in a case heard in the court of the Native Administration at Kenema. Plaintiffs claimed compensation from the defendant for using a certain area of bush over a period of years. It was established that the grandfather of the defendant came as a stranger to the district, was befriended by the plaintiffs' grandfather, and given bush to farm. He subsequently became headman of the village where he settled. The Court ascertained that this person was never regarded in the district as a big man, the implication being that he was not therefore in a position to hand on land to his heirs. It also came out that the village of which he was headman was merely a 'daughter town', i.e. an offshoot, of the town which the ancestors of the plaintiffs had founded (see Chapter V for elucidation of this point). The case was awarded to the plaintiffs and the defendant told that he must compensate them for use of their land.

[2] See Chapter I.

of the present ruling chiefs, heads of other 'crowning houses',[1] sub-chiefs, and their respective families. The senior members of this class are spoken of generally as 'big men'. The second class consists of subsequent settlers and strangers, usually from other parts of the country, and of the one-time domestic slaves. The term *ndɔ-bla* (aborigines) is applied, sometimes, to denote the first group in distinction to the people of the chiefdom as a whole.

The two types of tenure derive from what might be termed, respectively, primary and secondary settlement. As a general rule, the living memory is the only way of substantiating claims of either kind. The tendency is for the second kind to merge into the first. It will be convenient to call the class first mentioned 'land owners', and the second, 'land holders'. The main difference is in the extensiveness of the rights enjoyed over land. In the first case, the 'land owner' inherits land and has the right to transmit it to his heirs. The rights of the 'land holder' are limited to personal occupation and use.

Partly, perhaps, owing to the difficulty of making this distinction, and for other reasons, the Government apparently decided some time ago to drop the term 'owner' in connection with land tenure. It prefers to speak of 'land holders', and appears to regard the Tribal Authority as the actual 'owner' of land in a chiefdom.[2] This view is far from being in accordance with the native conception, and at the first meeting of the Protectorate Assembly in 1946, the Government was asked to state whom it regarded as the actual owners of land in the Protectorate.[3]

7. *Rights in Land and its Inheritance*

From the native point of view, an individual who acquires land by inheritance (*Poo logboi*—inherited bush) enjoys a complete set

---

[1] The term 'crowning house' popularly denotes a descent group which has supplied a chief at any time for the chiefdom concerned.

[2] See the *Protectorate Land Ordinance*, 1927, the preamble to which states that, 'Whereas all land in the Protectorate is vested in the tribal authorities, who hold such land on behalf of the native communities concerned'. A more recent Ordinance for the Acquisition of Land in the Protectorate (July, 1947) is even more explicit in specifically defining 'owner' as meaning a Tribal Authority.

[3] It goes without saying that native concern over questions of land tenure is very deep-seated indeed, as opposition to the recent Lands Acquisition Bill has amply testified. See also Chapter II, where it is recalled that, according to certain evidence offered to the Royal Commission of Enquiry into the causes

RICE-FARMING AND LAND TENURE

of rights over it.[1] These are qualified by the interest which his nearest of kin also enjoy in such property, and by his relation to the chief who, as *n dɔ-mahun gbei mui*, may be described as the 'over-looker' of all lands in the chiefdom. He has the right to the free and uninterrupted use of such land, to build houses and plant trees on it, to hunt game and catch fish, to cut timber, and to grow what crops he likes, and generally to use it in any way which does not contravene the laws and customs of the chiefdom. He may, also, with the approval of his relatives, delegate these rights temporarily to any outside person, provided that he accepts responsibility for such a person while the latter is on his land, and provided the arrangement has been sanctioned by the chief. The question of such responsibility comes mainly to the fore in the modern practice of leasing land to a 'non-native' of the Protectorate, such as a Syrian trader.

Such rights are continuous, and land passes down the male line of kinsmen as property. A man's heirs to land are, traditionally, in the first instance, his brothers: after his brothers come his sons, and then his daughters. The oldest brother was regarded as the important person in a group of kinsmen and the one who should take charge of the property. A more modern practice, however, is for sons to claim, and very often to be awarded, their father's property in the place of the deceased's brother. The change is partly the result of English laws in force in the Colony and of the action of some of the young men, more particularly literate ones, in appealing directly to the District Commissioner. Being less familiar, in some cases, with native law, the latter has either upheld such claims, or treated them in such a way as to make it difficult for the Native Authorities to reject them. It is also possible that Islamic customs of inheritance have had a similar effect in this respect.

In the absence of brothers, or if the man's children are still minors at his death; or again, with the agreement of his male relatives, the man's maternal nephew (i.e. his sister's son), may inherit the land. It reverts, however, on the latter's death to the

of the Mende Rising, one of the causes of the insurrection was the fear that by imposing a Hut Tax, the Government claimed rights to the land on which the houses were built.

[1] This form of land tenure might, perhaps, be described as 'freehold in entail', since, as mentioned in a later paragraph, such land may not be alienated outside members of the male line of kinsmen.

descendants in the male line of the original owners. The claim of daughters is subordinate to that of sons, particularly the eldest son, and neither sons nor daughters would be allowed to inherit, until they are full grown. In a polygenous society, where a single individual may have as many as two dozen sons, it is obvious that a strict division of his land between them all would speedily result in the most extreme form of fragmentation. Any tendency towards this is therefore avoided by vesting the title only in a single heir.

This means, in other words, that the 'ownership' of land involves a combination of individual and group rights. It means that all kinsmen in the male line have a right to land vested in its nominal owner, and this right they never relinquish, even if they leave the district. In addition, any trees they have planted, such as coffee, kola, etc., and the houses they have built, remain their personal property.[1] Trees growing wild, such as palm trees, are under the general concept of 'land', or 'bush', for which the single term, *ndɔgboé*, is used, and their usufruct is covered by the general rights possessed by the kinship group as a whole. Even the cutting of timber by a non-member of the group without permission is an invasion of those rights. The Mende make a verbal distinction between land on which people actually live and build their houses, and land used for farming. The former is *ndɔé* and the latter, as mentioned above, *ndɔgboé*, but there is no distinction between the two so far as the question of tenure is concerned. On the other hand, streams and rivers, and the fish in them, are not regarded in the same sense as land; nor are the wild animals which roam the bush. There is no restriction on using another person's land for hunting or fishing, and water may be drawn from a stream running through it without compensating him. It is customary, however, for any one setting traps, to consult the owner of the place on which he proposes to put them.

8. *Religious Implications of Land Ownership*

It is a well-known principle in West Africa that rights in land may not be alienated. Among the Mende, there is a variety of reasons for this rule. It is partly because group as well as personal

---

[1] The fact that 'commercial' trees of the kind mentioned above are regarded as personal property means that they may be planted and harvested on land belonging to another person, provided he gives permission. Such trees have no part in the ordinary conception of 'land'.

RICE-FARMING AND LAND TENURE

status is very closely bound up with the ownership of land, so that a descent group which entirely lost possession of its land would automatically lose, as a group, most of the prestige it had in the eyes of the community. This point is of particular importance in political matters. The more land a descent group owns, the larger will be the number of its 'tenants' and dependents, and hence the greater amount of political support it can command in chiefdom affairs. Loss of land will mean the automatic loss of most of its following.[1]

There are, also, the obvious economic advantages of land. But just as strong, perhaps, is the religious background and the fact that land constitutes a tie with the ancestors. The ancestors are buried on family land, and they continue to inhabit it. They are in constant touch with the living group of kinsmen through its senior members, and they look to their descendants to preserve the mutual heritage, which is the tangible link between the past, present, and future generations of the line. Such land has stored up in it the memories and traditions of the past, and its very possession recalls the obligations which the living owe to the dead. This sentiment is summed up very aptly in the words of a land-owner in the Bumpe chiefdom of Upper Mende:

'I did not get my land through my own powers. My great grandfather and his own great grandfather first had it. When God made the earth, all was just one. When God created beings, He made them to work on farms. These farms ultimately became their lands. So, I inherited my present bush from my forefathers.'

Thus, for religious, as well as social reasons, the necessity of keeping their land intact as common property acts as a constant stimulus towards unity and cohesion among members of the group concerned. Traditional customs and ceremonies, particularly those related to the cult of the ancestors, are strictly enjoined. A special premium is placed on attendance at funerals and meetings which have the effect of bringing more widely scattered branches of the group together. Neglect of the latter obligations is met by censure, and may even be treated by disciplinary action.

Occasionally, however, some cause of friction is responsible for the descent group breaking apart. Rather than allow the rift to become permanent, the matter may be referred to the chief with a view to his intervention and arbitration. If every effort fails, the

[1] See Chapter IX, also, on this point.

descent group concerned may divide into two or three different branches, so far as the holding and use of the common property is concerned. One important reason why such disruption is avoided as far as possible is because it encourages encroachment from outside. Small kinship units find it more difficult to maintain their claims against outsiders. They also lose the support of the wider group in financial troubles, and they can no longer enjoy the same benefits of mutual aid in working the land itself.

The tendency is for lands to become split up into widely scattered lots with increased settlement. The fact that land has been brought into cultivation from the earliest times under a shifting system means that the bush to which a given descent group lays claim is not necessarily a single area. It may consist of several portions, separated from each other quite often by large natural obstacles such as rivers and hills and by distances of several miles. Boundaries are recognized by local landmarks, like cotton trees, swamps, rocks, etc., and, sometimes, by fences.

9. *Rôle of the Head of the Kin Group in relation to Land*

As already implied, inheritance of land is synonymous with assumption of the headship of a kin group. In taking up his position the family head becomes trustee for the property, and the other relatives look to him to fulfil this dual responsibility. His first duty is to see that the land itself is used to the best advantage. He receives applications at the beginning of each farming season from those of his kinsmen who want to make their own farms. In allocating portions of the bush according to personal requirements and qualifications, he consults his brothers. Applications from a man's female relatives, such as daughters, are more likely to be considered favourably, as a rule, if they are actually residing in his household or the household of one of his blood relatives. The same applies to a daughter's son. If a daughter is living with her husband's people, she will probably be told to apply to them, if either she or her son wishes to farm. Nevertheless, the fact that a daughter's or a sister's right is secondary only to the male line means that a male individual has three more or less direct ways of gaining access to the use of land, viz. through his own father, through his mother and her brother, and through his wife's people.

The principle underlying actual use of land, as distinct from rights in its ownership, is very elastic. Considerations of local association, common residence, and the status and seniority of the applicant often over-ride considerations of kinship.

A sub-chief in Upper Mende country described some of the above conditions in the following words:

'I inherited my present bush from my father, and he inherited it from his own father. I have two brothers. They also inherited land from my father. I am head of the "family". When a stranger arrives and wants to "brush" (i.e. clear land for a farm), he should come to me and not to my brothers. I and my brothers "hang heads" (consult together), and decide to give him bush (to farm).

'If my brothers want to brush next year, they consult first with me before they make their farms. Any of my brothers' sons first consult with my brothers and they, in turn, consult with me, and I allot them land to brush. If my daughter wishes to make a farm, she consults me and not her husband. We of the "family" "hang heads", and decide whether or not we should allot her land. Or, if she wishes, she can go to her husband's people for land. Land allotted to my daughter should not be used by her son, except by my special permission.'

Though allocation of land at the beginning of each new farming season is the fairly general rule, it is not carried out in cases where the lands owned are very extensive, and where some kind of more or less permanent allocation was made during the life-time of the previous owner. This is the situation, sometimes, with well-established and well-integrated descent groups who own, to all intents and purposes, the greater part of the Section of a chiefdom. It means that the land in question may be divided into a number of 'blocks' between, for example, one or two of the brothers, or other senior members. The title to the whole area remains vested in the head of the group; but the individual holders make sub-allocations to members of their own households, or to other clients. Such allocations are subject, technically, to ratification by the head of the group; but he does not interfere with them. If one of the holders in question dies, the land reverts nominally to the head of the group, but a near relative of the deceased person may continue to administer and to farm it.

10. *The Position of the Chief*

The chief himself is referred to, sometimes, as *ndɔ mui*, meaning 'land man', or 'owner of land', in the sense of his being the ultimate owner of all lands in his chiefdom. This raises an interesting and controversial issue and its interpretation depends upon the way certain historical antecedents are judged. In order to put this matter into its proper context it is necessary to recapitulate the conditions already described in previous Chapters.

Prior to British intervention, the power of individual warrior chiefs was the main local factor, and conditions around them were determined largely by force of arms. Economic interests were forwarded mainly by securing slaves and plunder, and activities such as agriculture were of secondary importance. A chief who captured a town automatically dispossessed its inhabitants of their land by carrying them off as slaves, and quite often he took charge over the surrounding district. He might settle some of his warriors there, or the area might be abandoned. The only way of contesting his right there was by the sword.

The British domination of the country was secured by 1898, and agriculture had then replaced warfare as the principal form of economy. Interest in the holding of land which, it is probable, had previously been small, was naturally enhanced. The settled conditions gave uninterrupted tenure, and claims to local ownership came up for ratification. When disputes arose, the chief no longer had the backing of his warriors to decide the matter out of hand. Nor, if he took arbitrary action, could he then rely to any extent on support from the Poro society.[1] The chief's diminished authority limited his powers of appropriation and disposal[2] and led, in turn, to his being regarded more as the 'caretaker' of chiefdom lands than as their exclusive 'owner'. In other words, his interest in bush occupied by other members of the chiefdom became restricted to those rights of jurisdiction and arbitration which he shares nowadays with the Tribal Authority. He was still entitled, in theory, to allocate virgin bush.[3]

The general understanding, therefore, today, is that the chief

[1] For description of the political relationship of the Poro society with the chief, see Chapter IX.

[2] Evidence of the former exercise of such powers has already been cited in the present chapter and is quoted again in Chapter IX. It is also significant that the chief still retains a large number of traditional rights to animals and fish caught and killed in his chiefdom (see Chapter IX).

[3] It is doubtful if, apart from sacred bush belonging to the secret societies and inland swamps, any virgin bush remains in Mendeland. With regard to inland swamps, whether these have already been farmed or not, they belong to the owner of the land within whose boundaries they are.

RICE-FARMING AND LAND TENURE

and his kinsmen own and use land on exactly the same terms and conditions as any other member of the chiefdom. If the chief requires the use of more land than is already vested in his own descent group, he is expected to seek it in the same way as any other person, i.e. by 'begging' a neighbour or some other land owner for the loan of a piece of ripe bush.

Ordinarily, the application is presented with a *famalui*, which varies in amount from 2*s.* to 10*s.*, according to the size of the area to be cleared. In the old days, this 'greeting present' would take the form of a fowl and some rice to enable the people owning the bush to make a small sacrifice and thus inform their ancestors of the presence of a stranger. To omit the rite might offend the spirits and bring harm both to the owner and his temporary 'tenant'. It is usual, also, for the Town Chief to be informed of the arrangement. The person begging the bush is then allotted some ground to farm, and when the harvest comes round, he takes rice and a fowl, again, to the owner of the land. This latter gift is termed *seigbua lɔ*, or 'thanking present', and it enables the ancestors to be notified that the stranger has finished with the land. The transaction is now complete and the bush reverts to its actual owner, but the temporary user of it is allowed to harvest any cassada, cotton, etc., which he has planted and which matures after the rice crop has been taken in.[1]

A request of this kind from the chief would never be refused, but the fact that there is otherwise no special provision for him means that there is no equivalent in native law and custom to the European idea of 'crown lands'. The chief, acting on the advice of the Tribal Authority, may make various regulations about how land in the chiefdom shall be farmed. For example, he may decree that the various operations in rice-growing shall begin and end during certain months. But the chief is not allowed, in any circumstances, to dispossess an individual or his kinsmen of land, which they have occupied and cultivated over a period of years. A man's crime may be visited on himself or on his relatives. But apart from actual banishment, there is no way in which he can legally be denied access to his land.[2]

[1] Secret societies which require more bush in order to extend their premises are also expected to beg it from the owner.

[2] It is also worth mention, perhaps, that the tribute of rice paid traditionally to the chief from every farm (see Chapter IX) is merely an acknowledgement of the latter's jurisdiction over the land in question.

RICE-FARMING AND LAND TENURE

11. *Settlement as a Method of obtaining Land*

Some descent groups, who belong to what has been defined above as the 'land holding' class, exercise rights which are virtually indistinguishable from land ownership. This happens when the people in question are in special favour with the chief; when, under the present 'electoral' system, they succeed in becoming recognized as one of the 'crowning houses' of the chiefdom;[1] or when they have actually occupied and used land for a time as long as living memory. In such cases, the farming places they are in the habit of using are brushed and planted without application or reference to any outside person.

In the case of other 'land holders' whose position is less secure, or who are comparative newcomers to the district, a formal arrangement, and even submission, is required periodically, perhaps annually. For example, an individual arriving as a settler from another chiefdom, reports himself with a *famalui* to someone he knows and who will accept him as a 'stranger'.[2] In this case, the amount of the *famalui* varies according to the social status of the newcomer. His intending host refers the matter to his own relatives. The latter pass him on to the Town chief with a *famalui*, and from him to the chief himself.[3] The chief explains the laws and customs of the chiefdom to him. He must accept the same obligations as any other member of the chiefdom, such as taking his part in chiefdom labour, in road making, town cleaning, etc., and must pay the usual tribute. He has also to give periodical help on his landlord's farm, and should take him a gift at harvest time out of the proceeds of his own farm.

In other words, the 'stranger' incurs certain obligations for the privilege of using his landlord's land and of residing in the chiefdom. The landlord, for his part, assumes responsibility for him and acts as his advocate and protector in the event of a dispute. If the

---

[1] As explained in Chapter X, a number of anomalies have entered into the present system of electing chiefs whereby, for instance, a comparative stranger, who is wealthy and affluent, may sometimes work his way into the position of Chief.

[2] A 'stranger', in this sense, has a special meaning which corresponds, to some extent, to the English term, 'tenant'.

[3] One reason why a 'stranger' is sent to the chief is so that the latter is made aware of the person's alien origin. He will then be able to bear witness to this fact, should the stranger subsequently try to claim the land on which he is settled as his own property.

'stranger's' conduct is satisfactory, he is accepted as a permanent settler, and land is allotted to him year after year, without question. He is not permitted, however, to allow any persons, other than members of his own immediate family, to farm on such land, unless his landlord consents to it. Nor is he permitted to pledge any land allotted to him in the present or past. If he moves away, any houses he has built become the property of his landlord. He may, however, remove and take away with him doors, windows, and any other fitting. It is the same with respect to trees he has planted, though if they are of special economic value, he may be able to arrive at some agreement over them with the landlord. Alternatively, he can keep such property 'alive' by sending annually a 'shake hand' to his landlord. This signifies that he intends to return. The charge of his children also, if left behind, is taken over by the landlord.

Many such forms of settlement are permanent, and in the course of time, the settler, and more especially, his descendants, become identified with the group with whom they have settled to an extent which makes it virtually impossible to separate the issues in a land case. It generally happens that the settler or his children marry into the landlord's group. In such matters, so far as the use, apart from the title, of the land is concerned, the practical circumstances of the case are of as much importance as the theoretical principle of primary settlement. The fact, for example, that certain people had occupied and cultivated a piece of land over a long period, say, twenty or thirty years, would be sufficient justification for their being allowed to continue there. The most that the owner could claim would be the right to be consulted about the way in which the land was used. He might possibly claim, also, a share in the proceeds of its use. He would not be allowed to dispossess such persons without their agreeing to it and providing them, at the same time, with alternative bush, and even houses, in which to live.[1]

[1] The influx of 'strangers' leading, in some cases, to a large extension of some existing towns, or even to the establishment of a new town, is likely to produce a controversial issue in the future, when the land concerned takes on a more obvious economic value. Theoretically, of course, the land on which they have settled remains the property of their original landlords and the latter's descendants.

12. *Pledging of Land*

The practice of mortgaging and pledging—*Kpɔmbue*—land was unknown before the coming of the Europeans. Even today, it is still quite a rare feature in Mende country, except in cases where the owner, or some important member of his group, gets into debt to a serious extent. If he cannot find any other way of raising the money, he reports the matter to the chief with a view to getting help from all his kinsmen and dependants. If his relatives are unable to help him financially, they may allow him to pledge a certain area of land to a person who is ready to take over the debt. The amount offered in exchange for the pledge might be some £6 for two farming places for two years, i.e. to allow the making of successive farms during the time the debt is outstanding. If the bush is pledged for a longer period, the amount offered will be greater, but the pledge may retain usufruct, until the debt is repaid. The return he obtains from crops grown on the land is regarded as interest on the loan, and he can claim nothing more.

Usually, the pledge is regarded as outstanding until such time as it can be paid in full, and it may be repaid either by the original debtor himself, or by those who took up the debt on his behalf. If, after pledging bush, its owner is in a position to redeem it before the time agreed upon has fully expired, the person taking up the pledge is entitled to harvest whatever crops he has planted. This is to enable him to make good the interest on the money lent. However long-standing the debt, pledged lands remain, and are always considered, the property of the person who pledged them. The pledger is also regarded as the landlord of the pledgee. The latter is allowed to make full use of the bush itself, but any planted crops or trees, which the owner has put down, are either harvested by him or made the subject of a special arrangement with the person taking up the pledge.

13. *Leasing of Land*

The western practice of leasing land is entirely alien to Mende custom, though it bears some slight similarity to native methods of settlement and to the 'begging' of land. The important difference is that the 'begged' land is occupied only for a year, whereas a lease is usually taken out for a much longer period.

Another point of difference is that leases are sought for purposes which have no relation to farming, e.g. to build a store or a school, or for mining. The lessee must first obtain the consent of the land owner and of the chief. The District Commissioner acts as arbitrator in deciding the charge, which is assessed at so much per year. One portion of the 'rent' accrues to the land owner or occupier, another to the Treasury of the local Native Administration; and another to the chief. Before the institution of the Native Authority system, the amount was divided between the owner of the land and the chief. By custom, the head of the kinsmen concerned hands over their share to his younger brothers, and they are expected to return the lion's portion to him.

To be valid in the eyes of the Government, the lease must be witnessed and recorded. In the case of leases granted to Christian Missions, the lease runs for as long as 99 years and the amount is usually nominal. The amount assessed for Government leases varies, like that of leases taken out by Syrian and Creole traders for commercial purposes, according to a rough estimation of the economic value of the land. This is obviously much greater in well populated towns on the Railway Line than it is in the more rural areas.

However long a lease has to run, ownership of the land remains technically in native hands.

Access to land may then be summarized very briefly as follows. It is gained, in the first instance, through membership of a descent group which either 'owns' or 'holds' land. It may also be gained by 'begging', or by settlement and service with someone who himself is an owner or holder of land. It may be gained, finally, by taking up a pledge, or by leasing. To obtain land by taking up a pledge is, however, a rare practice, as compared with settlement and 'begging'; and so far as private transactions are concerned, the leasing of land for farming purposes is even less common in Mende country.

CHAPTER V

SOCIAL ORGANIZATION AND KINSHIP

1. *The Mawɛ as a Social Unit*

THE organization of life in the local community is shared by a number of social units whose nature ranges from the simple elementary family to that of the extended kind. For purposes of general description, however, the basic unit may be termed a household, and it is known in Mende as *mawɛ*.[1] It corresponds in the main essentials as to membership and function, to the joint family in that it is often three generations in depth and is relatively self-contained. Numerical composition varies very greatly, but a larger sized *mawɛ* may consist of one or two older men and their wives; some, or all, of their sons and daughters; husbands and wives of the latter; and a number of grandchildren. Such a household may also contain additional members in the shape of more distant blood and affinal relatives, as well as one or more dependants of the head of the household who are unrelated to the rest of the group. A small sized household, on the other hand, may consist merely of a man and his wives and their children, and one or two close relatives, such as his mother or sister. Properly speaking, however, a small sized household of the latter kind would not be spoken of as a *mawɛ*, unless the head or owner of it possessed at least four wives.

In fact, the social significance of the *mawɛ* can be appreciated only in terms of its traditional background of domestic slavery. In the old days, as mentioned in Chapter I, the slaves captured in

[1] The nearest English equivalent of *Mawɛ*, etymologically speaking, is 'our house', from *mu pelei*. In Mende, 'p' following 'u' becomes 'w', the 'l' is dropped, and the phrase, through a process of elision and contraction, becomes *mawɛ*. Thus, *mu pelei* = *mu wei* = *ma wɛ*.

war were set down to cultivate land for their masters, or to clear virgin bush. Houses were built for them, wives found among other slaves, and villages grew up adjacently, as a rule, to the house and compound of their owner. A single village, originating in this way, constituted a *mawɛ*, and might comprise as many as forty houses with a population of some 120 people. The slaves worked for the benefit of the owner of the *mawɛ*. He fed them out of the proceeds of the farms they made for him and his immediate family. Farmwork was organized on the co-operative activities of 'women's houses', or *pɛ waisia* (sing. *pɛ wa*). The *mawɛ*-owner housed his own wives and slaves in huts of their own. If there were a large number of them, more than one such *pɛwa* was required. Each women's house was responsible for making its own farm. A number of male slaves were allotted to it,[1] and they carried out the heavier work. The labour was supervised by the head wife, and in the case of a number of women's houses, each one was under the charge of a senior wife.

Sons of the owner of the *mawɛ* helped in its supervision until they were considered old enough to have charge of a *mawɛ* of their own. Then, provided they had their father's favour, they would be given a number of slaves with whom to start a *mawɛ* of their own. The sons remained directly under patriarchal control. It was rare for two full grown brothers to belong to the same *mawɛ*; because a brother, or any other member of a family of free men, considered it a humiliation to put himself under the domination of another person. Nevertheless, free men who had fallen on evil days, through debt or some other reason, sometimes sought the protection of another man's *mawɛ*. On the death of the owner of the *mawɛ*, the property was inherited, like other forms of family property, on patrilineal lines.

The system appears to have worked strictly in a patriarchal way. Individual *mawɛsia*, controlled by a number of younger brothers or sons, provided the head of the group of consanguineous kinsmen with produce and any labour required. He, in turn, upheld the interests and prestige of his juniors. The person in charge of a *mawɛ* was responsible for the welfare of his slaves and of the other members of his immediate household. In short, apparently, there was a delegation of patriarchal authority and paternal responsibility throughout the group. The kinship group concerned

---

[1] The complement is said to have been 12 male slaves to 12 women. It may be noted, also, that the *pɛwa* is sometimes spoken of as the 'family house'.

resided in the same or adjacent compounds. It is evident that its members were also connected with other extended families outside the local area, but historical data about the precise nature of the relationship are lacking. It is probably safer, therefore, to think of a system of extended kinship groupings rather than a system of kinship relationships. The Mende do not confine themselves to using a unilineal principle. A man's heirs are primarily his brothers in order of age, but custom traditionally includes cognatic as well as agnatic descent in certain circumstances.

The important point is that these main social features are retained, though in less rigid form, in the modern organization. For example, the present-day household of this kind is still, broadly speaking, both patrilineal and patrilocal. In other words, inheritance of the *mawɛ* itself, as a form of property, follows the male line and wives of male members usually reside with and become part of the household concerned. Membership of the *mawɛ*, today, is not, however, confined by any means merely to male agnates and their immediate families. The tendency is for affinal relatives, as well as close female relatives of the head of the household, to compose part of the unit and even to help manage its affairs. Perhaps this is because the *mawɛ* has primary significance as a farming rather than kinship institution. Nowadays, the organizing factor is not kinship itself, but common residence combined with genealogical connection.

2. *Domestic and Agricultural Organization of the Mawɛ*

A household of this kind, containing members of the extended family, usually occupies a group of adjacent houses, placed in the form of a circle and enclosing a compound. If the head of the household resides on the spot,[1] he has a 'sleeping house' for himself—a single roomed, round house. The younger women of the household also have their own house, which they share with the children; and there are one or two houses for the men, such as younger relatives and the 'workmen,' i.e. settlers and other dependents. There may be one or two more houses, in addition, which are occupied by older women, such as the head of the household's own

---

[1] Sometimes, a wealthy individual who owns a number of *mawɛsia* spends most of his time at his town house and has his farming households in several villages. In this case, he will visit the individual households only for the main operations during the farming season, or when some special occasion demands it. A younger brother, or other relative, resides on the spot and looks after the farming and other arrangements on his behalf.

mother, or the wife of his deceased father. The more old-fashioned 'women's house', or *pεwa*, is usually a large oval-shaped house with very solidly built mud walls, and contains a single room or 'parlour'.[1] In this, some eight or even a dozen women sleep on stick beds. About half a dozen children sleep with them on the beds, according to their size, or lie on mats on the mud floor. The room contains a hearth of three flat stones, where a fire is kept burning most of the day and even during the night, for purposes of cooking and warmth. Fishing baskets and other household paraphernalia hang from the rafters on which hampers of cotton, benniseed, etc., are also stored.

During the busy periods of the farming season, the household lives together communally. Food is prepared for the group as a whole under the direction of the big wife, who supervises its distribution. The etiquette is for her to carry the first bowl over to her husband, and he calls his age-mates to it. Another bowl is provided for the younger men, and a further one for the women. The younger children either sit and eat with the head of the household, or wait for the remnants. The womenfolk take it in turns to cook. At other times, outside the busy seasons, food is prepared separately by the women for their respective husbands and children, if the household is a large one.

The extent to which domestic help is mutually given in the larger kind of household depends entirely upon the degree of intimacy prevailing among its members. The same applies to the communal sharing of private property, such as dresses, lamps, eating utensils, etc. The use of certain articles, such as a shirt, and certain services are charged for, sometimes, by both sexes. Small 'dashes' are also given, particularly to senior members of the group, in recognition of help and advice.

To some extent, agricultural arrangements in the *mawε* continue the general structure and organization of earlier times, when the bulk of farm work was done by the slaves. In theory, the services of the members of the household are entirely at the disposal of its owner, as were those of the slaves. Their primary duty

---

[1] Experimentation in the building of women's houses has produced a rectangular type, consisting of a parlour and a single room for the head wife, and equipped with windows. The dimensions of three such modern houses at a town in Upper Mende were, in feet—24 × 40; 28 × 15; and 20 × 32. The older type has no windows and is entered by a side door at either end. One such house was approximately 18 × 30 feet.

SOCIAL ORGANIZATION AND KINSHIP

is to make his *kpaa wa*, or 'family farm', as it is also called. They are also expected to collect palm fruit and press palm oil for him, to build and re-thatch his house, keep his compound in repair, work on his coffee or groundnut plot, etc., and hunt and fish for him. In addition to their share of farm-work, the women have to spin thread as part of the domestic obligation.

In return for the proceeds of these activities, the head of the household provides its members with clothing at certain times during the year. The men are remunerated in this way at 'brushing-time', i.e. the start of the season, and at *Ramadan*, if the people are Moslems; the women at weeding time, at *Ramadan*, and again at harvest. The men may also be allotted small plots of ground on which to grow rice and cassada. These are known as *buleisia* (sing. *bulei*). Sometimes, the head wife, or other senior women members of the household, are also allowed to farm one of these small plots, and junior male members are expected to help them with the heavier work. The *bulei* is looked upon as a private undertaking, as opposed to the 'family farm', and the proceeds from it accrue entirely to the individual who makes it. The small crops grown, such as cassada, okra, and other vegetables, can be marketed locally. The women are expected to report any sales they may make and are usually allowed to keep the money. With it they buy some small piece of finery for themselves, or put it towards the society expenses of a son or daughter.

One of the main objects of the *bulei*, however, is to enable the person to feed himself and his wife and children, if he has any. On the other hand, though the proceeds of the *kpaa wa* are for the head of the household, they also serve as a general reserve for the whole household and provide seed for the next sowing.

In cases when the household runs on patriarchal lines, the head of it not only supervises farming arrangements, but has general jurisdiction over its members. He settles minor disputes, makes rules about the conduct of domestic affairs, and may impose small fines. He pays House Tax on behalf of adult male members and is responsible for their personal behaviour. This means that he may be called upon to settle a fine or debt. The money is taken out of the general proceeds of the season, which have been gained, for example, through the sale of palm oil and kernels. He may also advance bridewealth for a wife on behalf of the younger men.

In other cases, duties and services vary, or are more elastic. Sometimes, a smaller sized household gives its time exclusively to the making of the 'family farm' and to the other requirements of the head of the household. Traditional obligations are fulfilled more regularly in areas relatively remote from the Railway Line. Sometimes, the male members give only periodical help, for example, on the main operations on the farm, such as brushing, felling of trees, etc. Sometimes, they are allowed to cut palm kernels exclusively for themselves and are left to find clothes for themselves and their wives. In other districts, they may be available for two or three days out of the week, or they may divide work on the *kpaa wa* with work on their *bulei*.

3. *The Local Group*

The head of the *mawɛ* exercises domestic supervision over its members, but his control in this respect is subordinate to that of the local group of kinsmen, when major matters, such as allocation of land, are involved. This group is recognized under the expression *kuwui*, meaning literally 'compound'. This term denotes, primarily, that the persons concerned occupy the same or adjacent compounds in a town, and suggests that they have close connections with each other through blood relationship, marriage, and in other ways. In a limited sense, *kuwui* is simply the aggregate of the individual *mawɛsia* occupying a particular locality, but the ramifications from the point of view of kinship are more specific and complex. In every *kuwui*, there is a certain nuclear element which is supplied by the heads of the component *mawɛsia* and their immediate families. This nucleus consists of what are known as *ndehun-bla*, (lit. 'family people', see later paragraph), i.e. persons standing in close blood relationship with each other, mainly on the patrilineal side, who constitute a descent group for purposes of the inheritance of land and other forms of collective property. It comprises the central and focal portion of the *kuwui* and dominates it by virtue, as a rule, of being descended from its founders. It is also partly exclusive of other kin groups in the *kuwui* with which, however, it is invariably connected by ties of marriage.

This latter point and the fact that affinal relatives and non-relatives are frequently included in the *mawɛ* means that the *kuwui*, as a local group, is relatively heterogeneous. A further point is that the *kuwui* counts within its membership persons outside the physical boundaries of the 'compound'. This is the result of historical circumstances, already described. The nuclear descent group, or

SOCIAL ORGANIZATION AND KINSHIP

ndehun, in the *kuwui* claims ownership of various neighbouring villages outside the town, and this makes the village people members of that particular *kuwui*. In the latter case, the leading villagers, usually, are also members of the nuclear descent group, or *ndehun*.

The nature and extent of such kinship is shown by the following census data from a village in 'Middle' Mende country, which is part of a *kuwui* in the neighbouring town of Bo, some five miles away. In this case, X is one of the sons of the village headman and a member of the nuclear descent group. He may be used as a reference point for the purpose of describing and enumerating relationships. As members of the village were: X's own father and the latter's wives, including X's own mother; the six brothers and half-brothers of X with their respective wives and children; the two sisters of X living without their husbands; the five sisters and half-sisters of X with their respective husbands and children; the father of the husband of one of X's sisters, and his wives; the nephew (and his wife and children) of the husband of one of X's half-sisters, and his wife and children; the daughter of one of X's half-brothers, and her husband; a paternal aunt of X; and nine 'strangers', or 'village mates' of X, with their respective wives and children.

Exclusive of X himself, but including all the children mentioned, the total number of persons was one hundred and four. Of these, thirty could be reckoned in X's paternal kin; ten in his maternal kin; thirty-two were connected with X through marriage; and the remaining thirty-two had, as yet, no blood or affinal connection with him.

4. *The Rôle of the 'Kuloko'*

Each *kuwui* is under the social jurisdiction of its leader, the *kuloko* (from *kuwui*—compound and *loko*—hand, i.e. 'in whose hand the compound is'). Though the authority of the *kuloko* extends to the domestic affairs of members of the 'compound', he is expected to confine his rôle to the collective interests of the group. In the ordinary course of events, therefore, he constitutes the final court of appeal over family law and is expected to settle any dispute which seems likely to disturb general harmony. To his *barri* or to the veranda of his house, come the other elders of the *kuwui* in the evening to talk over the day's affairs, or any other matter affecting the relationship of the *kuwui* with the rest of the town. In the latter respect, the *kuloko* acts as the *kuwui's* representative and is the inter-

SOCIAL ORGANIZATION AND KINSHIP

mediary between it and the rest of the community. He, along with the heads of other 'compounds', constitute a species of town council under the presidency of the Town Chief. It is the duty of the *kuloko* to report back any matter of general interest to the *kuwui*, and to obtain, if necessary, their co-operation over it. One such matter for which the *kuloko* sometimes bears responsibility, today, is the collection of House Tax, which every *mawe* head is expected to render to him on behalf of his household. In former days, it was chiefdom tribute, which went on from the *kuloko* to the sub-chief.

Generally, the office of *kuloko* is reserved for the oldest suitable member of what has been referred to above as the nuclear descent group in the *kuwui*. In actual practice, however, it passes quite often to any one within the *kuwui* who has sufficient influence and popularity to impress the older members. Such a person is usually an older male, but even a woman may succeed to the position on her husband's decease, if the latter has been particularly outstanding as a personality.[1] A daughter is not usually appointed. Like other political and semi-political figures, the *kuloko* has a deputy, or 'speaker', whom he himself nominates, and who is usually a close kinsman.

5. *Interrelationship of Town and Country*

As already indicated, the nucleus of the *kuwui* is provided by the *ndehun-bla*—the group of consanguine relatives; thence derives its function. In other words, it fulfils some of the rôles which in other societies are performed by a clan, though the present emphasis should be laid more on the social and political than on the religious sphere. Thus, one of its major responsibilities, which is particularly relevant in the case of an agricultural people like the Mende, is to control the use of land. The *kuwui* has, also, a certain say in the marital affairs of its members, and holds a watching brief over their general conduct. Fundamentally, however, it is the main

[1] Sometimes, one or more of the 'big wives' of the Chief are put in charge of a *kuwui* to facilitate administrative control. There is an interesting example of this in the founding, in fairly recent years, of Mobai, as the Paramount Chief's new town in the Mando chiefdom. The first two compounds to be built were headed respectively by Madam Hawa Koma and Madam Lucia Makoto. The third compound was settled by people from a neighbouring town under their own male leader; but the fourth was placed under a third wife as it housed members of the Chief's own family group. Subsequently, when the town was fully established, the three women were replaced by men chosen by the compounds concerned.

SOCIAL ORGANIZATION AND KINSHIP

and most important buffer between the individual person and the larger community. These considerations may be exemplified best by the part of the *kuwui* in the wider structure of Mende society.

It has already been explained that the over-all picture of settlement in Mende country is one of small towns around each of which is spread a number of component villages. This combination of town and villages constitutes a social and political entity which, in the older sense, corresponds to what is officially termed, nowadays, a 'Section' of a chiefdom. The relationship of the *kuwui* to the total structure may be appreciated in the fact that the town, inclusive of surrounding villages, is a composite of individual *kuwuisia*. In the 'average-sized' and older type of Mende town, where the historical pattern still prevails, these may number between ten and fifteen.

The effects of this are significant in providing a wide basis of kinship for the political structure itself. The social cohesion of the *kuwui* rests on the factors of common residence and biological and affinal ties, but the latter are far from being locally exclusive. An obvious network of such ties and the reciprocal obligations involved also exists between the individual *kuwui* and the other compounds in a town, and it has the effect of creating a degree of wider social and psychological unity which is denoted by the Mende expression for it—*mbondawa-ji-hu*—'a community of kindreds'.

The same point is equally pertinent for the peculiar relationship which exists between town and countryside, and for the way in which the local group in the town is connected with specific groups outside, in the shape of villages and village people.[1] The effect of the mutual obligations obtaining is to make the village simply an extension into the countryside of the particular *kuwui* to which it appertains. The reason for this follows historically from the situation created by the 'tribal' wars, as well as from the more

[1] This pattern of town-village relationship has several parallels in other parts of Africa. In the case of the Nupe of Nigeria, the concentration of a large population in a single town leads to the foundation of 'daughter-settlements' by small groups. These 'colonies' are known as *tunga*, and normally they reflect the expansion rather than the breaking up of the 'mother-town'.

The phenomenon takes several forms; small groups move into uninhabited bush, to occupy virgin land and to found new settlements; immigrants from another part of the country choose to settle on the land which belongs to a certain village, and under its political protection; or the local big landlords settle their slaves and dependents on the land around the capital, in small hamlets. In the last case, however, the settlements represent not colonies of villages or towns, but private property farm settlements of individual landlords. cf. S. F. Nadel, *A Black Byzantium*. Int. Inst. Afr. Lang. and Cult., 1942, p. 36.

'normal' process of settlement. As already described, it was the custom to put captured slaves to work in clearing fresh land and to house them in villages adjacent to the already existing settlement. Land was also allotted to warriors helping in the defence of a town and to war-refugees. Sometimes, also, fresh villages were added to the *kuwui* through the initiative of individual members in seeking fresh places to farm and thus establishing themselves and their descendants at the sites where the clearing was made.

This last point, in particular, exemplifies the real nature of relationship between village and 'parent' *kuwui* which follows logically from Mende family law. According to this, everything acquired by a son is regarded as the property of his father or of the head of the group to which he belongs. This, in other words, would naturally bring a new village under the control of its founder's senior kin, and make its inhabitants responsible to the latter for whatever dues and duties were levied on the group as a whole. In short, therefore, decisions taken in the town as part of the business of the *kuwui*, as a whole, also affect the villagers and are communicated to them, as to town members, through the *kuloko*. This is done by calling the village headman and other village elders to the latter's house in the town.

6. *Subordination of the Village*

The social subordination of the village is, therefore, quite evident in that, theoretically, at any rate, the final word over its affairs rests with the people in the town. Nowadays, however, the extent of the latter's jurisdiction is modified by a variety of new circumstances. The result of modern conditions such, for example, as the construction of the railway and of motor roads has naturally altered the shape of local development, and the consequence is that some villages have assumed the size and importance of a town. In others, the exercise of social control by the 'parent' *kuwui* has lapsed through its decay in numbers and officiating personnel; or, sometimes, through the presence in the village itself of personalities sufficiently influential to offset outside authority.

Nevertheless, allowing for all this, the village is still regarded as a place which houses the socially subordinate members of society. There is still a tendency, for the historical reasons mentioned, to regard the villager in a disparaging way. He is considered as somewhat uncouth and 'green', and is still the first to

SOCIAL ORGANIZATION AND KINSHIP

be called for chiefdom and other levies. The villager, moreover, is rarely, if ever, literate, and may not even understand the Creole speech which, in towns on the railway line, has become almost a lingua franca. In short, the village is looked upon as a place to which members of the town can retire when they fall on evil days, or wish to remain out of sight during an illness. The older people finish their days there; and for an unsuccessful contestant of the chiefdom, whom a revengeful rival has bested (see Chapter X), it may be a place of exile.

This attitude has been enhanced by the modern development of the new towns with their western-style houses and mechanical appliances. So the Mende town and the countryside around it form really a single system of kinship. The town is made up of so many separate localities containing the 'compounds' of its inhabitants. With each 'urban' locality is associated one or more 'rural' localities, comprising villages and farm lands. These 'satellite' villages are scattered around the outside circumference of the town and are connected to it, like beads on a thread, by a series of winding bush paths which radiate out of the town. The distance between an individual village and the town ranges from one to five or six miles, and the topographical relationship of any one village with the part of the town with which it is socially connected is not always direct. Thus, the villages which are part of, say, *kuwui* A, may be interspersed by one or more villages which are part of, say *kuwui* B, or *kuwui* C. Their location depends on the historical circumstances of their foundation.

These points are exemplified on the attached drawing of the town of Moyamba and its environs in Kpaa Mende country. It should be pointed out in this instance, however, that the town and village relationship is depicted in terms of 'sections' and not 'compounds'. This is owing to the fact that various towns on the railway line have outgrown their former size and population, so that for the sake of administrative convenience the individual 'compounds' have been grouped together, according to locality and social connections, into larger sectional units.[1] This means that a particular 'section' of the town includes one or more 'compounds'.

[1] For this reason, in many of the 'newer' towns, it is usual to speak of the town concerned in terms of its sectional divisions rather than 'compounds'. The term 'section' corresponds, therefore, quite closely to the expression 'ward', which is commonly used in connection with the various parts of a town in other West African countries, e.g. Nigeria.

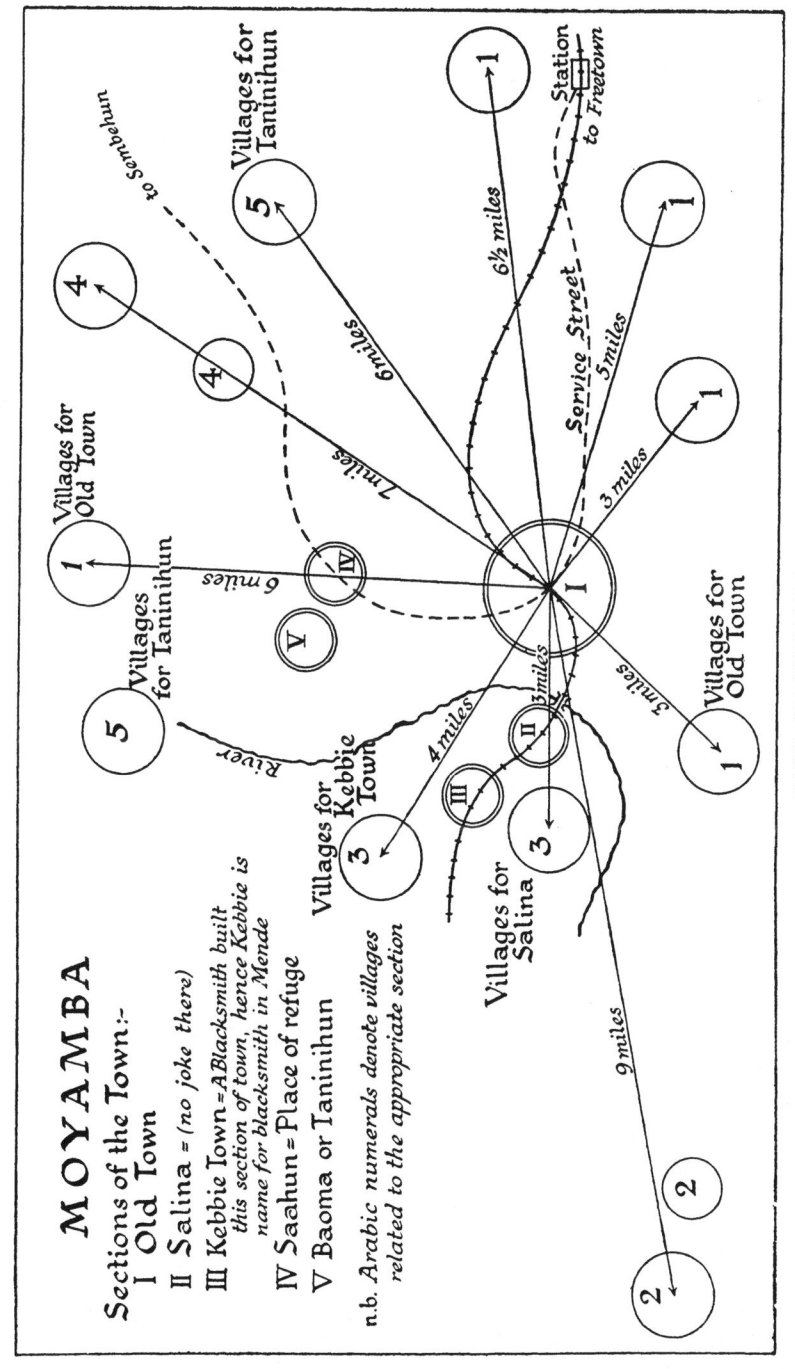

PLAN OF MOYAMBA

SOCIAL ORGANIZATION AND KINSHIP

The *kuwui*, then, both in the narrower sense of the local group of town or village, and in the inclusive sense of its members as a whole, provides the widest setting in which social activity, as opposed to political activity, can take place. What happens in conjugal relations may have interest for the *kuwui*, as a group, though it is more likely to affect the *mawɛ* immediately concerned. The same applies, though with less qualification, to matters, such as land, which may involve the wider group more readily. Groups larger than the *kuwui*, such as the Section of a chiefdom, or even the 'section' of one of the new towns, lack sufficient cohesion to exercise the same degree of social control. The institutions they encompass are political, or quasi-political ones. Because it stands mid-way between the larger political group and the immediate family and household unit, the *kuwui* provides, apparently, the most convenient form of social reference. Thus, it is noteworthy that the ordinary Mende man travelling in a strange part of the country will establish his identity by quoting the name of his *kuwui* and its big man, as well as the town from which he comes.

7. *Implications of Kinship Terminology*

As a corporate group, then, the *kuwui* occupies a position of central importance. Sociologically, its significance is the greater because terms analogous to 'family' and 'lineage' play a relatively small part in social identification, except in certain circumstances and among members of the ruling class and those who can lay claim to an ancestor of particular note, such as a well-known warrior. 'Lineage' is most likely to be used when the patrilineal principle is directly involved. Thus, in a chiefdom 'election', the appropriate reply to the question, 'On whose behalf are you contesting the chiefship?', would be *Nya baimbaisia* (lit. 'My lineage people', i.e. 'my ancestors', or 'line of descent'). Alternatively, the reply, *Nde gbembi*, 'My line of blood relatives', might be given.

The nearest equivalent of the term 'family' is *ndehun* (lit. 'brothership'), which implies the closest possible relationship of persons. *Ndehun* is widely used, and in the strict sense it denotes, as already indicated, the patrilineal relatives of the person using it, i.e. those entitled to share in the same family property as himself. These are the *ndehun-bla*—the 'family people'. Technically, the *mbondaesia* include a person's mother, as well as his wife's relatives. In quite common practice, however, use of *ndehun-bla* will include

SOCIAL ORGANIZATION AND KINSHIP

not only the speaker's mother within the category, but any of his mother's relatives with whom the degree of personal association is strong. It may even include, within the same frame of reference, someone originating in the same town as himself with whom there is no biological or affinal relationship, but with whom there has always been a close social connection. In the wider sense, therefore, 'family' relationship may be illustrated in more specific terms as follows, i.e. a person's *ndehun* will include:

His own brothers and sisters, provided they are by his own father.

His own brothers' and sisters' children of both sexes.

His own father and mother and other wives of his father.

His uncles and aunts, and their children of both sexes, on both the paternal and maternal side.

His grandfather and grandmother, and their children, additional to his own father and mother, on both paternal and maternal side.

His great uncles and aunts, and their children, on both paternal and maternal side.

His own children of both sexes, and any children they may have.

It may be noted that the *ndehun-bla* do not include wife and wife's relations; nor the spouses of sons and daughters and their relatives.

8. *Kinship Duties and Obligations*

Towards the *ndehun-bla* a person's obligations are well-known and obvious to all concerned. His relationship with all of them is formally, at any rate, as brother to brother, as son to father, etc., according to the generation and sex of the persons involved. They are entitled to draw on him financially and in other ways, if need be; just as, in necessity, he is entitled to assistance from them. Sometimes, this tacit understanding is made more concrete by a special family ceremony in which the kinsmen concerned agree, on oath, never to pledge or pawn family property to an outsider; never to allow any one of their members to suffer poverty, etc.

A person addresses his father's brothers as 'little father', his father's sisters as 'little mother', and *ndewe* refer to cross as well as parallel cousins. His mother's brothers and sisters, how-

SOCIAL ORGANIZATION AND KINSHIP

ever, are addressed as 'uncles' and 'aunts'. Traditionally, the father has complete control over his children which extends, as already mentioned, to any property they may acquire. He has full right to the labour of his son and to that of his son's wife, so long as they are both living with him. In return, the son is entitled to a share of his father's personal property on the latter's death. The mother usually passes on any personal effects, such as jewellery and clothes, to her daughters. The sense of emotional attachment and affection, for these reasons, is supposed to be strongest between father and son, and mother and daughter.

Though the pattern of a person's paternal and maternal duty is obviously strong, obligations towards the *mbondaesia* are hardly less stringent, largely because of the special relationship with his or her maternal relatives, i.e. the maternal uncles, the *kenyaisia*. In addition to inheritance of his father's property, a person is also entitled to share in, and use, his maternal uncle's belongings and has certain traditional perquisites, including the head of any animal his uncle kills. These privileges also include the right to 'inherit' his uncle's daughter, or his wife. Reciprocally, the uncle is entitled to full use of his nephew's services on his farm and in other ways. For example, by tradition he is also allowed to offer his nephew or niece as a pawn in discharge of a debt. In effect, however, this right existed mainly as an ultimate sanction on the nephew's or niece's proper show of respect.

There are certain sins and omissions, moreover, that only the uncle can pardon, and the latter's blessing is essential for the health and prosperity of both nephew and niece. In terms of family law, to disobey one's uncle is an even graver offence than disobedience of one's father and may provoke a more serious curse. In the latter case, the father's intercession is necessary to persuade the uncle to retract his oath. Its 'pulling' requires the presence of all the brothers and sisters of the person cursed. The father then presents the offending nephew to his uncle so that he can confess his sin. He (the father) also offers the uncle money, or a country cloth.[1]

---

[1] When this has been done, all the nephews and nieces prostrate themselves, holding on to their uncle's feet with both hands. The uncle then prays that they may all be forgiven the wrong they have done him and the curse removed. The nephew's mother then brings a bowl of water. The uncle takes some of this and blows it in a fine spray over the heads of all the nephews and nieces in front of him. He also smears a mixture of dust and water on their foreheads. This finally removes the curse; the uncle blesses them, and the family eat together as a group.

SOCIAL ORGANIZATION AND KINSHIP

A native explanation of this special relationship between the mother's brother and his sister's children is that since a brother and sister come from the same father they may be considered as one. Therefore, all that a mother gives her child is given also by her brother, and so her brother's displeasure or pleasure is the same as its mother's. The physical part of a person, i.e. his bones, flesh, etc., is provided by his father through the semen he puts into the mother.[1] The child's spirit—*ngafa*—however, is contributed by his mother. This explains why the blessing of the mother's people is so important to the child and why the father asks them to pray for the child when he takes it away from them. The mother is the child's 'keeper' in the same sense as a genie may have control over a human being (see Chapter XI, sect. 3). In praying to the ancestors, therefore, the spirits on the mother's side are first invoked, and those on the father's side last; because the father is the cover both for a person and his mother.

To his in-laws, a person's duty is generally to render assistance when required, and to fulfil certain specific obligations with respect to his wife's parents. He is expected to help on his father-in-law's farm, whenever he is called upon, and to show his sympathy in a marked way to his wife's family, when either of his parents-in-law dies, by a present that costs at least the price of a goat. In return, his father-in-law may allow him the use of land to make a farm or earn his living in other ways.

Broadly, a rather similar pattern of reciprocal obligation obtains also in the case of fellow townsmen and villagers, even if these categories settled originally as 'strangers'. Once they have shown willingness to associate with and take their part as members of the local group, their acceptance follows as a matter of course, irrespective of the question of kinship itself. The implication, very probably, is that for purposes of community life the factor of common residence is as decisive as kinship. Its effect, however, does not go so far as to create exogamous rules; for example, by forcing the person concerned to marry outside the village.[2] Nor does it confer 'legally' an automatic right to the use of local lands, though in

[1] This is explained further in the suggestion that it is the man who 'produces' the children; but in order for them to be seen it is necessary for him to join with a woman. 'The pen applied to paper produces writing.'

[2] In a sample of 75 wives in a small town, 32 were born there; 25 came from nearby towns and villages, and 16 from other chiefdoms.

SOCIAL ORGANIZATION AND KINSHIP

customary practice such a use would never be denied by the local group.

It is important, therefore, to give this latter factor of common residence its due weight. Even the ancestral cult, with its special and familial experience, is subject to modification in such circumstances. For example, in rites carried out in connection with the farm, it may be observed, sometimes, that the spirits invoked are associated primarily with the locality where the work is to be done. They are the former successful farmers of that place rather than, necessarily, the direct forefathers of the persons collected there to do them honour. The inference that might be drawn from this—that the ancestral and tutelary rôle is carried out in the capacity of *genii loci* as much as *genii familiae*—would add further point to this hypothesis.

CHAPTER VI

THE SOCIAL CYCLE AND INITIATION

A CONVENIENT way of understanding the general structure of Mende society is to consider the life of the ordinary individual. Each age has its special rôle. There are also *rites de passage* of varying degrees of significance, at birth itself, at puberty, at the birth of the first child, at widowhood, and at death.

1. *Infancy*

Broadly speaking, each important change of status is marked by a certain amount of training and ritual preparation which varies according to the sex of the individual. In the earliest stages, however, there is little distinction between the sexes, either in training or in their relation to the rest of the community. The arrival of a female child is greeted by the women with greater delight than that of a boy. They say that girls do not forget their mothers in time of need as boys do, and they prefer to train a girl. There is a cry of '*hooyo*' when a boy is born.[1]

A boy or a girl is named according to whether they are the first or a subsequent surviving child; for example, the first girl will be known as Boi. The children who follow her will be named after various ancestors or after important members of the descent group of either parent.[2] Boys are named four, and girls three, days after birth. The woman whose name a girl-child is to bear takes her out in the early morning, faces the sun, spits on the child's face, and

[1] This is to inform the menfolk that a future member of the Poro has arrived. '*Hooyo*' is generally used as a cry by initiates of this society.

[2] A boy who is given an ancestral name may be addressed by the term 'grandfather' by his relatives to avoid the disrespect of using the ancestor's actual name. If he has his own father's name, the father's brothers will refer to him as 'father's namesake'.

says, 'Resemble me in all my ways and deeds, because you are named after me.'[1] The boy's naming is done either by the father, the father's brother, or mother's brother. The boy is known as an infant as *heilopui*, a girl as *nyalui*. Though both may enjoy the considerable affection of the parents, their social significance is very small. Should the infant die, there is no formal and ritual 'crying' for it. The corpse is simply wrapped up in leaves and buried under a banana tree, or in some other place where it is customary to deposit rubbish. The mother sits on the heap of earth that has been dug away and pushes it backwards into the grave.[2]

2. *Childhood*

Children are suckled at the breast until they are about three years old. In addition to their mother's milk, they are fed from the earliest age on pap made out of yam or cassada, and sometimes on palm oil and rice. In general, there is little supervision of what they eat. They are given food quite irregularly, at the breast when they cry for it, or when other members of the household sit down for their own meal. Quite often, food is forced on them until the stomach is 'hard'. If the mother is ill, the child is suckled by any female member of the household who has milk, e.g. by another wife of its father, or by its grandmother. Children at this early age are carried around on the mother's back tied to it by a *lappa*. If a girl is the daughter of a chief, or of people living in a 'civilized' manner, she may be put into a cotton frock, even as a baby. Usually, however, children are allowed to crawl, and later, to walk about quite naked, except for a string with a charm attached to it round the waist, until they are about six years old. They are usually washed from head to toe at least once a day, and taught to relieve themselves in the bush. A girl-child remains in and about the compound and under the care of other women and older children of the household, until about six years old. The children learn to address all adults as 'mother' and 'grandmother', etc., according to age, sex, and social status.

[1] Names are also given according to the circumstances of the birth. If the mother has lost a previous child, the next arrival may be named in Mende, *Gilo*, in the case of a girl, and *Gibas*, in the case of a boy; meaning, 'let this one be saved'.

[2] This is done as a way of avoiding the witch spirit which is assumed to have brought about the child's death by entering its body.

THE SOCIAL CYCLE AND INITIATION

Almost from the time she starts to walk a girl-child imitates the habits of the older children and women in carrying a bowl or piece of cloth on the head; or she may lend an occasional hand at pounding the rice. She goes down to the farm with her mother and helps her to tidy up the field after weeding, or she carries up water to the men. A boy is more frequently with his father by this age. He eats with him and starts to imitate the men folk in their daily activities and in their way of talking.

3. *Puberty*

A child's proper period of training begins at about the age of six. A girl may undergo a mock initiation into the Sande society; in which case she follows the Sande women about in their 'extra-mural' activities, such as dancing; or she is sent away to relatives to be 'minded'. The boy, too, may be sent away to a relative, because the Mende fear that their children will be 'spoiled', if they remain too long at home. If a girl has already been 'given' as wife to a chief, she leaves her mother and lives in his compound under the care and instruction of his head wife. If their parents are educated, or ambitious for them in modern terms, both boys and girls may be sent to live with some person of well-known house-wifely qualities; or may be put into the charge of a Creole family in Freetown, usually with the idea of their attending school at the same time. Boys, and a smaller number of girls, are also sent direct into available Mission and Native Administration schools in the Protectorate, soon after this age. The boy who remains at home is circumcized at about the age of 10, and then begins to take some small responsibility in farming matters. He collects firewood for the house and traps small animals for the household pot.

Western education for a boy is approved, nowadays, to an increasing extent, but it is regarded with mixed feelings in the case of a girl. The disadvantage from the point of view of people living tribally is that the girl will probably become lost to them 'socially'. She may contract marriage with a Creole, or a native *pu-mui*,[1] thus foregoing bridewealth; she may be difficult to control on account of her new ideas and habits, and may speak disparagingly of the way her parents dress and behave. On the other hand, there is the

[1] *Pu-mui* = white man, i.e. a person who follows European ways, and hence one who would not observe the native custom over marriage.

THE SOCIAL CYCLE AND INITIATION

possibility of her making a good marriage with a chief, a wealthy trader, or some one in government clerical employment, and being better able, thereby, to help her relatives financially than if she remained on the farm. Generally speaking, most notable persons, such as chiefs, like to have at least one of their daughters 'educated', partly because it adds considerably to prestige to have such a girl about the place. It also helps the making of suitable unions of a dynastic kind. The daughter selected usually becomes the favourite of her father, if she is not so already. She is not expected to go to the farm, and is granted favours and privileges which her sisters do not share.

A girl who is being 'minded' remains with her guardian until she is old enough to complete her initiation in Sande.[1] In the meantime she acts as a personal maid and servant to her guardian. She prepares her bath-water, accompanies her to market, carries her loads, runs messages for her, and does a large part of the household chores. Generally, she is taught how to prepare and cook rice and other dishes and, sometimes, how to sew and do crochet work. She is also taught to defer to her elders. She lives entirely as a member of the household concerned and is subject to the same discipline and treatment as other younger members of it. Her guardians are responsible to the local community for her conduct and to her parents for her safe-keeping. Here is a typical nine-year-old girl's day:

a.m.
- 7.30– 7.45   Awakened and washed her face, arms, and legs.
- 7.45– 8.00   Greeted the elders and took out pans.
- 8.00– 8.30   Swept out the veranda and helped to clean up the kitchen, and washed pots and other utensils.
- 8.30– 9.00   Went out to market to buy food (cassada, etc.).
- 9.00–11.15   Helped the older women to wash clothes.
- 11.15–11.45 Helped the oldest member of the household (who is a petty trader) at her stall.

p.m.
- 11.45–12.5   Ate her midday meal.
- 12.5 – 2.30 Was given punishment and forced to sit at the stall.
- 2.30– 4.00   Still at the stall.
- 4.00– 6.00   Fetched water from a stream outside the town.
- 6.00– 7.30   Helped in the preparation of the evening meal.
- 7.30– 8.00   Cleaned pans.

[1] The popular name by which the Sande Society is known is 'Bundu'.

THE SOCIAL CYCLE AND INITIATION

p.m.
8.00– 9.00   Ate her evening meal.
9.00–10.00   Cleaned the kitchen, put away cooking utensils, and had a bath.
10.00–10.30 Listened to story-telling on the veranda. Went to bed.

Initiation into Sande is at the age of fourteen or fifteen. This, and, for a boy, Poro initiation, is perhaps the most important period in the life of the ordinary Mende person. By this time, a girl may already have been betrothed as a wife and, as such, is receiving periodical presents from her husband. During this stage, she is known as *Sande nya*. She keeps the name she was given at birth until the actual initiation, when she usually takes a fresh name, either of her own choice or to commemorate the circumstances of her career in the society bush. The first girl to be initiated in a particular session is known as *Kema*. The same considerations apply in the case of boys, whom it is a considerable insult thereafter to address other than by their Poro names. Sometimes, however, a Mende girl takes the name of the woman 'minding' her in compliment to the latter. Or, if boys and girls attend a Mission school, they may be baptized and given an English name, the effect of which is to mark them out as Christian and literate persons. Though some prefer to keep their native names, most of those who have attended school, or have been brought into contact with Creole influence, show a strong desire to imitate certain ways of any Creole friends they have. They copy their style of dress, and the girls emulate the fashion of brushing out instead of plaiting the hair, as is the native style.[1] Both sexes learn and use Creole forms of verbal expression[2] in ordinary conversation, and the girls generally make a good deal of effort to be thought '*Creole nyapoisia*'—Creole girls.

[1] For the sociological implications of all these points see the final chapter of this book. The practice of 'hair-straightening' is followed generally by Negro Americans in the United States, as well as by Negro people in other parts of the New World who have been influenced by the social and æsthetic values of Western culture.

[2] The claim has been made that this Creole medium of communication contains sufficient grammatical structure and vocabulary of its own to merit description as a language. The proponents of this view distinguish, however, between 'Creole', or *Krio*, as specifically developed in the Colony and the 'pidgin' English used by native speakers throughout the length of the West African Coast.

THE SOCIAL CYCLE AND INITIATION

This tendency has entered even into the Sande itself. At the end of their period of seclusion, the initiated girls make their customary and ceremonial return to ordinary life. They enter the town in procession wearing their newest clothes, which are not native-style *lappas* and head-ties, but European frocks and high-heeled shoes. Every girl, who can, carries an umbrella.

4. *Initiation and the Bush School*

A child's real training begins at initiation, and so the institution is worth studying. Let us consider first the boys who pass through the rites and syllabus of the Poro.

(*a*) *Preparation of the Poro camp*. A full Poro session lasts from November, throughout the dry season, until May, and during this period several sets of initiates may be taken. New initiates do not remain in the bush for more than a few weeks, as a rule, and in the case of schoolboys the time may be even shorter. Formerly, individuals might attend in the bush for a course of instruction which lasted several years, but the tendency now, apparently, is to restrict proceedings to little more than the bare requirements of initiation itself. A boy usually enters at puberty, though even younger lads may be taken, and there is nothing to prevent an adult person joining at the same time. The session is inaugurated by the senior members offering a sacrifice in the bush, in order to obtain the favour of the (Poro) spirits. Then a present is taken to the Paramount Chief, requesting his approval and patronage for the forthcoming session. The bush close to the permanent and sacred premises of the society is cleared as a temporary camp (the *kpanduinga*), and huts are put up to accommodate the initiates. There are no rites in connection with this operation and the camp can be moved about quite freely; but so long as the Poro is in session the ground in question is strictly out of bounds to non-members. Women who may be in the neighbourhood must give warning of their approach by clapping their hands. A road is then cut from this place to the town. Tall poles, connected to each other by ropes to which moss is tied, are erected along it, and at the spot where this passage joins the main road, the Poro sign, known as *ndimomoi*, is placed. In the meantime, the parents of the candidates have been preparing food for them.

(*b*) *Entry into the school*. On the eve of the session, Poro members meet in their house (*ngafa welei*) in town. It serves as a temporary

THE SOCIAL CYCLE AND INITIATION

residence and meeting place, and is a small round house with a mat screening the entrance in place of a door. The Poro men go round the town saying: 'We will dance tonight'. Then the Poro spirit himself is heard leaving the bush. He enters the town, making harsh nasal sounds, like someone groaning. His followers go from house to house taking out those who are to be initiated. The latter are escorted to the bush, and on arriving at the mat which hides its entrance from the road, they are met by an official. He puts a number of questions to which the appropriate answer is always 'Yes'. 'Could you carry water in a basket?', 'Could you uproot a full-grown palm tree with your bare hands?', etc. The officials then make as if to pull the candidate inside. The latter resists, but is drawn in at the third attempt. In the meantime, a great deal of drumming and noise is going on inside. It increases as he enters, and he is welcomed with shouts. He hands over his initiation fee, which consisted traditionally of a leaf of tobacco but is paid, nowadays, in cash, often amounting to as much as several pounds.

The boys, who are now standing in a ring, are greeted by the cry: '*Sokoti.*' They reply: '*Numo.*' This is repeated three times. One of the first sights they see is an official with the spirit's pipe in his hand. This individual does not wear any distinctive costume, but on the various occasions during the initiation period, when the spirit visits the town, he is its impersonator. The pipe is made out of cow horn, or is a curved stick with a hole in it. The pointed end has been pierced, covered with lizard skin, and a hole, through which the performer blows, has been cut through the skin. One horn of this kind is used in connection with initiation, and another kind is used by older members. The harsh nasal sound mentioned above is produced by this instrument. The effect is as if a wooden megaphone has been used. By stationing a number of men in different parts of the bush, each of whom speaks, in turn, through his horn, the effect is created of the spirit 'flying about the bush', as it is explained to non-members.

(*c*) *The marking ceremony*. Every boy must be circumcized before he is initiated, but circumcision plays no part in the initiation rite itself. If necessary, the former operation is carried out on the spot before the marks of membership are given. The boys are then given certain marks on their backs, according to the order in which they enter the bush. The first boy is known as *ndoinje*; the second as *lavalie*; the third as *petuja*; and the last as *gbonu*. Each boy is seized in turn by a number of the men. He is stripped naked and

THE SOCIAL CYCLE AND INITIATION

his clothes kept to wipe away the blood which flows from the cuts. Then he is thrown roughly on to the ground, and the appropriate marks are made, either by a hook, which raises the skin, or by a razor. If he shows fright, or tries to run away, his head is pushed into a hole which has already been dug for the purpose. During the operation, the 'spirit' plays loudly on his pipe and there is a clapping of hands, which drowns the noise of the boys' cries and prevents them being overheard by passers-by, especially women and children.

The initiation rite and the whole time spent in the bush which follows it symbolize the change of status. The young initiate is supposed to be 'swallowed' by the (Poro) spirit when he enters, and separation from his parents and kinsfolk signifies his death. The marks on his back are evidence of the spirit's teeth. At the end of his time, he is 'delivered' by the spirit and 'reborn'. Thus, the period in the bush marks his transition from boyhood to manhood, and as a result of the experience he emerges a fully fledged member of Mende society. The training he receives is symbolical as well as practical. It inculcates him with the deeper implications as well as the rules of the part he has to play as a man. It aims at teaching him self-discipline, and to rely on himself. He learns how to work co-operatively and to take orders from others.

(d) *The training.* While in the bush, the boys wear a garment of red netting. They must sleep in the camp, but are allowed out during the daytime, when not undergoing instruction, after the initial ceremony. They carry pipes about with them and utter wild cries to give warning of their approach. As a practical example of their training, the boys are allowed no modern equipment. Their material requirements, including part of their food, must be provided by themselves. They start by lighting a fire when darkness falls, and for the first night special songs are sung and no one is allowed to sleep. The next morning, the work is shared out, after the boys have been sorted out for training in terms of groups of the same size. The first boy who entered delegates the tasks. The second helps to make the spirit's pipes. The third is to sweep out the camp every morning. The fourth is to boil water for the elders any time it is required.

The boys are expected to bear hardship without complaint and to grow accustomed to it. They sleep at night on a bed of sticks under covering clothes which have been soaked in water, and they remain out of doors, if it rains. The singing and drumming lasts

THE SOCIAL CYCLE AND INITIATION

until one or two o'clock in the morning and the boys are awakened again at dawn. They are expected to get up and sing any time they are called. According to some accounts, training in hardihood also includes a certain amount of punishment play which is administered by the elders. Impossible requests are made jokingly to the boys as an excuse for inflicting pain on them and no crying is allowed. Sometimes, too, it is alleged, the boys are encouraged to steal food from neighbouring farms during the night-time, and to bring the spoils to the *Sowa* (head official) in the morning. The accusation of cruelty is generally denied, but other Poro members admit that a certain amount of stealing is carried out by the boys. They claim that it is severely punished, if detected, and is usually the result of some of the boys, whose parents are poor, going short of supplies from their homes. Occasionally, boys whose relatives cannot afford the fees demanded, work their way by doing jobs during the daytime on neighbouring farms. The money they earn goes to the officials.

In general, the training provided varies according to the length of time the boys are able to remain in the bush. It may include a certain amount of native law and custom, exemplified by the holding of mock courts and trials, in which the boys enact the rôles of their elders. Boys who can afford to stay for a length of time learn a good deal about native crafts as well as the ordinary duties of a grown man, such as 'brushing' and other farming operations, and cleaning roads. Individual specialists at making raffia clothes, basketry, nets, etc., sometimes go into the bush with the boys and help them to become proficient in the particular craft they choose. Bridge-building, the making and setting of traps for animals and fish, are also taught. On the social side, the boys learn drumming and to sing the special Poro songs. They practise somersaults and acrobatics, and altogether their experiences produce a strong sense of comradeship.[1]

The parents of the boys are expected to 'feed' the spirit, so long as their sons are in the bush. They give rice to an old member who carries it over to the camp. The basin is brought back clean,

[1] The drumming and dancing of the Poro boys can be heard throughout the dry season in such songs as the following: *Oh, gbenjiwaa leinga-oh!* (The large pot is cooking-oh!); *Gbengben nyɛkɛ ndoli nya ngotua kpu kɔwoma!* (The enticing waists of the women have sent me crazy!); *Pɔi lapo a gongo mɛɛ ganu ma, gomgo a fee!* (When the Poro boy meets grass in a corner, he passes it by as quickly as a squirrel!, i.e. he does not clean it out).

having been wiped with raffia. The spirit is supposed to have licked it clean. Another trick, performed to show the spirit's mysterious power, is the building of his house, the *ngafa-welei*. Some time in advance, the initiates erect a light structure of sticks and daub it over with mud. A canopy for a roof is made and thatch is cleverly tied to it. The walls are whitewashed and the house is ready. Then the spirit goes down to the town and announces that his own house has been burned; he proposes to build a new one within an hour. At the appointed time, the 'pre-fabricated' house is carried out to a conspicuous place and is planted over a pit, wherein the spirit sits, playing on his pipe. Non-members are then invited to come out and see the house and to wonder at this example of the spirit's skill.

(*e*) *The Initiation Rites.* The process of initiation is completed by means of three separate ceremonies, known respectively as *Ndahitie*, *Kpowa-mbei*, and *Kpia*. The opening rite is prefaced by a visit of the spirit to the town. He is accompanied by both old and new members. They dance there and return to the bush where the ceremony is performed, and the first 'warning' is given to the boys. The contributions of food which have been provided by the parents are brought forward, i.e. rice, fowls, and one bottle of palm oil per head. A fowl is seized, its head placed on a large stone and severed by another stone. It is then thrown to the members. All the fowls are killed in a similar way. While the head is being severed, an official says, 'Sokoti', to which the expected reply is given. This is repeated over each fowl in turn, and the ceremony is a warning to the boys to expect the same kind of treatment, if they divulge any Poro secrets to a non-member. Everyone agrees to accept and abide by the warning. Food is then cooked and eaten, and when the feast is over the crowd returns to the camp.

This marks the first ceremonial stage in the boys' initiation, and a similar rite is enacted about a week later. This is *Kpowa-mbei*, the literal meaning of which is 'non-members' rice'. The people in the town cook rice, and this time the smaller boys collect it from outside the bush. The spirit pays another visit to the town, and nets are spread over the house to catch him. He sounds his pipe to indicate his presence there, and immediately afterwards a second pipe is heard from the bush, suggesting that he has flown away. His interpreter leaves quietly in the crowd. The Poro group then returns to the sacred bush, and the ceremony proceeds.

The completion, or 'pulling' of the Poro (*Kpia*), is prefaced by

THE SOCIAL CYCLE AND INITIATION

a rite known as *Ngafa gohu lewe lei* (hitting the spirit's belly). The spirit is said to be reluctant to deliver the boys he has eaten and to whom he is expected to give birth, one by one. Force has therefore to be used upon him, and members strike him in the stomach.

The day before this is a busy one. Further contributions of food are collected. Everything used by the boys during their novitiate must be destroyed, so as not to be seen by the women. Their clothes and rags are packed into a large hamper, which will represent the spirit's belly. As night approaches, old members flock in from all sides, and at about 9 p.m. a large dance is staged in the town. At first, only the Poro spirit and the men take part, but after a while the spirit goes to rest in his house and women freely join in the dance, which goes on until daybreak.

For the initiates, however, this is a night of fear. They have been warned to keep awake lest they dream of the spirit. This would cause them to die in their sleep, and the idea is impressed upon them throughout the day. Their parents send them kola nuts to sustain them, and a large quantity of rice is eaten in order to ward off sleep. Then, at about 4 a.m., the *ngafa gohu lewe lei* begins. Like a woman in labour the spirit groans and sighs mournfully. His interpreter explains that the spirit is giving birth. The women clap their hands and the men reproach him for detaining their children so long. They threaten to beat him out of the town, unless he delivers them immediately, and pretend to be angry with him. Then, the hamper is dragged about while others belabour it with clubs. At each blow given, the spirit moans and leans against various objects, such as banana and paw-paw trees. Anything he rests against is pulled down by the men with large wooden hooks. Roads are blocked with branches of trees and a good deal of damage may be done to plantations around the town.

At dawn, however, the spirit takes a road out of the town and stops playing. He is said, according to one version, to have flown off into the depth of the forest to feed on the giant crabs of the forest lakes and will be away for a year. Before going, he asks for a new name to be given to him. Sometimes nets are spread around the bush the next morning to show the way he has climbed off into the sky.

As soon as the spirit is gone, the boys are hurried into the *kameihun* (the sacred part of the Poro bush) and everything in the temporary camp, including its huts, is burned on the spot. This means that the 'pulling' of the Poro—the happiest and long

THE SOCIAL CYCLE AND INITIATION

awaited day in the life of the initiates—has begun in earnest. Each boy is now told the final secrets he has to learn about the society, and he takes his final vow of secrecy. The boys are lined up in a semi-circle at the stones in the *palihun* (the deepest part of the bush) round the *Sowa*, or head official, and the *Mabɔlɛ*. (The *Mabɔlɛ* is the only woman official of the Poro and serves the boys as a matron.[1]) Moss and thread are wound round the boys' toes, so that they are all tied together in a continuous chain. On their heads they wear caps of moss and leaves of the umbrella tree.

The *Mabɔlɛ* stands in the middle, facing the sacred stones. She invokes the spirits of the society on their behalf, and prays that each new member may be as strongly attached to the society as the thread and moss which now bind them together. She asks that they may be productive of many children when they have wives. Prayers to the ancestral spirits on this occasion are addressed to former leaders of the society, not, of course, to the ancestors of the individual offering them. The method of communication, however, is the same as the general one, i.e. the ancestors are called in order of seniority, beginning with the oldest and finishing with the one who has died most recently. The prayers conclude with a general supplication. Thus: 'Father Siaffa, let it reach you; let it reach to Kanga; let it reach (lit. "be laid down") to the head, the great one (i.e. God). This is what *Leve* (an old name for God) brought down (showed us to do) long ago. These children, whom we are "pulling" from the Poro today, let nothing harm them; let them not fall from palm trees; make their bodies strong; give them wisdom to look after their children; let them hold themselves in a good way; let them show themselves to be men!'

As the *Mabɔlɛ* speaks, she dips a white fowl into a medicine, composed of leaves and water, and sprinkles the boys with it. Each boy holds out his tongue, in turn, and the *Mabɔlɛ* places some grains of rice on it in order to test his future. Holding up the fowl, she says: 'If this boy has ill-fortune before him, do not pick the grains.' (N.B. The fowl used has been starved of food since the previous evening.)

The chicken is then killed, as in the previous ceremonies, by severing its neck with a stone, and the boys are sprinkled with its blood. At the order to rise, they jump up joyfully, and cut away and throw behind them the moss and thread which bound them. They are now full members of the society; but their heads must be

[1] See Chapter XII.

THE SOCIAL CYCLE AND INITIATION

shaved bare of boyish hair. While this is being done, the *Mabɔlɛ* prepares the ceremonial meal. When it is ready, the *Sowa* rolls the rice, chicken flesh, and palm-oil prepared into lumps, placing each piece on the *Mabɔlɛ*'s foot. Then, one by one the initiates bend down with their hands behind their backs to take the food. She raises her foot three times to the boy's mouth, saying, '*Sokoti*', to which he replies, '*Numo*'. At the fourth time, he picks up the lump of food with his mouth and while he chews it the ceremony of swearing him in takes place. He is told that he will be choked by the rice if he reveals any society secrets.

When this is over, the initiates are given a general ablution with the remaining medicine before being taken to a stream for bathing. Each boy is seized in turn, one man holding his feet and another his neck, and he is lowered into the water. A fowl is demanded from the boy's father and he is kept there until it arrives. This is repeated four times and then the boy is given his new set of clothes. The boys dress in these and wear a head-tie over their shaven heads. The latter signifies that their heads have been broken by the spirit and are in process of healing. A further aspect of their re-birth is the new name they acquire and which is a mark of their entrance into manhood.

(*f*) *Completion of the Poro school*. When everyone is ready, the boys then march in procession to the town under a large country cloth. Their bodies have been smeared with burned palm-oil to give them a particularly fresh appearance. Parents, kinsfolk, and well-wishers come out to meet them, and the boys are led to the town *barri*, which has been specially prepared to lodge them. Gifts are brought out to them, and they remain there for four days, feasting heartily. Before they are finally discharged on the fourth day, as many pots of palm-wine as there are boys are taken into the *kameihun* for the farewell. The wine is supposed to be exclusively for the *Sowa* and *Mabɔlɛ*, but thirsty elders also flock in for refreshment. As the *Mabɔlɛ* takes up a pot of wine, the initiate who has contributed it, comes forward and kneels, facing the stones. The *Mabɔlɛ* prays for him, a small libation is poured on to the ground, and the Sowa pulls off the head-tie. The initiation of the new member is now entirely complete, and when all have been finally dealt with in this way, the Poro session itself is declared over.

In former times, should any of the boys die during the session, it was the custom to bury them secretly in the bush, and the parents were not informed officially until the session was over. Then, one of the Poro elders would go round to the mother's house and break a pot in front of her, saying: 'Of the pots you asked us to build, we are sorry to say that yours was broken.' There would be no 'crying' for the lad—the usual mourning custom—'because the mourners might breathe in some kind of disease'. Nowadays, any such deaths are reported and officially investigated.

5. *Initiation in the Sande*

In the case of Sande initiation a shorter description must suffice. Like the Poro society, the Sande is under the control of a number of senior officials, consisting of older women, who have attained the higher grade. These senior women are distinguished by the white head-tie they wear in public, and they are known as *Sowoisia* (pl. of *Sowo*). It is a status that must be achieved: that is to say, no initiate can proceed to the higher rank without undergoing a further period of training. This applies even to the daughter of a Sande leader, though as the latter's heiress she has the advantage of the various secret medicines. The principal official is the *Majo*.

The Sande is convened for initiation purposes about the same time as the Poro, but in a less formal way. Individual Sande women make themselves responsible for the institution and develop what might be described as a personal connection with various households and compounds within the local community. This means, in effect, that there may be as many as five separate Sande 'schools' within the same town. Occasionally, a fresh Sande group is started by some woman who is popular in the town. She must, of course, possess the necessary seniority and qualifications for the task. Quite often, the prelude is a dream in which the woman concerned learns of the whereabouts of certain important herbs and thus receives a 'call' to the work.

These individual Sande groups compete with each other, to some extent, for public patronage. Some enjoy a better reputation for the training they offer than others. The head woman, or *Majo*, of each has other senior women helping her with the 'curriculum', and the number of girls taken depends both on local support and the number of staff available for the purpose.[1] The total enrol-

[1] As this and succeeding paragraphs indicate, there is a fairly close similarity between the Sande school and the European type of 'finishing school'.

ment, however, is rarely more than thirty and, sometimes, is no more than half a dozen.

A girl, and even an adult woman, is admitted into the initiation school at any age. A girl who is as yet uninitiated is known as *gboa*. Age is estimated according to size, and after the girls have been divided up in this way they live in separate compartments of the bush. In addition to the initiates and women in charge, the ordinary session or 'school' includes a number of 'first grade' members who have re-entered the bush in order to take a higher degree and to qualify for the extra privileges that go with it. The session is convened by means of a circular sent round in the form of a small piece of tobacco—*sokolo*. This is a token of the head woman's hand in delivering any important messages. Fees, which may take the form of money, cloth, or other commodities, are also due at this time.

The aim of the Sande is much the same as that of the Poro school. It is to educate for the accepted pattern of life; and its methods, also, are symbolical in part. The girls are taught to be hard working and modest in their behaviour, particularly towards older people, and omissions in this respect are severely punished. As part of the training, their duties are to attend the senior members, fetching water and warming baths for them, etc. The girls themselves are allowed only cold water. They are expected to arise early in the morning, at the second crowing, and to greet all women of the higher ranks with a song, before proceeding on the domestic and other duties of the day. While in the bush, they are smeared heavily with clay and wear it on their faces and bodies for some time afterwards. This is a form of beauty treatment.

The period of seclusion may last up to 3 months, but nowadays it is usually much shorter. Prior to the final ceremony itself, the girls are allowed to move about in public, but under the supervision of one of their elders. The most important ceremonies are performed, in fact, immediately on entry. The first girl to be initiated is announced, and completion of the rite is celebrated by loud and joyful singing and the beating of drums, there being a special song for this moment. The *Majo* then sends back a piece of tobacco to the girl's parents as an official certification. The first girl, who is known henceforward as Kema, acts as head over the other girls for the remainder of the session.

During this early period of confinement great care is taken to keep the girls out of the sight of the rest of the community, and of men, in particular. Water and other necessities are brought into the bush by one of the older women until the wound, caused by excision of the clitoris, has healed. As the other ceremonies follow, the ban is gradually relaxed; but the girls must take a cloth out with them to conceal their heads if they meet anyone on the public road. Gradually, they appear more and more in public and pay an official visit to the chief and other big men, dressed in woollen embroidered jackets and woollen coloured caps. From the latter they receive small 'dashes' for their dancing.

In the meantime, the women taking higher grades have also completed their own appropriate ceremonies. The day on which the newly graduated members return to daily life is one of great rejoicing, which parents and relatives and all concerned share and celebrate. This also marks the final transition of the girls into full womanhood. They move in procession from their temporary camp, headed by the officials. The whole row of girls is covered by a canopy of large, good-quality country cloths which are held high over them by parents and older members of the society. In the old days, the girls would have been profusely decorated with jewelry and smothered in oil to make their skin glisten. Nowadays, as already mentioned, it is a point of honour for a mother to turn out her daughter in the latest modern style. Alongside the procession dance various 'spirits' of the society impersonated by officials wearing masks. When the town is reached the girls remain for a time in the town *barri* receiving the gifts which their friends and suitors bring them. Afterwards, each girl goes to her mother's house where a large chair has been placed like a throne for her, and there she sits in state for a time in all her finery.

The recreational activities of the Sande school are even more extensive than those of the Poro. Songs and dances learned in the bush are repeated and sung on all major occasions in the social and ceremonial life of the people. This largely explains, no doubt, the popularity of the institution itself. It is clear that a very marked spirit of comradeship among the women is engendered and passed on through its medium. Nor should the economic side be overlooked. Senior Sande women rely for a substantial part of their personal income on the perquisites gained from initiates and from fees and fines rendered by other individuals requiring the offices of the society. Moreover, the fact that a girl's initiation is important to the whole community means that the families concerned have a special incentive to earn extra money. Cash is

THE SOCIAL CYCLE AND INITIATION

required to secure the material necessaries, including food and cloth, which are essential if her relatives' prestige is to be upheld.

The net result of the latter point is that the expense of sending a girl through Sande is relatively large, and this in turn, as described in Chapter VII, affects the question of bridewealth. Alldridge[1] says that in 1901 the entrance fee was a bushel of rice, a fowl, a gallon of palm oil, a barrel of rum, and a 'head' of money at £3. This would suggest that the cost in those days was at least as high as it is today. Expenditure varies, of course, from district to district and is probably much greater in the larger towns where the social requirements are higher and where food, which is home-grown elsewhere, has to be purchased. There is also considerable variation in outlay on the part of parents, relatives, and prospective husbands. The items to be considered, in addition to food and clothes, include bush equipment, such as mats, enamel ware, etc., as well as subscriptions to the *Majo* and other officials. A rough estimate of the total budget, which was taken from one of the more rural areas, amounted to some £4 7s.[2] An estimate made in a more urban part of the country amounted to some £7.

But the Sande differs somewhat from the Poro in being fairly adaptive to the march of time. The traditional costume is indeed

---

[1] Alldridge, op. cit., *The Sherbro and its Hinterland*.

[2] Detailed particulars, in terms of the individual ceremonies, were as follows:

Mbele gbia hani (this is the initiation fee which is handed over to the officials for looking after the girl). It included 5s. to the Sande 'spirit'; 1s. to the *Ligbe*, another official, and one mat at 3d.

Sowo vewui ('rice for the head official'). This consisted of a daily ration of 4d. of rice; 2d. of palm oil; 3d. of fish; 2d. of condiments. It is cooked for each girl entering the bush and is regarded also as a small pot for the *Sowo*. On this basis, over a period of two months, it would amount to £2 15s.

Ndegbe lewe, or *Kpowa gowo wuilei* ('the gathering of the herbs'). The food costing about 1s. goes in this case to the officials.

Ndahitie ('quite fit'). This is the principal ceremony. After it has been performed, the girls are said to have graduated, and they can be seen in public. The cost of food in this case amounted to some 7s., and in addition there was a small present for the *Sowo*.

Gumihun. This is performed outside the town and behind the houses where the girls spend the night prior to the final washing. One bottle of English wine was provided at 4s. 6d., and there were various small presents for the Sande officials.

Bush equipment consisted of one second-hand cloth, two second-hand head-ties, and one new mat at a cost of some 9s.

worn in the bush, but the girls return to ordinary life dressed in the most up-to-date Creole fashions. Nor does the Sande scruple to advertise itself and the services it offers. The mock initiation of small girls of four or five years old with the object of getting them 'interested' is an instance of this. In general, there is a readiness to keep up with the times, even to the extent of compromising with traditional rites which are repugnant to modern ideas. It is claimed, for example, that the practice of excising the clitoris in initiation has been replaced by a small incision. It is equally significant that in certain areas of Mendeland, the Sande leaders have been willing to include educational experimentation in the customary programme. Under the supervision of a Government Medical Officer, girls, already trained in modern methods of mothercraft and hygiene, have been allowed to take part in the training in the Sande bush.[1]

6. *Social Implications of Adult Life*

Once initiated in Poro or Sande, the young man and young woman are ready to play their part in the adult life of any Mende community. Thenceforward, however, the course of their lives will run on quite separate, though complementary, lines. In addition to the practical and vocational training received, both sexes are assumed by this time to be familiar with the various social rules and etiquettes of everyday existence and are held responsible, in this respect, for any breach, particularly over marriage and sex laws and the code of hospitality. The former are described in Chapter VII. Etiquette varies in significance according to the circumstances. Generally, all younger persons are expected to show formal deference in addressing their elders of both sexes as well as political superiors. A wife, in approaching her husband, should bend with her hands on her knees, as should children in approaching their father. The men and the older male children take their meals separately and are served first by the women. Only the elderly women take part in religious ceremonies with the men; and Moslem women generally remain on the veranda of the mosque.[2] In public dances, the men compose one part of the circle,

[1] cf. M. A. S. Margai, 'Welfare Work in a Secret Society', *African Affairs*, March, 1948.
[2] Except in the 'newer' towns, the sexes customarily separate themselves also at Christian services.

THE SOCIAL CYCLE AND INITIATION

the women and children the other part. It is contrary to etiquette for men and women to walk side by side outside the compound; the man should walk ahead, followed by the woman. It is equally against etiquette for any show of intimacy, other than a hand clasp, to be made in public, even if the parties concerned are lovers. Women should not walk about alone, except on their domestic duties, and particularly not at night. If they do so, they may be referred to as *letay nyahanga*, ('walk-about women'), i.e. prostitutes. There is a strong joking relationship between brother and sister, but a brother who sits on his sister's bed may be held guilty of *simongama* (i.e. incest, see Chapter VII).

The relationship between husband and mother-in-law is in similar terms. A person may speak to and joke with his host's wife only after the latter has been formally presented to him, and the conversation is supposed to be restricted to domestic matters.

A man visiting a person in another town should send on word ahead and should accompany it with a 'greeting present' (*famalui*) and some such conventional message as 'Here is something to recognize me by'. On meeting, it is customary for both guest and host to give an account of all that has happened since their last meeting, before present business is broached and discussed. When the guest departs, he is expected to leave a 'good-bye present' (*kɔtu*) with his host. Travellers meeting on a road also enquire after each other's affairs after the preliminary greeting has been said, and are not supposed to part company until each other's news has been heard.

7. Manhood and Womanhood

In coming out of Poro in the old days, the young man usually started his career forthwith as a warrior, if he were freeborn. Nowadays, he usually returns to his father's people and is allotted a small room in his father's house or that of his father's brother. He joins with the other men in the activities of the farm and sits with them in the evening in the *barri*. These are his 'mates' and he addresses them by the term, *togbɛ*, which implies that the persons concerned were initiated at the same time in Poro. He is allowed to earn a little money on his own account by harvesting palm kernels from his father's bush. With this he buys clothes and other small presents for his mother. The next stage is for him to obtain

THE SOCIAL CYCLE AND INITIATION

a wife. Either his father selects a young girl for him, or else he finds a suitable girl nearer his own age who has recently been initiated. He informs his mother and other relatives about the matter, and if their consent is given, the courtship and contract on his behalf are completed in ways described in Chapter VII.

The girl of the same age, however, probably goes straight to the husband to whom she became betrothed either before, or at the formal ending of her Sande initiation. If she is her husband's first wife, she joins him as a member of his father's household. She works on their *kpaa wa* (family farm), and helps her husband to make his own smaller (*bulei*) farm. She probably sleeps in the *pɛwa* (women's house) of the head of the household and carries out her domestic duties under the supervision of the latter's head wife, whom she addresses as *Yei*. The other women of the household are her 'mates', and she calls them *mbaa*, if they are of approximately the same age as herself. She is expected to live and work as a member of the household group and her status among them is in accordance with her position as the wife of one of the younger men. In the meantime, the man, having demonstrated his ability and energy as a farmer, has gone on to acquire an additional wife and to obtain a greater standing in the group. Presently, he is ready to start a proper household (*mawɛ*) of his own.

8. *Improvements in Status*

In the case of a junior wife, it is the birth of her first child which brings her more respect. When she has gone three to six months in pregnancy, she ceases sexual relations with her husband and returns to her mother's house to await the arrival of the child. As it is her first pregnancy, a piece of white shirting about three yards in length is given her as a *lappa* on the advice of a soothsayer, as soon as her condition is noticed. A bell is attached to her clothes to warn off any (evil) spirits that may be around. If her abdomen is not enlarged after the normal time, the soothsayer is called in again. She confesses any misdemeanours to him and is recommended to seek out the party or parties whom she has wronged (see Chapter XII). There are no special rites or ceremonies corresponding with the months of pregnancy, but various prohibitions have to be observed. The expectant mother must not walk out late at night, and must avoid any possibility of meeting the *Ndɔgbɔ-*

THE SOCIAL CYCLE AND INITIATION

jusui (spirit) by going about alone in the bush.[1] She must always carry a knife about with her, since in her state of pregnancy she is regarded as a warrior, hence the expression *e longa koe hui* ('dying in the battle'), when a woman succumbs in childbirth.[2] There are no special avoidances in regard to food.

The arrival of the child also affects the status of the husband, though in smaller measure. He is expected to pay his wife's parents a formal call and to present them with a small gift, known as *kejɛ lui* ('ginger kola'). Should the woman abort, however, the soothsayer is consulted and may attribute the accident to an infringement of the rules of one of the secret societies. Any form of abortion is known as *moo mie*, and may also be put down to witchcraft.[3]

A woman marrying a man who already has a number of wives joins his household in the capacity, more or less, of a servant, unless it is a love-match. If she is a young girl, the head wife stands in the relationship of both mother and mistress to her and gives her instructions as to her duties and the times she should visit the husband. Three consecutive nights for each wife in turn is the etiquette. She takes her share in farm work with the other wives and, if her husband is a big man, in singing and dancing when he visits, or entertains friends. Any leisure time she has may be spent at needlework learned, perhaps, from a literate woman in the town.

Just as the status of a man rises with each additional wife entering his household, so does that of his first wife who assumes the position over them to which she is automatically entitled by virtue of her seniority. Provided she has a recognized position in the household, an older woman can always command the respect and services of those junior in years to herself. Here is how a woman aged about forty spent her day (*see next page*):

[1] It is of interest that these precautions are substantiated by modern medical findings to the effect that the ante-natal experience of the mother may have repercussions on fœtal development.

[2] In this case, the husband of the dead woman is tied to the *barri* and officials of the Sande society dance around, brandishing swords at him. It is considered that he may have used medicine against his wife, and she is not buried until he has paid a fine to the society.

[3] Non-literate women practise abortion very rarely because the desire for children is very strong; but a literate woman may sometimes induce an abortion for social reasons, or a prostitute to spare herself the inconvenience of pregnancy.

THE SOCIAL CYCLE AND INITIATION

a.m.
6.30– 7.00   Awakened and gave instructions for the day's work to the younger girls.
7.00– 7.30   Took a bath.
7.30– 8.15   Prepared the morning meal.
8.15– 8.45   Ate.
8.45– 9.30   Sent a small girl to market and began cooking the household's midday meal.
9.30–10.00   Was visited by a goldsmith and discussed a matter of some ear-rings with him.
10.00–11.00   Worked in the kitchen.
11.00–11.15   Made up her hair.
11.15–11.45   Dished up the food for the men and had her own meal on the veranda.

p.m.
11.45– 1.30   Engaged in needlework.
1.30– 2.30   Slept and a small girl combed out her hair.
2.30– 3.30   Was visited by a tailor who had done some work for her.
3.30– 4.00   Continued at needlework.
4.00– 5.00   Began cooking the evening meal.
5.00– 6.30   Sang while the little girl danced.
6.30– 7.00   Worked in the kitchen.
7.00– 7.15   Took a bath.
7.15– 8.00   Dished up the evening meal and ate her own.
8.00– 9.00   Supervised the younger girls in collecting and cleaning cooking utensils.
9.00–10.00   Listened to story-telling.
10.00   Went to bed.

By the time a man has reached a similar age (i.e. forty) it is expected that he will be in charge of a *mawɛ*[1] of his own, which may include not only his own immediate family but junior relatives and other dependents. No longer is he referred to as a 'small boy' —the term applied to a man who has only one wife, or who is unmarried. At this stage, he takes his proper place with the other elders of the town or village and is already eligible as a member of the chiefdom council, if his *kuwui* chooses to send him. The

[1] For a description of the full implications of this term, meaning 'household', see Chapter V.

THE SOCIAL CYCLE AND INITIATION

likelihood, too, is that he is considered a fit person to look after the ancestral rites of his own household, though the latter rôle is reserved more generally for a still older person, if available.

9. *Widowhood*

A woman who leaves her husband for any reason is known as *pla nyahe*, 'run away woman'. The ex-husband is termed *kpao hindui*. For a man to be without a wife, or a woman without a husband, is regarded as a very unfortunate state. This includes widowhood. The fact that the majority of women are married much earlier than the men means that a large number of women are predeceased by their husbands. The widow—*po nyaha*, as well as the widower, *poo hini*, has to undergo a number of ceremonies which are equivalent to a further *rite de passage*. Part of the function of these is to purify the person concerned before he or she has intercourse with another spouse.

In a case of this kind, water used for washing the soles of the deceased person's feet is kept, and on the eve of the third day after death in the case of the husband, or the fourth day in the case of the wife, it is poured on the ground in front of the house which the deceased occupied. An old woman beats this ground with a pestle until mud forms. In the meantime, the widower or widow has been kept apart from the rest of the community. The old woman takes hold of the person's hair and drags him or her round the house. Another old woman goes behind, pushing the bereaved spouse along like a reluctant sheep. Arriving at the front door, the widow puts her face near the mud and shouts to her husband that she is in trouble. Then the mud is smeared on her body, a basket is given her which she hangs by a string over her head, and in it she receives gifts from sympathizers. The most substantial present will be from the relative of the deceased who wants her. She then accompanies the old woman into the bush and rests her head on a plantain tree, then the old woman knocks the tree down with a pestle. The green plantain will be her food that evening, eaten boiled. The widow is also rubbed with mud, and she clothes herself in rags so that her husband will no longer desire her. Other women stay with her to prevent her sleeping that night: her husband might slip back and stay with her. The next day, she goes to the river to wash away the last thing that belonged to her husband, the dirt from the soles of his feet. She is now quite free.[1]

10. *Old Age and Ancestorhood*

In old age, the previous distinctions between the sexes no longer obtain for practical purposes. Elderly women as well as elderly men are generally treated with the greatest respect, and both play their part as the principal advisers and consultants in family and religious matters. In this respect, the senior member of a household, or of a descent group, frequently has a special rôle as the 'praying man', or *hɛmɔi*. Since the older people are regarded as being nearer the ancestors than other members of the living community, they have an obvious position as intermediaries between the two worlds. In the absence of written records, the senior generation plays a further important part, and in every town or village there are certain elderly men and women who are looked upon as the main repository of traditional lore and genealogical information. The ramifications of the latter point, as indicated in Chapter X, are of special significance in view of the extent to which political position in the ordinary Mende chiefdom is bound up with previous happenings and circumstances.

In addition to affairs of this kind, an older woman generally does a number of light duties about the house, such as spinning thread, preparing dyes, medicines, etc. These, and the other points mentioned above, are illustrated in the following brief account of a day in the life of a woman aged about seventy:

a.m.	
6.45	Awakened.
6.45– 7.00	Swept round her 'shop' and put out the articles for sale. Took a bath.
7.00– 8.00	Prepared rice-flour for a (Moslem) sacrifice.
8.00– 8.30	Went to the market and bought some further foodstuffs for the sacrifice.
8.30– 8.45	Took a leading part in the prayers said at the sacrifice.

[1] If the widower omits the ceremony for some reason when his own wife dies, he can perform it when another man's wife dies. The ceremonies are more extensive in the case of Moslems. The man's widows are put into his *barri* for forty days. Their hair is shaved off and they are verbally abused by the dead man's sisters. A man undergoes these ceremonies only on the first occasion that he is widowed.

THE SOCIAL CYCLE AND INITIATION

a.m.
8.45– 9.00   Distributed alms from the sacrifice to the Alfa, friends, and paupers.
9.00– 9.30   Had her morning meal.
9.30–12.30   Sitting at the 'shop'.

p.m.
12.30– 3.00   Slept.
3.00– 3.30   Ate a meal.
3.30– 4.00   Took a gift of sweet potatoes to an old relative in the town.
4.00– 6.00   At her 'shop' and singing quietly to herself.
6.00– 7.30   Went over to the house of another elderly female member of the group to discuss family matters.
7.30– 8.00   Had a bath and sat in her hammock smoking.
8.00– 9.30   Told stories to the smaller children.
9.30   Went to bed.

The final *rites de passage* leading to ancestorhood are celebrated in a person's funeral ceremonies. The most important of these—*Teindia-mei*, i.e. 'crossing the water'—are to enable him to make the journey into the new land. To enter it he is said to cross a river.

It is important in this connection to note that the ancestral status has its obligations, and part of the ceremonies performed are to prepare the person for them. Those who lived evil or useless lives are feared, as are all spirits, but their names are rarely, if ever, invoked. Equally relevant is the fact that these final rites are never omitted deliberately, whatever the position or the character of the person concerned. To do so would be tantamount to denying the deceased person access to the next world, and hence to invite the revenge of his spirit.[1] It is equally necessary that the deceased should be sent on his way with ceremonies appropriate to his earthly rank. He should also carry with him some token of his position. This explains, no doubt, the more elaborate rites performed at the death of a chief (see Chapter IX), and the custom

[1] It is also necessary, as Hofstra points out, that the person should be purified of any sins committed before his death. Hofstra instances a Section chief who died after being purified of a certain transgression. He enquired if this did not denote that the rite had been a failure, but was informed that it was necessary to enable the man's spirit to 'cross the river' (cf. S. Hofstra, 'Ancestral Spirits of the Mende', *Internationales Archiv für Ethnographie*, Band XXXIX, Heft 1-4, Leiden, 1940.

of depositing money and other personal articles in the grave. Unless the spirit is enabled to take up its proper status, it will continue to haunt those on earth responsible for its handicap.

But sometimes the grave is thought of as a big house which the deceased enters on being lowered into it. To dig a grave is spoken of as building a house. Generally, conceptions of the next world are of a rather vague kind. It is pictured, sometimes, as a clean town with white sand. Notions which are more specific are obviously influenced by Islamic teaching and cosmology. It is fairly clear, nevertheless, that the conditions of the natural world are continued in the hereafter. In addition to their tutelary rôle, the life of the ancestral spirits, as Hofstra indicates,[1] seems in many respects to be similar to that of the people on earth. They are held to cultivate rice-farms, build towns, etc. In other words, the spirits retain their anthropomorphic character. An informant exemplified this point by mentioning that his brother, who died away from home without his people's knowledge, appeared in a dream to one of their neighbours. He gave certain instructions about a leopard's tooth, which was found afterwards on the body.

An ancestor's status lasts as long as the dead are remembered, and this varies with social and political standing.[2] After this, the dead seemingly retire into their own limbo, though there is also some evidence to suggest a popular belief in re-birth and re-incarnation. In some cases, the finger of a dead man is pricked, or a string tied round his waist, so that he will be recognized when he re-appears. Children are also named, sometimes, after a particular ancestor, especially if they bear him any resemblance. All this seems to suggest some idea of the ancestral cycle being renewed.[3]

[1] Hofstra, op. cit.

[2] Hofstra points out, however, that we have to distinguish between the ritual and the psychological side of remembrance. Sometimes, the ancestral ceremony is performed simply to indicate to the community that the family concerned is in a position to make a large sacrifice. Sometimes, the personal factor transcends ritual bonds.

[3] Hofstra (ibid.) also recounts a fairly wide belief in the following cycle. After being created by *Levei* (God), people begin their lives in the sky. When they die there, they are re-born on earth. When they die on earth, they go to a place under the earth. There is, also, the process of being re-born and of moving to a place, which is repeated several times. In this way, a human being goes through ten lives. Hofstra's informants were unable to say whether the end of the cycle would bring the total extinction of the spirit. They were inclined to think that extinction would follow.

THE SOCIAL CYCLE AND INITIATION

On the other hand, similar practices, such as placing a splinter of wood beneath the nail of a dead child so that its parents may recognize it on its 'return', suggest merely the idea of re-birth without necessarily involving a full cycle. There is actually a strong fear of re-birth, when it occurs in abnormal circumstances, as, for example, in the case of a child dying in infancy.[1] It is considered that if the next child closely resembles the previous one, it is really a witch person which has killed its predecessor and come back to harm the parents.

[1] See the paragraph on childhood earlier in this chapter.

CHAPTER VII

MARRIAGE AND 'FRIENDSHIP'

1. *Social Significance of Marriage*

THE main factors which underlie the making of marriage among the Mende are social and economic.

As explained in the previous chapter, marriage is an integral part of the social cycle through which everyone is expected to pass. The marital state marks an automatic stage in the social progress of a person and is one kind of indication of his or her social status. Married persons constitute a definite and more senior category to those who are unmarried, irrespective of the actual age of the latter. An individual who, having reached a certain age, was still unmarried, would be quite 'out of status', and would be regarded as an oddity, and even with a certain amount of ostracism. This applies particularly in the case of a woman.

Marital status is generally arrived at with maturity. Every woman who has passed adolescence is expected to have a husband. In the case of a man, the conditions are more variable. In the old days, few men had the opportunity of obtaining a wife before they were thirty, or even thirty-five years of age, and had proved their hardihood and diligence. Nowadays, though the traditional objections to early marriage are not completely extinct, a man has more opportunities to secure the amount of bridewealth[1] through his own effort and so achieve a wife while still in his early twenties.

Additional wives are important because they increase con-

---

[1] The term 'bridewealth' is used throughout this chapter in a dual sense. It means the amount of money and/or goods required to complete a marriage. It is used later, also, to denote the total amount of money that a husband pays on account of his wife, i.e. it includes payments made before, and after, the legal contract.

MARRIAGE AND 'FRIENDSHIP'

siderably the social prestige of the husband and to some extent, also, that of his present wife. Indeed, socially, they may be essential. A person who has no more than one or two wives is spoken of as a 'small boy', and his subsequent success and standing are measured largely by the number of women he manages eventually to secure. To obtain wives a person must have wealth, and so polygyny on a large scale is a sign of affluence.

This is one of the main reasons why chiefs and other big men in Mende society usually have more wives than have commoners. It is the custom for persons who hope to gain the chief's favour, or to have a grandchild eligible for the chiefdom, to present a daughter to him. If he refused the offer, or did not add to his household from other sources, a chief would gain the reputation of being either a very mean or a very poor man. His political prestige would suffer and he would run the risk of losing the respect of his followers. In fact, the nature of the chief's position and the obligations of his office necessitate his keeping a large number of women for a variety of reasons. The chief is expected to entertain on a lavish scale, and this requires a large staff of cooks and servants, and musicians and singers. For example, a chief may have one wife to attend to the entertainment of visitors; another to look after his farm; another in charge of his private medicines; and a fourth to valet his clothes. To engage such a staff by marrying them as wives is the customary as well as the most economical way of obtaining their services.

As is the case in other African societies which carry on the cultivation of the soil by primitive methods, a plurality of wives is an agricultural asset. The work on the rice farm and in the palm kernel and oil industry is performed entirely by hand, and a large number of women attached permanently to the farming household makes it unnecessary to employ much wage labour. The heavier work, on a large farm, of clearing the bush and harrowing the ground is done with the aid of bodies of helpers from outside for whom it is customary to provide meals. Large quantities of rice and palm oil have to be cooked and the preparation, which includes threshing, cleaning, and parboiling the rice, is a job for women. These economic considerations colour the outlook of the Mende on farming affairs. In the more rural areas, it is considered that no one can make a proper farm unless he has at least four wives, and smaller conjugal units are sometimes denied full status as *mawεsia*, or farming households.

MARRIAGE AND 'FRIENDSHIP'

In addition to their work on the farm, which consists mainly of weeding, and on domestic chores, wives are economically useful in a variety of other ways. They do most of the fishing; they card and spin cotton thread; may be sent out to trade, or to keep a small stall on behalf of their husbands in the nearby town. The sale of 'garra' (dyed) cloths is a profitable business, and women who are skilled in dyeing are often put exclusively on the latter task.

So far, therefore, as the economic aspects are concerned, the old claim that polygyny represents a form of capital investment is as relevant to Mende country as to many other parts of the African continent. This is one of the main reasons for polygyny. The person who can afford it expends money, either on his own account or on account of some male relative, in order to obtain a woman's services. He invests, in other words, in the services of so many women and employs them in the running of his business. The women benefit from the social status they enjoy as wives and are protected and maintained. Their maintenance includes 'gifts' of clothing and, sometimes, of jewellery, at certain traditional times during the year, e.g. weeding time and harvest. Women who are sent out to trade, or who dye cloths, are permitted to retain part of what they earn; the remainder accrues to their husband or to the head of the household to which they belong. Sometimes, women are also a source of income in ways which are socially unsanctioned. A person who has intercourse with another man's wife is liable to render the husband compensation assessed, as a rule, at 30s. By deliberately allowing their wives to attract young men, some husbands are able to turn the misdemeanour to a profitable account.

Polygyny is popular, also, for other reasons. So long as a woman is suckling her child it is forbidden for anyone, including the child's father, to have intercourse with her. To do so may cause the death of the child. If there are a number of wives the long period of continence, which may last for three years, is obviated and there is more possibility of increasing the family. This point in itself is sufficient to guarantee the interest of older relatives in fresh marriages. It explains the readiness with which a father or an 'uncle' will subscribe to the expenses of a younger man, provided the latter has shown himself ready to observe customary obligations. Male children will be useful on the farm, whilst female children, other considerations apart, represent a potential means of increasing 'family' capital, through the bridewealth received for them. A

MARRIAGE AND 'FRIENDSHIP'

large group of kinsmen adds to both individual and collective security. Descent groups which own land look for reinforcements to maintain and carry on the property and to safeguard it from outside encroachment.

Quite apart from these considerations, most Mende men have a strong affection for children, as well as a keen desire to secure their own perpetuation through their offspring.

The fact that wealth plays a large part in marriage means that polygyny is mainly the monopoly of the older and well-to-do class. The younger and poorer men are either monogamists, or live quite often in a relationship of 'friendship' (see later paragraphs) with the married women, or with women who have left their husbands. Figures illustrating the fact that the majority of the women are shared as wives by the minority of the men have already been quoted in Chapter III.

The custom whereby wives are 'inherited' by the male relatives of the deceased husband also helps to maintain an uneven distribution of women, since the inheritors are often senior members of the group who already possess wives of their own. Nevertheless, all things considered, the size of the average polygynous family is probably smaller than is popularly imagined. Paramount chiefs may usually be regarded as an exception since a large establishment is obligatory in their case. Quite often, their households contain several dozen women. But it is doubtful if the ordinary well-to-do person and 'big man' possesses, on the average, more than three wives. The writer made this estimation in respect of Serabu, a Section town which is fairly representative of Mende country as a whole. In this case, out of twenty-three men, one man had eight wives; one man had seven wives; four men had four wives each; six men had three wives each; eight men had two wives each; two men had one wife each; and one man had no wives.

From the Mende woman's point of view, the main inducements to marriage, polygamic or otherwise, derive more directly from the cultural pattern. She is of very little account until and unless she has a husband, and even until she has borne a number of children. Widows, and other women who have lost their husbands, are looked upon as unfortunate. *Poo nyaha*, the term for 'widow', is used almost in reproach. Other women without a husband—*gbama nyahanga*—are looked upon as a social evil. It is considered that only a life of prostitution is open to them. In some chiefdoms, they are punished by fines if they cannot show someone, either a man or an older woman, who will stand surety for them.

Through marriage a woman obtains not only the respect of her fellows, but certain social and economic opportunities. If she is her husband's first wife, or if she is his 'love wife'—*ndoma nyaha*—she can look forward to extra privileges and perquisites, and to securing special advantages for her own children over those of her co-wives.

2. *Prerequisites to Marriage*

There are a number of social prerequisites of various kinds before a marriage can be made and consummated. Marriage may be contracted at any age, but a man may not consummate it until he has been initiated into the Poro society. Prior to this he is not regarded as a man, in the adult sense, and, strictly speaking, is prohibited from sexual intercourse with any member of the opposite sex. A woman must have been initiated in the Sande society, and must have passed her first menstruation. To have intercourse with an uninitiated girl is both an offence against the Sande and a form of 'woman damage'. Both of the parties concerned must be 'washed' by the latter society, and the parents and near kinsmen of the girl are entitled to compensation from the man or his kinsfolk.

The main consideration, however, from the prospective husband's point of view is to find money to offer for his bride. In the great majority of cases, he looks to his father and other kinsmen to meet the larger part, or even the whole, of his expenses in connection with his first wife. Subsequent marriages depend less upon the help which may or may not be forthcoming from relatives, and more upon the person's own ability to make an economic success of his career. This is bound up, as a rule, with his progress as a rice farmer, and the following is a description of the ideal pattern.

With the wife that his relatives have 'found' for him, the young man starts work on a small plot of land allocated to him by his father. The couple work together at setting traps and cutting down palm kernels on the old man's bush. After a time, there is enough money to look round for a second wife. The new wife is sent out to trade. Later, the man goes again to his father, or his 'landlord',[1]

---

[1] As explained in Chapter IV, a person who settles on another man's land becomes the latter's charge and owes him certain services on his farm in return for his 'landlord's' protection and financial assistance.

as the case may be, and asks for some small assistance towards the expenses of a third wife. In the following year, he says to his first wife who is now the 'big wife', 'I like such and such a girl. Let us make a bigger farm this year.' As soon as the harvest is over that year, he sells all the rice they have in the barn and so acquires the fourth wife.

3. *Prohibited Relationships*

There are, of course, certain restrictions in regard to the category of person with whom a man or woman may have intercourse, or marry. It is significant of Mende culture that these restrictions are determined ostensibly by the rules of one of the secret societies—the Humui—rather than by ideas of consanguinity and affinity. The 'moral' laws of the Humui control and regulate sexual conduct in general. Breach of certain of these laws is known as *simongama*, and it necessitates the 'washing' and fining of the offending parties. The nearest European equivalent of *simongama* is incest.

Broadly speaking, restrictions fall into three categories: (*a*) where connection with the woman would constitute *simongama*, which is a particularly heinous offence; (*b*) where connection does not constitute *simongama*, but is contrary to other laws of the Humui; and (*c*) additional restrictions which are peculiar to the particular descent groups involved. In general terms, it is *simongama* for a man to have sexual relations with any close relatives on the patrilineal side (including father's sister's daughter); with any descendants of the same mother as himself, irrespective of the paternity of such descendants; and with any close relatives of his existing wives. By special dispensation of the Humui, he may, in some cases, have relations with and marry his wife's sister after his wife has died. Generally, marriage with father's brother's daughter, i.e. paternal first cousin, is regarded as a social evil, and no children are expected to result from the union. Marriage with a second cousin on the paternal side is also unpopular, but occurs more often. A native explanation for the prohibition on first cousin marriage is that it avoids the possibility of marrying a half-sister unawares. This might arise if, as occasionally happens, two brothers, on intimate terms with each other, have been sharing each other's wives.

MARRIAGE AND 'FRIENDSHIP'

A man is prohibited specifically from having relations with the following categories of person, viz.

(a) His own mother, or maternal grandmother.
(b) His own daughter, or grand-daughter.
(c) His own sister, or half-sister.
(d) The sisters of both his father and mother.
(e) The daughter of his brother or sister, and the daughters of his brother's and sister's children.
(f) His wife's sister, or any immediate descendants of his wife's sister, while his wife is still alive.
(g) The descendants of his wife's brother, while that wife is alive.
(h) The daughter of his wife's father's brother.
(j) The sister, or any close relative, of any woman with whom he has had relations at any time, so long as that woman is alive.
(k) Any woman, irrespective of relationship, with whom his brother, or half-brother, has had intercourse.
(l) Any woman, irrespective of his relationship to her, who has suckled him.

Although, as mentioned above, *simongama* is generally committed in the case of a union between paternal first cousins, there are certain exceptions to the rule. This kind of marriage is contracted, sometimes, by chiefs and is known as *njoe*—'family marriage'. Its purpose is partly dynastic, and is rationalized in terms of the necessity for maintaining valuable property, such as land or important chiefdom secrets, within the same descent group. 'Family marriage' is also practised among the Humui society itself for similar reasons, i.e. to keep intact hereditary society secrets and medicines.

There are absolutely no restrictions, on the other hand, on marriage with a first cousin on the mother's side. Indeed this kind of union is favoured by the special relationship which obtains between the mother's brother and the sister's son. As already indicated, uncle and nephew have reciprocal duties and obligations towards each other, and the nephew has a claim to part of his uncle's property, and to his daughter or his wives. He may have connection with the latter while his uncle is alive, but if he does so, he forfeits his claim to his uncle's daughter; since to have relations with her, also, would constitute *simongama*.

MARRIAGE AND 'FRIENDSHIP'

By Mende custom, a son may also be permitted access to his father's wives, whilst the latter is still living; but an exception is made, of course, in the case of the person's own mother. This practice, however, is going out of use as the result of Islamic prohibitions.

In the old days, marriage between a Mende and a non-Mende person is said to have been very rare. Nowadays, relatively little attention is paid to the matter among commoners. There is little antipathy to one of their womenfolk marrying a 'stranger' though, as already mentioned, the Mende tend to look down on certain peoples, such as the Kono and the Kissi. The objection to strange marriages is stronger among the ruling class, partly on account of the supposed danger of introducing an outsider into the house. It is feared that the latter's relations may obtain a stake in the chiefdom itself. There are also some specific objections with regard to the Temne, the traditional enemies of the Mende, and when a Mende chief gave his daughter in marriage to a Temne chief, in recent years, the event was looked upon as a somewhat daring break with precedent.

Once physiological and social maturity is reached, there are no further restrictions of any kind on marriage. Sometimes, a person who is old and infirm marries a girl just out of Sande, and there is no prejudice against such a union. Marriage is possible between persons of any social status, with the exception of women who are Paramount Chiefs. A woman chief may not have a husband from the time of her accession. She is allowed, however, one recognized consort whom she may change at will, though such changes are not popular if they occur frequently. Her having relations with other men does not rank as adultery in this case.

4. *The Humui and Sexual Behaviour*

In addition to restrictions on marriage between certain categories of person, the rules of the Humui society prohibit specific kinds of sexual behaviour for the community as a whole. It is forbidden to have sexual intercourse with a girl under the age of puberty, or in the bush, during the day or night, with any person, irrespective of age and social and biological relationship. It is also forbidden to have intercourse with any woman who is nursing a child, or with any woman who is pregnant. Other sexual offences are for a brother to sit on his sister's or mother's bed, or a sister

MARRIAGE AND 'FRIENDSHIP'

to sit on her brother's bed. A man may not shake hands with his mother-in-law, or with the mother of any woman with whom he has had sexual relations. A wife may not visit her parents on the same night after intercourse.

The Humui lays down, in addition, a number of regulations regarding sexual hygiene. For example it is an offence for a woman to speak to, or to remain in the presence of any member of her own kinsfolk or of the kinsfolk of the man with whom she has had connection, until she has washed in the morning. If she comes into contact with any of her own or her husband's female relatives in this way, the offence amounts to *simongama*, and is dealt with as such. The implication is that the sexual act itself is extended by her action to proscribed relatives of the man. All women who have had intercourse during the night are required to wash before preparing food the next day.[1]

Breaches of these laws and regulations, whether deliberate or not, are regarded, in the case of *simongama*, as a serious offence against the relatives of the person concerned as well as against the society. It is believed that sickness and disaster will befall all concerned, and the guilty party must make compensation to the woman's relatives as well as to the Humui. The offence has also to be expiated in a ritual way. *Simongama* is regarded as particularly serious and disgraceful when it involves persons of note, such as a chief, and if a complaint arises the authorities try to settle it as secretly as possible. In one such case, the complainant, whose sister was given in marriage to a neighbour, alleged that the latter had intercourse with his two other sisters. He also alleged that this man had committed a further ritual offence in having intercourse with a number of his late uncle's wives, before they were 'out of the *barri*', i.e. before they had been ritually 'washed' after the death of their husband. The court which heard the matter in private session decided that a grave injury had indeed been committed and instructed the guilty party to compensate the complainant with an apology and the sum of £110 (which included expenses). He was also to relinquish his wife without, of course, receiving back bridewealth paid for her, and both he and the women concerned were to be 'washed' by the Humui.

More generally, however, an infraction of the Humui rules

---

[1] Another rule of the Humui, which has no obvious connection with sex, is that cold ashes in the hearth should be swept away before preparing food, and that stale food or drink should never be used.

MARRIAGE AND 'FRIENDSHIP'

comes to light through some one falling ill. Perhaps it is a child. The *tɔtogbemui* (soothsayer) is called in and consulted. After manipulating his stones and hearing anything the child's parent has to confess, he informs the latter that he has transgressed the rules of the society and must report to them. The Humui officials then deal with the matter.[1]

5. *The Legal Conditions of Marriage*

In former days, marriage in Mende society was regarded as a contract between the relatives on either side, and the man and woman themselves were only incidental parties. Nowadays, much more attention is paid to the individual wishes of the persons concerned. This is true chiefly of girls who have attended school, but non-literate women, too, are beginning to take the matter into their own hands. Extra opportunities to move about the country freely, to trade, and to earn money for themselves all add to this tendency. They are impatient, to an increasing extent, of the restrictions of farm life, and look for someone with a more regular supply of cash in his pocket than a husband whose entire earnings depend on farm work. The saying is: 'We cannot marry a farmer, who works to earn only by the year.' They prefer someone, like a clerk, who is paid by the month or by the week. The personal qualities and attributes of a prospective husband are also taken into account. He should be well built, and the colour of his hair and body should be black. He should have a smooth skin. He should be generous to the girl's mother.

Whereas, in former days, the consent of the girl herself would not have been considered necessary, today no marriage is valid unless it is agreed to by the girl as well as her father and mother. Agreement must be expressed publicly in the presence of some important person. If the girl's parents are dead or cannot be traced, the responsibility falls upon the nearest male relative, or the head of the household of which she is a member. This public consent is the essential condition. The giving of money and other presents and the performing of services on behalf of the girl's relatives are generally practised, but they are not absolutely essential to the validity of the marriage and may even be neglected in certain cases. Payment may be foregone, for example, in the

[1] See also Chapter XII, sect. 8.

case of women who are 'given' as wives to a Paramount chief; of a nephew marrying the daughter of his maternal uncle; of the daughter of one chief who is given to another chief; and (in former times) of a woman given in discharge of a debt, or of a freeman marrying a slave.

In such cases, it is sufficient for the man to 'show life'—*nde yui*. This means that he makes a small present of a nominal sum of money to the woman's parents. Their acceptance of it signifies consent to the marital union.

Nor is anything more than a nominal amount to 'enliven' the property required in the case of widows. A man's wives are 'inheritable' by his brothers, sons, and nephews. On their husband's death, the women are secluded for purposes of purification for three days. For Moslems, the period is forty days. During this time, they are required to make their choice among the deceased's relatives, who seek their favour by gifts. Their new husbands are then expected to 'show themselves' with a small present to the parents of the woman they claim. This procedure is known as 'climbing on the stump'—*tɛ gu kpe yei*.

6. *The Implications of 'Woman Damage'*

By virtue of the rights exercised over them, women contribute a number of services which the transaction of marriage transfers from one set of kinsmen to another. In becoming a man's wife, therefore, a woman comes under the control of him and his male relatives. Subject to customary conditions, marriage entitles them to the product of her services, in terms of children, and increment deriving from her work. Any infringement of these rights by outsiders, for example, by having sexual intercourse with her, is an encroachment on the prerogatives of the husband and his relatives, and has to be compensated as such. This largely explains the significance of the term 'woman damage' as applied when any person, other than those legally entitled to the privilege or expressly permitted it, has relations with a woman. In former days, the guilty party would be required to compensate all the relatives concerned as well as the woman's husband. Nowadays, however, the tendency in women's services and in property is for individual rights to take precedence over group rights. To an increasing extent the rule is for affairs of this kind to be settled directly with the husband. The change has been brought about largely

MARRIAGE AND 'FRIENDSHIP'

because now the obligation is more on the man himself to obtain a wife.

The same applies to 'woman damage' in respect of an unmarried girl. Until her marriage has been completed she is entirely under the control of her parents and their relatives and any sexual interference with her at this stage is an infringement of their authority over her. As already mentioned, if the offence is committed before, or at the time of her puberty, it is more grave and requires ritual treatment in addition to monetary compensation. Broadly speaking, therefore, there are three categories of 'woman damage':

(a) Having sexual intercourse with an immature girl.
(b) De-flowering a prospective wife without her relatives' consent.
(c) Having sexual intercourse with a woman of any description without permission of the person in charge of her.

(a) and (b) constitute infractions respectively of the laws of the Humui and Sande societies and require that the 'guilty' parties concerned should be 'washed' and fines paid to the societies in question. (c) refers to a grown woman, and the amount is payable to the person in control of her—usually her husband. If she is unmarried, it may be her parents, or even an older woman in whose care she is at the time.

Infidelity is detected by voluntary or compulsory confession. There are a number of occasions when a woman will confess voluntarily; for example, if she has quarrelled with her lover, or if he has left her for another woman. She may also confess, if she or her child become ill, since, in certain circumstances, sickness is thought to be the result of sexual misdemeanour. Another occasion is in the course of child-birth, if the labour is particularly long and difficult; because withholding the names of any lovers she may have means delaying the birth of the child.

The most general method of obtaining confession, however, is by 'swearing' the woman. This is done periodically, when a man has a large number of wives or when he suspects any particular one of infidelity. In order to carry out the swearing, he engages the services of a medicine man. The women are made to swear on the latter's medicine that they have not had connection with any man other than their husband. If, through fear of the consequences of the medicine, they refuse to swear, they are made to 'call', i.e. disclose, the names of their lovers.[1] Strictly speaking, wives must not be sworn without the consent of their parents and, in some chiefdoms, without the consent of the chief. In some cases, in order to avoid trouble with her husband and his relatives, the girl's own people obtain a confession from her of their own accord.

Wives rarely refuse to 'call' their lover's name. If they do refuse, they may be flogged or forced to 'swear' the man himself. This makes the lover reveal himself. When his name has been 'called', he goes to the husband and 'begs' him with a sum of money. If the husband is satisfied, he accepts it and the matter is settled 'out of court'. If the man denies the fact, which is rarely the case, or if he fails to satisfy the husband, the latter may take him to Court. The usual fine levied there is 30s. and, nowadays, such matters are invariably settled in cash. In the old days, a slave would be demanded, or if the woman were the wife of a chief or a warrior, the husband would endeavour to put the lover to death, and the woman would be severely flogged.

It is regarded as particularly disgraceful for a chief's wife to have connection with another man. If she does not confess, she may be sent back to her people and any money paid on her account is refunded. If the chief has not paid bridewealth for her, the girl's people lose his friendship. Generally, in the case of the wife of a chief or any other important man, the lover finds it preferable to settle the matter privately, and may have to pay an amount which ranges up to £50.

Sometimes, as mentioned in an earlier paragraph, the husband makes no objection to his wives having 'friends', provided the latter work for him. When the periodical test of his wives' fidelity takes place, he may tell the medicine man about the situation, and the woman is not discovered on account of that particular lover. If, however, the lover goes away, the husband may drop immediately upon him for damages. In other cases, the woman is actually forced, through her husband neglecting her, to find a man to support her.

Practices of this kind are regarded widely in Mende country

[1] Sometimes, a woman will go secretly to the medicine man and 'beg' an antidote to the medicine he is to use. The traditional method used was a more drastic one of extracting the truth. The medicine man would first rub a concoction of herbs and leaves over the woman's hands. A small iron rod, previously made red-hot, was placed in a pot filled with palm oil. The suspected woman had to thrust her hand into the oil and pull out the hot iron. If she failed to do this without being burned, her guilt was established.

as a growing abuse, and their spread is attributed to abolition of the older and sterner sanctions and to the introduction and extended use of money since the coming of the Europeans. Various suggestions have been put forward by the chiefs themselves for dealing with the situation, but there is apparently a strong reluctance to take any step which will detract from the rights and privileges of the husband. One chief is attempting to regulate the practice by trying each case on its merits. Before making an award, his Court endeavours to find out upon whom the woman was dependent for maintenance, and it disallows the claim, if the husband was taking no responsibility for her.

7. *Ways of making a Marriage*

The general method of contracting marriage is for the man and/or his relatives to present the girl and her relatives with a sum of money, and goods, such as country cloths. It is rare for a return present to be made, except in the case of literate persons following Colony customs, or of a Paramount chief who is too 'proud' to let his daughter go 'unaccompanied'. In the latter case, anything given with the girl is deducted from the husband's claim for expenses, should the marriage subsequently be dissolved.

The approach to the marriage contract is often a complicated one and is bound up with such factors as the object the person has in seeking a wife, his own status and position in society, and the age and social status of the girl or woman he has in view. Broadly speaking, marital unions fall into three categories from the point of view of the procedure involved, and these may be classified as follows: (*a*) *fale gbua nyahanga*—'mushroom wives'; (*b*) *kɔli nyahanga*—women 'found'; and (*c*) *ndoma nyahanga*—'love wives', and *kpao nyahanga*—'husbandless women'.

In the case of the first, i.e. *fale gbua nyahanga*, the procedure is a lengthy and cumulative one, hence the expression 'mushroom'. It may involve a considerable amount of money and is undergone, as a rule, only by chiefs and persons of wealth who wish to increase the number of women already in their household. The wife is betrothed while she is still a child, or even before birth. For example, a man who has a close friend, may ask him to let him have the next female child born. Instances of the betrothal of children are still fairly common; but the latter kind of arrangement is made very rarely, nowadays, if ever.

MARRIAGE AND 'FRIENDSHIP'

The full procedure over a 'mushroom' wife means that the prospective husband assumes immediate responsibility for the cost of and training of his future spouse. He begins by 'tying a rope on her wrist'—*ngεya lo tokomee*. In other words, he lays claim to her by a gift of, say, 1*s*. to the child's parents. Assuming that she is still an infant, he takes over a mat for her to lie on and a small country cloth to cover her. He cuts some wood to heat her bath water and provides some red oil and grease for rubbing her. His next expenses are at puberty, when he takes the girl and her parents as 'friends' (*ndiama lui*) by giving her, say, 5*s*., and her parents, say, 10*s*. Then he has to initiate her into Sande (*Sande wa gbi*). He gives her, say, three head-ties and a covering cloth when she enters the 'bush', and sends her the food and other necessaries in connection with every ceremony demanded by initiation. These expenses, including presents to the society officials, might amount to £4 or £5. After the Sande has been 'pulled', the girls are taken to the *barri* in the town, where they remain for a time. On this occasion, the prospective husband is expected to give the girl, say, 5*s*., and a further small amount to her companions, while they are 'standing the *barri*'. He also gives final presents on behalf of the girl to the Sande officials, say, 3*s*. to the *Majo*, 4*s*. to the *Ngafei*, and 4*s*. to the woman who acted as the girl's caretaker in the bush. He gives a special present of, say, 5*s*. to the girl's mother, which is known as *sowolui*. Finally, to the feast, which is held in the girl's honour on her return home, namely, *henjo mbie* ('cooking for the initiate'), he contributes one large cock, 3*s*. worth of rice, and gives 1*s*., as *famalui*, or 'greeting present', to the girl's relatives and, say, a further 2*s*. to the girl herself.

Then a meeting is held at which the final amount to be paid as bridewealth is decided upon. This is the *mboya*, and its purpose is to hasten the marriage. It consists of a lump sum in money, along with a quantity of goods of a traditional kind, such as country cloths. These are handed over to the girl's father and mother, and they allot a portion to one of the girl's *kenyaisia* (mother's brothers), who should also be present at the transaction and this formal recognition of the contract.

As already mentioned, *mboya* is contributed mainly by the man's kinsfolk. In the case of one young man, who married a girl aged fifteen, his father provided £2 and a country cloth; his mother, a small country cloth; and his uncles 10*s*. In another case, *mboya* of £4 10*s*. was provided by the man's father and brother each paying a half share. The recipients of the *mboya* are expected to re-distribute it among their own nearest relatives after each has taken a share for him or herself. In one instance, out of *mboya* of £7 and country cloths, the father retained £2; the mother £1 10s. and a country cloth; £1 10s. went to the mother's relatives; and £2 was divided among the girl's sisters and brothers.

After presentation of the *mboya*, all the parties present 'hang heads', i.e. consult together. The girl is called, and her father or her mother (more often the latter) says to her, 'Well, my daughter, So and So has brought *mboya* so that he can marry you, and here is the amount.' She hands the money to the girl, and goes on, 'You have taken the *mboya*, but are you willing to go to him? Will you stay with him in poverty and any other kind of ill-luck?' Provided the girl is willing to marry the man, she is expected to reply, 'I am ready to go to him, and so here is the money. You can keep it and use it as you like. I will do all I can to satisfy him.' This is a formal promise that her people will not be called upon to refund bridewealth as the result of her subsequent conduct.

The ceremony of handing over the *mboya* must be carried out in the presence of an important member of the town, such as the Town Chief. The prospective husband then presents the girl's mother with a cloth known as *dagba gulai* ('nursing dress'), and her father with a gown (*bla lome*), which is worth about 5s., and a mat. He gives 10s. to the girl herself, and a fee to the witness. He is now entitled 'to find the woman'—*wa-bi-nyahi goi*. Two days later, he sends round his big wife, or his sister, to the girl with a small present of, say, 2s. His messenger tells the girl's parents that the man's people want her to come and stay with them for a time. Acceptance of this present means that they are agreeable to her going. If it is not accepted, the *mboya* and *all* the previous expenses, which the husband has incurred, must be refunded to him.

Then the girl's mother spits on her daughter's hand, and she rubs the saliva on her forehead. The mother blesses her in this way, and prays that there may be many children—*Ngewɔ e gbɔ ma wu ndoloi gbotongɔ*. The girl is escorted away by dancers to her husband's house.[1] To make the marriage quite complete, the

[1] Moslems sometimes use a white bed sheet as a 'test' of virginity. The sheet is carried round to the girl's parents in the morning. If it is marked by blood, the husband makes them a present, and there is general rejoicing. This may be regarded, however, more as a ritualistic feature than a genuine test, since the husband is usually informed of his wife's condition in this respect when she comes out of Sande.

husband should make a very small and nominal present (it may be no more than one penny) to the girl's parents. It is known as 'life kola'—*nde vu lui*—and it signifies that he takes responsibility for her life. Should he omit this, her people may raise a complaint if the girl dies soon after she has gone to him and his group. He may have to pay them a large amount in compensation.

The expenditure of this form of marriage and transaction varies, of course, with the social status of the person. In the case of a Paramount chief, *mboya* may amount to several hundreds of pounds. Sometimes, part of the initiation expenses are met by the girl's parents. Some parents prefer to put their daughter through Sande on their own account to avoid the possibility of having to re-pay a large sum, should the marriage subsequently break up.

The procedure in the case of the second category, *kɔli nyahanga*, or women 'found', is much the same as with *fale gbua nyahanga*, but it begins after the girl has left Sande. The man first approaches the girl with some reasonable amount of money and 'takes her as friend', i.e. obtains her consent. The girl is expected to report his advances to her parents. Alternatively, he may send his sister or his big wife, if the latter is not a jealous woman. It is etiquette for the girl to refuse these initial approaches. The man's emissary assures her that she will be well treated.

As before, the girl's father and mother have then to give their consent before a witness, and the man 'lays kola'—*tolo la*—i.e. gives them a nominal amount of money. If they accept this, it is a guarantee of the betrothal and is spoken of as a 'fence'—*kulie*, because it protects the girl from other men. Then a further meeting is held at which the amount of the *mboya* is agreed upon, having regard for the expenses which the parents have already incurred over their girl's initiation. The prospective husband may consent to defray all, or part of these, and the amount is included in the *mboya*. Like 'mushroom' marriages, this kind of union is usually a prerogative of the wealthier class of person.

In the case of *ndoma nyahanga*, the third category, no amount is paid even nominally as *mboya*. The majority of poor men's wives come under this heading. It also includes women who have run away from their husbands on account of a lover with whom they are living, and a few educated women who consider it derogatory to have money paid for them. In former times, women given in discharge of a debt—*kpomba nyahanga*—would also be classified in the same way.

Daughters of Paramount chiefs, for whom no money is paid, constitute a further addition to this class. Chiefs sometimes give their daughters away for reasons of prestige, or to mark their appreciation of lavish hospitality they have received from a fellow chief.

Generally speaking, marriage of this kind begins with a 'friendship' arrangement. The man speaks privately to the woman, and they begin to co-habit. Such a relationship is common mainly in the railway line towns, where women who have left their husbands largely congregate for purposes of trading. The matter may, or may not, be mentioned to the woman's parents; but if they take notice of what is going on, the man begins to 'feed' them with small presents—*hinda wanda*—and they will probably not raise any objection, particularly if he helps them on their farm. This means that he will not be sued by them for 'woman damage', but any children resulting will belong to the woman's people and not to him. If the man wishes to take the matter any further, he is expected to 'show life' with a small present to the parents. This, provided the parents are agreeable, converts the 'friendship' into proper marriage, and the woman is regarded thenceforward as his wife.

Usually, no bridewealth is called for in the case of women whose previous marriage has been dissolved, because the relatives are unwilling to run the risk of having to make further re-payments. A poor man may undertake to work for the parents of a woman on condition of their agreeing to regard him as her husband. If she leaves him after he has worked for some time, he has no bridewealth to re-claim, but he is entitled to retain any children she has borne him. He is entitled, in addition, to some amount of compensation for his services, but may not marry off any of the female children without their mother's knowledge.

'Friendships' of an unsanctioned kind occur when, as described above, a man with a number of wives connives for economic reasons at their keeping lovers, or when a man wishes to have occasional relations with a woman. In the latter case, if he wants her at his house for the purpose, he sends one of his wives to 'call' her. If he goes to a house other than the one in which he or his wives are living, the intervention of the wife is unnecessary.

The main constituents of proper marriage may be summed up,

MARRIAGE AND 'FRIENDSHIP'

then, as follows. No marriage is valid without the consent of the woman's parents, and the man has no right to her and can make no claim on her account, until they have recognized him as her husband. Until the parents have been formally apprised of his intentions, his relationship with the girl is technically one merely of 'friendship', even though she may be referred to as his 'wife'. The presents he gives her up to this time, i.e. up to the time when the parents are notified, are known as *boya hani*, and he can re-claim them only from the girl. If he has been living with her and she dies, the parents can fall on him for 'life kola', i.e. compensation. Marriage with the first category mentioned, i.e. *fale gbua nyahanga*, is not fully complete until the final payments of *mboya* and 'life kola' have been made. If the man has relations with the girl before this has been done, he risks losing all rights over her, as well as any expenses he has incurred on her behalf. His only course is to 'beg' her relatives with a gift. This explains why parents do not always insist on *mboya* being paid in full at the time of the betrothal and will accept it in instalments. If another man has intercourse with the girl in the meantime, it is for the parents to sue him for damages in order to recoup themselves for the damages which the 'husband' will be entitled to claim from them.

Should some act on the part of the girl or her relatives make completion of the marriage impossible, e.g. through the girl changing her mind about the matter and going off with someone else; or through her parents deciding to give her to another person, the 'husband' is entitled to a refund in full. This will include every item and form of expense he has incurred, including gifts and expenditure on Sande. Alternatively, another woman may be substituted by the parents, providing all the parties concerned are agreeable. This happens, sometimes, if the wife dies soon after the marriage has been completed. The woman's relatives will choose this course the more readily, if their son-in-law has been 'good' to them, i.e. has helped them extensively on the farm and with other services. In that case, the relatives 'look round the house', and a girl who has not been suckled at the same breast as the deceased woman—to avoid *simongama*—is found. Failing this, the amount of returnable bridewealth is reckoned according to the length of time the deceased woman was with her husband.

Women who are substituted in this way are known as *wata nyahanga*.

8. *Marital Obligations*

The wife's duty is to obey and satisfy her husband in every way possible. She is expected to defer to him in everything except purely domestic matters, and traditional etiquette requires her to approach him on bended knee. If she comes into the household as a junior wife, however, she is under the immediate control of her husband's big wife and takes her orders directly from the latter.

The husband's obligations towards his wife are to maintain her so long as she remains with him and to provide her with clothing. He is expected to treat all his wives in the same way, though an exception is made in the case of senior wives. If he gives an article of clothing to one wife, the other should receive the same kind of article, but it need not be the same in pattern or value. Wives retain a large measure of control and influence over their own children, and the fact that there is a special relationship between the latter and their mothers' brothers creates a situation which is extraneous, to some extent, to the patriarchal structure of the household.

As mentioned in Chapter V, a husband is expected to help his wife's parents on their farm and in other ways. Any general services he gives are also counted in his favour with respect to the question of returnable bridewealth. His wife's parents have no specific obligations of a reciprocal kind towards him.

9. *The Dissolution of Marriage*

Generally, no question of dissolution of marriage arises so long as the wife gives satisfactory service. If, however, the husband wishes, for any reason, to put an end to the matter, he simply sends the woman back to her people and makes a public declaration to the effect that she is no longer his wife. Thenceforward, he has no further responsibility for her; but provided the step was taken by him and not by the woman, he has no claim for refund of bridewealth. He may even be required to render a *kɔtu* or 'good-bye' fee to the woman's parents in compensation for the loss of her virginity. He may retain any children, other than those at the breast. In actual fact, very few marriages are ended in this way, i.e. through direct action on the part of the husband. As a general rule, if the wife is unsatisfactory, he can find some indirect way of putting the blame on her. For example, he may neglect her or

MARRIAGE AND 'FRIENDSHIP'

treat her roughly until she is glad to run away from him. Viewed, therefore, in this way, it is the grounds which are legitimate for re-fund of bridewealth rather than the grounds which are legitimate for dissolution of marriage which are significant.

A husband may dissolve his marriage and claim re-fund of bridewealth for the following reasons:

(a) Desertion; for example, when the woman returns home of her own accord and refuses to go back to him; or when she goes off with another man. To cease to work for the husband also constitutes an act of 'desertion' on the wife's part.

(b) Continued infidelity, whether with one man or a number of men. A husband will rarely send away a woman whom he does not want to lose for an occasional infidelity. It is considered an offence against him and as an indignity, but not as particularly disgraceful, as a rule.

(c) Practise of witchcraft by the wife, or by the wife causing the death of her child by giving it to a witch who 'eats' the child's spirit.

(d) Abusing the husband's parents.

(e) Refusal to co-habit.

Barrenness does not constitute sufficient grounds for dissolution of the marriage. A woman may leave her husband without rendering her people liable for re-fund of bridewealth if he is persistently cruel to her; or if he commits *simongama* with one of her near relatives. Infidelity on the part of the husband does not, of course, constitute reasonable grounds; nor, theoretically, does impotency. Impotency is considered shameful, and for this reason it may be possible for a wife to return without difficulty. It does not, however, prevent a man taking and having any number of wives. In the circumstances, however, they are usually allowed to co-habit with a relative of the husband, such as a nephew, or even to have lovers of their own. If the husband is unable to maintain his wife, she may return home, but she still remains his wife. In the event, however, of another person having relations with her, the husband has no claim for 'woman damage'.

The fact that the woman's relatives have usually received a share of the bridewealth gives them an interest in keeping the marriage intact. Otherwise, they may be called upon to remit money which they have already put to use. Similarly, the fact that the man's relatives have often made their contribution to his expenses entitles them to a say over the treatment of the girl and is a check, sometimes, to undue harshness on the part of the husband and his relatives. They realize that they may forfeit their money, as well as the general services of the girl, if she runs away. In other words, the interests of both groups lie in keeping relations between husband and wife as stable and as amicable as possible.

The general rule, which is unaffected by the reasons for dissolution of marriage, is for the woman's children to remain with the husband or his people, until they are grown up. They are considered as members of his group. There is nothing to prevent their living subsequently with their mother; but if they do so, they run the risk of losing rights in their father's personal property, and his people may be reluctant to let them use their land. If the children are very young, an arrangement may be made whereby they remain with their mother until they are old enough to walk. When the daughter marries, the father receives the bridewealth, but the girl's mother and uncle are entitled to a share of it in the same way as if the mother were still with their father.

10. *Re-Claim of Bridewealth*

Desertion by the wife is the most frequent cause of marriage coming to an end, and most claims for re-payment of bridewealth derive from her refusal to return to her husband. If every effort to persuade her is in vain, the husband enters his claim at the Native Court. The bridewealth, as already indicated, constitutes for practical purposes the sum total of expenses he has incurred over the woman in question. In his claim, he is allowed to count presents and services to her and to her parents and relatives both prior to, and after, completion of the *mboya*. Any gifts or presents from the girl's people form a contra-account and are deducted from the husband's final reckoning. The following details, which are part of a claim for £26 7s. in respect of a woman called Mattu, give an idea of the social obligations involved in the marriage transaction as a whole. The items include a head-tie and tobacco given to Mattu when the husband first met her and valued at 5s. 3d.; the amount of 9s. 9d. given on the occasion of her first Sande ceremony; the amount of £2 representing the value of a gift of palm kernels to her uncles; some £5 on account of clothes supplied in connection with the Sande initiation; 5s. 6d. given at the death of one of Mattu's relatives, Tamba, and a further £6 given in connection with the funerals of other relatives; and various sums of money representing about two dozen separate small gifts to Mattu and her mother and mother's relatives.

Currently, there are several methods of settling claims and cases of this kind in the Native Court. The first task is always to decide if the marriage is a 'legal' one, i.e. that it had the consent of the woman's parents. These juridical methods and procedure involved are described, however, in Chapter IX, and so it is unnecessary to include them here.

CHAPTER VIII

THE POSITION OF WOMEN

1. *Women's Position a Paradox*

THE social position of women is somewhat paradoxical. On the one hand, there is obviously no doubt that they are subject to a great deal of male control; in the first case, of the group into which they are born, and in the second, of the men to whom they are married. In the eyes of the 'law', a woman is generally looked upon as a minor and, except in certain circumstances, is not allowed to sue on her own account in court. Legally, she cannot be held directly responsible for her actions and, if married, is supposed at all times to be under the authority of her husband, or of one of his male relatives. The implications of the last point affect her position still further. Any work she does is, strictly speaking, for the sole benefit of her husband and his relatives, and, therefore, if she earns any money through trading, for example, she may retain it only with his consent. Any goods or articles she possesses, other than personal items of clothing or pieces of jewellery her husband has given her, belong to him, and can be claimed at his death by the relative who inherits his estate. Even jewellery, if it is particularly valuable, may fall into this category.

Again, the husband may have as many other wives or other women as he wishes or can acquire; the wife is expected to remain faithful to him alone. The children she bears belong to the husband and his group, and remain with them if the marriage is dissolved, irrespective of the cause of its dissolution. In a general sense, the woman remains in the background in public affairs even when

THE POSITION OF WOMEN

the issue in question affects members of her own sex.[1] Further, as mentioned in Chapter IV, the sexes have very little contact with each other once the stage of puberty is reached. Thereafter, the women are expected to keep quite apart from the men, to wait on them, and to confine themselves to domestic duties.

If the apparent situation of social separation and female inferiority were the real one, there would be no doubt as to the subservient rôle of the women. The facts of the matter, however, are not such as to justify the idea either that women are merely 'slaves', or that male superiority is only a sham. As is the case in most preliterate societies, the rôle of Mende women is complementary rather than subordinate to that of the men, and in performing it, they obtain political as well as social compensations which are substantial enough to offset most of the nominal disadvantages. At the same time, it has to be admitted that their influence operates, in the main, indirectly and beneath the surface. The Sande society, which carries almost the entire responsibility for the training and social indoctrination of the female side of the community, is an example of this. In organizing society business, the *majo* and other senior officials are in a position to determine to a great extent the whole question of women's behaviour and attitudes towards men. Sande regulations concerning matters of sex and social conduct are as binding on men as women and cannot be altered without the consent of the society's leaders. In other important societies, too, such as the Njayei and Humui in particular, women hold hereditary offices and are the principal leaders.[2] Thus, if only through the part they take in this field, individual women are in a position to grant or to withhold favours and services which are important to the opposite sex. Similarly, the office of *Mabɔlɛ* in the Poro society, which is held by a woman, commands the highest respect and has an integral rôle in the ceremonial life and purpose of that association.

Nor is the influence which women can bring to bear on public affairs limited to society matters. This is particularly evident in the case of older women who happen to belong to an important family. Provided they have the appropriate qualities of ability and the

---

[1] There was an interesting example of this point in the opening of a maternity centre, sponsored by one of the Native Administrations. Except for the mid-wives themselves, no woman approached within thirty yards of the surrounding throng of males.

[2] See Chapter XIII for the further implications of this point.

THE POSITION OF WOMEN

experience of age, they may be put in charge of family affairs. This means that, as trustees for lands and property, their influence in the community is as great as any male head of a group of kinsmen, and that, as such, they are equally eligible for political office, such as village or town headmen, and members of the Native Administration. Women occupying such posts will be found in many chiefdoms, and in such capacities their voice is as good as any male of the council. Even more significant, as described more fully in Chapter IX (q.v.), is the fact that, in some cases, women are appointed as Paramount chiefs and that in some chiefdoms the institution is, or has become, quite a regular one.

Nor is this respect paid to women, particularly older women, inconsistent with the native outlook. The Mende acknowledge that there are 'sensible' women, and it is clear that social status depends, in this respect, more upon age than upon sex. The Mende themselves explain this by saying that they look upon a woman as a man when a certain age is reached. Thus, it may come about that a chief's senior wife is sometimes put into a position of trust in the chiefdom which ordinarily would be filled by a male relative of the ruler.[1] Similarly, women of rank, such as the sisters of a chief, are accorded socially the same consideration as any of the big men of the chiefdom. For example, when an important visitor arrives, they may take precedence after the chief himself in greeting him.

It is not only women of the upper class who manage to hold their own with the men. It is hardly necessary to point out that polygyny does not always place the wives at an individual disadvantage in relations with their husband. A group of them may combine on occasion to make his life almost unbearable with petty irritations until he has acceded to some general demand. Particularly under present conditions, a man with a large number of wives finds it virtually impossible to keep account of the comings and goings of each one of them. Any two may join together to keep each other's secrets and to cover up each other's movements.

2. *Tensions between the Sexes*

As already noted,[2] one of the effects of polygyny on the social structure is to apportion most of the women among a relatively

[1] For an example of this see Chapter V, footnote p. 103.
[2] See Chapters III and VII.

small number of men. This makes it difficult, particularly in larger households, for some of the women to satisfy their desire for children with their own husbands. It also explains in part why the institution of 'friendship' is so common. Often, as already mentioned, the arrangement is connived at, if not encouraged, by the husband, particularly in areas where male labour is scarce, on the understanding that his wife's lover gives service on the farm. The practice is not a new one; but the increased ability of the young men to move away and the difficulty of bringing them to book, if they subsequently avoid their part of the bargain, provoke many and bitter complaints about present laxities in morals. The older men assert that adultery was relatively unknown before the country came under British rule. In former times, it was possible to deal effectively with both parties. They could be severely flogged, and a warrior would not hesitate to kill a man he found tampering with his wife. Nowadays, if the lover were as much as stocked, he would probably run straight to the District Commissioner. Many of the young men who help to cause the trouble are in European employment, and for this reason the aggrieved party is often afraid to lay a complaint.

In more general terms, therefore, the developing situation is symptomatic of a state of social disruption in which the rôle of women is only incidental, and to which the contributive factors are largely external. The construction of the railway line and of motor roads has made movement between and from the tribal areas easy and, in creating commercial centres, has provided increased opportunities for women to earn their living by trading. Money can also be earned at the mines in several parts of the Protectorate, and the recent War has been the conclusive factor in putting wages and cash into the hands of a section of the community, including the women, among whom its possession was previously uncommon. The paying of war-time allotments to the wives of soldiers serving abroad was a special novelty. Allotments ranged between 7*s.* 6*d.* and 43*s.* 6*d.* per month and amounted, perhaps, to some 22*s.* on the average. Sometimes, individual wives were able to double the amount by making 'friendship' with another soldier and sending along a sister, or some other woman, to pose as his wife at the District Commissioner's Office. Some women took the chance, with the connivance of the soldiers, to repay bridewealth, and followed their new 'husbands' when they were removed for training to other parts of the country. In addition, quite a large number of the women, like the younger men, moved away on their own account to find work at wage-rates in the Colony in various ways connected with the war.

The fact that women have become accustomed, not only to the use of money, but to regular money payments, affects their attitude towards marriage, even in the more rural areas. As mentioned in the previous Chapter, they say: 'We cannot marry a farmer, who works to earn only by the year.' They prefer someone who, like a clerk, is paid by the month or by the week. The consequence is that some men, who would ordinarily stay on the land, are forced, in order to obtain wives, to take up labouring or any other paid job they can get, in the town, and put in what time they can on their farms over the week-end. Farmers find it increasingly difficult to obtain assistance, except at wage-rates, and are obliged in some districts to pay women as much as men for a day's work. In a few cases, even wives have got on to their husband's pay-roll. One chief, who prides himself on keeping up with the times, reported that he paid his head wife £10 per year, his second wife £5, and two other wives, who cook for him and fetch his bath-water, £2 10s. each.

3. 'Husbandless Women'

The resulting breakdown in the older order of things is reflected concretely in litigation over women which provides a large part of the business of the native courts.[1] Another result, particularly evident in towns on the railway line where women who have left their husbands or families mainly congregate, is the special popularity of friendship in place of proper marriage. These 'husbandless women', as the Mende call these unattached women, travel up and down the railway line as trade and other interests direct. Their air of freedom and sophisticated ways induces up-country girls to copy their habits, and attracts young men, and even boys, to follow the same roving life as themselves. Older men hope to secure their services for economic purposes, such as trading. They are regarded as a social evil, mainly because their presence causes fights and 'palavers', and occasionally leads to serious damage when a jealous swain, finding his 'friend' together with another man, sets fire to the house. Many of them combine petty trading with a semi-commercial form of prostitution.

[1] For figures on this point, see Chapter IX.

THE POSITION OF WOMEN

Data regarding some three dozen women of the latter kind indicated them to be of varying tribal origin, and included Creoles. About three-fourths of the group were estimated to be below the age of thirty; ten could read and write; only nine out of thirty-four had resided in the same town for longer than a year, and about half that number were in the habit of making frequent visits to other towns. About half the sample were living with relatives; the others rented accommodation, paying about 17*s*. per month on the average for it. Five out of the thirty-four were 'married'. Some ten of them employed young boys, whom they paid some 15*s*. per month and whose duty, among other things, was to find and escort clients to them. Contacts with the opposite sex were made personally in other cases, or in the ordinary course of trading. The women were remunerated by 'drinks' and clothes, as well as in cash, and a very rough estimate of earnings averaged between £11 and £15 per month. The extent of the remuneration was either left to the client or varied according to class.

The clientele of these women includes a variety of individuals, but mainly the semi-literate class of clerk and artisan. European soldiers in transit were also catered for. Where a group of such women share the same house, the arrangements approximate those of an organized brothel, with the exception that personal choice is exercised over customers, the sign of acceptance being a head-tie thrown over to the person accepted. In one such house, the women had more or less permanent 'friends' who, however, gave way when business necessitated it.[1]

The fact that pecuniary considerations are replacing occupational and traditional ones in determining the status of the women strikes right at the heart of the indigenous structure. Prestige and patriarchal authority rested formerly on the ability to control, as well as to possess, a large household. The growing custom of rewarding services by payments of cash represents one form of response to the demands of the new situation. In other cases, alternative methods, in terms of a more generous distribution of clothes and dress materials at the traditionally prescribed seasons of the year, have been adopted. For example, in the case of sixty-

[1] Women of this kind are known, in Creole speech, as 'rally girls', or 'ark royals' (the latter term being popularized by a 'Coast' song in connection with the British aircraft carrier of that name). The term 'rally boys' is also applied to the youths who do the procuring. The fee, which is sometimes charged customers for the latter service, is spoken of as the 'tow-rope'.

four farming households of varying size and importance, the average expenditure on making the farm itself, i.e. cost of hiring and feeding labourers, seed, and implements, was some £13; whereas an average amount of some £14 was spent by the head of the household on clothes, most of which went to the womenfolk.[1]

The reaction to all this of the older men who, as the principal polygynists, are mostly affected, is sometimes less liberal. They take steps to restrict the movement of women about the country. The departure of wives for whom they have given bridewealth may represent quite a serious loss in gross capital. 'Chiefs', remarked a member of this class, 'do not get wives for nothing.' Chiefdom bye-laws have been framed accordingly. An Upper Mende Native Administration enacted that under penalty of fining, every woman, young or old, must have a husband or caretaker; wives must not be allowed to stay away from their husband's house with their parents for more than a month; if a wife does stay away in another chiefdom, it is the duty of her husband to see that she returns and of the husband and village headman to inform the Paramount Chief immediately if she runs away at any time. The parents are also allotted a share of the responsibility.[2]

In a more general way, the situation probably helps to account for the reluctance of official native opinion to admit a Government scheme for modernizing the Sande society for welfare purposes.[3] In certain parts of Mendeland, opposition to this has been expressed strongly on the grounds that it meant male interference with 'women's business', though there is no question of a male person actually entering the Sande bush itself. One of the reasons given is that 'it makes the women too proud'. As explained later in Chapter XII, the same situation also goes a long way towards accounting for the popularity of Islam among the upper class of native society. The stricter sexual code for women that this religion enjoins and the relative success of the Mandingo and Susu men, as Islam's principal adherents, in exacting obedience from their wives and keeping them under control, are all points that appeal to the Mende polygynist. In emulation, possibly, of these

[1] This represents an expenditure of about £2 on each woman.

[2] At a chiefs' conference, it was resolved that women strangers in a town should be 'signed for' by their landlords with 5s., payable to the Native Treasury. They were to stay with their host until called for by the husband or his representative, and the husband would repay the host his 5s.

[3] As mentioned in Chapter VI.

precautions, some Mende husbands who are Moslems, and some who are not, apply practical methods of surveillance by enclosing their compounds with high walls, by taking what amounts to a roll-call of their womenfolk at nightfall, and by locking them up after dark. It is possibly for the same reason, also, that the custom of building the ordinary 'women's house' without windows is maintained, i.e. to prevent the women getting out or anyone getting in at night-time![1]

In other cases, attempts are made to deal with the situation by restraining the men. At one chiefs' conference it was agreed that seduction leading to a woman being separated from the husband should be punished by a fine of £5, the woman to be 'sworn' if she refused to name the seducer before the court, and that the onus for refund of the bridewealth should be laid upon the lover rather than upon the woman's relatives as is the present custom in cases of dissolution.[2] The matter is complicated, however, by the reason already mentioned, namely, that wives are sometimes used as decoys to entrap unpaid labourers for their husbands.

4. Difficulties of the 'Literate' or 'Educated' Woman

Literate, or 'civilized' women, as they sometimes prefer to call themselves,[3] are as yet few in number, but their position is an important index to current developments in the social structure.

There are rather more than 2,000 girls at present in school from the Protectorate. Two-thirds of the Protectorate schools are run by the Missions and are situated mainly in 'urban' areas, so that the mere process of attending them brings the country-bred girl into a more sophisticated environment in which, to a large extent, the criteria of social attainment involve dressing according to European modes, using European types of furniture, food, etc.

[1] On one occasion, when watching a public dance in a chief's compound, the writer had with him a powerful electric torch which he flashed over the dancers. He was earnestly requested by the chief to keep the light focused on the latter's wives who were taking part in the performance.

[2] It is recorded that when this subject of 'woman palaver' was introduced at the conference, it was hardly possible, for a time, to keep order.

[3] The term 'literate' is used in preference to 'civilized' because of the difficulty of defining the latter expression sociologically in a few words in the present context. A number of non-literate women follow habits and customs similar to those of the literate class. See Chapter XIII for a fuller discussion of this question.

THE POSITION OF WOMEN

She is also brought into further contact with part-western, part-Creole social values and notions of respectability. Her experience probably convinces her, if only for social reasons, of the inferiority of the old ways of life, but rarely provides her with the means, on her own account, of obviating them.[1] Most girls do not go further than Standard IV in school, and a few gain qualifications sufficient for the only careers, nursing and teaching, open to women in the Protectorate.[2]

The natural and obvious alternative is marriage, but here again prospects are limited, partly by the nature of the new conditions. European standards of living set a target which most literate members of the opposite sex find it difficult, in terms of their earnings as clerks or teachers and of obligations to their relatives, to reach.[3] They are obliged in choosing a wife to consider not merely questions of companionship. Others, who are Moslems, are unwilling to accept a girl whose religious outlook and ideas about her own position are different from their own. The assets of the literate girl, her western traits and habits, her ability to read and write and to sew, are social rather than economic in the present context and even inferior in the latter sense to what the non-literate woman can usually offer. A non-literate woman is not only less expensive to maintain in her general requirements, such as clothes,[4] but can be sent out to earn money by trading, *garra*-dyeing, etc. She makes fewer demands on her husband's attention, and is less likely to raise any objection, if the occasion arises, to the introduction of additional women into the household. The latter point may be fairly significant as it appears that polygynous marriage is still frequent among the literate class. Thus, out of a sample of 62 literate husbands, 38 were polygynously, and 24 monogamously, married.

The result of all these factors is, in some respects, to make the

[1] For a further description of the implications of this point, see Chapter XIII.

[2] A small number of Protectorate girls attend secondary schools in Freetown, and recently a Mission school in the Protectorate has started a secondary class for girls.   [3] See Chapter XIII.

[4] In the case of 16 literate husbands, the estimated average amount spent in a year by the wife on clothes was £16 6s. compared with an estimated amount of £8 9s. spent on the wives of 19 non-literate husbands in the same town. The most costly single item in the case of the literate women was footwear, in the case of the non-literate women, *lappas*. This distinction is sociologically of some significance, as will be seen from Chapter XIII.

literate woman more, rather than less, maritally dependent. Another point militating against her position is that provision for cases arising out of marriage is the same for literate persons as it is for all 'natives' of the Protectorate. In other words, if a literate woman has been married in native fashion, i.e. by bridewealth, she can be claimed in the same way as any other woman by her husband's relatives, should he predecease her. If, on the other hand, the marriage has been contracted in church, and no bridewealth is given, it may not be recognized subsequently by the native court as 'legal'. This means that in the event, at some later time, of desertion or ill-treatment on the part of the husband, the wife may be 'non-suited' in the matter and have no proper claim on either him or his relatives to support her. The general circumstances of the marriage, in terms, for example, of the absence of bridewealth, may have estranged her from her own people, and she will have to make submission to them before they take her back.[1] In any case, returning to them may mean going back to a life on which she has learned to look down and for which she has neither desire nor aptitude. The non-literate woman's position, in similar circumstances, is uncomplicated by comparison, and parting from her husband is unlikely to present her with any special or economic difficulty.

The whole question is influenced still further, so far as western forms of marriage are concerned, by the attitude of the Missions which is somewhat variable. Some missionaries definitely discourage giving of bridewealth on account of its concomitants of 'inheritance'. Apparently, the Roman Catholics will perform the Christian ceremony provided the man is baptized; the woman need not be. The Methodists, the other principal Mission, will 'recognize' marriages contracted in native fashion, but will not perform the Christian ceremony unless both parties are members of their church. Neither denomination allows polygyny, and if a man wishes to be married in church, he must put away any other wives than the one he wishes to marry there.

The main difficulty, however, quite apart from legalities, is that the literate woman, now, is called upon to live in changed circumstances. In the larger and extended type of family, in which most of this new class have actually grown up, the personal

[1] I am indebted to Mr. J. S. Fenton, C.M.G., until recently Secretary for Protectorate Affairs, for some interesting comments on the present and future possibilities of this matter.

relations of man and wife are of less significance than under modern conditions. Marital disputes are settled 'in the house', in terms of the family group, which also accepts the main onus for decisions taken. Guidance and advice are available on the spot, and both parties are responsible as much to those around them as to each other, for their actions.

Very often, the situation of literate married couples is almost opposable to this. The job of the husband probably requires his working in one of the larger towns. This automatically removes one, if not both, of the partners from kinship and local associations to an environment in which such sanctions as exist in the shape, for example, of the Mission are of a less personal, or of a quite nominal nature. Nor does the intermingling of Christian and Moslem social controls make for consistency in this respect. The consequence is that the wife, being answerable for her conduct to far fewer people, is laid open readily to the charge of indiscipline. Disharmonies and disputes are enhanced by the fact that their social training has equipped neither spouse with the necessary pattern of marital behaviour, which would enable them to make the series of personal adjustments to each other demanded by the new and conjugal conditions.

All this is aggravated by the surrounding circumstances, including the necessity to make a material display. The fact that literate men, a large number of whom are unattached, greatly outnumber women with similar habits and tastes to their own, places a special premium on female sophistication and a fashionable attire, and adds to the popularity of 'friendship' as a solution in both a pre- and extra-marital sense. Traditional differences between the sexes tend to persist beneath the surface of western traits, and the fact that women, whether they have been to school or not, are usually much below the educational standards of their husbands,[1] reinforces existing incompatibilities. Though it is changing, it is still largely the custom to spend leisure time apart, the men meeting to play cards or drink together, the women to sew and gossip.[2] The sexes come together for dances, however,

[1] Out of a sample of 25 literate husbands, 23 had been educated at a secondary school, and two at primary schools. Of their wives, only two had been to a secondary school, nine to primary schools, and the remainder were non-literate.

[2] Recently, the Bo African Club, which is the most important centre of literate social activity in the Protectorate, opened its membership to women, and women take a prominent part in its functions.

though the difficulty of finding someone to look after the children often prevents the man and wife going as a couple. The latter point seems a fairly clear indication of the extent to which the extended type of family is breaking down.

CHAPTER IX

THE CHIEF AND HIS CHIEFDOM

1. *Basis of Political Authority*

THE social processes of settlement and the interrelation of town and village have been described in Chapters I and V. Factors of this kind underlie the political organization of Mende society. The earlier pioneers of Mendeland, the hunters, farmers, and warriors, established settlements which grew, with the arrival of fresh family groups, war-refugees, and slaves, into small towns of varying size and importance. The towns, in expanding, developed surrounding villages each of which was connected through kinship, and in other ways, with a particular section of the town's position.

In simple terms, each of these towns and its dependent villages may be regarded as a single political unit. At the head of it was a chief who, in the old days, was essentially a warrior; and in the time of the 'tribal wars', it is probable that there were very many of these petty rulers whose suzerainty did not extend beyond their own town and its environs. It is obvious, however, that the process of political development did not stop here. It took the form of warfare and conquest, as well as more peaceful methods of expansion, and the result is that, today, the basic political unit is a 'section', comprising a number of towns and villages; and a number of sections made up the modern chiefdom. Each section is headed by a section chief, or sub-chief, who is supposed to be the oldest and most suitable person in the male line from the original 'founders' of the territory in question. Similarly, the chiefdom is headed by a Paramount chief, who is supposed to be the oldest and most suitable person in the male line of the descent group claiming jurisdiction over the various sections contained within the chiefdom as a whole.

The basis of political authority in either case hinges mainly on the term 'founder', about which there should be no misunderstanding. To found a chiefdom, or the section of a chiefdom, has two implications which usually go together. The first involves the question of settlement. A person who opens up virgin country is considered to acquire certain rights over it. In the course of time, with the growth of the original habitation, these rights take on a political form which includes jurisdiction over the people living there. This explains why most holders of political office in a chiefdom are descended from the former settlers who, in many cases, were allocated land in return for services rendered to the local warrior chief. Thus, out of forty-eight persons holding minor political positions, mainly as Village Heads, in the present day (1946) Kakua chiefdom, thirty-three are the direct descendants of men who had the favour of Momo Gbotɔ, the great warrior of the Bo area. Three of the latter had served him as spies, three as farmers, five as warriors, three as hunters, one as a medicine man, and the remainder had proved themselves useful after arriving either as war-refugees or as prisoners of war.

The further implication of 'founding a chiefdom' involves judicial and administrative rights which have been obtained through conquest and intrigue. In this case, to 'carve out' a chiefdom by force of arms constitutes simply another method of founding it.

2. *Political Confusion following British Protection*

But in the modern Mende chiefdom additional considerations greatly complicate the indigenous processes. In declaring their Protectorate over the Sierra Leone hinterland, the British consolidated what they believed to be the existing political boundaries between the various local rulers with whom they had already signed treaties and made other forms of contact. In fact, British recognition of indigenous political arrangements was quite arbitrary both prior to, and following, their actual Proclamation,[1] and the probability is that quite a novel situation was created in

---

[1] An obvious example of this was the international boundary agreed with the Liberian government, which placed part of Mende country under British rule and part in Liberian territory.

various local areas of native administration. In some cases, the relations between ruling houses, which involved a relatively wide region of political alliance and control, were ignored and the territories concerned were treated as separate and individual parts.

The British also put all the native rulers whom they recognized as 'Paramount Chiefs' on the same footing, so far as political status was concerned. This meant, in some cases, that a local ruler who had previously been paying fealty to his neighbour, now ranked equally, in British eyes at least, with his former overlord. In addition, the British signed treaties with, and recognized as chiefs, a number of persons whose position and standing in the chiefdom concerned was of a very minor and subordinate character. The status of other native rulers was misrepresented or misunderstood through mistakes, deliberate or otherwise, on the part of interpreters. In some instances, too, the Government awarded the chiefly staff of office to persons whose only claim to the territory concerned lay in the fact that they had managed to bring in House Tax for it. Again, in the early days, the Frontier Police virtually created chiefs out of persons who won their favours or were useful to them.[1] A large number of chiefs were deposed after the Mende Rising and it is said, in some instances, the people put forward women as their representatives under the belief that the British would not take vengeance on them.[2] Other persons, who were merely successful traders, bribed their way through the appropriate native channels to the notice of the Government.[3]

3. *Partition of the Mando Chiefdom*

These various factors and circumstances, which are antecedent to the modern Mende chiefdom and its rulers, appear to be illus-

[1] Madame Yoko, the well-known Kpaa Mende chief, who owed her success very largely to the support she received from the Frontier Police, is a good example.

[2] This consideration has been held to account, in part, for the existence among the Mende of an institution virtually unique in preliterate society, i.e. of women holding full executive power as rulers (see also later paragraph).

[3] Possibly, further confusion arose more latterly out of the opening of the Bo School for the training of the sons and nominees of chiefs. A number of chiefs, who were apprehensive of the Government's intentions, sent boys, sometimes slaves, who had no proper connection with the ruling house. The latter subsequently, and perhaps not unnaturally, claimed the honour which had been thrust upon them.

THE CHIEF AND HIS CHIEFDOM

trated by the following account of the Mando chiefdom in Upper Mende country. It is compiled from documents left by the late Paramount Chief Bai Comber, who was an educated man and the first Protectorate chief to sit as a member of the Sierra Leone Legislative Council. He was the son of Kabba Sei, whose name has already been mentioned in connection with earlier events in this part of Mendeland.

'About 1901 or '02, the portion of Kabba Sei's dominion known as Vahun (Guma) with the exception of Bomaru, now in the Upper Bambara chiefdom, was ceded to Liberia. In the days of the tribal wars, blocks of chiefdoms came together for mutual protection against aggression. Reconstruction of the country by the British Government gave rise to many rivalries and opportunities for revenge. Individuals snatched what power and position they could. Influence was misused and the British authorities misled. Following the cession of Guma, mentioned above, Sub-chief Bawbaw Tamba of Jolu asked to be recognized as Paramount Chief. This was an act of revenge against Kabba Sei on account of the latter's refusal to sign a petition for Nyagua's return (from exile) from the Gold Coast. Nevertheless, it was upheld by Government.

'The recognition of Dia as a separate chiefdom divided the Mando chiefdom into two unequal parts—Bomaru on the eastern, and the remainder of the Mando chiefdom on the western side. The end of the Mando-Upper Bambara amalgamation, a few years after the House Tax War, also gave Chief Kutubu of Upper Bambara a chance to become Paramount Chief, and he successfully persuaded old Gbagba of Bomaru to back him. Kabba Sei was getting old and feeble and was unable to check these developments. In this way, the Mando chiefdom declined.

'Mando, Upper Bambara, and Malema were usually in amalgamation, and the three chiefdoms and Bomaru and Dia collaborated at various times. The following order of leadership has been unanimously given by Bunduka of Leuma, Kabba Sei, Gbagba and Dowi of Bomaru, Paramount Chief Manyeh of Dia ... (and others):

    Farley of Mando—Potolu
    Sangoi of Guma—Vahun
    Foreka of Bomaru
    Yaku of Baiwalla
    Kabba Sei of Mando—Gohun

'It was during Kabba Sei's time that the country fell under British administration by the Treaty No. 119, which he signed at Baiima. The Treaty chief of Malema, Duawu Niemy, was first uncle of Kabba Sei, and the Treaty chief, Momo Babaho of Upper Bambara, was his first cousin.

'Up to the time of the Treaty, the three important chiefs of the Upper Mendes were Nyagua, Kabba Sei, and Kai Lundo. The general desire to acquire new lands and extend their influence bred ill-feeling among them at one time or another. They never, however, came into actual conflict with each other, and the differences between them were easily settled and did not develop into feuds. The misrepresentation which resulted in the deposition of Kabba Sei for a short time would have been refuted had Kai Lundo been alive at the time. He was one of the few friends who knew Kabba Sei and his qualities. Conscious of the extent of his own influence and of the strength of the warriors he commanded, Kabba Sei gave way to none but the Europeans. His warlike methods were succeeded in the latter part of his reign by peaceful ones.'

4. *Succession to the Chieftainship*

As indicated above, political authority has its basis in the dual principle of land ownership and military conquest and supremacy. This principle is given expression in terms of certain descent groups, who as *ndɔ-bla*, or 'aborigines', of the chiefdom concerned, claim hereditary right as its rulers and leading officials.[1] The more important offices concerned, in addition to that of Paramount Chief, are those of the Speaker of the chiefdom and the Sub-chiefs. These form the political hierarchy, which is assisted in local terms by Town chiefs and Village headmen. In certain cases, even at the present day, the composition of this hierarchy is integrated to the extent of most of the principal offices being held by members of the same descent group. This may be illustrated by the ruling house of the Mando chiefdom. The attached chart shows the lineage of this house and the living members (underlined), who hold office at the present day.

Throughout these political positions the rule of patrineal inheritance holds good, though it is subject to modification in the

[1] See Chapter IV for the bearing of land tenure on political status and authority.

LINEAGE OF RULING HOUSE MANDO CHIEFDOM

(Showing offices—Paramount Chief, Sub-chief, etc.—held by members of this house. Living members underlined.)

```
Mondor, P.C.
├── Joe Mahei
│   (S/C. Levuma)
│   └── Genda
│       ├── Siaffa Gbaigela
│       │   (S/Sp. Levuma)
│       ├── Amara Bunduka
│       │   (S/C. Levuma)
│       ├── Moiba Ngokoe
│       └── Bunduka
│           (S/C. Levuma)
│           └── Ganuahengor
└── Kpana Farley, P.C.
    └── Kabba Sei, P.C.
        ├── Bai Comber, P.C.
        │   ├── Sei II
        │   │   (Kuloko, Mobai)
        │   ├── Sei Comber I, P.C.
        │   └── Ali Farley
        │       (Member District Council)
        ├── Sandy
        │   (S/C. Mobai)
        └── A. Comber
            └── Momo Farley
                (S/C. Mobai)
                ├── Aruna
                │   (T/C. Gohun)
                └── Siaffa Poogo
                    (V.H. Mobaiwulo)
```

180

case of the Town chief and Village headman. According to tradition, however, the post of 'chief', as ruler of the chiefdom, is to be regarded strictly as the possession, in the male line, of the descendants of the original founder. A native version of the matter elucidates this point in the following way:

'When a chief died in the old days, a gift of ten heads of money (i.e. slaves) was made by his family to the chiefdom to obtain their favour before appointing the new chief. Had the previous ruler been tyrannical, the amount of the gift would be larger. The royal house was then called upon to show the people their new chief. It was the rule for the dying chief to nominate his successor, and the name of the person would be kept a secret as long as possible in case of harm befalling him. He was usually the first-born, but might be another son of the late chief, if the latter's mother stood in higher favour. In any case, the nomination was independent of the wealth of the individual, and quite a poor man might be chosen. In some cases, a series of brothers followed each other as chiefs, before the son of the first brother was appointed. The idea in this—that the sons of the former chief stood in closer relationship to him than his son's sons—denoted the guiding principle of inheritance. In default of a suitable successor, there was nothing to prevent a woman, such as a daughter of the late chief, being appointed, and even a daughter's child had a right to succeed in the absence of nearer heirs in the male line.[1] Sometimes, a powerful warrior or other person of influence would act as Regent chief during the senility of the actual chief, or during the minority of the rightful successor, but this conferred no right either on him or his descendants to inherit the chiefdom.'[2]

[1] There is an interesting example of this in the present ruling house of the Simbaru chiefdom. The first chief, Sangewa, was succeeded by his daughter's son, Bavore, who was followed by his son, Gamanga I. The latter was succeeded by his sister's son, Ngeigba Hinga. Following the latter's death, the line reverted to Gamanga's branch, and the office was occupied in turn by the latter's sons, Ansumana and Kalilu. The present chief is the son of Kalilu.

[2] There are many examples of this last point in the history of Mende chiefdoms. For instance, Momo Gbotɔ, a powerful warrior in Middle Mende, acted as Regent during the minority of Hotagua, the son of the previous chief, who subsequently became Paramount Chief of the Kakua chiefdom and signed a treaty with the British in the 1880's. Quite often, the practice of regency resulted in usurpation, or at attempts at usurpation of the chiefdom concerned.

5. *Duties and Perquisites of the Chief*

The primary rôle of the chief was as the military protector of the people who followed him. One of his main tasks, therefore, as leader in war was the recruitment and organization of his warriors. Not only his own success and prestige, but the safety of his people depended on his skill in this respect and on the individual prowess of those whom he led. He was also responsible for the civil as well as military administration of the chiefdom, and acted as the principal adjudicator in the case of complaints and disputes. To perform the latter task, he held court, periodically, in which he was assisted by the principal men in the chiefdom, including the Speaker, sub-chiefs, and the important elders. His obligations also included the entertainment of strangers, and a wide dispensation of help and hospitality to needy members of his own chiefdom. Finally, he acted as general patron of the more important secret societies, such as the Poro and the Sande, and was expected to sponsor the various ceremonies called for in connection with the ancestral cult and related forms of worship and propitiation.

The means of discharging this office and of upholding its dignity and prestige were supplied by a number of customary forms of service and tribute from the chiefdom. The first of these was *ndɔ-yenge*, or chiefdom labour, which meant that the chiefdom, in terms of levies of workers from the individual sections, had the responsibility of making the chief's *manja* (rice) farms. In the same way, the chiefdom supplied labour for the purpose of keeping the chief's compound in good repair, or of building a new one if need be, as well as clearing main roads, etc. In addition, the chief was entitled to a small proportion of the rice and palm oil produced on every *mawɛ* in the chiefdom. This was collected through the sub-chiefs. There were also various customary presents. When the chief visited one of his sub-chiefs, the latter was expected to 'put down the chief's hammock'—*mboma hitie*—by offering him a fairly valuable gift, such as a number of cows, and entertaining him and his followers on a lavish scale. The chief also had right to certain animals killed in the chiefdom, such as the leopard, and could claim, in some cases, a small 'dash' from any one tapping palm wine.

A further and more important source of income was the fees and fines gained in the hearing of court cases. In some instances, there were also special levies for the purpose of entertaining important strangers.

THE CHIEF AND HIS CHIEFDOM

6. *Councils*

These hereditary prerogatives of the ruling house were subject, however, to a certain amount of popular control, partly through the Chief's Council, and partly through a Chiefdom Council, where the latter existed. There was, also, the still greater force of the Poro society operating extensively behind the scenes, about which more will be said in the following paragraphs.

The chief's own council was composed of the Speaker, the sub-chiefs, and a number of the big men of the chiefdom, who were related to the chief, or were his particular friends. Its restraining influence was probably less, therefore, than the full chiefdom council, which comprised all title holders in the chiefdom, including the Speaker, sub-chiefs, and their deputies, the headmen of larger towns and villages, and representatives of the principal *kuwuisia*. Theoretically, the Chief was supposed to consult this body over any measure affecting the chiefdom as a whole, and was responsible to it for his actions. In fact, owing to difficulties of communication and for other reasons, the probability is that it was rarely convened as a full assembly and that the Chief ruled with the help of his own council. Moreover, in the main, it is probable that in the last resort, he relied largely on the support of the Poro society to ensure the maintenance of customary law and behaviour.

7. *The Rôle of the Poro Society*

Indeed, the Poro society was, in all likelihood, the means by which a uniform system of government and set of customs was possible among the large number of politically separate and remotely scattered communities of Mende country. The society instilled general awe of a religious kind, and derived its power entirely through the intercourse which its senior officials claimed to have with the world of spirits. They impersonated the latter with the aid of masks and other paraphernalia.

There is little doubt, in other words, that Poro law surmounted the local administration of the chiefs in several respects. Its symbols, as sign of peace or call to war, were understood and obeyed all over the country. The instance, in this respect, of the initiation of the Mende Rising, has already been quoted. Common action was effected on such a wide scale by placing the whole country under Poro oath, before its actual object was known.

THE CHIEF AND HIS CHIEFDOM

After this, everyone was bound to adhere to whatever plans had been decided upon in the Poro inner council, hence the expression used in this connection—*ngo yela*, 'one word' or 'unity'. As an arbitrator in chiefdom disputes, the Poro acted through an armed band of its officials, masked as spirits, whose intervention was sufficient to overawe any party refusing the society's decision. Prohibitions placed in the name of the Poro on the harvesting of palm fruit or on fishing at certain seasons were ignored only at the greatest peril. The Poro also regulated trading practices and fixed prices at which various commodities should be sold[1] and at which certain services, for instance, a day's load-carrying, should be performed.

It is obvious, therefore, that the connection between this society and political authority has always been very strong and that the two mutually reinforce each other. Indeed, in so far as the Mende chief is a purely secular figure, lacking the ritual sanctions with which chiefly authority is associated among the neighbouring Timne people, it might well be held that the Poro is his religious counterpart in the field of government. Since the Chief's function as a ruler is largely derived from his rôle as a director and leader in time of war, his ability to command and to exact obedience was based, therefore, on physical power and personality and not the mystical sources from which the Poro derives its voice. Nor has the Mende chief any religious or ritual duties to perform which are other than presidential. He is expected to sponsor certain public ceremonies, but not to officiate in them. In fact, any attributes of a religious kind that the Chief possesses are merely those which any senior participant in the ancestral cult also shares.

This apparent lack of religious elements in the business of administration is remedied by the Poro in a number of ways. For example, the society signalizes the respect due to secular authority by parading at the funeral or coronation of a chief its principal and most sacred spirit, the *Gbeni*, which ordinarily 'comes out' in public only on the most important type of occasion. At the funeral, the *Gbeni* proceeds to the grave of the dead chief and bows over it. It has to be 'bought off' by a sum of money from the chief's family. The same ritual is performed for all political figures,

[1] Recent evidence of the Poro's intervention in commercial matters is supplied in G. W. Brown's paper, 'The Poro in Modern Business', *Man*, 1937, No. 3.

THE CHIEF AND HIS CHIEFDOM

including sub-chiefs, and not merely for the Paramount Chief. A further point is that the chief, when dying, is taken into the Poro bush for medical treatment. His death is subsequently announced from the roof of his house by an official of the society. It is to be noted, however, that the chief is not buried in the Poro bush itself, unless he happens to be a relative newcomer to the chiefdom. He is usually buried within his own compound; it is considered that he 'belongs' to all his people.

The chief, in turn, as the society's official patron in all matters external to its secret business, is expected to uphold Poro interests whenever they come into conflict with the views of Moslems and, nowadays, even the Government. In recognition of these services and of his official position, he is given a customary present from the society, whenever it holds a session. Traditionally, the chief was also entitled to the assistance of Poro initiates in working his rice-farm. Nowadays, he is expected to pay for such services in cash.

The upshot of all this is that no person can hope to occupy any position of authority in the chiefdom without being a Poro member and receiving Poro support. It is probable, in the old days, that each fresh successor to the chiefly office needed Poro approval, and the contemporary situation is much the same. It is evident, today, also that the 'election' (see next chapter) of the new chief is previously deliberated in the Poro bush and may finally be decided there by swearing members of the Tribal (chiefdom) Authority, who constitute the 'electoral' body, on Poro medicine.[1] In former times, too, the Poro helped to maintain the dignity of secular rule by decreeing that disputes affecting important members of the community should be heard privately in the bush by a Poro tribunal, the identity of whose president was kept secret. Nowadays, also, serious 'palavers' concerning the chiefdom as a whole are talked over in the bush, irrespective of whether or not they come up for public attention, or the official notice of the Government.

8. *The Chief's Court and Court Procedure*

Nowadays, the chief's court is organized on lines which, in several respects, owe more to western than indigenous custom.

[1] One method of carrying out the appropriate 'swear' in such a case is to oblige each member of the Tribal Authority to jump, in turn, over the carcase of a sheep which has duly been sacrificed to the Poro spirits.

Cases are heard and judged by a 'bench' which consists of the chief, or of the Speaker, as chairman, and a number of sub-chiefs, tribal authorities, and other big men. The latter sit in rotation, i.e. the members present at one session are replaced by other sub-chiefs, tribal authorities, etc., at the next session. The court usually sits either once or twice in the month at the chief's 'capital' town. Sometimes, it goes on circuit and holds its meetings by turn at the various section towns.

As already indicated, under the British Administration, the court is restricted to cases which, from the point of view of English law, are mainly 'civil' and which involve quite minor offences. Though a District Commissioner or a higher court can revise its judgements, the native court has complete jurisdiction over all cases involving native law and custom with a few specific exceptions, such as cases involving 'illegal societies' like the Human Leopards.[1] The majority of cases heard, therefore, concern debt, and 'woman palaver' in its various forms. A smaller number of cases concern claims over land, and there are occasional complaints over the unauthorized use of medicines, etc. On the basis of an analysis of some two hundred cases heard in the courts of six Mende chiefdoms, it is estimated that about half the total number of cases heard in the ordinary court concern claims for the settlement of debt or for compensation, amounting, on the average, to about 10s. in each instance; and that about one-third of the total concerns claims for 'woman damage', or for repayment of bridewealth.

Before a case is heard, both plaintiff and defendant are required to pay a small sum into court on account of *Summoning* and *Hearing Fees*. Fines are also levied in certain instances, for example, for creating a disturbance in the town or for contravening a native law, and these, together with summoning and hearing fees, constitute quite an appreciable income. Nowadays, members of the tribunal are paid through this account for their services.

The traditional method and form of court procedure has already been outlined on a previous page. In the modern form, the suitors in a case are summoned by the chief's messengers to appear on a certain day. The case opens with plaintiff and defendant each making his statement to the court. Both parties are required to swear on chiefdom medicine, before doing this. The

[1] See Chapter XI for a description of certain 'illegal' and anti-social practices in a similar respect.

medicine is administered by the Chiefdom Clerk. Privately owned medicines are not allowed in court or for the actual procedure. The nature of the medicine used varies widely. In some cases, it consists merely of a box containing a number of medicines which have been confiscated by the authorities on account of their 'illegal' use. The parties to the case are required to touch this box whilst making their affirmation. Sometimes, they are required, at the same time, to taste salt; or to place one end of a pair of bellows in their mouth, the belief being that the medicine will cause them serious harm in the event of a lie. Moslems swear on the Quran, and persons professing Christianity are allowed to take an oath on the Bible.

The court may decide to question both plaintiff and defendant both during, and after, their statements. Both parties are allowed to call witnesses, who are sworn likewise, in support of their cases, and they are allowed to examine each other's witnesses. Members of the court sometimes deliberate among themselves during the hearing, and this is the usual practice after all the statements and evidence have been heard. The 'chairman', who is either the Paramount Chief, or the Speaker, then announces the verdict and the amount of the fine, if the latter is called for.

The court sitting is open, of course, to members of the public, but nowadays they do not take part in the proceedings, as was formerly the custom. Most cases are heard meticulously and with great regard to detail, particularly if they involve some question of land ownership, or concern the matter of bridewealth. An example of the latter kind may serve to illustrate at least one aspect of judicial treatment.

The first task in settling claims for the return of bridewealth is always to decide if the marriage is a 'legal' one, i.e. that it had the consent of the woman's parents. The court has to reckon with the reluctance of some parents to admit that their daughter is, in fact, 'married'. For instance, in presenting their daughter to a chief, they may say merely, 'Here is a servant for your house'. The woman, also, has to testify that she is unwilling to return to her husband. The wife's family are the responsible parties whatever the cause of her desertion; but if another man is involved, they may expect him to pay a large part of what is due in terms of refundable payments. This is counted in his favour, if he wishes to remain with or to marry the woman in question. Women, themselves, are not allowed to sue in a bridewealth case, unless they are elderly and influential people, because only such women have authority to contract a marriage on their own account. These points are important in the 'newer' towns on the railway line, where quite a large number of arrangements are made of which the parents are not officially informed. Such unions do not progress 'legally' beyond the stage of 'friendship', as indicated in Chapter VIII.

There is a tendency, therefore, for some courts to judge matters of the latter kind in a less formal and more 'moral' way. They take into consideration the length of time the couple has been living together as man and wife. The woman's home may be in another part of the country, and this avoids the difficulty in calling witnesses to the marriage to court. Another sign of the times is that in one court, the woman's family are required to make a deposit before the case can be heard at all. This is to obviate the possibility of the woman's father decamping to another chiefdom and the consequent trouble and expense of sending 'shake hands' to other chiefs in order to secure his return.

Once the preliminaries in a case of this kind have been settled, the general procedure is for the person claiming repayment of bridewealth to bring forward his account. As already described in Chapter VII, he may claim for the sum total of expenses he has incurred over the woman in question. He may include all presents and services to her and members of her group, but he is not allowed to claim for her maintenance, nor for that of any of her relatives who may have visited him. Any gifts from the girl's relatives form a contra-account and are deducted from the husband's final reckoning. First, the woman's parents are sworn and asked, item by item, if they agree to this estimate. Each item they agree is allowed the claimant, but if they deny any item or part of it, the amount in question is deducted from the total sum which is eventually awarded. Some courts, however, deduct only half the amount denied. For example, if £50 is claimed and the relatives deny £20 of it, an amount of £40 is finally awarded.

In most cases, as might be expected, the list of items on the account is very extensive and contains a wide assortment of gifts and services of the most trivial kind. All of these the husband has carried very carefully in his memory from the time of the first approach to his wife. Literacy has converted the memorizing of such matters into a question of book-keeping. In one claim, contested between a literate plaintiff and non-literate defendants, the latter complained ruefully of the long and meticulous record produced against them. The comment of the court members, themselves non-literate, was, 'Well, if you allow your daughter to marry a "bookman", this is the kind of thing you must expect'! In view of the fact that the hearing of cases of this kind takes a large part of the court's time, attempts have been made in a number of chiefdoms, either to discourage the bringing of them, or to shorten the procedure. In one chiefdom, the rule is that a claim must be enumerated in full on the same day as the reckoning is begun, otherwise it must be started afresh on the next court day it can be heard. It is hoped that the parties concerned will make a further effort at reconciliation, in the meantime, rather than undergo the extra trouble, tedium, and expense. In another chiefdom, the Chiefdom Clerk goes through the account with the claimant and a representative of the girl's family, and the amount is agreed on by the usual method of swearing, before the case is heard officially in court.

One chiefdom requires the registration of every marriage on payment or completion of the *mboya* (see Chapter VII), and subsequent payments are disregarded. The amount, which must be agreed by both parties, is officially recorded. It represents the sum to which the husband is entitled in the event of his making a successful claim at a later date. The average amount of 'bridewealth' in a sample of 147 cases entered in this instance was £9 3s. 4d.

9. *Social Insignia of Chieftainship*

The Mende chief is a relatively 'democratic' figure, nowadays, in that he mixes freely in various ways with his people, and may even take part in the manual work on his own farm. There are various social insignia and special characteristics of the office, however, which mark him out from ordinary society.

The first of these is the chief's own house and compound. The modern chief's house usually has a zinc roof in emulation, it would seem, of the official type of European bungalow. Its walls are usually of wood, or of mud blocks, instead of the native style which consists of wattle and daub. Usually, too, the chief's compound is surrounded by a mud wall, about eight feet in height. All these features are a sign of wealth and social status in that zinc is costly material and mud walls require extra labourers to build. The walls

THE CHIEF AND HIS CHIEFDOM

also ensure a greater degree of privacy, and were needed in the old days for purposes of extra safety. Within the compound are sufficient houses, some of them also built partly on modern lines, to accommodate the women of the household, some of the chief's nearer relatives and friends, and important visitors. Very often, the compound also contains the chief's private *barri*, or resting place; an ancestral shrine; tombs of the chief's ancestors, etc., as well as kitchens and latrines. It is usually the largest household enclosure in the town for the very good reason, if for no other, that for any other person to build a larger one would be disrespectful to the chief himself. The attached sketch indicates the kind of way in which the compound of a chief in Middle Mende country is laid out.

A further important sign of the chief's status is the large number of women members of his household. Most of these are his own wives, and they include cooks, singers and musicians, and household servants. Most of the women concerned have specific duties in connection with the chief's official position. The remainder of his wives are likely to spend most of their time in his villages on farm work under the supervision of a senior woman. Chiefs who are in the habit of entertaining Creole, or native guests following western customs, sometimes have a special woman to cater for their needs in respect of food. The domestic household, as a whole, is under the charge, of course, of a senior wife.

In the old days, the wearing of leopard's teeth was a sign of royal rank and of membership of such a family. Nowadays, the Mende chief usually makes little display in ways of this kind save on formal occasions, such as the visit of a fellow chief. In the latter case, it is customary for one of his followers to carry the long wooden staff, which is the official emblem of chiefly status, and for other emblems, such as an elephant's tail, to be borne. It is also etiquette for the chief to be accompanied by a crowd of courtiers whenever he walks or moves outside his own compound. On a formal visit he will be followed by a group of women singers and male drummers, whose duty is to extol the praises of him and his host. It is contrary to Mende custom to use personal names in addressing a person, and in the case of the chief, it is a serious offence to mention his name publicly at all. To do so constitutes grave disrespect and carries the further suggestion that the person using it is working some medicine against the chief. The approved title of address is *marda*—'grandfather'; the title of 'chief—*maha*,

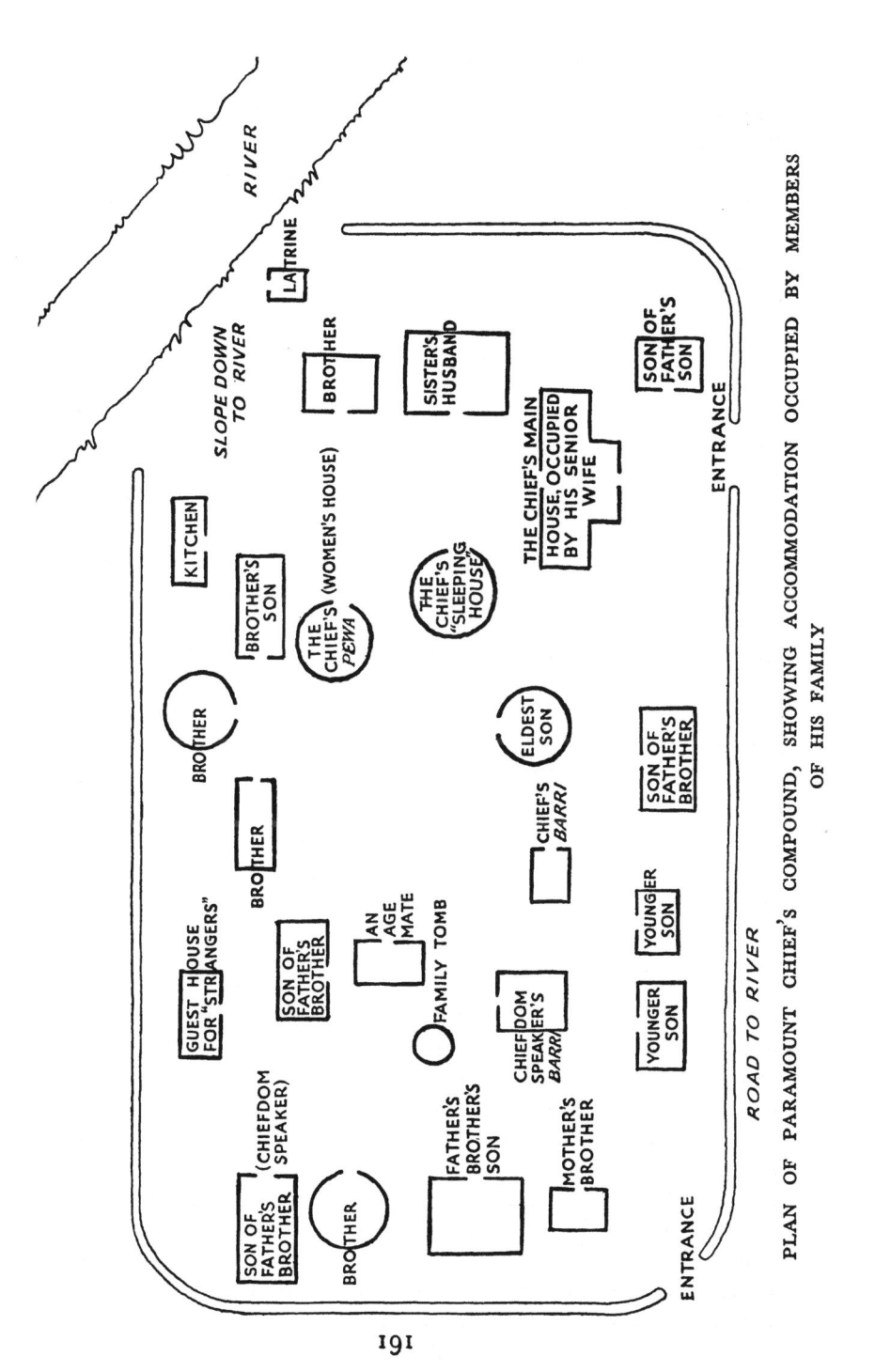

PLAN OF PARAMOUNT CHIEF'S COMPOUND, SHOWING ACCOMMODATION OCCUPIED BY MEMBERS OF HIS FAMILY

is applied more frequently to other leading officials in the chiefdom, including, on occasion, even the headman of a large village. A person approaching the chief, including the younger members of his own immediate family, is supposed to move towards him with body bent and with hands on knees, and to uncover his head.

Ceremonial observance, however, is most marked at the chief's death which, as the following account indicates, provides an occasion for both public and private ritual.

'When the Chief at last comes to his end, the family is told that the sickness is serious and that the Chief would like some well prepared food. A goat and a bushel of clean rice are sent. Each member of the Tribal Authority is expected to give some silver or brass money and two or more country cloths for his burial.

'In the meantime, no one is allowed to "cry". The people are merely told that the Chief is seriously ill. There is a great quietness in the town with the people passing silently up and down. Messengers are sent to call all the big men in the chiefdom and nearby Paramount Chiefs, because the latter are required to wash the body.

'The relatives are then informed and asked for money and supply food—goats, sheep, and fowls. When the Paramount Chiefs arrive, they ask for the big men of the chiefdom to tell them about the whole course of the Chief's illness, and they show their sympathy to the family by gifts of money. The Chiefs then visit the body which has been placed in a special house in the charge of a member of the family. In the olden days, Chiefs were buried in the beds of running streams to prevent the body falling into the hands of invaders.

'The Chiefs then permit the corpse to be washed. According to country fashion, the head is shaved and the body wrapped in a number of garments and country cloths. Moslems shave the head and wrap the body in a shroud, consisting of six yards of shirting, with a number of country cloths to cover it. In the meantime, the grave is being dug and a small shelter constructed beside which followers of the Poro "spirits" stand drumming. The leading relatives of the deceased are then called and they decorate the grave with fine cloths.

'This work is done in the dead of night and the actual burial takes place at about 3 o'clock in the morning. If buried in country fashion, the corpse is laid flat in the grave with the head upright.

Money, already donated, is put into a pot and placed by the side of the dead man. The grave is then filled completely with earth. The money is a greeting present to the new country to which he is going and to enable him to build a house there.

'The Chief's death is still kept secret from the public and anyone heard "crying" for him is heavily fined. About half an hour later, however, word is given that *Gbeni* will be "out" dancing that day. A cannon is loaded and taken up to a hilly place where its sound will be heard afar, and the hunters also go up there with their guns. By about half-past five, most of the women of the town are in the Chief's compound ready to "cry", and along with them will be various Poro "spirits". Then at a given signal a man with a loud voice climbs on to the highest roof in the compound and calls out four times, "The unexpected always happens. A few days ago we took the Chief to a medical bush. We did all we could for him and prayed our fathers to release our leader. But all our efforts were in vain. Your Chief is dead". At the fourth repetition, the cannon sounds and the people start the "cry", the women loosing their hair, rubbing mud on their faces, and others shaving their heads.

'One of the Poro "spirits" then goes first to the house where the Chief is buried, and thence to every house in the town, announcing the Chief's death. At each place he is given a present. Another Poro spirit, the *Wujei*, goes round the town dancing and is also given money. After this, every Poro man is ordered to the bush so that the *Gbeni* can "come out". Amidst great beating of drums, the *Gbeni* eventually appears and goes first to the burial place, where he remains until the family has given him money. The *Gbeni* then leads a great dance throughout the town and this continues until he retires to the bush at sundown.

'By this time, the town is full of strangers who have arrived for the ceremonies, and during the evening the followers of the other Poro spirits go round demanding money, cows, and sheep for their coming out. Early next morning, the *Ngafagoti* and the *Wujei*, accompanied by their followers, and drummers, visit the burial place again and inform the people a second time of the Chief's death. Then they return to the burial house in which a white country cloth has been spread, and the crowd collects around, singing.

'These Poro spirits remain out with their drummers until the fourth day, when the *Gbeni* re-appears. This time, it is earlier in the morning, between 4 and 5 o'clock. In the meantime, many cows and other livestock have been killed and many bowls of rice prepared. This food is taken to the Chief's compound and distributed among the people. These ceremonies are repeated on the seventh, and again on the fortieth day after death, in the case of a Moslem.'

Very often, the chief has a number of special medicines, which are his private property, to safeguard his life and health from witchcraft and other misfortunes. In the old days, it was customary for a trusted attendant, the 'Bearer of the Chief's Life', to have charge of these medicines. This function of personal protection was, and in some cases still is, shared by the chief's *mori*-man, who acts as special adviser and assists the chief to carry out public sacrifices, when the occasion arises. Most well-knit and important descent groups in the chiefdom, including the ruling house, usually observe some specific prohibition over food or the killing of certain animals. So far as can be gathered, however, there is no totemistic connection or implication in this, and its only social function is to heighten family consciousness and loyalty.

For news and general intelligence concerning events and affairs in the chiefdom, the chief has to rely largely on those most closely about him. Such persons include those members of his immediate family, whom he can trust, and certain friends and followers. The latter, quite often, are traders and others whose business takes them frequently about in different parts of the chiefdom. These people are known as the chief's 'gossipers'—*nga fa bla*. The group most closely connected with the chief and those who take care of him by, for example, tasting his food, are spoken of as the chief's 'eyes and ears'—*mahei mahun gbei bla*. Though the circumstances are different, it is just as important, nowadays, as in former times, from the chief's point of view, to be fully acquainted with all that is going on around him. Invariably, there are rival parties trying to discredit him, with or without just cause, in the eyes of the Government, and his main hope of obviating them may lie in his ability to prepare some prior counter-charge. A particular method of attacking the ruling house is to raise a scare of cannibalism in the country which, even if eventually proven false, carries the temporary implication that the chief is condoning the practice of securing human fat in his chiefdom. Another, and more frequent method, is to have the chief accused of using forced labour or some other form of extortion.

10. *Women as Chiefs*

The almost unique part which women play in the political life of the Mende merits special attention. Both at the present day and within historic times, women have occupied the post of chief on exactly the same basis of power and authority as men. There is a contemporary example of this in the case of Madame Yewa of Blama chiefdom, and a number of others, like Madame Matto, wife of the warrior chief Faba of Dodo, and her daughter, Madame Humonya, of Nongowa chiefdom, as well as Madame Yoko of Moyamba, have had significant careers as rulers. Instances of women occupying lesser positions in the chiefdom, as members of the Tribal Authority, are also quite numerous; and they, too, take their places for political purposes on the same terms as men. In fact, the only restriction on a woman holding chiefly office follows logically from the laws of family inheritance. As chief, she may not take a husband, though she may, of course, have a male consort. The reason for this, quite obviously, is to ensure that any children she bears will belong to and remain in her own descent group.

For practical purposes, therefore, the question is not to decide whether women rule as chiefs, but how far matriarchy may be regarded as indigenous. On this, both historical information and native opinion itself is uncertain and the opinion of informants divided. It is argued, by some people, that, as mentioned earlier, women were put forward by the people to obviate the vengeance of the British after the Mende rising; and, again, that individual women won their position in return for favours to the Frontier Police.[1] It has even been suggested that the Mende chiefdoms concerned deliberately decided to emulate the British institution, after hearing about the great power and prestige of Queen Victoria.

A number of women, it may be noted, appear in records of treaties prior to the declaration of the Protectorate, and they include 'Nyarroh, Queen of Barri Country', as a signatory in Treaty No. 113 of 1890; 'The Magao, Queen of Lubu', in a Treaty of 1869; 'Regbafri, principal lady of Manho', in Treaty No. 78 of

[1] This is claimed specifically in the case of two women, Nancy Tucker and Betsy Gaye, who ruled as chiefs from 1886–98.

1872; 'A Lady of Sherbro Island', in Treaty No. 66 of 1861; and 'Fony-Lady of Mano Bagru', in Treaty No. 68 of 1861.[1] In refutation, however, of the important political rôle which this evidence implies, it might be said that the information has been misinterpreted or misunderstood. For example, a woman leader of one of the secret societies would certainly possess considerable power and influence in a local area and this might be taken, though inaccurately, as a sign of political position by those who sought her signature to the treaty concerned.

On the other hand, it is necessary to weigh two alternative considerations against all this. The first is that in a number of cases the founders of specific chiefdoms are traditionally cited as women. The modern chiefdom of Maje is an instance of this. The second and more important point is that Mende law itself, as already indicated, recognizes female inheritance of family property in the absence of a suitable successor in the male line. The latter would be sufficient to explain the occasional incidence of a female ruler in a chiefdom. It is insufficient in itself to explain the claim that certain chiefdoms have the institution as a regular one.

11. *Other Political Figures*

(a) *The Speaker*. As already indicated, the second person in the political hierarchy is the chiefdom Speaker, or *Lavalie*. It is possible that the office originated in the original leader appointing one of his followers as deputy. Sometimes, it was a sister's son. In any case, the practice seems to have led to the establishment of regular Speakers' 'houses' (just as there were regular chiefs' 'houses') from which the Speaker was invariably chosen.

The Speaker has two principal functions in the chiefdom. First, he is essentially the chief's deputy. He takes over these duties whenever the latter is ill, or absent from any public occasion. In such an event, the Speaker officiates in full capacity and with entire responsibility for the chiefly office. Secondly, the Speaker is the main intermediary between the chief and the chiefdom, and complaints and disputes are brought initially to his notice for transmission, if necessary, to the chief. Part of the Speaker's rôle, in this respect, is to act as a 'sounding board' to public opinion on the one hand; and on the other, to let the people know if the chief should depart, in his actions, from traditional custom and practice.

[1] I am indebted to Mr. J. S. Fenton for these particulars.

THE CHIEF AND HIS CHIEFDOM

The Speaker is also responsible for passing the chief's orders and instructions down to subordinate officials, and is essentially in this respect, as the title of his office (from *La*—mouth) implies, the chief's 'mouthpiece'. The general practice, in the event of any particular command, is for a messenger to set out with the Speaker's walking-stick, as a sign of his credentials, to each sub-chief in turn. It is for each of the latter, then, to see that the message is implemented in his particular section of the chiefdom. Similarly, in the general assembly of the chiefdom council, it is customary for the Speaker first to inform the gathering of the business of the meeting, before the Chief himself addresses it.[1]

The Speaker's duties make him, in fact, a kind of 'chief of staff' in the general business of the chiefdom. Partly for honorific reasons, and partly for the sake of convenience, the office is sometimes duplicated, in the larger chiefdoms, and the second Speaker deputizes, when necessary, for the first Speaker. Nowadays, the influence of the Speaker is felt mainly at the time of an interregnum, when he usually acts as Regent Chief until the appointment of the new ruler. In this capacity he is in a position quite substantially to determine the success or otherwise of a particular candidate. Nor is it unknown, in present circumstances, for the Speaker to command a rival following to that of the ruling chief with the effect that this has for jeopardizing the latter's standing in the eyes of the British administration. For this reason, it is good policy, sometimes, for the Chief to secure the appointment of a person who is a stranger to the chiefdom. Occasionally, too, a chief finds it useful to obtain a Speaker who is able to support him financially.

(*b*) *The Sub-chiefs.* The section, or sub-chiefs, who come next in order of precedence, hold a position in their locality which, as already explained, is similar to the Paramount in more local terms. Structurally speaking, the area of their jurisdiction constitutes virtually a sub-chiefdom, and it is governed on lines similar to those in the larger unit. Before the British revised the practice, the Sub-chief held his own local court and, like the Paramount Chief, was entitled to various tributes and services from the people

[1] After the chief has spoken, the Council retires and consults together, giving its opinions according to Sections. Note, in some of the respects mentioned, the similarity of the Speaker's rôle with that of the *Linguist* in the case of the political institutions of the Akan people of the Gold Coast, cf. J. B. Danquah, *Akan Laws and Customs*, 1928.

of his Section, in making his farms, repairing his compound, etc. He was also entitled to a proportion of the rice and other produce which he sent on from his Section to the Paramount Chief.[1] In addition, the Sub-chief, as well as the Speaker, was entitled to a share of the fees and fines gained through hearing cases in the Chief's court.

(*c*) *Town Chiefs, Village Headmen, etc.* The remaining officials of the chiefdom are the Town Chiefs and Village Headmen. In a number of the towns which at the present day have outgrown their normal size, there are also Town Section Chiefs over the individual wards. The main duties of all these functionaries are to maintain law and order in their respective localities, to settle minor disputes, and to find accommodation for strangers. They are entitled to various small perquisites, which include the customary 'greeting' and 'goodbye' presents from all visitors and 'dashes' from all who seek their help and advice. They also receive a share of the fees and fines, if they sit as members of the chief's court. Finally, there are the local elders, or heads of 'compounds', whose function, as already described, is social rather than political except in so far as it is linked up with the official machinery of taxation.

In summary, then, the political organization of a Mende chiefdom has been derived mainly through the practical requirements of military expediency and taxation. Through the sub-chiefs, the Paramount Chief exercised general control over the system as a whole and was responsible for keeping its administration intact. But the emphasis was rather on local management of affairs. The individual Sections merely contributed their due share of 'taxes' in return for the benefits of protection or of plunder, which they received in common. The efficiency of the system was bound up with a number of other factors which were political only in their effect: first, the whole structure of kinship and descent; upon which the political organization itself was based and which was mainly responsible for its internal operation; second, the external influence of the Poro society with its overall supervision of local factions and of public conduct in the widest sense.

[1] The Speaker had a similar prerogative which he could exercise in the Section whence he was appointed.

CHAPTER X

MODERN METHODS OF GOVERNMENT

1. *Modern Methods of appointing the Chief*

THE picture of Mende political organization presented in the previous chapter may help to understand the kind of system which has come into being since the British took over. In many ways, this is quite a different one. It is largely because British methods of colonization have been concerned in recent years, as in other parts of West Africa, more with the development of political institutions than any other aspect of native culture.

This point may be exemplified firstly by reference to succession to the chieftainship. Nowadays, this question is settled by electoral methods rather than by direct inheritance. Elections are, of course, a British innovation which would appear to have been adopted for expediency. It would clearly be very difficult to sift and validate certain claims to a chiefdom solely on the lines of indigenous custom. Indeed, in many modern Mende chiefdoms, the office of chief has been occupied at various times by members of quite unrelated descent groups to an extent which makes it nearly impossible to associate a single uninterrupted dynasty with it.

In the confusion and dissension of the rival claims of several and separate 'houses', it appears, therefore, that the Government took the course of opening the matter to popular decision. Candidature was adopted as the appropriate method and has become a regular institution in all parts of the Protectorate. This means that whenever a chiefdom becomes vacant, any person who considers that he has a right to the chief's office may put forward his claim.

MODERN METHODS OF GOVERNMENT

A day is appointed, and it is left to the Tribal Authority, as representative of the people, to sift the rival candidates and to decide, with the assistance of outside chiefs, appointed by the Government as Assessors, which of them owns the rightful title. Before giving the person selected its official recognition, however, the Government expects him to be put forward with the more or less unanimous vote of the Tribal Authority.

Today, therefore, the appropriate chief-appointing mechanism is the Tribal Authority and the Government's part in the matter, in theory at any rate, is only supervisory. Actually, it is rather more than this in that the senior Administrative Officer in charge of the election holds a preliminary hearing of the candidates in open court, and decides which of them shall be allowed to retire with the Tribal Authority for the final selection. The persons concerned must be in direct descent from previous *bona fide* rulers, including Treaty Chiefs whom the British recognized at the inauguration of the Protectorate. Moreover, in furthering the democratic notion that the rightful claimant should also be the most popular candidate, individual administrative officers appear to have employed a variety of devices which bear very little relation to the indigenous system. For example they have sometimes made a preliminary reconstruction of the Tribal Authority on the basis of proportionate representation according to the numerical strength of the various Sections; sometimes, representatives have been included for every twenty payers of House Tax. One officer conducted an election on the principle of an 'open vote' by 5,000 heads of (family) houses.[1]

One result of this new form of procedure, which was probably unavoidable, has been a considerable encouragement of candidature. Sometimes, as many as nine claimants have come forward from the same 'ruling house'. The most significant outcome, however, has been to put quite a novel complexion on the chiefly institution, in terms of the wider social opportunities, thus afforded. It has also imparted an additional meaning to the use which can be made of money for the purpose of bribing the appropriate authorities. Candidates often try to solicit the support of members of the Tribal Authority in this and in other ways, such as promising to advance them in office, if successful. Similar approaches are

[1] As explained previously, family houses, or *mawesia*, are social, not political units, and if their heads are members of the Tribal Authority it is by virtue of their seniority in the larger and inclusive kindred, or *kuwui*.

made sometimes to the Assessor Chiefs and the interpreters; and the practice is extended, on occasion, to anyone associated with the Government officer in charge of the matter, on the assumption that the latter's influence is really the decisive factor.

A further result has been to create an extra demand for the services of medicine men of all kinds. Candidates may pay, sometimes, as much as £50, and even more, for the various charms, etc., which these practitioners in the supernatural are able to supply. A Kono 'witch's cloak', for example, provides an infallible means of creating sufficient personality in the candidate to convince the electoral body.[1]

Altogether, the modern process of 'succession' offers a lively set of proceedings. Long before the actual day, candidates are busy about the chiefdom, and even among neighbouring chiefs, in canvassing support. Indeed, the business of 'nursing a constituency' may be said to begin long before the decease of the ruling chief.[2] Some potential successors to the office try to impress the chiefdom by their generosity, by boastful words, by some signal act of bravado or hardihood, such as deliberately insulting some important but rather unpopular personage, or by spending the night in the cold water of a river.[3] All this 'bluff' is very characteristic of certain admired patterns of behaviour in Mende culture. At the election proper, it is particularly important that the candidate should 'know the history of the country', i.e. genealogies and personal biographies of its founders and their descendants. For this reason relics of all kinds which have significance in this respect, such as a Government staff,[4] are zealously retained and kept hidden away

[1] See, also, S. Hofstra's description of this feature in 'Personality and Differentiation in the Political Life of the Mendi', *Africa*, Vol. X, 1937, pp. 436–57.

[2] There is some logic in this as it has been estimated that the average duration of a chief's reign is no more than seven years.

[3] During the writer's stay in the Protectorate, a Mission church was deliberately burned down in a chiefdom which is strongly under Moslem influence. It is significant, perhaps, that the person suspected of the arson was a candidate in a forthcoming election.

[4] The British awarded a special staff to some of the earlier chiefs with whom they signed treaties. These points indicate very clearly why many of the older men and members of 'ruling houses', in particular, are always reluctant to discuss the question of family history. There is always the chance that the information will be useful to a rival, who may either distort it to suit his own case or find some means of discrediting its validity. In the proper sense of the term, therefore, genealogies have a considerable economic value in themselves.

by the descent group concerned, so that they can be produced in triumph at the psychological moment.

It is evident, too, that the occasion provides a formal opportunity for the public airing of personal grievances and the long standing grudges which individual groups hold against each other.[1] The climax is reached with the successful candidate being paraded round the town, while his supporters cry in defiance to those whom they have defeated, 'We have "scraped" it from them; "scraped" it clean from them!' The new chief is then prostrated, almost naked, on the ground and the staff of office placed over him. This signifies that thenceforward the country is under his care and jurisdiction. The wives of the unsuccessful candidates burst into mournful cry, and their husbands take money, cattle, and rice to 'beg' their future ruler.

2. Introduction of the Native Authority System

In taking over the Sierra Leone hinterland, the British chose to administer it through the chiefs and gave, naturally, no official recognition, save in a negative sense,[2] to the secret societies. To a large extent, therefore, changes brought about administratively to Mende political institutions are reflected in the altered status, significance, and implications of the chief's office. Many of these changes have been purposely designed, partly to regularize native practices, or to bring them into line with European notions of equity and good government. A more positive aim has been to balance and distribute power and authority more evenly in the chiefdom. The effect, in one sense, has been to make the chief's position more secure and, on the other hand, considerably to curtail his privileges and prerogatives.

Thus, although the chief no longer fears deposition through the Poro or through 'tribal wars', one of the Government's first actions was to ban slave-dealing and to encourage 'legitimate' trade in its place. This, in removing one of the chief's main sources of wealth,

---

[1] This may be illustrated by the remarks of a candidate in court who said, 'I am not claiming to be chief but only showing I am a right born of the country. I want to warn whoever becomes chief not to flog me. I am not claiming to be chief at all. I could not pay even a court fee. . . .'

[2] For example, as early as 1897 the Poro Ordinance forbade the placing of the Poro sign on palm trees, etc., on the grounds that the chiefs were using it to hold up trade in their own interests.

made his followers less dependent upon him. His personal position and authority were decreased, in addition, by restrictions on the power of native courts, which debarred the infliction, previously exercised, of capital punishment for various offences, including witchcraft, as well as murder and homicide. Both directly and indirectly, Government influence affected not only the older form of court procedure, but modified very considerably both penalties and the imposition of fines and hearing fees. It also limited the native court's jurisdiction, as already mentioned, to cases which are mainly 'civil' and it provided a right of further appeal.

A further series of wider changes in the political field affect even more directly and substantially the indigenous structure. These include the gradual conversion of 'chiefly' authority into 'chiefdom' authority, and they have culminated in the *Native Authority* form of government, modelled on Nigerian lines. Officially, it is now the Tribal (Chiefdom) Authority, i.e. the former Chiefdom Council, and not the Chief, which is responsible for the administration of justice, public disbursements, etc. The chief himself is merely the principal executive officer and judicial authority in the chiefdom. In chiefdoms where the system has been set up, *Native Treasuries* have been instituted and the customary tributes and perquisites of the chief, such as rice, cash, chiefdom labour, etc., have all, with a few small exceptions, been commuted and are now paid directly into them. In other words, the chief and other officials obtain their emoluments as officers of the chiefdom. The hearing of cases has been abolished from the courts of sub-chiefs and has been limited to the chief's court, known as the Native Administration court. The money collected there in fees and fines also goes directly into the Treasury before the court members receive their share.

This new system of Native Administrations was started in 1936, and by 1945 rather more than half the total number of Protectorate chiefdoms had been reorganized, including two-thirds of the Mende chiefdoms.

A further step, also on Nigerian lines, with the official purpose of encouraging and training the community in the management of its own affairs, is the institution of *Chiefdom Estimates*. After consulting together, the Chief and Tribal Authority are expected to draw up an annual budget of the chiefdom's financial position in terms of *Revenue* and *Expenditure*. *Revenue* includes the various amounts derived from Chiefdom Tax[1] which, in the old days, largely took the form of tribute to the chief; Court Fees and Fines, etc. *Expenditure* includes administrative costs, such as the personal emoluments of the Chief, Speaker, Sub-Chiefs, Chiefdom Clerk, etc., and of items in connection with chiefdom development, such as roads or a school.

The two following sets of estimates, the first for a large and the second for a small Mende chiefdom, in 1945, show the nature of current budgets and indicate the kind of business which comes nominally within the sphere of Native Administration.

The larger chiefdom estimated a *Revenue* of £2,456 and an *Expenditure* of £1,537. The bulk of *Revenue* was to come in terms of £604 from Chiefdom Tax; £850 from Fees and Fines collected in Court; £742 from the sale of rice grown on the chiefdom farm; £151 from a Government Grant; £125 from school fees, etc. *Expenditure* was to amount to £1,186 in administrative costs, including the emolument of the Chief at £220, of two Speakers at £60 each, and of eight sub-chiefs at a total of £77. £227 was to be spent on *Re-Current Development* and £124 on *Extraordinary Development*, including the cost of a certain amount of sanitation, upkeep of a school, a road, and the chiefdom farm. The smaller chiefdom estimated a *Revenue* of £471 and an *Expenditure* of £423. The bulk of *Revenue* was to come from Chiefdom Tax at £184 and Court Fees and Fines at £200. *Expenditure* was to amount to £384 in administrative costs, including the emolument of the Chief at £80, of the Speaker at £20, and of two sub-chiefs at £18. £9 was allocated to *Re-Current*, and £30 to *Extraordinary Development*.

Differences, in amounts allocated for 'Development' by the larger and smaller chiefdoms, are obviously wide. Six Mende chiefdoms budgeted sums exceeding £200 for Re-Current Development and exceeding £500 for Extraordinary Development. But the average amounts were in the neighbourhood of £100 and £140 respectively.

Under the new system, the Tribal Authority is encouraged to meet together in full assembly more often than in the past. It is expected to hold a number of sessions, during the course of the year, in order to discuss matters affecting the chiefdom as a whole,

---

[1] Chiefdom Tax is based on a rebate of 4s. out of every 9s. in House Tax, which is collected on behalf of the Government from every adult male person owning a house in the chiefdom.

and to consider and enact new legislation, when desirable, on local matters. The following is an example of the minutes of a meeting of one of these Mende Tribal Authorities. The chiefdom in question is headed by an educated and very able Paramount chief.

'The Tribal Authority met at —— and the opportunity was taken to hold a meeting at which the following points were discussed:

'1. *Complaints.* (*a*) Sub-chief Amadu Gobeh of —— Section. A bitter complaint was made against this sub-chief not long after the election. He was alleged to put a swear on the whole section which was considered unlawful. The matter was investigated by the Paramount Chief at —— and Amadu Gobeh was found guilty. Thereupon he was suspended, and the Paramount Chief promised to refer the matter to the Tribal Authority to decide the necessary punishment to be inflicted. Since then, Amadu Gobeh has been going about here and there trying to sow seeds of discord and to bring about another political upheaval. He recently visited —— in another section and told deliberate lies about this to the Paramount Chief. We are therefore of the opinion that this man should be removed from the post of sub-chief and propose to put this into effect . . .

'3. *Porro and Bundu.* We are of the opinion that these should be put in recognized towns and that the names of all those initiated should be sent in every case to the Paramount Chief for record.

'4. *Farming.* It is observed that there is a lateness everywhere in swamp and upland farming this year. We ascribe this lateness to (*a*) attempts to avoid bird-driving which an early harvest involved; (*b*) palm kernel and oil industry. We are aware also that this lateness brings about a poor harvest in rice, bad burning and the present shortness of native cotton. To remedy this, we propose to issue an order in January next year for all brushing to begin in that month, so that burning may take place in March and sowing early in April. While farming is actively in operation, 'porro' to be placed on all palm trees in the chiefdom. It is observed, also, that a lot of young children are just left to roam about the village during the day. We think this is bad and parents should be warned always to take their children to the farm as youths and girls of ten upwards are most useful on the farms. . . .

'5. *Public Health.* We are of the opinion that it is necessary to open three other stations in the chiefdom for registration of births and deaths. If this is done we shall do everything in our power to get every birth and every death registered. In recent years, a practice of filing the teeth among young men and women has sprung up. The operation is very painful and it is highly probable that this is injurious to health. We propose to discourage this. . . .'

3. *Later Developments in Administrative Organization*

The policy of the British Government is to interfere as little as possible with native life, but it is significant, though not surprising, that the process of 'municipalizing' some political institutions should have had repercussions elsewhere, e.g. on leadership. However, this 'municipalization' must be looked at from all points of view. When the British took over, in 1896, there was a large number of more or less separate chiefdoms and 'sub-chiefdoms'. There was no important central authority, little uniformity in political status, and the extent of individual sovereignty was very variable.

It is possible that the British found this rather high degree of political fragmentation convenient, and out of military and administrative expediency in the early days even encouraged it.[1] At all events, very few amalgamations have been effected during some fifty years of British control, and today the picture in the Protectorate is of some 200 separate chiefdoms of equal political status. Each of these is an independent 'state' on its own and entirely self-contained, so far as administration is concerned.

To the prospects of further political development there are obviously two main drawbacks. For one thing, the political isolation of so many independent units makes common consultation difficult. It also handicaps the people in co-ordinating their own opinion. Further, chiefdom revenues are extremely small for the most part, and administrative costs, particularly in the smaller chiefdoms, are correspondingly disproportionate to the amount available for developmental purposes. Part of the former difficulty, however, has lately been obviated by the institution of District

[1] This seems to be exemplified by the 'splitting up' in 1919 of the former large Kpaa Mende chiefdoms into more than a dozen separate chiefdoms. It should be added, however, that the more recent policy of the Government has worked mainly in the other direction.

MODERN METHODS OF GOVERNMENT

Councils. These Councils consist of two representatives from each of the chiefdoms making up an administrative district of the Protectorate. One such representative is normally the chief, and the other is appointed by a full meeting of the Tribal Authority. He need not necessarily be a member of that body. The prime purpose of the District Council is to consult together on local matters and to make recommendations on them to the Government.[1]

The District Council also elects two representatives to the Protectorate Assembly. This is a still more recent institution and consists of all the representatives sent to it by the District Councils, along with the senior Government officials in the Protectorate and four African members nominated by the Governor to represent interests not covered by the District Councils, such as Missions and Trade Unions. The purpose of the Assembly is to advise on matters referred to it by the Governor, including proposed legislation affecting the Protectorate; to consider matters referred to it by the District Councils; and to advise on the expenditure from the Protectorate Mining Benefits Fund.[2] Its duties also include the election of three of its members to the Legislative Council.

These Councils and the Assembly undoubtedly serve a useful purpose. They afford an opportunity for matters of local interest to be discussed with relation to common needs, provide the central government with fresh ideas and suggestions for reform, and air grievances, which otherwise might go 'underground'. The District Council usually winds up its proceedings with a number of resolutions, which invariably include appeals for the building of more roads, schools, dispensaries, etc. In its short life, the Assembly has also shown quite a militant attitude towards the central government in, for example, refusing resolutely to agree to official proposals for the public acquisition, in specific circumstances, of Protectorate lands. Considered, however, as a pyramid which the Legislative Council crowns, the system of government has at least one main drawback. It has yet to provide adequate representation for the newer classes of educated and able people who are not members of the chiefly group. It is significant that, as yet, few

[1] Though proposals for the convening of chiefs on regional and tribal lines were laid down in the earlier Ordinances of the Protectorate, there appears to have been little encouragement of the idea until recent times. Prior to the inauguration of these District Councils, however, a number of educated chiefs took the initiative in organizing conferences on their own account.

[2] cf. *Sierra Leone Sessional Paper No. 7 of 1945*, 'Administrative Reorganization of the Protectorate'.

commoners have found their way through the District Councils to the Assembly.[1]

4. *Some Anomalies of the Administrative Situation*

The economic anomalies of administration present a more difficult problem, and outside amalgamation of chiefdoms on a fairly wide scale there appears to be no way even of mitigating it. The idea of amalgamation tends to be strongly resisted by those whose main stake is in the existing set-up. Yet the position is clear and its ramifications can be appreciated from the following figures, which are based on the Estimates for 1945 of some seventy chiefdoms, mainly Mende ones. The average revenue per chiefdom is £1,100, of which an amount averaging some 65 per cent will go in administrative costs, mainly as personal emoluments to chiefdom officials. For example, in the case of thirty-six Mende chiefdoms of representative sizes, the average emolument of the Chief alone amounts to some 19 per cent of the total revenue. Of the seventy-odd chiefdoms mentioned above, eighteen estimate their income at less than £600. As shown by the budgets already quoted, this leaves virtually nothing over for local development, even over many years.

In the light of future development, the existing structure of chiefdoms can therefore be regarded only as a temporary expediency. Perhaps a breathing space is required in which a more effective system of government can be satisfactorily evolved. The Native Administration scheme was introduced against a background of widespread non-literacy. The Tribal Authorities themselves prove this. From figures which the present writer obtained, only fourteen out of three hundred Tribal Authorities, comprising six Mende chiefdoms, had received any form of schooling. In 1936, when the N.A. scheme was started, the percentage of children of school age at school in the whole Protectorate was only some 3 per cent; today it is about 4 per cent, though in the Mende area it is slightly higher than this. Moreover, the extent to which the changes and new opportunities provided by the revised constitution are understood, or are at all meaningful to those whom they are supposed mostly to affect, is probably not very great. In moving around villages, the writer found little evidence that the new position in respect, for instance, of chiefdom labour was

[1] See a later paragraph for a further comment on this point.

appreciated. The ordinary villager feels that his relationship is with the chief, not with the Native Administration. If, therefore, he makes any complaint to a Government officer, it is his chief whom he is reporting and whose displeasure he expects to incur if the complaint misfires.

In particular, the section of society whose interests are deeply vested in the traditional way of life, naturally suspects or is definitely hostile to any effort made to alter it. The significance of modern methods of hygiene and sanitation is something yet to be learned and an innovation may be opposed simply because it is novel.[1] As a young educated chief, who had endeavoured continuously to obtain the collaboration of his big men in drawing up the Chiefdom Estimates, pointed out, 'They just say to me, "O, go away, and don't bother us with white man's business." '[2] To many, too, the newer regulations come as a form of regimentation which, as one young Mende man recently returned from the War put it, was 'just like being in the Army—left turn, right turn!'

The net result, at any rate, is to bring out very clearly the significance in the matter of adequate leadership and of a fair standard of education. The chiefdom minutes quoted above illustrate this. A very great deal clearly depends on a high level of personal integrity. Far from being a cure for the results of almost universal non-literacy, the N.A. systems tend, in such a context, to place a special premium on the mere possession of literacy, and, hence, on occasion, to offer rare opportunities to any educated person unscrupulous enough to take advantage of them. This is shown most obviously in the case of defaulters who have had charge of the collection and recording of certain funds. It tends, also, in chiefdoms where the Chief himself is non-literate, to place an extraordinary and quite anomalous degree of power and responsibility in the hands of the Chiefdom Clerk who, though nominally the most subordinate official of the Native Administration, is the only member of it required to be able to read and write.

[1] One informant sarcastically remarked to the writer that the very idea of the Government doing anything to help was new in itself, hence the popular lack of comprehension.

[2] Chiefdom Estimates are subject, in any case, to the approval of the Administrative Officer, and in many cases are substantially revised, or even virtually reconstructed by him. In the circumstances, this point robs the idea of most of the educational and psychological importance the practice is supposed to possess.

MODERN METHODS OF GOVERNMENT

The Chiefdom Clerk is, in fact, an interesting example of how aspects of the older institution have taken on a new form. The duties which the Clerk now performs are very like those of the Speaker in the previous order. They consist in keeping Court and other chiefdom records, in supervising the assessment and collection of House Tax, in collecting Court fees and fines, in acting as the chief's secretary and his general go-between with the Administrative Officer, and in a great many miscellaneous tasks, the significance of which depends on the relative literacy of the Chief and Tribal Authorities. In more extreme cases, therefore, he is virtually the 'manager' of the chiefdom, so far as the machinery of the N.A. is concerned. He is also, in terms of the amount and responsibility of the work, easily the most poorly paid official, at a salary of between £20 and £40 per annum.[1]

In some important respects, official limitations on the former prerogatives of the Chief are a substitute for the balance of political power which, in former times, might have been maintained through the Poro society. Nevertheless, it is a moot point as to how far the chief's office can be divested of its traditional significance without undue loss of the popular respect which, in the present transitional and otherwise leaderless stage of cultural development, is its most valuable asset.

The answer depends largely on whatever interpretation, as expressed partly in Government policy and partly in the attitude of its officials, is to be put on the exact relationship of the Chief to the central authority. Is he to be, as some of the educated people already say, a kind of unofficial Civil Servant without, however, the recognized status and prestige of the latter? Or is he to have the rôle, which tradition suggests, of leading and adapting his people and their institutions in the way demanded by modern circumstances? In either case, both the chief's position and its context require clarification and re-definition. They have to be assessed, for practical purposes, not only from the angle of native culture. There is the sociological effect of British domination and the implicit and widespread acceptance of certain western

---

[1] Needless to add, many Chiefdom Clerks are fully alive to this anomaly in their position, including its disproportionate lack of status. As one of them put it, he was now receiving 50s. per month 'after being at the beck and call of the Chief for 10 years'. The Clerk will point out, also, that although the older men about him still call him a 'small boy', they are, in fact, mostly very jealous of the influence he exercises.

standards of value. Judged from the latter point of view, whether it be a matter of salary, educational attainments, or previous occupation, the Chief cuts a very poor figure beside the Administrative Officer, who is described officially as his 'guide, philosopher, and friend'.[1] In point of fact, the power of the latter over the chief is very great for a variety of reasons and the nature of the relationship is fully appreciated, in its wider and hierarchical context, by the rest of his people.[2] They are all aware of the ultimate sanction which, if exercised, means the chief's deposition.

Not unnaturally, the situation and its psychological concomitants affects inevitably the relations of the chief with his people. If they are at all familiar with the N.A. system, they realize, for example, that the very amount of the Chief's income is subject to Administrative consent. In their eyes, he tends to be accountable as much, if not more, to the Government, as he is to them for his general actions in the chiefdom. One of the educated chiefs voiced this particular point when he wrote:

'In the olden days, the Paramount Chief was the recognized Tribal Head of his people . . . the D.C. being an Adviser. But . . . since the introduction of the N.A., the power of the Paramount Chief has passed on to the D.C. The majority of the people have been misled into the belief that the Paramount Chief is no longer the Traditional Head, but merely a paid Figure Head whose word could not stand against that of the D.C., even though the latter's ideas of Native Traditional Law is nil. . . .'[3]

[1] The average salary of Mende chiefs is about £240 per annum. Rather less than half the total number of Mende chiefs—a far greater proportion than in any other 'tribal' group—have received an elementary education, and a few have also attended secondary schools. Out of 37 chiefs, mainly, but not exclusively Mende, 14 were in clerical employment, mainly Government, before their election as Chiefs; 10 were 'farmers'; 3 were traders; and 3 more were chiefdom Speakers; the remainder followed a wide variety of occupation, such as carpenter, goldsmith, hammock boy, vaccinator, catechist, motor boy, etc.

[2] Preaching before a Chief and his Court on the danger of disobeying the will of Allah, a Moslem 'Alfa' made this point evident in the following words: 'When you disobey a Chief and fall into his grip, you feel you are in the grip of a District Commissioner, and not a District Commissioner, but a Divisional Commissioner, and not a Divisional Commissioner, but the Governor, and not the Governor, but the great King of England. . . .' cf. K. L. Little, 'A Moslem Missionary in Mendeland', *Man*, August, 1947.

[3] Document.

MODERN METHODS OF GOVERNMENT

The result, quoting this particular Chief's point of view, is that whatever initiative he takes tends to be abortive from the start, because he is never sure of the support of either party.

'Since it was explained to the people that under the N.A. system the Chief could no longer exact chiefdom labour from them they can no longer be persuaded to undertake any improvements for themselves. If I try to encourage education in the chiefdom, either the D.C. will not approve the expenditure in the Estimates, or if I ask the people to build a school on their own account, the D.C. will say that I am using forced labour.'[1]

A further consideration is that British rule, in itself, tolerates powerful rivals to the Chief's authority whom he no longer possesses traditional means of suppressing. The probability is that his very election created and left behind defeated candidates whose jealousy is still smouldering and who are continually on the watch for a chance to take their revenge. He is equally in fear of being misrepresented by them; whether, on the one hand, he tries too zealously to implement some official policy which contravenes 'country law'; or tries, on the other, forcibly to bring home to the Government some deeply felt grievance.[2]

At the same time, the Chief, like other big men, is still expected to maintain certain traditional aspects of his position, however small the chiefdom. He is still looked upon as the 'father' of his people, and is expected to uphold their prestige and his own by supporting a large number of dependents, dispensing hospitality, and entertaining strangers, and in patronizing chiefdom institutions. Yet, he and the other big men are limited to a fairly definite proportion of what the chiefdom can produce in tax and the Court in fees and fines, and to a commutation of traditional privileges and perquisites which, though fairly comprehensive, does not, perhaps, allow sufficient for the native obligation to relieve

---

[1] Document.

[2] It is believed fairly widely among the Chiefs and educated people in the Protectorate that the Administrative Officers are in the habit of encouraging malcontents in a chiefdom to bring forward complaints, such as charges of extortion, against any chief who is not sufficiently complaisant in his response to official 'advice'. Whilst there have possibly been individual instances of this, it must also be pointed out that such complaints have not always, and of necessity, to be 'manufactured'. It is hardly necessary to add in this connection that the position of the Administrative Officer himself is no less delicate and difficult in such circumstances.

want and poverty.[1] One of the effects, therefore, is to encourage the bringing of cases to Court. As already mentioned, about one-third of these concern claims for 'woman damage' and for re-payment of bridewealth.

It is not surprising, therefore, that some of the practices and abuses complained of are driven underground. In some cases, the chief has been known to exact labour from the chiefdom by means of an understanding with the sub-chiefs which enables the latter to exercise the same opportunity in their own sections. Another method, which has been used, is for the chief and the leaders of the Poro to inaugurate a chiefdom session of the society, stipulating that each village shall supply a given number of candidates on each of whom a substantial entrance fee is levied.[2] In other instances, cases heard in Court have not been officially recorded, and the fees and fines have been pocketed. Allocation of leases, assessment and collection of House Tax, etc., have also been known to provide illegal perquisites.

5. *The Present Political Trend and its Possibilities*

Thus, it is not a simple matter to sum up in a few words the direction in which Mende political institutions are moving. One general and obvious conclusion is that the 'slack' between native custom and modern practice has not been adequately drawn in. External, as well as internal, factors and circumstances have to be taken into account. In respect of the latter, we have already noted the relatively secure, though modified, position of the Chief, and the increased emphasis which is now laid on chiefdom as opposed to chiefly authority. This has given some basis, at least, for a more popular participation in local government. Similarly, the trend towards opening out succession to the office to a wider section of society is both an economic spur and an incentive in the same direction. The disadvantage of the first in a situation which is still very fluid, is that it tends to deprive the Chief of a large part of his natural rôle as a leader. The disadvantage of the

[1] cf. J. S. Fenton, in the Report on his visit to Nigeria, describes the basis on which this commutation was estimated, and also provides an excellent account of certain aspects of the native system of administration.

[2] It should not be assumed from this that all Poro sessions organized on the basis of the chiefdom involve extortionate practices. The situation does indicate, however, that so-called native customs are, *sometimes*, simply a cloak for operations which are illegal by native as well as European standards.

second is that it brings about a considerable amount of internal dissension and disruption when, for example, a temporarily successful 'house' may attempt to 'break' its rivals and put them out of the running for subsequent purposes, by raising up old 'palavers' and Court cases against them. It also promotes and encourages the practice of graft, and creates a good deal of scepticism regarding the political insight of the central government itself.

There are alternative methods of meeting these main difficulties. One way would be to make the chief and higher officials directly, as well as indirectly, responsible to the Government. In that case, the Government itself would have to assume most, if not all, of the responsibility for their selection and, preferably also, their training.[1] The other way would be to leave the political position more or less as it stands for the present, but to raise the rate of literacy with all possible despatch. Ultimately, the political problem will probably resolve itself in ways acceptable to the present 'democratic' trend, and this will necessitate quite a new equilibrium of forces in local government, with the chief playing, no doubt, a more honorific though still important part in the local executive.

This latter consideration is borne out by the lack of sufficient recruits for the system as it is still constituted. It has to be remembered that western ideas and ways exercise an increasing attraction for most of the younger generation over the traditional and restrictive features of native life. Financially, native politics have little to offer. There is no position in the chiefdom, save that of the chief himself, which can compare with even a third grade clerkship in Government service. A second grade clerk, whose salary ranges from £160 to £200, is actually on a higher scale than many of the chiefs themselves.

Most of the educated people, it is true, retain quite a close connection with, and play an active part in, family affairs. Many show a 'patriotic' interest in native institutions by sponsoring performances of native dancing,[2] by wearing native clothes on specific occasions, and by deploring the deteriorating effect on native life of certain western and Creole habits.[3] A number, while earning their living as traders, teachers, and farmers, are also Tribal Authorities. Others make their influence felt on chiefdom matters

---

[1] This first suggestion, it should be noted, implies a relatively 'static' view.
[2] See also Chapter XIII.
[3] The Creole habit which is most deplored is that of expressing superiority towards the native person. See also Chapter XIII.

MODERN METHODS OF GOVERNMENT

by rendering advice, writing letters, etc., and by interceding, sometimes, on behalf of relatives in senior chiefdom posts. But, in general, the impression gained is that the literate class generally takes little formal part in the political life of the chiefdoms. One simple reason for this is that their work very often necessitates their living in places at some distance from their own chiefdom. Again, a large proportion of them are in Government service and hence are, or feel that they are, debarred from taking any official part in native affairs.

Whether means can be found under the new institution of District Councils of obviating these difficulties remains to be seen. At present, the belief is strong among this group as a whole that the Government does not want them to have any proper share in political development. There is, in any case, a certain amount of resistance on the part of the tribal people themselves to the idea of educated participation, though it is usually neutralized in places where the chief himself is a literate person. To add to the feeling of dissatisfaction and unrest, many thousands of demobilized soldiers have returned from the war, bringing with them some of the experience gained outside the country. Their attitude towards the situation is adequately expressed, perhaps, in the remarks of one who informed the writer that he was going back to his farm, but would be looking forward to improvements in the older order of things. He would not be content, to the same extent, to take instructions from the older people and would not 'put up' with practices like 'woman palaver' and other forms of 'extortion'.

These factors, coupled with the rapidly growing force of African nationalism, are already straining the not very elastic structure of tribal political institutions to the breaking point. In other words, rather speedy means will have to be found of associating these younger and newer elements in the situation more positively with the business of government. This applies to central as well as local administration.[1] It is not going too far to suggest that a form of municipal organization is already due in some of the large towns on the railway line. In the more 'rural' areas, too, similar changes cannot be far off and the only logical reason for delay—non-literacy—is one which could be remedied quite speedily given official encouragement and support.

[1] Since these remarks were written, it seems that more positive encouragement has been given officially to the question of literate representation in local government.

CHAPTER XI

RELIGION AND MEDICINE

1. *Introduction*

ONE of the oldest anthropological controversies, into which the present writer does not propose to enter at this point, is when and how precisely to distinguish between 'religious' and 'magical' behaviour. One tempting way out of the difficulty is to avoid the dichotomy altogether, and to speak simply of a people's attitudes towards the 'supernatural'. But this merely shifts the onus of classification. Where, aside from western definitions of the matter, do 'natural' phenomena end and 'supernatural' phenomena begin? The problem is no less difficult among the Mende than with other preliterate people whose every day attitudes and behaviour in this respect are largely a derivative of their general conception of the world about them.

In the case of the Mende, this conception governs and determines their reaction and adjustment in almost every aspect of the cultural life, though to a varying extent. It seems to be based on the physical environment in which, presumably, traditional belief mainly developed its roots. This physical environment consisted, until recently, of thick and almost impenetrable bush and forest in which the traveller who strayed from the narrow and foliage enshrouded path might get lost for ever. It was a place where wild and dangerous animals, like leopards and snakes, lurked, and where even more dangerous human enemies frequently lay in ambush to attack the unwary. It was a place where the pursuit of game was both difficult and dangerous. Above all, it was a place in which sudden heavy storms and floods added fresh uncertainty to the arduous and unending labour of hewing down and clearing giant trees, scratching the earth with simple, hand-made tools, and finally tearing away the rapidly and ever growing weeds from the few grains or vegetables which the effort had produced. In short, it was an environment in which very many factors and circumstances were of a kind to enhance the inexplicable, the mysterious, and the dreadful. Consciously or unconsciously, the sentient mind must have been made continuously aware of its inadequacy, and must have realized its inability to cope with, let alone control, its surroundings by material means alone.

Precisely what the processes of rationalization are in such circumstances goes beyond present speculation. For sociological purposes, the manner in which man 'adapts' himself psychologically is immediately relevant only in so far as it throws light on the nature of the adaptation itself. Basically, the Mende adaptation (and this is probably true of all forms of 'primitive' religion) involves a positive acceptance of the world or 'universe' as it is found. This is fully inclusive of phenomena that are regarded as inexplicable and unpredictable. Put more explicitly, the Mende adaptation[1] clearly acknowledges these and other phenomena and, in so far as they are active and manifest, supplies its own working interpretation of them. Finally, the Mende adaptation provides its own system of techniques for dealing with them. Such a system does not claim complete efficiency, but it offers what might be termed a reasonable and working hypothesis of 'supernatural manipulation.' These points, or rather, principles, can be made more specific in the following terms.

2. *The Supreme God*

In the beginning, there was *Leve*, spoken of nowadays as *Ngewɔ*. *Leve*, or *Ngewɔ*, may be directly translated as (Supreme) God.[2] All life and activity, in both a material and non-material sense, derives from him. *Ngewɔ* created the world and everything

---

[1] I speak of 'Mende adaptation' only because I am writing about religion among the Mende, and not with the object of claiming as specifically Mende an 'evolution' of religious belief which is shared in very large measure by neighbouring peoples. It is evident that such an 'evolution' must have been preceded, culturally speaking, by a great deal of cross-fertilization. I do wish, however, to indicate that I am writing of Mende religion, so far as it is possible to perceive it as indigenously distinguishable from Islamic beliefs and practices which are also part of the present cultural context.

[2] I have thought it best to qualify use of the term 'God' because of occasional references the Mende make to other deities, such as the Earth.

in it, including not only human beings, animals, plants, and so on, but spirits also. In addition, He invested the whole universe with a certain non-material kind of power or influence, which manifests itself in various ways and on specific occasions in human beings and animals, and even in natural phenomena, such as lightning, waterfalls, and mountains. He is the ultimate source and symbol of that power and influence, but though all-powerful, he is not an immanent being. Like most African Supreme Gods, having made the world, he retired far into the sky. He has little immediate contact with the affairs of human beings, though he still sends the rain to fall on his 'wife', the Earth (*Ndoi*). This relationship of the deity to the objective world is further rationalized in the Mende saying that 'God is the Chief'. The ordinary Mende commoner does not approach a chief directly, but uses a 'big man', or someone who has the chief's ear, as an intermediary.

Little is known about the exact nature of *Ngewɔ*, because no one has ever seen Him. He is not entirely unapproachable, however, and sometimes a prayer may be addressed directly to Him. Indeed, it is customary to end most supplications with the expression, *Ngewɔ lama*—'God willing'. But contact is made more often through the medium of a 'spirit', in Mende *ngafa* (pl. *ngafanga*). 'Spirit' is a generic concept which can be specified broadly in terms of four categories, namely, ancestral spirits; 'genii' (*dyinyanga*); secret society spirits; and miscellaneous spirits. In ordinary conversation, no other term than this generic expression is used, and a descriptive phrase has to be employed to signify the nature of the particular spirit to which reference is made; for example *Ngafa nyamu*—evil spirit. Sometimes, the special name by which the genii in question is known may be used. The Mende say that they know these various spirits are around because people dream of them.

3. *Ancestral Spirits*[1]

The first category, the ancestral spirits, are of course the spirits of the dead. Their habitat is essentially local, and they usually inhabit the district where their living successors dwell, and particularly the houses, compounds, and farming places of the

[1] For a more detailed description of the ancestral spirits, see S. Hofstra's article, 'The Ancestral Spirits of the Mendi', *Int. Arch. f. Eth.*, Band XXXIV, Heft 1-4, Leiden, 1940.

latter. Occasionally, however, they appear in a dream to a person even when he is away from home. They are regarded as members of the families concerned, and for this reason, if for no other, are the spirits with whom there is the most universal and common contact. For a similar reason, and because communication with them is comparatively easy, they are the most general link between human beings and the supernatural world. As members of a particular family, or descent group, they retain a strong and continuous interest of a proprietary kind in property belonging to the family, and in family affairs and activities. In consequence, and because they rank as the family's most senior members, they expect to be consulted about any important matter of family business. As senior members, they also expect a share of the respect and affection due to all older living members of the family, and also to partake to some extent in its material prosperity. In return, they extend their blessing on its members and are generally responsible for their welfare. As a general rule, ancestral presence is not materially visible, but as already mentioned, they appear in dreams and are readily recognized.

Usually, the ancestors do not consist of individuals beyond two generations previous to the eldest members of the present family. In family relations, they have the status of grandfather, and are addressed by that term. They punish the neglectful and disobedient, and are particularly severe on breaches of discipline and of the duties which members of the family owe each other and its head. Not only a person's own ancestors, but the ancestors of other people may be vengeful towards him if they are wronged during their lifetime. When he becomes conscious of their anger, such a person should go to their nearest relative with a small 'shake hand', and ask the relative to pray for his forgiveness. The relative will then make an offering at his ancestor's grave at which the offending party should be present.

Ceremonies in connection with the ancestors, or approaches to them, are carried out by the head of the family or its oldest member. Very often, there are special places, such as the foot of a large cotton tree between whose roots a small wooden shelter is placed. Such a spot is known as *hɛma*—praying place—and it is here that the *hɛmɔi*—prayer-leader—and the other members of the family congregate so as to make their offering. A fowl and some rice are brought forward, and the *hɛmɔi* addresses the ancestors somewhat in this manner: 'Well, grandfathers, we are here now and we beg you to accept these gifts.' All then return to the village and partake of a meal together, which finishes with palm wine and general rejoicing. The food left at the ancestral shrine is eaten up by birds or by passing strangers, and this is a sign that the ancestors have taken it and are pleased. If it has not gone by the next day a further ceremony must be performed. These sacrifices and ceremonies are usually carried out in the early morning; possibly on account of the implications of vigour associated with the beginning of the day.

Invocations of this kind are generally the result of someone dreaming of an ancestor, or of a run of misfortune and illness in the family.[1] The ancestors are angry and wish to be fed. It is assumed that the sick person has offended them in some way. The two ways of appeasing them are by the ceremony of the 'red rice' —*mbagboli*—and by the 'laying of the plant'—*hɔwei*

The 'red rice' ceremony is usually performed by the head of the family, or by the mother or 'big wife' of the sick person. Two pieces of tobacco are carried to the graves and a supplication is made on the 'offender's' behalf in words like the following:

'Ah, grandfathers, I have come to you! Momo is the person ill. The soothsayer tells me that you are angry with him because he has not fed you for a long time. Do you, ancestors, kindly pardon him. He is a small boy; he has no senses yet. I have come now to beg you. My heart is now clear. The sky above is also satisfied and the earth below is also satisfied. Every day that passes, we ask that you people should always be our leaders and should not leave us unprotected.'

Next morning, all concerned carry cooked rice and a fowl. There must be no pepper in the food, lest it make the hearts of '*nduwumoi*'—the dead—very hot and increase their anger. The person officiating then approaches the grave and says the following prayer:

'Old father, Jina ... let this reach you; old father, Abu ... let this reach you. The food I promised to give you is what I have now brought. Let no bad thing happen to him (the sick person), and even to us (the members of the family), let nothing bad happen to us.'

The rice is then mixed with the liver of the fowl and put on

[1] The regularity with which ancestral rites are carried out appears to vary considerably. Some groups make a number of routine offerings during the year. Others do not appear to sacrifice without some special cause.

RELIGION AND MEDICINE

the grave. Water is next poured out for drinking with the words, 'Please, the water.' Those standing by then eat the rice. All close their eyes, and at the word of the officiant they open them again, saying in chorus, 'In your protection let our eyes be open for something sweet in the future.'

The *hɔwei*[1] ceremony is performed when the graves of the ancestors are at an inconvenient distance away. Similar prayers are recited, but the rice is usually put on two crossed leaves (the *hɔwei*), and placed on the public pathway. In order to ascertain if the angry spirit is appeased some rice is placed on the offender's tongue, or palm of his hand, and a fowl is brought to peck it. If the fowl declines the grains, it is a sign that the spirit is still angry, and the offender has to provide further presents and his elders to make further intercession on his behalf.

It is of interest, also, to note that in connection with these ancestral rites, the children are given their food first at the communal meal. They are said to be 'nearest' the ancestors, 'having done them least harm'.[2]

4. The 'Dyinyinga', or Genii

The genii, or *dyinyinga*, may be described, for the most part, as nature spirits. They are usually associated quite definitely with natural phenomena, such as rivers, the bush, etc. They are specifically recognizable in anthropomorphic terms and possess, very often, well marked human tastes, emotions, and passions. Like human beings, they are responsive to approach and solicitation, but their favour is not won in the same ordered way as that of the ancestral spirits, and it cannot always be relied upon. The obtaining of it depends mainly on the personality of the individual concerned rather than on precise rules of conduct. In any case, though contact and intercourse with them may be productive of great good fortune, it is also fraught with a certain amount of risk. The individual must act boldly. Either he obtains power over the genie, or the genie takes control of him. In the latter case, he may be obliged to do the genie's work; or, to retain its favour, may have to sacrifice something to which he is very much attached, such as

---

[1] The *hɔwei* plant is also used in connection with the 'begging' of the uncle when the nephew has offended him (see Chapter V).

[2] A parallelism might be observed here with Christian dogma regarding the innocence of little children.

his own first born son.[1] Genii appear to some persons and not to others, and very often they make their appearance at night time when a person is sleeping. Their relationships with human beings can be of the most intimate kind and may extend as far as sexual intercourse.

Though the genie is conceived of spiritually, it can turn itself into a human being and is often perceived in such a form by the person who encounters it. Linguistically, the Mende term *dyinyinga* probably owes something to Arabic and Islam, but there are no spirits of the air as in popular Moslem belief. Most genii are white in colour, and it is possible that this attribution, also, has been derived from outside; for example, from the appearance of the Portuguese, who were the first European people to make contact with aboriginal society. Even today, Europeans are spoken of quite often as genii.

The following examples illustrate the strong degree of association of this kind of spirit with natural phenomena. The *Tingowei*, for instance, is a long being in the form of a golden chain, which is seen only by people to whom it shows itself and who hear the sound of its chain. The links of the chain may be espied as lying on the top of a granite promontory. Persons passing by in their canoes are tempted to seize it, and their boats founder on the rock. Those who see it from the land may become mad. The *Tingoi* appears as a beautiful siren-like woman with a soft, white skin. She lives in the deep water of a river and is seen, sometimes, perched on the brow of a rock combing out her hair with a shining golden comb. She is usually amiable, and the person who knows how to approach her in the correct way obtains considerable riches. But the approach must be made at the right moment. You should steal upon her from behind and snatch away the comb. She will come to you pleading for its return with every possible artifice and blandishment; but to let her have it back means

[1] In an interesting case of parricide concerning a Mende boy who killed his father under, it was claimed, the influence of spirits, we have an illustration of this point. From the angle of abnormal psychology, such behaviour might, perhaps, be classified under the category of 'possession' (cf. S. Hofstra, 'The Belief among the Mendi in non-ancestral spirits and its relation to a case of parricide', *Int. Arch. f. Eth.*, Band XL, Heft 5-6). As Hofstra points out, however, such cases cannot be understood solely in psychological terms. The belief in spirits forms part of native thought, so that some persons, already for that reason, are sooner disposed to undergo supernatural experiences than members of western culture.

death, or poverty for the rest of your life. You must steadfastly refuse every new request, and should burn the comb and put the ashes on the cooking stones in your house. Every time the *Tingoi* calls on you, you should double your conditions and find some fresh pretext for refusing her. The *Njaloi*, too, lives as a rule in deep waters (lit. *palie*—deep places). He owns towns full of treasure. Canoe-passengers must pay him a due. Those who know how to deal with the situation strike a bargain, and at night-time he returns their gift. The *Njaloi* has a bright coloured stone, which gives a brilliant light, in his forehead.

The *Ndogbɔjusui* is the best known genie. He lives on the top of a mountain by day, and roams the bush and bush paths by night. He appears as a man with a white skin and a long white beard to lonely travellers, whom he tricks into following him deep into the forest. The only way to get the better of him is to answer his questions in a contrary way. For example, if the *Ndogbɔjusui* asks, 'Whence do you come?', you should reply, 'From the moon'; if he asks, 'What you want to eat?', you say, 'Stones'; 'What do you use to carry water?', you reply, 'A fishing-net'. Then he takes a net, fills it with water, and when the water runs away, he leaves you alone. The questions he asks are aimed at and intimate the actual thoughts of the person interrogated. But the latter must never say what is truly in his mind. If he fails in this, he may stray in the bush for days and be given up as lost. If, on the other hand, he answers with sufficient subtlety, the *Ndogbɔjusui* rewards him well.[1] The *Ndogbɔjusui* is also associated with the bush in an agricultural sense. The steatite *nomoli* which the farmer turns up when he is hoeing in old bush are looked upon as the genii's handiwork and can be used to make the rice prosper. On the other hand, the farmer clearing virgin land must be careful lest he offend the *Ndogbɔjusui* in any way. If he does so, and any calamity follows, the only way is to propitiate the spirit.

Another genie that lives on land is *Kaikonjo*. He used to cause a great deal of mischief around Bumpe and in the Sherbro area, but was put to flight by *Kaswela*, a water spirit from Bonthe.

Broadly speaking, relationships with the genie category of spirit are on a personal rather than social basis and involve no regular cult of worship and propitiation, as in the case of the ancestral category. There is some exception, however, which

[1] This illustrates in an allegorical way quite an important psychological principle in the Mende cultural pattern.

follows from the genie's close association with regular and seasonal phenomena, or activity, such as the overflow of a river or farming. One example of this is taken from Manina in the Upper Mende country.

The town of Manina, it should be explained, is situated on the river Lagula, and during the month of September the Lagula overflows its banks. Someone in the town dreams of this happening, and the soothsayer interprets it as a warning that the general behaviour of the people has angered the genie of the river. If the latter is not propitiated the whole country will be flooded. The chief sends word of this out to neighbouring towns and villages and appoints a day when the necessary sacrifices can be performed. These take place at the end of the month when enough rice has been taken in to make the affair a success. The soothsayer or, sometimes, a *mori*-man, enumerates the kind of articles required, such as sheep, fowls, fish, palm oil, and salt, but not pepper.[1] A council of the Paramount Chief and Section chiefs decides on the amount that each part of the country shall provide, and the cooking utensils are carried secretly out of the town during the night previous to the day of the ceremony to a spot on the upper part of the river. This contains some large stones and tall trees which are the abode of the spirit and is the place where the cooking must be done.

In the meantime, everyone proposing to attend the ceremony has been warned that he must cross the river before daybreak. If anyone steps into the water on the actual day, the spirit will refuse the offering. When morning comes, the people move out of the town towards the river, carrying with them the necessary food. The procession consists only of men, however, as women are not permitted on such an occasion. Even cooking, which is the normal duty of the latter, is done by men and they prepare two separate portions. One lot, consisting of specially selected materials, is for the spirit; the other for the people. Particular care is taken not to cut the throat of the fowl intended for the spirit's pot. This fowl is usually the largest one available, and it is cooked together with the hearts and livers of all the sheep offered. The cooking done, the whole assembly proceeds to the stones and seat themselves on

[1] As mentioned in a previous paragraph, it is considered that the burning taste of pepper makes it an unsuitable offering. Sheep are offered instead of goats, because it is believed that a sheep is more 'blessed' than a goat. The latter point is probably explained by Islamic influence.

the ground. The soothsayer acts as master of the ceremonies and, before 'feeding the stones', he calls out three times. He then calls a fourth time, '*ngiye wai*', meaning 'big hill'. In response comes a call from the bush, usually like that of a cock. It is uttered by a man whom the soothsayer has concealed there the night before. The answer is taken, however, as a sign that the spirit is present, and the soothsayer continues with the offerings. To test if they are acceptable or not, a white kola nut is split and the two halves thrown into the air. If the inner portions show uppermost on landing, the verdict is favourable and the people return joyfully to the town. Failing this, an enquiry is made to find out if any rules of the ceremony have been violated, and a further sacrifice is made. Some days later, when the volume of water has substantially subsided in the river, it is taken as a sign that the spirit has been successfully propitiated.

5. *'Nameless' and Mischievous Spirits*

The third category of spirit is also closely associated with the natural environment, but lacks the fairly specific identity of the genii and is usually nameless. Possibly, these spirits should logically be included, as Hofstra's explanation of them suggests,[1] with other spirits of dead people.

These spirits are thought of, however, as mischievous and troublesome, and they are reminiscent of the troll of Scandinavian mythology and the 'little people', or fairies, of Keltic mythology. In a sense, therefore, they stand in apposition to the genii who, in terms of West European folk lore, might be likened to the 'big fairies', such as the Keltic Lugh and Angus Og. The Mende have a fairly general belief that their country was formerly inhabited by dwarfs—*tombuisia*—and that their dwelling places are still indicated by ant hills. These *tombuisia* also occupied caves and woods to which the same term—*tombui*—is given. Such places are regarded with awe. Since the *tombuisia* were the original owners of the country, it is expected that they will be jealous of the present users of the bush. This explains, perhaps, the reason for various ritual precautions taken throughout the farming season with the object of warding off or exorcising certain so-called evil spirits.[2]

[1] cf. Hofstra, 'Ancestral Spirits of the Mendi', op. cit.
[2] On various occasions in the course of preparing the farm for cultivation, medicine, etc. is thrown into the adjoining bush with the saying, 'that's for

On the whole, however, these 'nameless' spirits and 'bush devils' as they are popularly termed in translation are less feared than the genii and other types of *ngafa*. The main impression is that they are merely meddlesome and trouble-makers. They are accountable for minor misfortunes and afflictions, such as a bruised toe or a badly scratched arm, while the farmer is working in the bush. For reasons of this kind, small offerings are made occasionally to them, and a *sawei*, a (purifying) medicine is scattered around the farming places in much the same way as a European housewife might spray disinfectant round a room in order to cleanse it of flies and mosquitoes. A certain amount of purposiveness is attributed to these spirits, but they are un-moral to a characteristic degree.

6. *Spirits of the Secret Societies*

The fourth and final category of *ngafa* is of far greater importance and the most difficult of all to classify with satisfactory clarity. This is the 'spirit' associated with various secret societies, in particular, the Poro and the Sande. In this case, the conception exemplifies what appears as a more or less conscious attempt to endow spiritual force and power with an active personality, achieved by means of masks and various kinds of body gear. In this conception spiritual power has been 'canalized' for purposes of social expression and action. Objectively, the power thus personified is simply a social construction depending upon the collective behaviour of the members of the cults subscribing to it. In the minds of the people, however, the supernatural qualities of the (society) spirit are intrinsic to it. 'The (Poro) *ngafa* was made by God and not by man', was the reply of a Mende man to a comment on the apparently material origin of the 'spirit', and taken at its literal value, this remark leaves no doubt regarding the religious status of the phenomenon in question.

the evil spirit'. Hofstra's explanation, which is very feasible, is that 'evil' spirits as such comprise, in the first place, the spirits of people who already had a bad character, or are persons for whom funeral ceremonies have been omitted or improperly performed. He also postulates a further group of *ngafanga*, who are not really evil spirits, but who led a somewhat wandering life, or remained outside family life. For the latter reason, when rice is offered in the usual ancestral ceremony, some rice is also thrown on the road for them in particular. This latter group and the rite in question correspond to the category under discussion in the text.

There is, in fact, little doubt from the point of view of the Mende that the secret society spirit belongs as much, if not more, to the 'metaphysical' plane as any other category of *ngafa*. This is shown partly by the complex attachment of cults and by the psychological attitude towards cult activities.[1] The quality of awe and respect shown towards this kind of spirit and its cult-paraphernalia is emotionally distinct from that evoked by other spirits. It signifies, perhaps, that although materialization of the society spirit is necessary for social action, there is nothing lost thereby in supernatural content.

7. *The Nature of 'Hale' or 'Medicine'*

It may be gathered, therefore, from the foregoing that the 'spirits' provide in various ways for the Mende man some degree of personalization of the more distant, more abstract Being, known as *Ngewɔ*. Of the nature of *Ngewɔ* he knows little and, in consequence, is uncertain of the way to 'handle' Him. The spirits generally possess certain 'human' qualities which he appreciates and with which he can deal by means of flattery and propitiation. Nevertheless, and this point must be stressed, the spirits owe their influence, as well as their existence, to the power with which *Ngewɔ* invested the universe.

This power, which *Ngewɔ* has left behind and which derives from Him, is a further and very important conception. Like *ngafa* it is also generic. It is expressed in the term *hale*, usually translated as 'medicine'. In common parlance, and in a specific and rather limited sense, this word denotes any physical object or instrument employed to secure certain ends by supernatural means. Such a reading, however, tends to conceal the fact that the object concerned is impregnated with a supernatural force which is external to the object itself. It is significant, for example, that in swearing on a stone, or on anything else 'that *Ngewɔ* made', the Mende believe that the 'spirit' in the object will be helped by *Ngewɔ* to carry out the purpose of the swear, or to inflict punishment on a wrongdoer. With the latter, in particular, the issue is left deliberately in the hands of *Ngewɔ*, hence the common expression, 'Oh, I leave it all to God'.

It would be more appropriate, therefore, to regard *hale* as something which is generally latent, and which requires only a

[1] These latter points are described in more detail in Chapter XII.

special kind of action or special circumstance to become actively manifest. In essence, *hale* is entirely non-moral and 'neutral'; but it may be manifested as 'good' or 'bad', as positive or negative, according to the person who uses it and the way it is used. Theoretically, anyone may use medicine,[1] but the conditions require persons who are specialists in its production and employment, because *hale* is potentially dangerous as well as potentially valuable. Mishandling of it may bring down harm on its manipulator and those associated with him. Moreover, the best results are obtained by those who have the skill and knowledge to use it.[2] Just as *hale* can be used on behalf of anyone, so it can be used against a person.

First and foremost among these specialists in supernatural power come the officials and senior graduates of the secret societies, like the Poro, Sande, Humui, etc. Then there are the individual 'technicians', like the *halemui*, or medicine man, and the soothsayer, diviner, and so on, down in order of respectability to 'mori-men', witches, and owners of 'bad' medicine.

8. *Practitioners in 'Hale'*

An important sociological distinction has to be made, however, between the various categories and the work they do. The function of the secret societies is essentially a socially approved one. The ends sought and the work undertaken under their ægis, either in a corporate sense or through their accredited representatives for individual purpose, are to be regarded as socially beneficial. It may be something as specific, on the one hand, as the cure of a person's illness; or the furthering, on the other hand, of the general welfare and prosperity of the community. In this respect, the rôle of the secret society is somewhat analogous to that of a corporate medical service as opposed to private practice. In theory, remuneration is made as a payment to the society itself; and the skill of society officials, derived from their membership of the institution, is a form of cult property which can be

[1] The common use of *hale* is rationalized by the popular saying that since 'God' is so far off, it is up to everyone to find what means he can to help himself.

[2] As explained later, a medicine becomes very closely associated with the personality of its owner and user. It has to be tended and 'nurtured' carefully. Part of the technique in the case of specific medicines consists in 'talking' to them in a certain way every day.

used and imparted to outsiders only in terms of the society and under its auspices.

The medicine man *halemui* and others of his kind, on the other hand, are essentially private practitioners, though they may sometimes be employed for a purpose which has communal implications, such as the preparation of a rice medicine. They are engaged for, and serve, individual and personal ends rather than public ones. Their knowledge is their own personal property, and they can pass it on to whom they like and at whatever price they can obtain for it. Usually, techniques and medicines are handed on from father to son, or to an apprentice.

Occasionally, however, someone quite outside the 'profession' has a dream and compounds a new and successful medicine as the result of it. Dreams, in fact, play a large part in this respect in establishing the necessary credentials of anyone dealing in medicine. They are also an important element in the soothsayer's or diviner's technique; in that he uses them largely to 'diagnose' both illnesses and social situations, for the benefit of those employing him. Sometimes, indeed, he uses his own dreams not only to interpret present events, but also to warn people of some future calamity of which they are unaware. This invariably calls for a propitiatory 'sacrifice', according to his dictates. Moslem practitioners and preachers also employ the same device as a means of enhancing their personal reputation and of spreading the faith.[1]

In view of the medicine man's individual rôle, the kind of engagements he fulfils are not necessarily of the sort to produce socially beneficial results. The same applies to the '*mori*-man', who is classified within the same category.[2] They both undertake anything from a love potion to a cure for a headache; or from a talisman which will secure successful candidature at a chiefdom 'election', to a 'swear' which will bring about the downfall of a

[1] cf. K. L. Little, 'A Moslem "Missionary" in Mendeland', *Man*, Aug., 1947.
[2] Broadly speaking, a medicine man is simply a professional worker of medicine, and the term is elastic enough to include the '*mori*-man'. As the latter term denotes, however, the '*mori*-man' is a person professing Islam who purports to work by means of various Islamic paraphernalia, such as inscriptions in Arabic writing, beads, verses from the Qur'ān, etc. He also employs the aid of numerous charms and talismans associated with the occult side of Islam. Largely through his professed connection with that religion, the *mori*-man enjoys greater prestige than other ('medical') practitioners in many communities.

rival. At the same time, they have a recognized status in the community which is implicitly acknowledged on specific occasions, for example, in the hire, for judicial purposes, of the particular medicine they own. As described on a previous page, they may also be called upon to perform various communal ceremonies in connection with the propitiation of certain genii.

Nor, in the general sense, are medicine men and similar practitioners of this accredited category held personally responsible for the outcome of their work, unless it is patently antisocial in character. If the victim of it has any complaint to make, he should lay it primarily against the person who hired the medicine man. It is the former who incurs the main liability. The existence of *hale* has, in fact, legal and official recognition, and the medicine man is regarded simply as an agent in the matter.

9. *'Bad' Medicine Men and Witchcraft*

In contrast to the above mentioned categories, there are other exponents of medicine, including persons owning 'bad' medicine—*hale nyamubla*, who are regarded quite definitely as anti-social. They have absolutely no legal protection; and it is the duty of every member of the community who knows their identity to bring them to the notice of the authorities for proper treatment and punishment. Until quite recently, and the belief still lingers in the more remote parts of Mendeland, witchcraft was often suspected when anyone died in unusual circumstances. Every person associated with him was regarded as a potential witch. After the funeral ceremonies, the uncle of the deceased gave permission to the 'washing man'—*ngua-moi*—to examine the intestines of the corpse. The left side was cut open and the spleen taken out and dropped into a pot of water mixed with leaves. If it sank to the bottom it was conclusive proof that a witch-spirit had entered the man and caused his death. The body was then buried under a heap of stones with a stake through it to prevent the spirit wandering and harming other people. If the liver sank half-way in the water, it indicated that the dead person was partly a witch—*hubonɛi*. He could detect witchcraft, but could not perform it himself.

A witch-spirit—*honei*—sets out, sometimes, to kill a child, but is thwarted. Instead it enters the child and they grow up together, so that the child becomes a 'witch person', or 'witch host'—

RELIGION AND MEDICINE

honamui. He will always deny this, though he really knows it to be a fact. The movements of the *honei*, or witch-spirit, are controlled by use of a certain leaf which is picked by the *honamui*, when he wishes the *honei* to go out at night time. The *honei* can travel about independently of the *honamui*, while the latter is sleeping, on bats and owls.

A particularly clear example of the illicit operation of *hale* is provided in the case of *ndilei* medicine. This is a medicine which can be transformed into a boa-constrictor by the witch (person) owning it. It is a mineral substance whose Mende name is *tingoi*, and it is hollow inside. It can be bought from its existing owner, if the latter wishes to rid himself of it. Disposing of it, however, carries a very grave risk, including death, because the medicine becomes an integral part of its temporary owner. This is because the latter becomes virtually the slave of the medicine in return for the work which it does for him, and is slavishly subject to its will. A way of getting rid of it is through the *kema-bla* who, as witch-finders, have an antidote for witchcraft and can distinguish the evil thing in the dark. Another 'antidote-people' are the *kondo-bla*. They can provide a counter-medicine—*kondo-gbandei*—to witchcraft. This is made out of a small piece of bamboo cane, and when hung over the door, or over a child's bed, it has the effect of 'shooting' the witch. The witch's only hope of salvation lies in confession to the soothsayer. The latter refers him to the *kondo-moi*, i.e. the leader of the *kondo-bla*, who requires him to surrender his 'leaf'. This deprives the witch of his power. He is then treated by the *kondo-bla* for his sickness.

In terms, then, of the work done, the owner of the *ndilei* and the medicine itself may be regarded as one; since the owner becomes a witch through association with it. He may have acquired it for the purpose of avenging himself on someone who has wronged him. But once under the medicine's power, he is committed to the life of cannibalism which witches lead.

This witch cum boa-constrictor (*ndile*) works always by night and feeds on the blood of his victims by sucking it vampire-like out of their throats. Usually, his attentions are fatal, and he has the power, also, of causing infantile paralysis in children. The *ndilemoi's* first step is to secure some article which has any kind of association with his intended victim. This may range from a piece of clothing to anything picked up from the latter's farm. Without it, the witch has no means of attacking the artery. The medicine itself is then buried close to the victim's home—outside in the bush or even at the doorway of his house, in any place from which his house can be seen. From there, it is transformed at the appointed hour into the boa-constrictor.

The Speaker of an Upper Mende chiefdom related this account of his experiences with a 'boa-constrictor':

'One day, he noticed an old woman among some rice bundles at a farm. She was moving about stealthily and eventually unwrapped a triangular shaped object from a piece of shirting. She then pointed it towards each part of the compass in turn, touching her breast with it after each movement. After hiding the object under the rice, she went away. The Speaker went over to the bundles, and on putting his hand down to examine the object, received a violent shock which bowled him over. He saw a bright light, rather like a rainbow, and it flashed on the neighbouring farm house. Presently, the old woman returned and repeated her actions. Being suspicious, he reported the matter to the Chief. The Kema-people were sent for, and in the old woman's house they found the object in question. Along with it was a head-tie belonging to a woman in the town, as well as a collection of stones equal in number to the houses in the village. The woman to whom the head-tie belonged became paralysed soon afterwards. The old woman herself was sworn, and she, too, died soon after this.'

Fear of the 'boa-constrictor' is very wide and is not limited, by any means, to the non-literate section of Mende society. It is a fear which is particularly contagious, and which is caught very readily in a large town. The sudden and unexplained death of a child coupled, perhaps, with the presence in the compound at the time of a woman who is a stranger to the place is sufficient to start it; especially if the stranger's actions have been remarked on as eccentric in any way.[1] The fear is the greater because it rests,

[1] During the writer's stay there were, at least, two alleged instances of *ndilei* medicine in one of the larger towns. Both of these arose, apparently, out of the death of small children. On the second occasion, the rumour grew so strong that very few of the town's inhabitants would venture out of their houses after darkness had fallen. Many individuals reported instances of being chased by 'cannibals' and the rumour gained further strength through the subsequent disappearance of a young boy from the house of a well-known trader, and through the appearance in the town, at a late hour, of the car of one of the Government officials. The owner of the latter, it was alleged, had already been involved in a case of cannibalism in another part of the country and was renewing his activities locally in this respect.

very occasionally, on objective fact in that associated outbreaks of 'cannibalism' still occur, the object being to obtain human fat for the purpose of re-invigorating certain medicines.[1]

Though such events do not form any part of the regular institutional pattern of Mende society, they are significant enough to be regarded as an important example of the anti-social operation of *hale*. It is possible that, in former times, the securing of parts of the human body formed part of certain religious practices. Nowadays, however, it is symptomatic more of political undercurrents. When it occurs, it has generally two motives behind it. By the possession and secret use of cannibal medicines, an individual, or group of individuals, obtain enough prestige and power to terrorize a local community for their own ends, which may consist in the exaction of money or political privileges. Or a cannibalistic murder may be committed for the purpose of casting suspicion, in the eyes of the British administration, on some local political figure, such as the Paramount Chief. By discrediting the latter, the murderers hope to secure his removal.

10. *The 'Bɔfima'*

A further very powerful and anti-social medicine of the same kind is the *Bɔfima*. This is made out of the skin from the palm of the human hand and sole of the foot and the forehead. There are also parts of certain organs, such as the genitals and the liver, as well as a cloth taken from a menstruating woman, and some dust from the ground where a large number of people are accustomed to meet. It also contains some rope taken from a trap from which an animal has escaped; the point of a needle; and a piece of a fowl's coop.

All the above items are made up into a bundle and put into a bag, or they may be parcelled up in leaves. Attached to the bundle is a number of strings, perhaps as many as seven. Tied to the end of each string is a hook, sometimes of wood, sometimes of iron. When the owner of the medicine wishes to know if he can

---

[1] One such outbreak occurred at Segbwema in 1938 which, as in a more recent instance at Kenema, necessitated Government enquiry and action. There was an earlier and more serious outbreak in Sherbro country, in the Imperri chiefdom, which in 1912–13 required the stationing of troops at the town of Gbangbama. cf. K. J. Beatty, *Human Leopards* (Hugh Rees Ltd.), and R. G. Berry, *The Sierra Leone Cannibals*, with Notes on their Customs.

safely embark on a certain line of action, he will take the *Bɔfima* out into the bush and throw it with the strings attached into the undergrowth. If, on withdrawing the bundle the strings come away freely and do not get caught, he feels safe in continuing. If, however, the hooks get caught in the branches and are difficult to withdraw, the matter is left over.

The *Bɔfima* requires periodical 're-invigoration', otherwise it will turn on its owner and destroy him. Some *Bɔfima* medicines have to be renewed annually; others more often. The success and power of this medicine depends on the parts of the body mentioned above. The oil, which is prepared from the fat of the intestines, is used to anoint the *Bɔfima* itself, and is also used as a rubbing medicine to bring good luck and to give the person so treated a fearsome and dignified appearance. The oil is sold, therefore, as a side line, and it may be bought by people who are not, in the proper sense, in league with the owners of the medicine. The report is that it is sold in small scent bottles for amounts varying from £5 to £20 to people who can afford it.[1]

11. *Practical Uses of Medicine and other Medical Paraphernalia*

Both the secret societies and the individual practitioners operate very largely by means of medicines (to use the term in its more specific sense), and to 'work medicine' is the verbal equivalent in this respect. Physically speaking, an ordinary medicine is generally a compound of herbs, mixed with other natural ingredients, such as soil and leaves, the whole being saturated

---

[1] Renewal of the *Bɔfima* requires, of course, a fresh human victim. Before setting out to obtain one, the *Bɔfima* is consulted, and if all is well its owners proceed. Persons are hired, sometimes, to carry out the deed. The tactics are to wait on a straight stretch of the road at night-time. A member of the party climbs into a tree from which he can obtain a good view, and he waits there hidden by leaves. The others hide in the bush at the foot of the tree. They go into action as soon as the look-out spies a lone woman or child coming down the road. First, one of them will make a friendly approach to the traveller, making sure that she is alone. Then, the woman's mouth is clamped by a pair of pincers to prevent her screaming, and the jaw is dislocated on each side by blows from a hammer. After killing the victim the required parts and fat are taken from the body and the corpse is buried in the swamp.

The fat must be turned into oil by a woman who is not allowed to touch food until her work is completed. She must wash her hands very thoroughly before eating.

with water. Medicines of this kind are known as *saweisia*, and are employed ritually for 'washing' certain social offences and crimes, as well as for the cure of physical ailments. Other medicines, particularly the kind used forensically, may consist of a wide variety of miscellaneous objects, like cowries, old razor blades, ribbon, feathers, animal fat, human nails, etc. Often, the ingredients forming the medicine are tied up in a piece of cloth, or may be contained in the horn of an animal, a sheep, or a goat. There appears to be no rigid rule in regard to the choice of materials, though unusual objects are preferred because, it would seem, they possess some extra quality through their abnormality.

An essential part of the technique of 'working medicine' is that the objects should deliberately be set aside: one is tempted to say 'consecrated', for the purpose in view. Once the medicine man in charge of the work has done this, the objects themselves are impregnated with power and become effective media for its transmission. As such, their potency varies with their previous and present associations and with the medical prestige of the persons compounding them. In other words, they may be likened metaphorically to electric batteries. They are charged with energy.

As already indicated, medicines constitute, according to their nature, a form of private or of collective property, and they may be inherited or loaned in the same way as other forms of property. Individual medicines, such as the *Ngelegba*—Thunder medicine, and the *Tilei*, which eats away a person's nose—are known far and wide, and their possession and use are vested in the families owning them. Other medicines are owned collectively as chiefdom or society medicines. They may be used only for public purposes or for business which is of specific concern to the society. Chiefdom medicines consist, sometimes, of a collection of erstwhile private medicines which have been confiscated because their owners were using them in a nefarious way. The fact that they can be 'municipalized' in this fashion illustrates the point, made in an earlier paragraph, about the 'neutral' nature of *hale*. It is also significant in this respect, that as a generic concept, *hale*, has to be designated specifically in terms of the way and according to the purpose for which it is used. Thus, *numu bao hale* is a medicine that can care, i.e. one intended for protective purposes; *kpoi hale* is a drinking medicine, i.e. for medical purposes, in the sense of a physical cure; *sondu wa hale*, a medicine for 'swearing'.

The supernatural property which medicines of this kind possess and which renders them dangerous for ordinary handling, along with the way in which they are compounded, puts them into a somewhat different category from other quasi-religious and magical paraphernalia. For example, *lasi-moi* (in Creole, *sebe*) which is best described as a talisman, may consist of a piece of Arabic writing sewn into cloth. Its efficacy seems to derive exclusively from the prestige of its Moslem manufacturers as practitioners in the supernatural. A very similar type of function is also performed by the *nessi*, which is also made by *mori*-men. A verse from the Qur'ān is painted on a smooth wooden board shaped rather like a shield, and the writing is washed off with water into a bottle. It has the effect of bringing good luck to its possessor.

The so-called 'sacrifice' is another aspect of the use of *hale*, and its purpose is generally propitiatory and protective. In the case of the *kpakpa*, it is something which is communally 'set aside' with the object of warding off potential danger to the chiefdom, as a whole, or to a group of individuals, such as a particular family. It consists of a number of articles collected together on the advice of a medicine man or a *mori*-man. It is used, sometimes, in Court cases as a means of turning what would be otherwise an adverse judgement into a favourable one.

Another form of 'sacrifice' is the *saa hani*—a white rag hung from the rafters of a house or tied to a pole outside it in protection of its inhabitants. This, however, is a peculiarly Moslem trait. A further type of 'sacrifice', which has more in common with the western meaning of the term, is the custom of slaughtering a goat or fowl as a way of propitiating ancestral or other spirits. Examples of the latter have already been quoted in full. In general, however, the practice of 'sacrificing' contains a good deal that is neither symbolical nor imitative. Its implications are mainly compulsive and coercive. A person who is in trouble, or is fearful of getting into trouble, goes to the soothsayer and the latter instructs him as to what he should 'set aside'. It may be a hoe or a knife. Nor are the objects in question by necessity of any special economic value. The person concerned simply places them in a corner of his house or compound. 'Sacrificing' is associated with a wide range of objective—from paying off an old score, to curing illness in a child.

In addition to its employment in the protection of life and health and in promoting prosperity, medicine has a very important forensic function. It is an essential part of legal procedure and the main way of attesting evidence. It is also used widely in safe-

RELIGION AND MEDICINE

guarding public and private property from theft, and in detecting criminality.

In Court, medicines are administered in a large variety of ways which range from the tasting of salt to the blowing of a pair of bellows. As indicated in Chapter IX, both plaintiff and defendant must be sworn in this way before their statements can be taken. They declare—'Oh, big medicine of the such and such chiefdom, may I die if what I say is not true!' Or a medicine may be used for the purpose of confirming a verbal promise. The person concerned swears on the medicine that he will carry out what he has undertaken. Again, a person whose property has been stolen denounces the anonymous thief and invites the medicine to bring the culprit to disaster. In all these cases, the implication is that the medicine itself will serve as the instrument of justice: it will be the means of restoring the moral equilibrium. Swears made in the last-mentioned way, however, can be 'pulled', i.e. removed, if either the person who made the swear, or the owner of the medicine used for the purpose, can be persuaded to do the 'pulling'. In such a case, the verbal injunction contained in the original swear is simply reversed.[1] Properly speaking, however, use of the medicine in this way for detective and punitive purposes requires the sanction of the chief. The same applies to another and more

[1] The procedure in this kind of swear and use of medicine is as follows: The person concerned takes up his medicine, then shaking a rattle and calling out publicly that if the wrong-doer does not confess his misdeed, he will 'submit the matter to God', he makes a tour of the village. If there is no result to this apparently charitable action, he proceeds to the cross-roads, and having placed his medicine in the middle of the way, pronounces somewhat as follows in a loud voice:

'I, myself, do not know the man who has wronged me, but you know him, my powerful medicine. Go search him out, and take revenge on him. As for you, you vile thief, whoever you may be, man or woman, slave or freeman, chief or commoner, listen to my voice. May your liver drop into powder—may your heart fall to pieces—your hind-quarters stop working—may you be impotent—may your wife be barren, and your blood run through two holes. May snakes bite you and the boa-constrictor eat you—may God curse you. If you go by water, may the spirits turn your boat over. If you are caught in a storm, may lightning from the sky strike you. When you go to sleep at night, may you never awaken. May any illness you have burst your inside and split open your belly. When you go to your wife, may you embrace a corpse. May death cut you down now and for ever, and may you never return to life.'...
In the reverse procedure, the swear is removed with the words—'May this swear be removed and no harm come to you'—*Sundu frloi foloŋ hinda nyamu gbi a gbiwie*.

RELIGION AND MEDICINE

elaborate method of detection by the *gbatui* medicine which involves the use of hypnosis.[1]

Finally, the general part that the secret societies play in the control and manipulation of supernatural power needs to be stressed. In the old days, it is possible that it was even greater and that it excluded much of the 'private' practice evident nowadays on the part of *mori*-men and other individual exponents. Even to-day, the regulation of sexual and social conduct and the supervision of a good deal of political and economic activity is still vested in them. In all this, the special society medicines take an essential part which is detailed elsewhere.[2] The Sande medicine, for example, is to propagate and foster womanly virtue and character, and to 'wash', i.e. cleanse and purify, women when they fall short in those respects. The 'Sande corner'—a screened off portion of the house occupied by the principal woman of the society—contains the society's medicine and is therefore a place of particular sanctity. An intruder there will incur not only the severe displeasure of Sande members, but the additional disability of a

[1] The *gbatui* medicine is the property of the medicine man hired to undertake the enquiry into, say, a theft. It consists of a stiff piece of elephant or hippopotamus skin. The medicine man is assisted by a medium whom he first hypnotizes by rubbing the palms of the latter's hands and his arms with a medical preparation. To the crowd of onlookers which has collected, the medicine man then explains the work he is about to do and enlarges on the efficacy of his medicine for the purpose, indicating the hypnotic condition of his assistant as proof of this. He may then demonstrate the medicine's powers further by getting the crowd to secrete a ring on one of its members whilst he (the medicine man) is not looking. He then unearths the ring by sending the medium with the *gbatui* in his hand to the person who has the ring.

After this preliminary performance a space is cleared for the medicine man and the medium, and a stool is placed on the ground between them. Everyone who is suspected of the theft, or who may have any connection with it, is made to sit on this in turn and is interrogated by the medicine man through the medium. The *gbatui* is still in the latter's hand, and he is told to strike the guilty person with it, or to make a sign of his innocence. This procedure may be extended by a process of elimination designed to clear circumstantial evidence. For example, the medicine man tells the medium to strike the stool if the thief is a woman, or entered the house by a window, is a stranger, etc. Assuming the thief has still not been disclosed, fresh suspects are brought forward. If the medicine man is genuinely at a loss and in danger of losing the respect of the crowd, he may eventually order his medium to strike a person whom the previous enquiries have disclosed as being unpopular or particularly suspect. Such a person may be a stranger, or a person of another tribe.

[2] See Chapter XII.

RELIGION AND MEDICINE

swollen stomach. Only the society itself, using the medicine which caused it, can 'pull' this effect.

Enough, then, has been said to indicate that *hale* is generally inclusive of rites, drugs, and sacrifices. Conceptually, it is not too much to claim that it is implicit in most of the religious and magical life as well as the religious programme. It lies basically at the edifice of society and its supernatural significance is aptly summed up in the Mende saying—*Hani na gbi tongo e hale a numu lo hu*, which can be translated broadly as 'All that is consecrated medicine takes possession of man'. Manifestation of this latter and final aspect is particularly evident in certain social states and conditions which, objectively, are the result of special physiological circumstances. Thus, women who are pregnant or menstruating are 'dangerous' in the sense that to make contact with them is harmful to all the parties concerned. The dead body of a member of any of the societies can be safely handled only by the deceased person's colleagues.[1] Sickness, too, is often a sign of (ritual) contamination and requires confession and purification before the patient can expect to get well again.

[1] This applies also in respect of persons who are twins. There is a species of cult associated with this type of biological relationship.

CHAPTER XII

CULTURAL RÔLE OF THE PORO AND OTHER SOCIETIES

1. *The Secret Societies as Cultural Arbiters*

THE foregoing description of the organization of religion and medicine in Mende society would be incomplete without some detailed consideration of the secret societies. These institutions, as already indicated, are of primary importance in determining ritual behaviour and affecting social attitudes, because the sanctions in nearly every sphere of the common life derive from them. The principal societies involved, in addition to the Poro and the Sande, are the Humui, concerned with the general regulation of sexual conduct; and the Njayei, concerned with the cure of certain mental conditions and the propagation of agricultural fertility. The Wunde, concerned largely with military training, is popular among the Kpaa Mende, but appears to owe its origin mainly to the Timne neighbours of the latter. These societies are not exclusive, of course, to the Mende, but are shared widely, with the exception of the Wunde, with peoples in Liberia as well as with the adjacent Sherbro, Krim, Gola, etc.

Through their staff of hereditary officials, masked 'spirits', and rituals, the secret societies canalize and embody supernatural power. Collectively, they provide an institutional structure which bears resemblance to the medieval church in Europe; but with one or two important differences. Like the medieval church, they lay down various rules of conduct, prescribe certain forms of behaviour, and are the sole agency capable of remitting certain sins. On the other hand, both their control over supernatural power and their regulation of lay conduct and behaviour is, to some extent, departmental and even a matter of specialization.

CULTURAL RÔLE OF THE PORO AND OTHER SOCIETIES

That is to say, particular fields of the cultural life and their regulation tend to fall within the exclusive province of specific societies. The combined effect, however, is a pattern of life which is influenced very largely by the secret societies.

The traditional basis and general structure of these societies may be well illustrated from the Poro. It goes without saying that there is much local variation. In Mende country alone one is frequently told that the Poro is 'strong' in this place and 'weak' in that. Elsewhere, among the Temne for example, it is said virtually to control the chiefship in some localities; in other places its effect is negligible or entirely absent.

2. *Traditional Explanation of the Poro*

Whether the Poro originated with the Mende themselves is unknown. There are linguistic similarities with Sherbro over a number of cult terms,[1] but its diffusion from an earlier and more distant source is more likely. The matter, however, remains one for speculation. Migeod suggests that the expression '*Purrus Campus*', which is found on the oldest medieval maps of Ptolemy, should be translated literally as 'poro bush'.[2] He thinks that this is an indication of the society's considerable antiquity. A more credible, though less historical, reference to the institution occurs in the word 'purrah' in the writings of various eighteenth-century visitors to Sierra Leone.[3]

Other authors have suggested that the Poro was brought into Sierra Leone by the Vai people from Liberia; or that it spread from what is now French Guinea into Sierra Leone with the Temne, who came as a fighting legion of the Baga from Futa Jallon.[4] If the last is true, it is possible that the Poro is a derivative of the still older cult of Si'mo, which Butt-Thompson claims is the foundation of other important societies, like the Egbo of Nigeria, found as far down the coast as Angola.[5]

Without discounting the value of traditional accounts of its origin, it is clear that, so far as Sierra Leone is concerned, the Poro antedates the 'tribal wars' in that country. For this reason,

[1] The Mende word for 'Poro' is *Poe*, meaning literally 'no end'; 'far behind'.
[2] cf. F. H. W. Migeod, op. cit.
[3] cf. Lt. John Matthews, *A Voyage to the River Sierra Leone* (1788).
[4] cf. W. Butt-Thompson, op. cit.
[5] ibid.

a number of rationalized explanations have to be discarded. For example, it has been suggested that the society originated out of men banding themselves together in secret to obviate slave-raiding parties from which they hid in the bush; or, that during the tribal wars, the war-chiefs found it convenient to hold their councils in the bush, where they would not be overheard by the women, or by eavesdropping spies of the enemy. Another, and even less likely explanation, is that it was feared at one time that pregnant women, looking on the faces of individuals deformed by syphilis, would give birth to children who were similarly deformed. It was arranged to hide such diseased people deep in the forest where they would not be seen by the women and children. One of the sufferers was appointed to speak for the others, and he gave warning of their approach when they came to beg for food. As time went on, the number thus isolated increased, and it was decided to starve them out. The method of decreasing them was not told to the women and children, and the syphilitic people died out altogether. Years afterwards, an instrument was invented to imitate the voice of such a person for the purpose of frightening the women and children.

The main characteristics of the society are, however, exemplified in two traditional accounts which are related widely among the Mende themselves. One is that the first Mende chief was very powerful and his people thought that it would lead to a general disruption of the whole tribe, if his death became known. It was decided to keep the matter a secret. It so happened that the chief had an impediment which caused him to speak in a nasal tone, and so a suitable person was found to impersonate him. He was sworn to secrecy on a very strong medicine. Gradually, others were also told, and sworn likewise.

The second, and more extensive, traditional account is, that a very long time ago, there lived a certain wealthy old man who had many wives and children. He owned a large amount of bush and the people for miles around regarded him as their big man. Unfortunately, he contracted cancer of the nose and his voice became harsh, but musical, in tone. This was the first case known of such a disease, and the old man was put away in a forest near the town. His head wife and his youngest daughter were the only members of his family to tend him. The other big men of the district visited him freely to talk over important matters, but women and young people were forbidden to see him. One day, the men consulted

CULTURAL RÔLE OF THE PORO AND OTHER SOCIETIES

together to usurp his lands, and they agreed to kill him, his wife, and his daughter. In order to deceive the other wives and children in the town an instrument which would produce the same tremulous sounds as his voice was devised. A wood carver hollowed out a stick and a small piece of skin was bound over its smaller end. Returning to the town, the men then informed the people that the old man had changed into a spirit and that his wife (*Mabɔlɛ*), and his daughter (*Gbonu*) still tended him. Whenever the men wanted to make a feast, they would pretend to take the old man to visit his wives and children in the town. A brother-in-law of the man, acting as an interpreter, would herald the news of his visit, and the women and children would rush into their houses, the former clapping their hands in appreciation of it, but in great fear. Then the interpreter would announce the old man's needs: rice, goats, palm-oil, etc., and these would be amply supplied. At other times, the men would break into the barns and seize what they required for the feast.

This account recapitulates further institutional features of the Poro by suggesting that the particular bush in which the old man, his wife, and daughter were buried became known as *kameihun* (*kamai*—to meet around), because the men met there around their leader. In due course all the old man's property was acquired and the children themselves grew up to be men. It was then decided to introduce them to their father, and this constituted the first session of the society. Another bush was selected, and huts were built there to accommodate the young men, because they were not allowed to tread the sacred ground of the *kameihun*. This temporary abode was known as *kpandoinga* (*kpandohu*—void), because it was void of the secrets of the society. One by one, the young men were introduced to their 'father', impersonated by the 'spirit' (*ngafei*), who would be squatting on the trunk of some large tree with the pipe of office, the so-called Poro horn. Marks of membership were then cut on each youth's back.

3. *Structure of the Poro*

As already explained, the primary function of the Poro is to equip every Mende man for the part he is to play in community life. In this respect, however, it is necessary to distinguish between two different aspects of the society's organization. In the primary and social sense, it provides merely a course of training which, though symbolical as well as practical, does not carry the initiate beyond a very junior stage in society affairs. All control of society business proper is vested in the senior members. The latter consist of hereditary officials and those who have risen to a position of seniority by a further and fairly extensive period of instruction. There is, actually, no permanently existing Poro in the sense of a continuous and uninterrupted round of society activities. Members are called together at indefinite times for the attainment of specific objects, and when these objects have been gained, the 'poro'[1] breaks up or dissolves. Even the annual initiation school for new members is no exception to this rule or principle.

Nor does the Poro possess any centralized form of organization.[2] It is called together and organized locally through the medium of what, for lack of a better term, might be called 'lodges'. These 'lodges' are quite independent of each other, so far as their administrative and specific activities are concerned. At the same time, they operate along lines and carry out rituals and practices which are substantially the same all over Mende country. In other words, if a person has been initiated in one area, he will be admitted to a society gathering anywhere else and, according to his particular society status, may participate fully in whatever is going on in the place he visits. The general rule is for every important town, and even village, to make its own 'poro'. Sometimes, as indicated in Chapter IX, the chief will call a general meeting of Poro people in his chiefdom when a matter of special importance arises, which concerns either the society or the chiefdom.

As already described, status and position in the society depend upon the person successfully undertaking a further course of training which enables him to pass to a higher degree. Any one of male sex may attain a higher grade, though the leading officials, the *Gbeima* (most senior) and the *Sowa*, who comes next, hold their positions through hereditary right. Women, who are initiated, become members of the society in the same way as a man, but they are not allowed to proceed to any higher grades and, with one exception, are not allowed to occupy any official posts. The fees,

[1] There is a fairly clear, but subtle, distinction to be made between the Poro as a society or general institution, and a 'poro', which is a gathering of Poro members called together for a specific object.

[2] For a detailed comparison of the structure of the Poro in Liberia, see G. W. Harley, 'Notes on the Poro in Liberia', Papers of the Peabody Museum, Vol. XIX, No. 2.

which every initiate must pay and which are due, also, from members moving up to a senior grade, are paid to the officials and distributed among the senior members. The latter organize and are responsible for training given in the bush. The duty of junior members is simply to implement whatever decision is arrived at by the elders. They are never consulted by the 'senior Poro', and have no power to initiate Poro action in any form. These junior, or ordinary, members of the Poro are known as *So hinga* ('Those who are entitled to procreate'). As already explained, until he has been initiated in the society, no Mende man is considered mature enough to have sexual intercourse or to marry.

4. *Women as Poro Members*

Women are admitted as members of the Poro under specific conditions. There are certain individuals, known as *Sami*, who have an hereditary connection with the society and who, irrespective of their sex, must be initiated. Any woman who becomes a Paramount chief must also be initiated, but she remains a junior member. Women who suffer from barrenness may be initiated as a means of obtaining a cure. Barrenness is regarded as the result of some infringement of Poro rules, and the woman concerned is escorted into the society's bush by a young boy, known as *ngegba* (*ngi gba*—I am different). On their arrival, the Poro spirits are invoked and asked to release the woman from the curse they have laid upon her, and to pass it on to the boy. Such a woman is then called *bolemui* from *Mabɔlɛ*, the only woman official of the society who herself is responsible for the invocation. The Poro session on such an occasion lasts only a very short time, perhaps from 5 a.m. to 4 p.m., and both the *bolemui* and the *ngegba* are given only a very elementary form of instruction and a few cuts on their backs, as marks of membership. In the course of time, however, the *ngegba* becomes a full Poro man.

The office of *Mabɔlɛ*, according to tradition, derives from the first Poro 'spirit', the old man mentioned above. Before he was put to death he decreed that a woman should be co-opted in the society in memory of his wife, who had this name. The *Mabɔlɛ*'s duty is to take part in certain ceremonies, additional to the one just described, and to act as matron to the young initiates during their course of training. She is held in the highest respect and, when the Poro session is over, she takes charge of the 'spirit's' pipe and the razor, which is used for marking the initiates. She hides them securely above the rafters of her house in the town. Originally, it is claimed, no woman other then the *Mabɔlɛ* was admitted. Any woman who learned a Poro secret, or, who knowingly or unknowingly trespassed on Poro bush was severely punished along with members of her immediate family. The 'spirit' rushed to her house followed by an angry crowd of members, razed it to the ground, and cleared away all the rubble so that no trace was left. The victim herself was then taken to the bush and roughly treated. Nowadays, however, such women are forced merely to undergo initiation. They retain their membership of the Sande of which no man may become a member. All other women are strictly excluded from any form of contact with the Poro, and no woman may see the dead body of a woman, who is a member, or of an important male member.

5. *Poro Spirits*

The paraphernalia of the society, drums, medicines, masks, etc., are usually kept in a house in the town. In addition to the principal spirit, the *Gbeni*, there are several subsidiary spirits which, however, do not possess the terrifying qualities of the *Gbeni*. These are the *Ngafagoti*, the *Yavei*, the *Jobai*, and the *Dagbadaii*. The *Gbeni* may be seen only by society members and even they are in danger, if they approach too near to him. The *Gbeni's* costume consists of cloth and leather. He wears a leopard skin, and carries medicines, including Arabic writings, and glass accoutrement, in addition to his leather mask. As already described, the *Gbeni* appears in public only on the most important occasions. His coming is announced by the *Wujei*, who precedes his appearance from the bush, and by the long, drawn out cry which is the characteristic Poro call. Each spirit is attended by a number of followers; those of the *Gbeni* being the smartest Poro boys. There are attendants (*mboleisia*), a broom-holder (*kpangbahoumoi*) who sweeps the road in front of the spirit, drummers (*mbili-yeisia*), a bugler (*buvemui*), and a number of individuals beating sticks (*kokondeiyai-bla*). The followers wear head-ties, head-dresses of animal skin, and a head-tie is wrapped round the body in the form of a tunic: short trousers of country cloth are also worn. The *Gbeni* is 'pulled' out of the bush by the *mbolesia*, and the crowd following turns about according to the way the spirit faces, in order to avoid coming in

CULTURAL RÔLE OF THE PORO AND OTHER SOCIETIES

front of him. The other spirits are mainly for amusement. They usually remain out and dance after the *Gbeni* has retired. The *Dagbadaii*, however, is also dangerous from the point of view of women and children. Its function is largely satirical. Accompanied by its followers, it parades the town and chants comments on the conduct of any townspeople, including notabilities, against whom there is any popular grievance or complaint. Its followers reply in chorus and repeat the spirit's words, which, as is the general rule, are uttered through a megaphone. Special drums are used in connection with Poro business, and while the society is in session no other drums may be beaten in the town.

6. *The Sacred Bush of the Society*

The sacred bush of the society is usually adjacent to the town, and is invariably surrounded by high cotton trees which give to the place an appearance of both majesty and mystery. This spot, as already mentioned, is known as the *kameihun*, and it is here that members meet to discuss society business. In the heart of the *kameihun* is the *palihun* (in the deep[1]). This is a clearing, where are four large stones, which mark the place where the founder of this particular bush was buried. It is sacrilege to enter this place wearing any kind of footwear,[2] because it is here that prayers are offered to the spirits of the society and that the most important ceremonies, including the final graduation of new members, are performed. The *kameihun* also contains the graves of past leaders and notable members of the society. Its establishment entails special rites which, in the old days, are said to have included a human sacrifice of a man and a woman. They were buried in a standing position and the grave was marked with the stones mentioned above. Many goats and fowls were also killed, and a great feast took place amidst general rejoicing. The officiating person was the oldest man in the community, preferably a warrior. After this, the spot was held for ever in the greatest veneration, and only the *Sowa* and the *Mabɔlɛ* could tread this particular ground.

[1] The deep parts of the river and of the sea are believed to be the abode of the spirits of the dead. The term therefore indicates that the spirits of deceased members live in a similarly removed spot.

[2] As mentioned in Appendix I, the possibility of this prohibition being due to Moslem influence should not be overlooked.

7. *Secret Society Operation of Medical and other Services*

To revert now to the more general question of secret society function, the various rôles performed in community life can be summarized under four main headings, viz.:

(a) General education, in the sense of social and vocational training and indoctrination of social attitudes.
(b) Regulation of sexual conduct.
(c) Supervision of political and economic affairs.
(d) Operation of various social services, ranging from medical treatment to forms of entertainment and recreation.

Of the first three of these rules, enough has already been said under previous headings to indicate the part of the societies in cultural arbitration and specialization.[1] It only remains, therefore, to describe the fourth category and to show how similar effects of a social and psychological kind are also involved in these further activities.

Since disease is frequently held to be the result of some breach of ritual or society rules,[2] the proper body to effect the cure is the society against which the sick person has offended, and which possesses the appropriate antidote.

Generally, the course of treatment has several stages. The first thing for the patient to do is to consult a soothsayer. He has a bag of stones, each of which represents the various ills from which humanity suffers. In the course of manipulating his stones, the soothsayer asks his patient if he remembers having broken such and such a rule or done such and such an act. He tries to get the patient to confess some great or small misdemeanour which might be interpreted as a concrete offence against known rules and regulations. If the patient denies any such offence, he is told that he is lying or has forgotten the matter. Eventually, the soothsayer informs him of the particular society against which he has transgressed and tells him that the only way to obtain a cure is to make full confession to them.

The person reports there and the final stage is for him to be

[1] See Chapters VI and VII.

[2] It should not be inferred, of course, that illness is never attributed to a natural cause. As Hofstra points out (op. cit. 'The Ancestral Spirits of the Mendi'), there are many cases of illness and causes of death, for example—senility, when in the first instance a natural cause is looked for and where ordinary (natural) medicines will first be applied. When the illness does not respond to natural remedies, however, the soothsayer or diviner is called in.

CULTURAL RÔLE OF THE PORO AND OTHER SOCIETIES

ritually washed by the society concerned, or to be made a member of it and formally initiated. The decision rests on the nature of his offence and the rules of the given society. Sociologically, the reason for initiation is fairly obvious. Through the offence the individual has committed, e.g. trespassing on society bush or coming into physical contact with any of the secret paraphernalia, he is considered to have acquired a measure of the society's own special power. The surest way of preventing his divulging what he has learned to outsiders is to place him under the same oaths and obligations as are incumbent upon members of the society themselves. This also obviates the possibility of his making unauthorized use of society secrets and of setting himself up among the public as an unofficial practitioner. Once initiated, however, the fame of any medical work he does redounds to the credit of the society as a whole rather than to him as an individual person.

There are a number of physical and physiological complaints which fall specifically within the province of certain societies. The example of barrenness and its treatment through the Poro has already been cited. Illnesses of various kinds in the case of a man may be traced to his having intruded in the Sande bush during the period of the girls' initiation. He may be able to obtain a cure by paying a fine to the society and being washed by them. A really serious illness may be attributed to the person concerned, or to someone closely connected with him, having committed *simongama* which, as already explained, constitutes the most serious breach of Humui laws.

An advanced grade of the Humui also specializes in medical as well as ritual washing and is known as *Kpékalay* (literally, 'the heart of the razor') on account of the razor used in the ceremony. The upper part of the patient's tongue is scratched with a razor or needle to wipe away all impurity. It is this category which, along with the 'house' Humui, deals with *simongama*.

Insanity, and other forms of mental complaint, are put down to breaches of the rules of the Njayei society. The complaint results from the sufferer having trespassed on Njayei bush, or from his having seen the dead body of an important member of the society before it was ritually purified. In such circumstances, initiation is the only cure, unless the person is already a Humui member. In that case, he undergoes treatment without initiation into the Njayei. There are reciprocal arrangements between the two societies, and the members address each other as 'brother' and 'sister'. This is not surprising in view of the fact that the respective functions of the two societies overlap in certain respects. For example, the Njayei deals, along with the Bongɔi section of the Humui, with persons who have broken the prohibition on sexual intercourse in the bush.

Membership of the Njayei, like that of the Humui, is also gained when the person concerned dreams of the Njayei medicine, or 'wrongs' one of its elders. There are also hereditary members. The Njayei group meets in a round house which has distinctively speckled walls. Non-members may enter this, but not the special corner where the medicine is kept. As is also the case in the Humui, the leader is a woman. She has charge of the sacred boa-constrictor whose flesh is taboo to all members. When this animal dies it has the same ceremonial burial as a senior member. In addition to treating the mentally sick, the society supplies medicines for making the farming bush fertile. Sometimes its services are employed by the Chiefdom Council for this purpose. As mentioned in Chapter X, certain Njayei ingredients can increase a person's self-confidence and develop his 'personality'; hence their use in elections for the chieftainship. If the successful candidate is already an Njayei member, he may then spend some time afterwards, secluded in the Njayei house, in order to confirm and consolidate his future chances of luck and prosperity. This particular custom, it may be noted, bears some resemblance to the ritual '*kanta*-ing' of the Timne chief after his crowning.[1] There is a further striking similarity in that the Njayei cut off the head of a member when he dies and bury it with the next person. This practice is also followed in the burial of Timne chiefs.

Most forms of native therapy include the prescription of special medicines compounded mainly out of certain kinds of herbs and leaves whose remedial value is of a physical, as opposed to psychological, character. These are applied in ways which vary from ritual sprinkling of the body to external application as poultices and internal consumption as drinks. The Humui, in particular, makes a prolific use of these materials, and for this reason the leader of this society is known as 'leaf person'.[2] The bush sacred to

[1] cf. Esu Biyi, 'The Timne People and Their Kings', *J.A.S.*, Vol. 12, p. 190.
[2] Leaves are also used in the ritual washing of a deceased senior member. The body may not be seen by non-members until a medicine, containing leaves and herbs, has been sprinkled over the corpse, which has been carefully guarded in the meantime.

the Humui serves as a kind of hospital in this respect, and small children may be taken there for treatment.

All medical work is virtually the prerogative of the secret societies, particularly the Humui and Njayei; but not quite all. There is, for example, the Kpa society which any adult person can join. The function of the Kpa is confined to the treatment of minor complaints, such as eye trouble, toothache, etc. In many villages, there are certain large stones, known as *kpaa-gotui* at which the *Kpa-bla,* or Kpa people, carry on their work. A man may apprentice himself by applying to the leader of the Kpa, and after learning the use of herbs and medicines, he returns home and sets up his own hospital and dispensary.

Rules of health and hygiene, as already indicated, are implicit in many of these secret society prohibitions. Yet another instance is the ceremonies performed by the Sande on occasions of abortion, birth, and still-birth. In the case of the last, the women of the town collect herbs in the bush under the directions of a senior official. Returning, they sprinkle all the houses in the town with this lustral medicine, and this must be done before further child-bearing can proceed with success.

8. *Entertainment and Recreation*

Additional to the spirits which inspire awe, most of the secret societies have one or more ancillary spirits whose function is mainly of quite a secular kind. It is to provide entertainment. Usually, the appearance of these spirits in public signalizes some important ceremony, such as a funeral. The individual impersonating the spirit wears a wooden mask and a cape of raffia which is extensive enough to cover his entire body, because it is absolutely essential that no part of the person should be revealed. The spirit, escorted by attendants and followers, usually visits every big man in the town and squats in various grotesque poses in front of his house. It then proceeds to parade about the town, attracting spectators and causing amusement wherever it goes. By-standers with a position of social prestige to maintain hand over money to the spirit's followers.

The performance of these 'amusing' spirits, as they are popularly termed, is mainly a matter of miming and mimicry. But in the case of the Sande dance the entertainment is on more elaborate lines. It is a great honour to impersonate the Sande spirit in this

CULTURAL RÔLE OF THE PORO AND OTHER SOCIETIES

instance and one which is reserved for higher grades of the society. Additional to the carved wooden mask, which is dyed a deep black and is the effigy of a human face, an outer garment is worn. This is densely covered with hanging strips of wood fibre sewn on to a foundation of black cloth. Black stockings are worn, and tiny bells hang from some of the strings of the dress. The spirit carries a small whip of stiff grass and is accompanied by an 'interpreter'. Communication between the two is made by means of signs with the whip, and the interpreter explains the spirit's meaning to the onlookers.

The Sande spirit has a special dance which she performs as a *pas seul* to the beating of a *sangbei* (drum) by a male drummer. Her attendant keeps a careful watch while she dances in order to adjust any disarray in dress which might give away the spirit's human identity. One of the most disastrous things that could happen would be for the mask to fall off when non-members, or those of a lower grade, are about. The consequences would be serious, for the spirit would be bound to take revenge. Secrecy is enhanced by giving the spirit some personal name which is either complimentary or which suggests a virtue, so that the real name of the impersonator goes unmentioned.

The style of the dance includes a darting and skipping movement taken almost at the run, like the preliminary strides of an expert skater on the rink. There are side to side inclinations of the head and shoulders—both turned in opposite directions and complicated pirouettes on the balls of the feet. While waiting to dance, the spirit feigns restlessness, scatters the crowd about her, and has to be 'pacified' by her attendant. The dance itself usually takes place in the chief's compound in the midst of a large gathering of townsfolk and visitors, and the entertainment invariably includes special exhibitions of dancing of an even more spirited and acrobatic kind than the spirit's own costume allows. If the occasion is a particularly important one, women singers provide additional musical accompaniment with their *segbura* (calabash rattles), and there may be a number of male drummers. The dance is started by the leading singer—*ngolɛ nje* (singing mother), shaking her rattle and intoning the opening verse of a song. This is taken up by her fellow singers and they reply in chorus. The drummers then join in.

These special exhibitions are performed by a picked group of younger Sande initiates. They dance as a group, or in individual turns. On finishing, the solo dancer is greeted with enthusiasm by the older women. The dancing costume in this case consists of bunches of palm leaf fibre suspended by bangles round the arms and legs, and knicker-bockers of native or European cloth. The practice of 'dashing' the dancers with money after each turn is an important part of the institution and one of the ways in which a person wins and retains social prestige in Mende society. The donor walks into the full view of the assembly to hand over his contribution. Alternatively, the dancing girl drops her head-tie on to the lap of some important spectator and he is expected to return it with money.

CHAPTER XIII

THE MODERN SOCIAL TREND

1. *Factors Promoting Social Change*

A CURSORY examination of contemporary events in tropical Africa suggests that one of the main features of native society is the desire for a higher standard of living than is materially possible to the majority of individuals living under a tribal system of economics. This is borne out in countries as far apart as Tanganyika and the Gold Coast. It is reflected in a good deal of political unrest, and is shown by widespread and popular movements from the country areas to the mines and to the towns and, in fact, to almost any place where money can be earned. It is demonstrated concretely by an emulation of western forms of dress and housing, and by an urge to acquire technical and industrial skills of a western kind. European currency, schools, and modern methods of travel and transportation by railway, lorry, bicycle, and steam launch aid the process since they enable a person not only to move away from, but to earn a living for himself outside the traditional organization of kindred and tribe.

In Sierra Leone, in general, and in Mendeland, in particular, these modern desires and incentives are the product of many factors besides the two World Wars which affected the rural societies of tropical Africa hardly less than those elsewhere. In Sierra Leone, however, the psychological and cultural change was not properly set in motion until the beginning of the present century. Anxious as were the inhabitants of the hinterland in pre-Protectorate days for gunpowder, rum, and a number of other goods that the British traders, Creole and European, could supply, they had little or no use for the non-material traits of Western culture. It was strictly against etiquette for a chief to use anything but the native language in front of his people, and persons who emulated western habits in any way were jeered at and ridiculed.

Probably, it was the unchallengeable political and military superiority of the British, coupled with the extension of a money economy throughout the Protectorate, which was the most significant factor. Money itself came rapidly into use as a standard of value and medium of exchange. Native producers who had previously bartered or made a more or less direct exchange of their palm kernels for Manchester cloths were now paid in cash. The Government required its House Tax in cash, and in the construction of the Sierra Leone Railway the up-country labour employed on the 'navvying' was also paid in cash. Undoubtedly, all this helped to stimulate the demand for 'cop-por', as Alldridge noted when he returned to the country in 1905. It was the one thing that everyone valued. On his previous visit, a few years before the Mende Rising, he found persons treating English gold sovereigns as curiosities and playing with them as if they were marbles. He also recalls that in the old days silver coins were melted down for ornaments.[1]

In addition, the opening up of the country for trade and evangelization and the gradual enlargement of the Administration itself helped to bring Protectorate people in much closer contact with western ideas and values. The native youth who joined a mission station as catechist or scholar, or who took a post in a Government or mercantile office or store automatically divorced himself in a large measure from tribal life. He speedily discovered that to gain acceptance in his new surroundings it was necessary to emulate some, at least, of its standards. From this, to the next stage of actively seeking recognition in western or westernized circles, was only a short step. Once taken, however, it had wide repercussions on other members of native society because of its implied association with the ruling race. Those who took the step gained extra prestige and in so doing they spread the idea of western habits and western ways the more rapidly among the rest. Finally, their success stimulated a special incentive towards western education as the obvious gateway to similar opportunities.

2. *The Significance of Literacy*

It is largely for the latter reason alone that in the present and

[1] T. J. Alldridge, *A Transformed Colony*, London, Seeley, 1910.

changing conditions of Mendeland and Sierra Leone, as a whole, literacy stands out as a social factor in its own right. Ability to speak English is more than a cultural characteristic, because it means that one of the main disadvantages under which the ordinary native person labours in dealing with Europeans and European culture has been overcome. No longer has he to rely on the goodwill of a third party to state his case. No longer is he restricted to a traditional rôle which he may, or may not, wish to fulfil.

Sociologically, the advantages accruing from having attended school are equally important, but not all of them obvious. A few years at school place the individual on the fringe of a new society. They introduce him to experiences as a literate person which are all the more meaningful through the fresh cultural allegiances thrust upon him. He is made conscious of his new status of literacy in two ways: on the one hand, by the pride he has in displaying the traits of a superior class, for example, in the reading of a book or newspaper in public; and on the other hand, by the reaction of the non-literate people in characterizing him as a 'white man' and as one toward whom they will behave thenceforward with some doubt and suspicion. In effect, he becomes a 'social hybrid'.[1] Lacking confidence in an unfamiliar rôle, he is inclined to turn more to persons in the same marginal position as himself, than, as traditionally, to his own kindred for what he needs in reassurance and moral support. But being geographically more dispersed, the new ties he makes tend to be less intimate than the old ones and depend, to an increasing extent, on the holding of vocational aims in common rather than on the complex of mutual interests and activities which bind together the local group. Moreover, taking an effective part in the literate world usually involves a physical separation from non-literate society or, at any rate, from that section of it with which, in the shape of home and family, the ordinary young man has closest connection.

[1] The implications of this point are appreciated by many of the native people themselves. One of the chiefs commented: 'What is the present object of teaching English ...? It takes Mende children a long time to learn the language, affects far too few to have much effect educationally, and those who get the least smattering of it think they know everything when they don't even know their own people. Either keep a child at school for ten or twelve years, and let him learn the English ways thoroughly, or leave him alone!'

3. *Some Features of the New Society*

In addition to articles of European clothing, the minimal needs of a 'civilized' person include a certain amount of manufactured furniture—a bed, a table, and chairs. His friends will expect to be entertained with European-made drinks and with cigarettes instead of with palm wine. His wife, too, is likely, to an increased extent since the war, to demand a regular supply of pocket money and the means of carrying on petty trade of her own. These ambitions are modest by external standards, but to satisfy them requires European currency in larger amounts and at more regular intervals than most young men can obtain by remaining on the land and working for their fathers or the head of the family. The alternative —a job in the town—increases economic liabilities still further. It puts an extra premium on sociability, a house or rooms may have to be rented, and food, which previously could be taken home from the farm, has to be bought in the market or at the shops at commercial prices.

Some idea of the discrepancy between rural and urban standards may be gained from the following figures. In the case of twelve 'urban' families, comprising Creole and native clerks, carpenters, etc., and their families, the average size of household was 2·1 men, 2·0 women, and 1·0 children. The average annual expenditure per household was about £79, of which nearly half was budgeted for food, about 14 per cent for rent, and about 28 per cent for clothes. In the case of thirteen 'better-off' urban households, comprising senior clerks, factors, etc., the average annual expenditure was about £125, of which some 42 per cent was budgeted for food and some 16 per cent for clothes. It is socially significant, perhaps, that the amount spent on clothes is relatively much larger in smaller incomes than in larger ones.[1]

If these particulars are contrasted with the earnings of people working on the land, the result is striking. According to data relating to sixteen farming households in a relatively prosperous area of the palm belt, the average income, derived from the sale of produce such as palm kernels and oil, rice, cocoa, etc., was

---

[1] For example, in a further sample of nineteen men, who had an average income of some £73 per annum, the proportion spent on clothing the husband and his wife, or wives, was estimated at some 33 per cent, as compared with some 15 per cent in the case of sixteen husbands with an average income of some £194 per annum.

estimated at some £64 per 'family farm'. The average expenditure incurred in production, i.e. in the hire and feeding of labourers, cost of equipment and seed, was some £33 per farm. This also included the cost of clothes, which the head of the household presents to its members on customary occasions during the season and which amounted to about 15*s.* per adult person, including the family head himself. Out of the general proceeds, in return for the work the members of the family do, the head of the household is also expected to help its members in their personal affairs, such as debts, bridewealth, ceremonial obligations in regard to their in-laws, etc. The average composition of these households, including the head but excluding children under puberty, was 8·5 men, 10·5 women, and 4·0 children. Leaving the women and children entirely out of the matter, the difference between £64 and £33 represents an average amount of rather less than £4 per man for the purposes mentioned above. It is true that individual members of the household are usually allowed to do a certain amount of work for themselves, including the marketing of palm kernels, etc., and possibly petty trading and other odd or occasional jobs. Senior members of the household, too, may sometimes expect a small increment in court fees and in return for their patronage. But, allowing for all this and including in the account the £4 referred to above, with the 15*s.* for clothes, it is doubtful whether the gross income of the average male would amount to as much as £10 per annum in monetary terms. There is the government house tax of 9*s.* to pay out of this and, in any case, younger members, because of their junior status, would be likely, as a group, to receive less than the average. Shelter, and food—which is mostly home grown—have, of course, to be reckoned in, but what is sociologically important in the present context is the amount of income which is actually available and spendable in ways demanded by the social situation as a 'civilized' person.

4. *Sources of Social Ambition*

Life in the rural areas and the business of making a farm are both bound up intimately with the tribal system. Non-literate as well as literate young men who have had extensive experience of conditions outside it are likely to find the older controls, particularly the long track of seniority, very irksome. Some of them, who might otherwise be disposed to remain in the villages, complain of the jealousy of their more influential neighbours—of chiefs who will not suffer anyone in their chiefdom to make a larger farm than themselves,[1] of cases of victimization when a man is known to have gained a little wealth; of the 'raking-up' of old 'palavers', and of other methods of extortion, such as repeated claims for 'woman damage' under the guise of native law and custom, and, last but not least, of the continuous and economic burden of relatives and friends in a local community.

Nor, as indicated in Chapter X, does even a senior post in the native administration itself compare very favourably, either in status or increment, with the better jobs in government clerical service and the mercantile firms. Factors employed by the latter may make between £400 and £500 per annum. The resulting trend is socially as well as politically away from tribal affairs and tribal life. The younger generation, both in conversation and on paper, indicated to the writer the growth of a strong feeling of national consciousness. This is often coupled with personal ambition. For example, one young man, aged nineteen, stated:

'My mind is not actually made up for my profession, I feel that our country is vastly in need of men like doctors, engineers, agricultural teachers, and I am prepared for any of these, once I am of use to this Sierra Leone and (am) one of the people who will raise it from its present place to a better and more improved standard. This is the debt I feel I owe to my country, and unless it is paid, I will not be a happy man.'

Expressions of this kind betoken a degree of energy and restlessness which appears to characterize most of the younger people, including the women. Many of the returned soldiers, for instance, have gained a fairly definite picture of what they want in the way of future careers. Most of them wish to improve their material conditions. The army has accustomed them to a plentiful supply of food and to such useful trades as mechanical engineering, telegraphy, etc. Some who have served with the Royal Army Medical Corps have acquired skill as hospital nurses and dispensers. The experiences they relate in the village *barri* and at the market give extra point to the Mende proverb, *Numu ɛ jesia lɔ ah gilɔ yɛ ngi nje, mehɛ yengɔ yakpe mia nengɔ* ('One who has not travelled thinks it is only the food cooked by his mother that is sweet'); a sentiment which aptly describes the increased mobility of Mende society.

[1] Alldridge, op. cit., also makes this point.

THE MODERN SOCIAL TREND

Women can now obtain money for themselves, if necessary outside the patriarchal system of family or kindred. Trading, when it involves movement and travel from one part of the country to another, also promotes new cultural experiences. Psychologically, the contrast between the new and older conditions of living is of considerable significance. Until recently the more remote parts of Sierra Leone had changed little since the Europeans entered the country. The social cycle was more or less intact. Birth, marriage, and funeral ceremonies were unaltered. The ancestors were worshipped and secret-society regulations observed (as they still are to a large extent), and the other religio-magical sanctions retained their old force. Few, if any, of the more impressive inventions of western civilization—such as mechanical and electrical devices—had penetrated far from the railway line, and knowledge of them was merely second-hand. Restraints on women and young men were still fairly strong; domestic slavery, for example, was not officially abolished until 1926. For an individual whose mental horizon has hitherto been bounded almost literally by the bush path around his village, the contrast afforded even by an up-country trading station may be extreme, particularly if it comes at an impressionable time in his life.

One young man described his first walk round a town in the following words:

'I became a sort of idiot as we moved along, for I stood to gaze at whatever English-made articles I have never seen before, for example, cycles, motor cycles, and cars. I took a very keen interest in gazing at two-storey buildings, I admired people moving in them, and I often asked my brother whether they would not fall from there. . . .'

The effect of seeing and moving among strangers for the first time may be equally significant, as is indicated by the following experience of another young man. He was taken from his village at about the age of eleven by his uncle, a government clerk, to a native town about forty miles away.

'My ideas . . . gradually changed . . . for I knew nothing of the world, and I did not think there were any more people beyond the town limits of Largo and Kenema. I only knew of one tribe, Mende, to which I belong and all my people and the inhabitants of the towns around. . . .'

THE MODERN SOCIAL TREND

A train, or the engine, may be a frightening as well as a wonderful object when it is encountered for the first time, and a third young man relates his boyhood reaction to a ride in the following words:

'At the start of the engine I could not even open my eyes to see what beautiful things may be of interest to me. I was in that restless condition until we got to a station. The engine piped again, but this time I was encouraged by a friend to brave it out. On looking out I was stupefied at seeing, and at once assumed that everything else moved with us as we rode on.'

It is also worth remembering that until quite recent times the European himself, with his white skin and different complexion, was thought to be some kind of genie. Early European travellers relate how, on occasion, the people crowded round the hut where they were resting, or even crept into their tent to touch and feel their skin.[1] Something of this attitude, which is not derived directly from the European's official position, still remains, at any rate in places removed from the motor road and railway line.

In the circumstances, therefore, it is not surprising that 'England', the place where these new and wonderful things were made, the home of the 'Europeans'—the ruling class—and the place, moreover, where the successful doctors and lawyers of their own race obtained their training, should be conceived in popular imagination as an El Dorado and 'Land of Opportunity'. Fourteen out of thirty-four older secondary-school boys voluntarily indicated their strong desire, and even intention, of continuing their studies 'overseas', that is, in the United Kingdom. One of them wrote: 'I have already given it as a solemn oath that in due course I shall visit the shores of England for the safety and upkeep of our country'. Ambitions of this kind, indeed, are typical of the general attitude of these members of the younger generation, including the women, whom literacy has placed on the initial rungs of the social ladder. There is evidently a wide conviction that almost any kind of educational qualification obtained in England is a certain guarantee of subsequent success, particularly in government service. It is almost as if the mere touch of English soil wrought a subtle alchemy in the individual's personality and his future prospects. It is hardly necessary to add that many of the notions which are popularly held regarding social life and

[1] cf. Alldridge, *The Sherbro and its Hinterland*, as already quoted in Chapter II.

conditions in England are, at the least, as inaccurate as those held by the majority of English people regarding conditions in West Africa. Perhaps the most common assumptions are that, in England, education is available to everyone, almost without exception, to a university level; that the government controls everything: it finds you a good job and helps to maintain you; and that nearly everybody in England has a 'white-collar job' or has something to do with machines.[1]

5. *The Creole as a Cultural Medium*

The general interest in European civilization and the desire to attain it places special importance on the rôle of Creole people settled in the Protectorate. They are regarded as representatives of Europe. These Creoles as descendants of the original settlers of Freetown and the Colony, have, in fact, been in close touch with England for a long time. They have carried on a variety of professional, clerical, and industrial occupations for more than a hundred years, and so they have evolved a system of social classes. Despite some increase in the number of Protectorate schools and in opportunities for young men of the Protectorate to gain employment with the government Creoles still hold the majority of the better and more responsible jobs in public service all over the country. The Provincial Administration is a possible exception. The 'better-off' class of Creoles have always emulated a European way of life, and their standards have provided an increasing incentive to the native people up-country since the suppression of the Mende Rising in 1898.

More significant, therefore, than any religious idea which the missionaries, both European and Creole, have carried to the Protectorate, is the desire which attendance at a mission school arouses for social acceptance in a world governed by part-European, part-Creole notions of civilized behaviour. The meaning of 'civilized', so far as the native person himself is concerned, varies according to whether he is literate or not. In the eyes of the non-literate man, a 'civilized' individual is a 'book man', 'one who knows book', that is, one who can read. In a more general and quite neutral sense it also means someone who practises European ways or someone who has given up farming and who earns his living in some other way

[1] A boy wrote: 'There are special people in England called "the Government"; these people have spread all over the British Colonies.'

than on the land. It has, in addition, the favourable implications of 'knowledgeable', 'well travelled', 'neat in appearance', and 'generous with money'. In literate eyes it denotes a person who practises European ways—but with the very strong implication that such ways are the 'right ways', in the exact sense in which Sumner interprets the term 'mores'.

European ways, therefore, carry the stamp of the administrative class, and so they have great prestige. The European officials themselves, of course, have the assurance of authority and of a higher income than is enjoyed by most members of the African community. Their status is symbolized effectively in the Court Messengers (native police) who attend them, and they are given immediate attention and precedence in the shops, at the railway station, and in the post office. In the stores they are allowed behind the counter to select what goods they require and are given priority, as a rule, in any article which is in short supply. They have immediate access to any non-European person in a town, including the Paramount Chief. They are generally saluted by the raising or removal of the hat and are addressed as 'sir' by many literate Africans.

All this increases the social distance between them and the Africans, particularly as European officials usually live at least half a mile, and sometimes a mile, from the nearest native dwelling. It means that their habits are difficult to emulate except in material and other forms which can be visually observed. Of their personal ideas and outlook little is known except at second hand, but the design of a European bungalow or the topee and trilby hat, khaki shirt and shorts, in the case of the men, and the two felt hats, one inside the other, worn by some European women as a protection against the sun—these are often imitated. The same applies to some extent to items of European diet, such as tinned fish and meat, and to articles of European furniture and ways of arranging it.

In the field of interpersonal relations or in other fields, such as religious worship—in which the European official rarely participates—the Creole missionary, clerk, trader, or teacher fills the gap, supplies his own code of etiquette, and sets a standard of social attainment which in spending, educational accomplishments, and cultural mannerisms is intermediate to that of the Europeans and the native people. For instance, Creole traits which have been specifically accepted include the Christian profession of religion and regular churchgoing; the use of 'marking rings' and 'engagement Bibles' in the preliminaries of marriage; and, in the case of women wearing the hair straight instead of in plaits.

European and Creole cultures are largely identical. This makes it difficult to say which is the more significant; but data which were collected in regard to the cultural traits of some two hundred Creole and literate native persons in Bo may help to clarify the results of Creole-native contact. From these it would appear that, in descending order of their popularity, the most widely spread western characteristics and habits, as distinct from native ones, are in style of dress, religion, profession, leisure-time activities—including games and club affiliations—marital status (i.e., monogamy as distinct from polygamy), food-taking habits, style of house decoration, and marriage ceremonies. So far as could be gathered from the same particulars, every native individual undergoes a certain amount of 'creolization', or the process of taking on Creole habits, once he begins to dissociate himself from tribal life. Needless to add, creolization is more evident, as a rule, in the case of persons who have attended school, but even illiterate persons become creolized to some extent by using the Creole speech, or Krio as it is termed,[1] and by adopting Creole dishes, such as foo-foo.

The tendency also shows itself in social selection. There are instances of Moslem men, polygamously married in native fashion, putting away their wives in order to secure a Creole bride. To facilitate this, they undergo Christian baptism and exchange their Arabic and native names of, say, Mustapha or Lansana for English and Christian ones such as John or Joseph. The culmination is reached when an individual who has been born and bred in the Colony and has adopted a Colony name actually succeeds in 'passing' as a Creole.[2] Another way of expressing social ambition is to adopt the *Krio* language.

6. *The Effect on Group Relations*

This general process, and intermarriage in particular, takes place in a context of group consciousness and of a certain amount of resistance from the parties concerned, i.e. Creole and literate

[1] cf. V. E. J. Buckle, 'The Language of the Sierra Leone "Creo"', *Sierra Leone Studies*, Vol. XXI, 1939.

[2] The *Sierra Leone Census*, 1931, also alludes to this point in attempting to account for a fairly substantial and unexpected rise in the Creole section of the population since previous censuses.

THE MODERN SOCIAL TREND

native. A Protectorate girl may be taken severely to task for going about with a Creole man and censured for marrying him. No objection to a Creole man's having a Protectorate 'friend' is raised by other Creoles, but he runs some danger of criticism and loss of status if he marries her. This is because there is some tendency to regard the native from the point of view of the Creole's European social heritage. A Creole may refer, sometimes, to native people as 'aboriginals', or as 'uncivilized'—expressions at which the latter, if they are literate, take considerable umbrage. The native man retorts by disparaging the Creole's historic rôle as a landless newcomer—and as the 'son of a slave'. He resents intensely what he regards as the Creole habit of 'looking down' on the Protectorate and may instance an occasion when a Creole individual, with whom he was on fairly intimate terms up-country, has refused to recognize him at his (the Creole's) home in Freetown. Creoles, on their part, sometimes object to a native's speaking to them in English instead of *Krio*. To speak English is to associate one's self with the ruling European class, and the implication is that in using it, the native man is claiming social superiority over the Creole whom he addresses.

Use of *Krio* among Creoles themselves has the effect of strengthening their own feeling of cultural and group solidarity in the face of Protectorate aggression.[1] It is also a mark of a category of person socially superior to the less well educated and less wealthy Protectorate individual, who adopts it, sometimes in order to identify himself with the Creoles.

At the bottom of the scale the situation is similar. There distinction is between non-literate Africans on the one hand, and literate Africans. For sociological purposes the wearing of shoes and stockings and some proficiency in the use of English, as against going barefoot and speaking *only* a native language and/or *Krio* are sufficient, though minimal, criteria at which to draw the line between the two groups. There is a certain amount of antipathy between them, though for reasons which are slightly different from those which predispose Creole and literate native rela-

[1] For example, in government departments in Freetown, which are staffed mainly by Creole clerks who resent, in some cases, the intrusion of Protectorate individuals into an occupation which, until fairly recently, was virtually a prerogative of their own.

Feeling has been considerably enhanced, more recently, by the question of relative Protectorate and Colony representation in proposals for the reconstituted Legislative Council.

tions. The ordinary non-literate person is less frustrated by being socially excluded from the 'civilized' world than by being denied access to its material advantages. He is envious of the better clothes, the larger supply of enamelware and other goods which a literate person can usually manage to acquire. He resents having to use the literate man as an intermediary in order to make himself intelligible to a European. In addition, he is inclined to suspect the literate people of 'betraying' him to white men over native custom. He is conscious, moreover, of a certain superiority in their attitude towards him and towards his manual occupation.

The literate native person is well aware of this attitude, but his own reaction is largely defensive. The more ambitious he is, the more likely is it that his family has to support him, particularly in an economic sense. Usually, therefore, he is inclined to accommodate himself as far as possible to non-literate opinion in the various ways demanded of him, such as attendance at family ceremonies, funerals, etc. Creoles, however, have less to lose and are less inclined to compromise, particularly over native customs which they regard as undignified or degenerate.

In general, there is a wide social and economic gap between Europeans and the African community in the Protectorate, and mutual antipathies are not so obvious as they are in the Colony. The non-literate and poorly educated native people generally accept without particular question the socially superior position of the Europeans and even 'prefer' them in some ways to the Creole. Better educated Protectorate individuals and many Creoles, however, tend to comment adversely on the aloofness of the Europeans and speak bitterly about the extra privileges and higher standard of living which they enjoy. The European official, in return, usually prefers the 'bushman' and is inclined to attribute whatever failings he finds in the literate native to the latter's association with Colony people. Between other Europeans, who are mainly missionaries, and the African community as a whole, relations are much easier. Antagonisms are not absent from either side but are expressed more on personal than on racial grounds.

7. *A Structural Analysis of the Situation*

These considerations and the fact that differences are socially recognized in the ways described above provide us with the means of analysing the present trend in structural terms. We may regard

'European', 'Creole', 'Literate native', and 'Non-literate native' as the labels of four fairly distinct classes. These are marked off from each other by various forms and degrees of social distance, the most obvious of which is the residential separation of the European and the deference paid him by the rest of the community. Moreover, the fact that the classes in question are esteemed according to their possession of appropriate educational, occupational, and other traits means that they can be arranged in order of social precedence. For example, the European class, by virtue of its political position and the prestige attached to European behaviour, is in control of the system as a whole. The basis of classification is similarity of occupation, wealth, and education, modes of life, a similar stock of ideas, feelings, attitudes, and a feeling of belonging to one group.

(a) *The 'European' class.* Members of the European class do administrative or supervisory work. They all finished their education at either a university or a secondary school. They are nearly all in receipt of an annual income of more than £400. They dress in shirts and shorts during the day and don trousers and, very often, mosquito boots in the evening. They have food habits more or less in common and also share recreational interests in tennis, bridge, drinking, etc. They share rather similar attitudes towards the Africans, which include a taboo on intermarriage and, to a substantial degree, on eating together. This feeling of belonging to one racial group, coupled with such a high degree of social exclusiveness, suggests that the term 'class' has some implications of 'caste'. It is less relevant, however, in the case of missionary members of the group.

(b) *The 'Creole' class.* Most members of the 'Creole' class have attended a secondary school. Occupationally they are to be found in the higher grades of the government clerical service or are senior schoolmasters, factors for European firms, or members of the clergy. They earn from about £200 per annum upward. Members of this class profess either Christianity or Islam, usually the former. They practise monogamy, follow the social etiquette of the better-off people of the Colony. On the whole, this class contains relatively few natives of the Protectorate. Protectorate individuals who qualify for it tend to form a separate, though not exclusive, clique of their own. Class consciousness is felt mainly in the appreciation of the superior standard of living which they as a class enjoy over the rest of the African community and in their greater knowledge of the correct etiquette of social behaviour as compared with the class immediately beneath them. Most of its members adhere either to Anglicanism or Methodism, and regular attendance at church and participation in church activities are regarded as desirable behaviour. Monogamy is almost a *sine qua non*, but a certain amount of extra-marital licence is permitted. Houses are sometimes furnished elaborately with a full selection of European articles, including pictures. Older persons play games such as whist and bezique; the younger ones, tennis, football, and cricket. The women are largely engaged in household duties, including minding children for relatives. One or more servants are always employed,[1] sometimes to look after the younger children. At other times the women do needlework.

The sexes mix freely and come together for mutual entertainment on occasions like weddings and christenings, which are usually celebrated with some ceremony. Drinks like bottled beer, whiskey, and gin are generally offered; palm wine is drunk rarely and is scarcely ever offered to a guest. The men wear European clothes on all occasions, i.e. khaki or white shirts and shorts in the office, lounge suits for more formal gatherings, and evening dress or dinner jacket for dances. The women usually follow the Colony style of a head-tie and print frock during the daytime and on most weekdays, though some women wear hats. On Sundays a silk dress with a hat and stockings are worn: long frocks are *de rigueur* for dances. The sexes usually take meals together, and popular dishes are foo-foo, Joloff rice, salad, etc. Rice is treated as a staple, but tinned foods, particularly fruit, are often eaten also.

In the largest town in the Protectorate the social activities of this class are institutionalized in an 'African Club', where there are a small library and facilities for reading, dancing, games, and dramatic entertainment. Membership is restricted to persons of African descent, and prospective members have to be proposed and seconded. The entrance fee is 10s. 6d., and there is a monthly subscription of 3s. Dances are held on most public holidays and attract visitors from towns on the motor road as far distant as thirty miles. Cost of admission to these functions varies between 2s. 6d. and 5s. Women come free, by invitation. There is a swing band and a full European programme of rumbas, waltzes, fox trots, and lancers is followed. 'Literary evenings' and similar meetings

---

[1] 'Servants', it should be noted, include older children who, according to custom, are being 'minded'.

comprise lectures or talks, given, as a rule, by members of the European community or by individuals of note who may be travelling through the town. The club also sponsors and organizes athletic sports and entertains strangers on the occasion of an inter-town football match. The various club offices are keenly contested, and the club's invitation confers a degree of social prestige on the recipient.

(c) *The 'Literate Native' Class*. The 'Literate native' class consists in the broadest sense of every other African who has been to school or who can speak English with a reasonable amount of proficiency. It is sociologically inclusive, therefore, not only of the majority of educated Protectorate people but also of the lesser educated, less wealthy Creole.[1] He is to be thought of more accurately, perhaps, as a member of the same social group as the literate native persons concerned. To a large extent, it is 'Protectorate conscious', but literate native people and the Creoles who move with them are alike in being distinguished from the non-literate and tribal group.

The range of this class is wide enough in income, occupation, and cultural characteristic to permit some sub-division. The upper stratum would include junior clerks in government service, members of the staff of the railway, artisans, motor drivers, and male and female nurses. Their level of income is from some £50 per year upward. The same stratum includes a large number of Moslems as well as Christians. The latter are often converts of the Roman Catholic or of the United Brethren in Christ Missions, a project of American Moravians. Marriages are polygamic as well as monogamic. Houses are decorated and furnished in the European style so far as the means of the individual allow. Social activities are generally similar to those of the 'Creole' class, and some 'Literate native' individuals belong to the club mentioned above and take a prominent part in its activities. Members of the 'Literate native' class also take a lively interest in Moslem festivals and sponsor and participate in exhibitions of native dancing and games. Native dress is worn on such occasions and, sometimes, after the day's work is over. Otherwise, the class follows as far as it is able the dress habits of the Creole. Similar considerations affect the question of meals and the etiquette of social intercourse. Individuals whose wives are non-literate eat separately or with their male friends.

[1] This classification needs qualification, however, in the case of the lesser educated, less well-off Creole who, irrespective of circumstances, still tends to consider himself superior to the Protectorate-born person.

They are not accompanied, as a rule, by their wives to any European type of occasion, such as a dance, unless the latter are literate.

The other stratum of the 'Literate' class comprises individuals in clerical employment outside the government, such as assistants to Lebanese, lower technical grades on the railway, tailors, mechanics, and the permanent but non-clerical staff of government departments. It also includes senior members of the Court Messenger force (if literate). A rough estimation of income would be a minimum of £25 per year. This stratum is predominantly native, but there is a sprinkling of individuals from the Colony. The womenfolk are generally non-literate. Customary behaviour is largely on traditional lines, and material equipment is limited to a few articles of European manufacture, including domestic utensils, along with native-made beds and stools. The native form of religion is practised in addition to Christianity and Islam among this group, and some of them belong to the Ahmaddiyya sect of Islam. A relatively large number of the individuals concerned are single young men, who rent a room or a house, which they share with other men. They drink palm wine and the cheaper South African wines. Food is prepared in native fashion and is invariably eaten separately from the women. It usually consists of native dishes, such as palm oil 'chop', but tinned foods are used occasionally, along with bottled cooking fats.

A large number of the 'Literate' class as a whole have been initiated in the Poro society, and some of them continue to play a part in Poro activities. Generally their social life is institutionalized also on more modern lines. For instance, in the town to which reference was made above, there are the Hunter's Society and the *Ogugu*, in addition to two societies, the *Almania* and *Tarancis*, which exist as mutual-aid societies as well as for the purpose of sponsoring native dancing. The Hunter's Society is limited to male members, and its purpose, as the name implies, is the hunting and shooting of game. Meetings are held once a week at which members pay a subscription of 6d. Rifles and shotguns owned by individual members are used communally to secure fowl and deer in the swamps outside the town. The *Ogugu* is confined to Aku people, as Yorubas are called in Sierra Leone. Most of its members have married local women. A subscription of 1s. a member per month is collected, and the society has its own medicine, which is used for skin complaints.

Communication between members of this class as a whole and with the Creole class is carried on in a native language or in *Krio*. English is generally used only on a formal occasion, such as a speech; in connection with a specific form of European activity, such as a game; or in contacts with Europeans, principally of an official or business kind. Among the 'Creole' class, *Krio* is generally used, but English is also used, on occasion, in conversation with another African, if the latter is a stranger of some importance.

The fact that every native member and many Creole members of the 'Literate' class have either a wife or relatives who are non-literate is enough to guarantee their continued connection in one way or another with tribal society. By virtue of their education and official position in the government, a number of literate native people play a large part in family affairs. Some of them retain an active interest in the question of succession to a chieftaincy and find it essential to maintain local contacts, if only for the sake of 'nursing their constituency'. The result is that their advice and help are often in demand. They are expected to contribute lavishly to family ceremonies, particularly at funerals, and may be made responsible for the care and education of younger brothers or nephews.

(*d*) *The 'Non-Literate' class.* The fact that the conditions which make for prestige among the literate sections of Sierra Leone society operate to a smaller extent among the non-literate people might constitute some objection against their being included in the hierarchical system. On the other hand, it is out of their ranks that the literate native class is mainly recruited. In addition, the non-literate people as a social class are clearly characterized by facts and circumstances which have already been enumerated and which include, as well as non-literacy itself, similarity in occupation—which is farming—in traditional and tribal customs, in a lower standard of living than the rest of society, and, to some extent, in consciousness of themselves as a specific group. In other words, if the principle of stratification is extended to their case, they constitute, from the point of view of numbers, the very broad base of the social pyramid.

8. *Conclusion*

Thus, it may be said in summary that there are signs of a new social system in Mendeland and the Sierra Leone Protectorate.

THE MODERN SOCIAL TREND

This system, as a whole, comes from the new values brought by a capitalist-money economy and it has its main basis in literacy and the opportunities afforded by literacy. It is at a very embryonic stage, partly because differences in income are small. Primary schools have been in existence in the Protectorate for barely two generations, and secondary education, so far, has touched only a very small proportion of the population. This means that considerations of heredity which help to determine the form of more developed systems of class have not yet become important. Social mobility still depends largely on personal qualities.

These social changes illustrate the dynamism of the acculturative process. The process itself may be summed up in four broad propositions: (1) An increasing number of individuals no longer acknowledge the tribal and other sanctions to which they were formerly subject. (2) Older values and forms of social prestige are being replaced by new ones. (3) There is a growing tendency for an individual's social position to be assessed with reference to the community rather than to his own family. (4) The kind of relations between individuals who gain their living in some western form of employment is giving rise to a type of social structure in which status is assigned increasingly according to factors, such as income, occupation, and education, which originate in a western system of values.

The social situations which these propositions summarize may be seen, in turn, as functions of the gradual spread of the western market economy.[1]

[1] cf. Karl Polyani, *The Great Transformation*, for an historical examination of this economic aspect of social change in terms of the self-regulating mechanism of the market economy.

APPENDIX I

THE PART OF ISLAM IN MENDE LIFE

It will be obvious from the foregoing chapters of this book that persons professing some connection with Islam play quite an important part in the general organization of Mende religious and magical life. The rôle of the *mori*-man, as a practitioner in medicine, has been mentioned more than once. One of the main reasons why Islam, in a popular form, has made such strides among the people of Sierra Leone is clearly its readiness to adjust itself to the indigenous system. This is amply demonstrated by the presence of Moslem traits in many otherwise indigenous ceremonials. It is borne out even in the Poro bush where, for example, footwear is prohibited in entering the sacred places. There is the further instance, among non-Moslems, in the ceremony known in Mende as *teindia-mei*—'crossing the water'—which is the culminating point in a person's burial rites. Here, again, one finds substitutions of popular versions of entry into the Islamic Heaven in terms of 'crossing a bridge'.[1]

Broadly speaking, the regular profession of Islam is confined to two sections of society in Mendeland. These are the ruling classes and the immigrant Mandingo and Susu traders. The latter are Islam's principal exponents and disseminators. Historically, the connection with the ruling class may be accounted for, partly, through a number of present chiefs being themselves of Mandingo origin. There is also the probability that in early times military prestige and Islam were closely correlated. Though the former war-chiefs were not necessarily Moslems themselves, most of them

[1] A large number of the proper names in general use among the Mende are corruptions of the names of Moslem saints and locally well-known 'holy men' and Moslem big men, viz. Siaffa from Mustapha; Luseni from Alhusaine; Momo from Mahomet; Adama from Adam, etc.

appear to have employed a Moslem 'priest' as regular adviser and worker of medicine on their behalf. Their success as warriors and conquerors was largely attributed, therefore, to the latter's special power over medicine, though the fact that the priest was, or called himself, a Moslem was probably, at first, quite incidental.

However, the association no doubt grew and developed with the consolidation of the chief's own position. Probably, it has also been helped by the comparative wealth and skill of the Mandingoes and Susu themselves and by the respect they enjoy as traders, dealers, and goldsmiths. The latter group is also particularly effective as a prototype; in that they are invariably ostentatious in the practise of their faith. No less significant, in this respect, in the eyes of the Mende upper class is the fact that the Mandingo and Susu are observably more successful in keeping their womenfolk out of the way of other men and under general control. In the social disruption of present times this is a consideration of importance for those who have 'invested' heavily in wives. If a Mandingo or Susu wife commits adultery, she is ostracized for a time by her husband and his relatives, and is made to feel that she has done something shameful. Her husband is stricter, too, in demanding obeisance from her, and does not allow her to take part in public gatherings, other than Moslem feasts and ceremonies. If she has occasion to visit the house or home of her parents, she is accompanied by a male relative of the husband. It is generally noteworthy, in fact, that Islam lays down a more rigid code of sex morality than is sanctioned by indigenous belief and very often the preaching of the Imam in the mosque is to the effect that women should be obedient to their husbands in order to be fruitful— *Nyahanga, a goo wu hinga wɛ!*

On account of these and similar reasons, it is a mark of prestige in non-literate Mende society to profess Islam.[1] Among the small European-educated group, however, Christianity usually comes first in this. Of those chiefs who are Christians, most find it politically expedient to support Moslem practices in various ways and to treat the Moslem Imam and 'Alfas' with the greatest respect. Sometimes, disputes between Moslems which would ordinarily be

[1] Significantly enough, this popularity of Islam is combined with more than tacit disapproval of the Ahmaddiyyah sect which is trying to proselytize the Protectorate. The Ahmaddiyyah allow women in the mosque alongside the men, discountenance large scale polygyny, etc., and it is not surprising that their followers are drawn from the poorer class of society.

settled in Court are handed over to the Imam for treatment and judgment. In fact, in general, it would be fair to say that the ordinary Mende ruler exercises a good deal of tactful catholicity in religious matters. Whilst anxious to offend neither Moslems nor the Christian Missions, he is also expected to keep up ancestral and other cults, not merely as religious institutions, but because they are an essential part of the indigenous body of custom which it is his traditional duty to maintain.

It would obviously be a mistake, therefore, necessarily to assume that Moslems in Mende society are strict adherents of the code they profess. If the ordinary Mende man abstains from alcohol and restricts the number of his wives, there are economic reasons as well as the stricture of the Qur'ān to be considered. It is noteworthy, too, that the Islamic features most markedly and generally observed are those which recapitulate significant traits in the existing cultural pattern. Funeral rites and other opportunities for conspicuous consumption, and feasts which afford a chance for conviviality and entertainment are the occasions when Islamic procedure comes mainly into operation. The ceremonies which mark the ending of the great fast of *Ramadan* are an obvious example of this in bringing out Moslems and non-Moslems alike. This may be illustrated by the following short description of the day's events at Bo, the largest town in Mendeland.

'Dancing, which marked the ending of the fast, commenced in the town about 8 o'clock the previous evening. The women also began to prepare food for the morrow.

'The fast was broken at 6.30 the next morning, and the majority of people in the town were soon engaged in ironing clothes, cleaning out their houses, cutting their hair, and bathing. By 8 o'clock most of them had already donned their newest and finest clothes. It is the custom of farmers who are Moslems to present clothing materials to the members of their households at this season of the year. By 9 o'clock there was a general move to the praying field a short distance outside the town. Various big men took their families and friends up there in lorries which they had specially chartered for the occasion. The Paramount Chief arrived about the same time in a hammock followed by his courtiers, and he was given a seat in the front. The remainder of the townspeople took up their position alongside him and behind him, ranged according to rank and *kuwui* and with the elders in front. The crowd was estimated roughly at about 1,000 men and 400 women.

'The assembly was called to prayer at 9.15 by the Aladan. All turn towards the east. The Imam leads the prayer and the Aladan repeats it in a louder voice. Allah is praised seven times with the people standing and posturing. Quotations from the Qur'ān follow and the congregation prostrates itself on the ground. Then, the Imam is helped up onto a platform and preaches a sermon. He tells the people how the day should be spent. They should sacrifice something to God, and give alms to the poor and gifts to the friends who call on them. But they should not steal another person's money to do this. He then gave a brief history of the Fast itself.

'After the service was over the crowd broke up in joy and excitement, and there was a rush to greet the Imam. The press was so great that the Chief let him ride in his own hammock back to the town. The people then moved back to their homes, taking care to use a route different from the one they had followed up to the praying field. The Imam was taken first to the Chief's *barri* in the latter's compound, and was greeted there by the Chief. After this, the big women of the town left, escorted by their followers, and the Imam returned to his own house with a large crowd following him.

'In the meantime, the goats, sheep, and cows are being slaughtered, as a sacrifice, in the compounds of the leading men in the town.[1] The meat is shared out in the compound and portions of it are sent round to friends and relatives. The poorer people are allowed to help themselves to the special rice cakes which have been made. Whilst this is going on, parties of singers are being formed. These are mainly composed of women, all of whom wear the same style and colour of smock and head-tie. Led by drummers and rattling their "shake-shakes", they visit neighbouring compounds where they are given small "dashes".

'At 2 o'clock, the *Tarancis* society starts its display of native dancing in the main *barri*, and the *Almania* begin to perform on similar lines in another quarter of the town. These dances and the singing parties continued their activities until 8.30 p.m., when the rain started, and the singers congregated in the verandas of houses.'

Finally, this further account of the burial of a Moslem woman, who was a 'big woman' of the town, helps to illustrate how Moslem

[1] At a very conservative estimate, about 8 cows and 28 sheep were killed, representing in value about £100.

and indigenous custom are intermingled in the funeral rites, and how at the same time the customary features of singing and dancing continue to play their part.

'Fatmatta, who was the head of an important *kuwui* in the town, died at 9 o'clock in the morning. "She wouldn't be helped on the way", i.e. died very slowly, was the comment of one of her relatives. Her passing was marked by beating the chiefdom drum in the chief's *barri*. Within the compound all was quiet, with members of the family going silently about their business. The late woman's husband, a man of about 65, was already showing signs of mourning; his clothes were disarrayed. The women had already started to wash the corpse. Their clothes, also, were in disarray, with the smock leaving one shoulder bare. Some, as they approached the death chamber, took off their head-ties and tied them round the waist, as is the custom when a special effort is required. Others had their *lappas* folded in a bundle on their heads.

'At about 9.40, the crying "broke" as a long plaintive wail from the room where the corpse was lying, covered by a sheet, on the bed. About fifty women were seated inside, by this time, on chairs and on the floor. They were all of them wailing, some louder than others, and falling into an occasional paroxsym. This went on for about half an hour, but it ceased altogether on one of the age-mates of the deceased saying that the dead woman had asked that there should be little weeping. In the meantime, a number of newcomers had arrived. Each took off any footwear she was wearing as she entered the room and joined in the crying. Presently, those inside began to chant verses from the Qur'ān. These were sung very softly.

'Male visitors and members of the family stayed outside the room and one or two lit cigarettes. Visitors continued to arrive, including a local Hadji and one or two prominent Moslem elders. Each saluted the relatives with the customary half clasp of the hand. A literate person present was asked to write a note to the Chief informing him that it had been decided that a certain person should act as temporary head of the *kuwui*. The proper person to succeed the late woman was away in another part of the country. A subscription list of sympathizers was then opened, and each person on entering or leaving the compound dropped coins on to a plate giving their names to the scribe, who entered the amount on a piece of paper. They were classified according to whether they were relatives, fellow Moslems, or "well wishers".[1] Fresh and more sporadic outbursts of weeping followed from the room and were succeeded by a recital of the dead woman's history by some of the age-mates, which included the main events of her life. The chanting was then resumed, accompanied by a rhythmic flicking of the thumb against the first finger and dropping of the fist on the palm of the other hand. The woman's husband continued to make periodic appearances clutching his head and groaning. Seeing him, a brother of the woman broke forth with the cry, "My sister is gone!"

'The more important visitors now began to arrive, headed by the Chief himself, who was related to the woman. After greeting the relatives, he told them that their choice of a temporary head was a foolish one as the person was a gambler. He then pulled out a large pile of coins and handed over an amount of £20. The Speaker followed with a much smaller sum, commenting aside that these were some of the expenses of a Mende man. Chairs were brought for the Chief and other important visitors and they took up their place on the veranda. The widower was then led away to be consoled by the women. A member of the family sent word for a sheep to be bought and the singing started afresh.

'It continued until nearly 4 o'clock, the time fixed for the burial. In the meantime, a group of women singers arrived and proceeded to dance round the dead woman's house.[2] Then, the Chief and principal Moslems in the town took their places in the funeral procession and the corpse was brought out and placed on a wooden bier under a white shroud. This gave members of the crowd standing around the opportunity to come forward and say if anything was owed them by the deceased.[3] Various relatives,

---

[1] The amount of 'sympathy' displayed over the total ceremonies realized some £85 in monetary terms. A large part of this sum was spent on the purchase of animals for sacrifice and to feed the mourners and other guests. The balance went to the dead woman's children and grandchildren.

[2] The dancing and singing are quite 'secular' in style, and it is doubtful if any direct ritual implication can be read into the performance. Probably, it may be explained as (a) to lighten the hearts of the sorrowful and (b) in celebration of the new status which the dead person is in process of attaining.

[3] It is the custom for a person's creditors to help in his funeral ceremonies, and the acceptance of their presents by the family means that the latter also accept the obligation for any debts. A peculiarly Moslem custom is to make public forgiveness at the graveside of any wrongs the deceased person committed during his lifetime to the individual who recites them.

including the husband, also said their last words to the corpse. The procession then moved off to the Moslem cemetery about half a mile outside the town. It was headed by the leading Moslems carrying the bier and singing sorrowfully. At the cemetery, the women stayed about fifty yards away from the grave which was already prepared. A daughter of the dead woman brought forward a young boy, the deceased's grandson, to pluck away the shroud, but she was told that the custom was no longer followed and sent away.[1] Country cloths were removed from the body and sent back to the house. Prayers were then said by one of the Moslem "big men" present; a number of men let themselves down into the grave; the corpse was lowered after them, and green leafy branches were dropped on top of it to shield it from the earth which followed.

'As the crowd moved back to the house, the women singers who had accompanied the procession, danced through them and then around the neighbouring houses, when the compound was reached. Outside the house, a number of pestles and mortars had been left, formally displayed on the ground. The female mourners returned to the late woman's room, and more singers arrived. Then three large portions of rice flour crowned with kola nuts were brought out and shared among any who cared to partake of them. A female sheep was brought forward and was held down whilst its throat was severed with a knife. Whilst this was going on, the people around stooped to the ground, holding out their right hands with palms extended in the direction of the "sacrifice", and touching the ground with their left hands.[2] Some touched the sacrificer to associate themselves more closely with the proceedings. A "big man" came forward and proceeded to skin and cut up the carcase of the dead animal.[3] The various portions, liver, intestines, etc., were then sent over to the heads of neighbouring "compounds". In the room inside the house the women continued to cry, whilst parties of women outside continued their dancing and singing.'

[1] The actual custom is for the youngest male member of the family to remove the shroud from the corpse. He walks over the bier three times for a woman, or four times for a man, before taking it back to the house. If he turns his head on the way, he will see the deceased. The shroud, which is of plain white country cloth, is then dyed and he wears it as a garment.

[2] It was explained that the purpose of this particular rite was to prevent the decomposition of the corpse.

[3] Needless to say, skinning an animal is a skilled operation and is taught to specific persons in the Poro bush.

THE PART OF ISLAM IN MENDE LIFE

As is usual with Moslems, these ceremonies and sacrifices were repeated on the seventh and fortieth day after the death, as well as on the third day, when the 'indigenous' funeral rites are concluded.

APPENDIX II

THE *BONGA*-TRADERS

DRIED fish, mainly *bonga*, are the basis of the 'soup' with which the Mende savour their rice and other carbohydrate diets, and it provides the principal form of animal protein in their food. A qualitative analysis of a sample of such a soup showed the presence of monosaccharide sugar, protein, fats, cellulose, water, sodium chloride, phosphorus, calcium, and nitrates. The soup consisted of *bonga* fish, okra, palm oil, salt, pepper, and onions. About half of it was composed of water and roughage in almost equal parts, and proteins comprised another quarter.[1]

Meat is eaten, sometimes, in the shape of small bush animals and deer and leopard; but apart from hunting and trapping the only animals 'killed' are cows, goats, sheep, and fowls on ceremonial occasions. Cows are brought by lorry from the north, mainly from Kabala, and from French Guinea via Kailahun. They are slaughtered in the large towns on the railway line and, sometimes, at places on the motor roads. But market meat, as such, is bought and consumed only by the wealthier town population and does not find its way into the villages.

So far as Mende country and much of the interior of Sierra Leone is concerned, fish is obtained largely from fishing grounds off Sherbro Island and outside Shenge and around Plantain Island. It is usually dried at these centres of production before it is taken up-country by lorry, launch, and rail (see attached map). Broadly speaking, the processes of distribution are: (1) from fisherman to local trader, who sells in the adjacent markets of Bonthe and Shenge; (2) from local trader to up-country traders, who sell in

[1] I am indebted to Mr. O. Bassir of Bo School for this analysis.

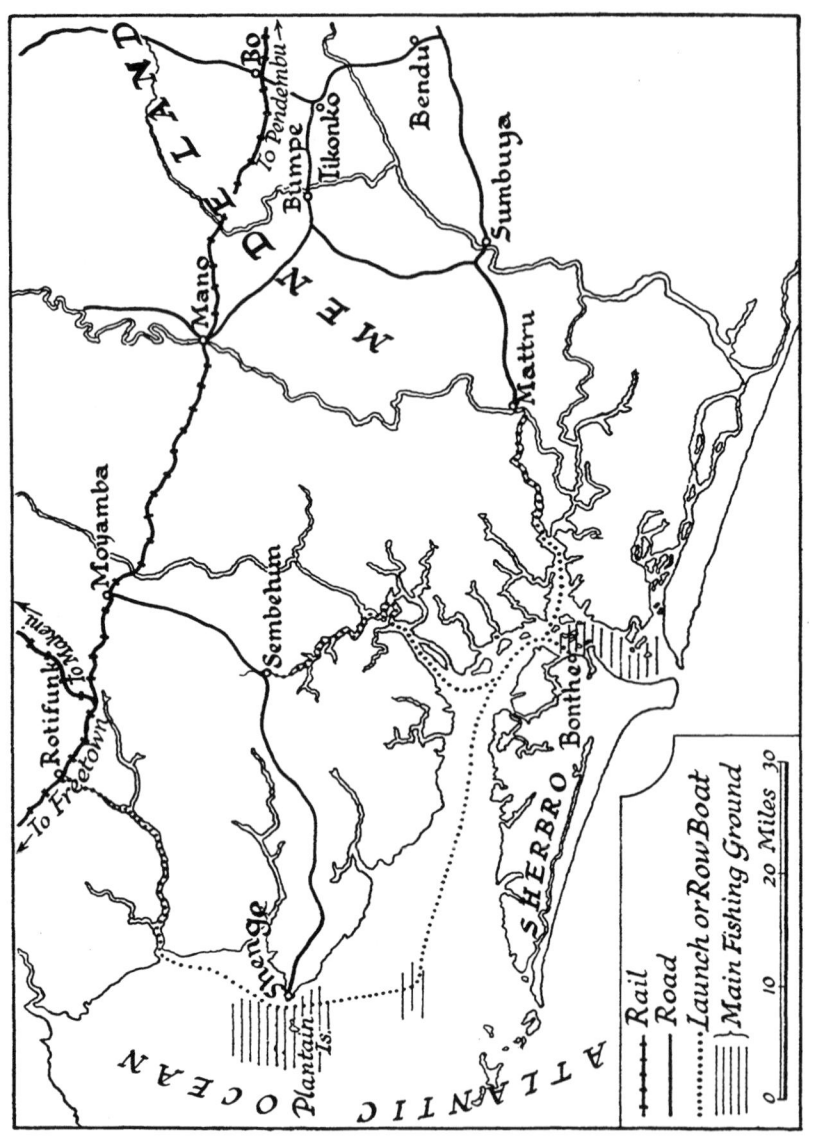

MAP OF COASTAL FISHING GROUNDS

THE BONGA-TRADERS

turn at large up-country markets, either direct to the consumer or to small local traders who, in their turn; (3) sell at local markets in the bush.

The fishing 'ports', Bonthe and Shenge,[1] are therefore the primary centres of distribution; the up-country markets in towns like Moyamba, Mano, and Bo, (see map) on the railway line are secondary centres; and the much smaller 'bush' market in surrounding towns and villages is the third and final centre of distribution. Sometimes, however, there are two intermediate stages; in that up-country traders from towns further up the railway line may buy supplies at a point between their own town and the 'port'. Examples of this are traders from Segbwema, about 200 miles up the line from Freetown, buying at Rotifunk or at Bo.[2]

It will be convenient briefly to describe the industry and marketing process at Bonthe and at Shenge in turn.

The Trade at Bonthe. The supply of fish coming into Bonthe market is regulated, of course, largely by seasonal and fishing conditions. In the height of the tornado season, i.e. at the beginning and ending of the rainy period, only shore fishing is possible in most places. The principal fish caught throughout the year are as follows:

January:	*Adari, bonga, nguangua* (a small-tailed fish).[3]
February:	*Adari, bonga, nguangua.*
March:	*Nguangua.*
April:	*Nguangua.*
May:	Catfish.
June:	Catfish.
July:	'Frupper', skate, barracuda, 'spanish'.
August:	'Frupper', skate, barracuda, 'spanish'.
September:	*Adari, bonga,* 'frupper', 'spanish', barracuda.
October:	As above, and also mackerel, catfish and 'krocoss'[3]
November:	*Nguangua,* adari, and much *bonga.*
December:	*Nguangua,* adari, and much *bonga.*

The fishermen themselves live in villages along the coast, mainly south of Bonthe, and on small islands between Bonthe and

[1] Rotifunk, which is about two days by rowing-boat from the coast, might also be regarded as a 'port' for the Shenge grounds.

[2] Alternatively, as at Shenge, up-country traders may do their business directly with the fisherman.

[3] It is understood that *nguangua* and *krocoss* are Creole names.

the mainland at such places as Yonni on the mainland and Lema, Momboya, Mema, Sham Point, etc.

The following methods of catching fish are practised in the Bonthe area:

(1) The fence (*kulie*) method. This is used where the creek joins the sea. A small fence of sticks about two and a half feet high is constructed. It has a trap door in which the fish are caught on the ebb tide.

(2) By casting nets to which a wooden float is attached. The fisherman stands upright in his canoe to cast the net.

(3) By 'save' boats. A log of wood about two feet long, or a broken calabash, to which lines are attached is anchored by a heavy weight in the sand. The owner of the lines inspects them every seven or ten hours.

(4) Fishing with lines. A number of hooks are attached to lines which the fisherman ties on his wrists or ankles and trails through the water as he paddles his canoe.

(5) A wire netting is set out in a semi-circular form against the inflowing tide and the fish are caught on the ebb, when the tide recedes. This is one method of catching both *bonga* and *adari*.

Usually, the curing of the fish is done by the fishermen, and the fish are left on the beach to dry in the sun after they have been smoked and salted.

Fishermen in the Bonthe area usually own and fish from individual canoes which are about sixteen feet long by nearly two feet wide. These cost 6s. each and are made by canoe-makers. Each man who owns a canoe works independently and makes no contribution to the head of his group of kinsmen.

The fishermen sell their fish at the villages to traders, mainly women, who come over to them by canoe. On the mainland, they trek over on foot. Some of the better-to-do traders bring carriers with them to transport their baskets. When conditions are favourable an individual fisherman may sell as much as £10 to £20 worth of fish in a week (1945). At one village close to Bonthe, *bonga* were being sold at eight or nine for 6d. This was in the month of February. On one of the islands, six *bonga* (uncured) passed for 3d. Transport by canoe costs the trader 6d. per journey, and 6d. is charged as freight for each basket. The transaction between the fisherman and the trader is always in cash, except at isolated islands where manufactured goods are not available and little food is grown. At such places *farinha* (graded cassada) is bartered at the rate of one cigarette cupful for two *bonga*. Occasionally, fishermen take their fish into Bonthe market themselves and sell it in order to buy manufactured goods, such as pans and pots, tobacco, vests, wine, etc., which they sell to their fellow fishermen on the return.[1]

Chiefdom regulations in regard to fishing forbid the acceptance of advances from traders to avoid indebtedness on the part of the fishermen. Traders making contact with a fisherman for the first time, however, give him small presents of tobacco, salt, etc. to gain his good will. A further regulation forbids traders rushing out into the sea to meet incoming canoes owing to the danger of this practice.

Though other articles are also sold in Bonthe market, fish is by far the most important commodity there. The market opens at 5 a.m. every day; and by 8 or 9 o'clock all the fish has been sold. The prices of fish appear to vary quite considerably. Early in November, for example, baskets of fish were making respectively £10, £8, and £5, according to their size. The smallest sized basket contains about nine hundred *bonga*; the largest sized one contains about forty dozen *adari*, or about thirty dozen 'frupper', or *nguangua*. The largest sized basket of *adari* was making £15 to £20, and 'frupper', £10 to £17.

Up-country traders from Bo, Kenema, Segbwema, etc., who buy fish in Bonthe market have to pack the fish themselves. Sometimes, it is also necessary to have the fish smoked before they are sent on the next stage of the journey to join the railway line at Moyamba via launch as far as Sembehun; or travel by lorry to such towns as Sumbuya and Bo via Mattru by launch (see map). The journey from Bonthe to Mattru takes about seven to ten hours according to the speed of the launch and the tide. Launches are operated by Syrian traders and the Government. The journey to Sembehun takes slightly longer. At Mattru, the traders take a mail lorry, or a privately owned lorry which is making the journey to Bo, 58 miles away, or Sumbuya, 20 miles. Fish travelling via Sembehun may be joined on the journey to Moyamba and the railway line by consignments from Shenge, which also travel (in the dry season) by lorry. Most fish consigned up-country takes this route.

The quantity of fish imported through Bonthe depends on the

[1] Fish for Freetown is taken round the coast, sometimes, in large wooden row-boats, or may be railed via Moyamba.

season of the year, as well as on other factors. Some particulars are available in the case of the Mattru route. In the course of 4 days in February, twenty-six large baskets, eight medium-sized ones, and nine small-sized baskets of *bonga* were landed at Mattru. The approximate value of fish leaving Bonthe per week is said to be between £200 and £300.

In addition to the cost of the fish itself, the following expenses would be incurred by a trader from, say, Bo, in connection with his business:[1]

	£	s.	d.
Lorry fare, Bo to Mattru		5	0
Freight of empty basket		1	0
Launch fare, Mattru to Bonthe		2	6
Porterage of basket of fish from Bonthe market back to launch.		1	0
Freight of basket on launch (small basket, 5s.)		7	0
Return fare on launch for self.		2	6
Porterage launch to lorry at Mattru			3
Lorry fare, Mattru to Bo		5	0
Porterage, lorry to lodgings at Bo			5 (or 6d.)
Porterage from lodgings to Bo market			6
	£1	5	2

The price at which *bonga* are eventually sold and retailed is affected not only by costs of transportation, but by the proximity of the market concerned to sources of local fresh water fish and by the possibility of such a market having more than one source of dried fish. Mano, for example, is supplied from Bonthe via Mattru and Moyamba, and from Shenge via both Rotifunk and Moyamba. At Mano, a great deal of fresh water fish is obtained during the dry season from the adjacent river Taia, and this means that although Mano is further from the sources of production than other markets, the dried variety may actually be cheaper there at certain times. These conditions may be exemplified by a number of retail prices for *bonga* in the month of February. The price in Bonthe was 3d. for four; in Sumbuya, 3d. for three; in Bo, 3d. for one; in Mano, 3d. for two; in Tikonko, 4d. or 5d. for one; in Bumpe, 3d. for one. The two latter places, Tikonko and Bumpe, are off the railway line.

The Industry at Shenge. *Bonga* is the main type of fish obtained

[1] Estimates based on 1945 figures.

from the Shenge area, where fishing is carried on in the open sea in Yawri Bay, around Plantain Island, and off the coast of the Shenge (*Shenke*—play with the head) peninsula.

The main season for *bonga* here is between May and October. During the same season, 'mollet' and mackerel are also caught. Very little fishing is possible in the months of June, July, and August, when the south-west wind is strongly blowing.

The fishing here is carried on mainly by Temne people from Masimra; and they are estimated to comprise about three-fifths of the population around Shenge, which is put at a figure in the neighbourhood of 900. The fishing-boats are individually owned, and a man may own, sometimes, three or four. He hires a 'captain' for the boat and engages three or four other men to do the fishing. The proceeds are divided on the basis of the owner of the boat taking half; the 'captain' takes the larger share of the other half; and the fishermen take equal shares of the balance. Sometimes, under an alternative arrangement, the owner of the boat takes all the fish and pays the men hired in cash for their share of the catch. The men usually remain with him until they have acquired boats of their own. The boat itself is a sea-going craft, about fourteen feet long and about six feet at the waist. It can be rowed and sailed and is used to transport fish and passengers up the creek as far as Rotifunk.

The fishermen live in small villages, locally known as *shimbeks*, which are situated along the beach a few miles outside the town of Shenge. There is a small market at Shenge itself, but most of the business is done directly with the fishermen themselves. The buyers and their agents from up-country come over to the villages for this purpose. Some of these people live in houses in Rotifunk which the fishing community built, originally to store fish and lodge strangers. They pay the fishermen rent at the rate of 2s. 6d. per week for their accommodation, and having arrived in Rotifunk as strangers, they have naturally become the regular customers of their landlords. Relatives of the fisher people live in Rotifunk and look after this side of the business, i.e. renting accommodation, 'coaxing' buyers, etc.

In this Shenge fish trade, there is a practice of paying money in advance for fish. When the boats return to the shore about sundown, there is of course an eager rush to them on the part of traders to take delivery of their fish. The fishermen also find it more convenient to let the buyers do their own smoking. This operation is carried out in special low-roofed huts adjacent to the fishermen's own houses. The huts are about twenty-four feet square with a large fireplace, and the limited amount of window space ensures that the fish stacked in the corners receive a profuse volume of smoke.

During the rains, the road between Shenge and Sembehun is impassable for any motor traffic, and so between May and November most of the fish is taken in the fishing boats as far as Rotifunk. It also travels, sometimes, over to Bonthe via the island of Ndema. The journey to Rotifunk, as already mentioned, takes two days and the latter trip takes two days to Ndema and a further day from there to Bonthe. The fare charged per passenger to Bonthe is 3s., with 5s. freight for a large-sized basket and 2s. for a small-sized one. The price of *bonga* at Rotifunk (early November) was £7 for the largest sized basket, and £4 to £5 for a medium-sized one. A large-sized basket of *adari* was making £10 and contained some forty dozen fish. It is estimated that about £600 worth of fish is sold weekly in Rotifunk market, mainly to buyers from up-country towns.

During the rains a certain amount of direct exchange of rice is carried out in this district, when Mende people bring down amounts of two or three bushels and barter them for fish at Shenge. Some of these Mende have remained in the area and there is now a community of about 150 persons, who have been settled there, more or less permanently, for the past ten years. They are not serious fishermen, but are attached to the Timnes. They do odd jobs for them, in return for which they are given fish to hawk along the Sembehun-Shenge road. These Mende people also earn their keep by weaving and basket-making.

APPENDIX III

THE COST OF A COUNTRY CLOTH

ONE of the best known and most generally used articles in Mende life is the native made 'country cloth'. This is a cotton cloth of varying size and it is woven by the people themselves. It is used ceremonially as a gift in, for example, bride-wealth payments, and is also a standard of value and medium of exchange in commercial transactions. It is used, in addition, for purposes of decoration; as a garment; and as a covering cloth in bed. A well made and artistically designed country cloth is an object of considerable aesthetic value.

The cotton used in the weaving of the cloth is usually planted and grown alongside the rice crop. Several types of cotton are used, the principal ones are known by the native terms *quande*, *fandewai*, and *nduli*. *Quande* is a russet colour, the others are white. The cotton is teased on a bow-like implement and carded by means of a steel card, the latter being a European made tool. It is then spun out by hand on a piece of wood which is rotated on a plate. One hand spins the spool, whilst the other controls the thread. The thread is spun in two different sized spools. One, exclusive of the stick, weighs about 1½ lb., and the other about half that weight. A woman takes about nine days to spin a spool of the former kind and its commercial price, nowadays (1945), is between 2*s*. and 3*s*. Formerly, it cost 6*d*. to 1*s*. If colours other than the natural white and russet are required, the next process is to dye the cotton. Blue is the most popular colour and, given fine weather, it takes four days to dye the thread a light (Cambridge) blue, and about a week to dye it dark blue. The dye most generally used is obtained from the roots of a plant known as *surie*, which grows wild in the bush. A number of other plants are also used. A European proprietary brand (Libby) is also used.

THE COST OF A COUNTRY CLOTH

Dyeing is a skilled trade and its secrets are guarded carefully by the women who carry it on. Such women communicate the process only to girls who follow them and serve as apprentices. A few pounds weight of the roots used are cut into pieces and boiled in water. The mass, when cold, is poured into a larger iron pot, known as the *garra* pot, which is left out of doors. The shade of colour desired is obtained according to the quantity of water added after the roots have been boiled and the length of time they have been left to soak after boiling. The longer they are left, the darker the shade. The material to be dyed is then put into the *garra* pot and left there for some hours. After this, it is washed in the dye for a further length of time and finally hung out to dry.

When it is ready the thread is handed over to the men for weaving into cloth. This, too, is a highly skilled trade which is performed only by men who are specialists at it. There are various methods of weaving as used by the Mandingo and Gbandi people, as well as by the Mende and other peoples indigenous to the Sierra Leone region. At the Mende loom, the weaver moves along the lines of thread, which are pegged out for him. Mandingo and Gbandi weavers sit in a fixed position and draw the cloth in, as it is woven, over a roller.[1]

The strips woven are about five inches in width and their length is determined by the size of cloth required. There are four different sizes. The first, about three yards long, is used mostly by the women, and, sometimes, by the men in the villages as a dressing cloth. The second is nine yards in length and is known as *kula-hinei*, or 'male cloth'. It is used for clothing and cover at night. The third is the *gba'le*. It is about fourteen yards long and is used as bed covering. The fourth is the double *gba'le*; it is about twenty yards long and is used as bedding. Generally, it is found only in the houses of chiefs.

It takes the weaver about two days to complete the first size; about three and a half days the second size; about six days the third size; and about two weeks the double *gba'le*, when the weather is fine, as in the dry season.

The approximate commercial prices at which these different sizes of country cloths are sold are as follows (1946): The smallest

---

[1] As already mentioned, the reader should consult M. C. F. Easmon, 'Sierra Leone Country Cloths', W.A.P. 110, for a full description of the technical processes of weaving and for further particulars regarding types and styles of country cloths.

THE COST OF A COUNTRY CLOTH

size at 15s.; the second size at 25s.; the single *gba'le* at 35s.; and the double *gba'le* at 60s. Omitting the cost of the cotton and of dyeing, it is estimated that the weaver himself would receive 2s. 6d. out of the first size; 4s. out of the second size; 8s. out of the single *gba'le*; and 15s. out of the double *gba'le*. It is estimated that the double *gba'le* requires about twelve spools of cotton.

Usually, the spinning of the cotton is done by the weaver's wives; but in its separate stages, the cost of the double *gba'le* can be estimated as follows:

	£	s.	d.
Twelve spools of cotton at, say, 2s. 6d. each	1	10	0
Cost of dye		15	0
Weaver's fee		15	0
	£3	0	0

BIBLIOGRAPHY

HISTORICAL AND GENERAL

ADDISON, W., 'The Palm-nut tree and its uses', *Sierra Leone Studies*, 1918, No. 1.
    'The Wunde Society', *Man*, December 1936, Vol. XXXVI.
ALLDRIDGE, T. J., *A Transformed Colony* (London, 1910).
    The Sherbo and its Hinterland (London, 1901).
BANBURY, G. A. L., *Sierra Leone, or The White Man's Grave* (1888).
BANTON, M., *West African City* (London, 1957).
BEATTY, K. J., *Human Leopards* (London, 1915).
BERRY, R. G., *The Sierra Leone Cannibals, with Notes on their Customs*.
BLYDEN, E. W., *Christianity, Islam, and the Negro Race* (London, 1889).
BOURNE, H. R. Fox 'The Sierra Leone Troubles', *Fortnightly Review*, 1898.
BROWN, G. W., 'The Poro in Modern Business', *Man*, No. 3, 1937.
BUTT-THOMPSON, F. W., *Secret Societies of West Africa* (London, 1929).
    Sierra Leone in History and Tradition (London, 1926).
CLARKE, ROBERT, *A Description of the Manners and Customs of the Liberated Africans* (1843).
COLE, J. ABAYOMI, *A Revelation of the Secret Orders of West Africa* (Dayton, 1886).
CROOKS, J. J., *A History of Sierra Leone* (1903).
DAVIS, R. P. M., *History of the Sierra Leone Battalion of the Royal West African Frontier Force* (Freetown, 1932).
DAWSON, JOHN, 'Therapeutic Functions of Social Groups in Sierra Leone', *Bulletin of British Psychological Society*, 17, 56, 1964.
EASMON, M. C. F., *Sierra Leone Native Cloths* (1914).
EBERL-ELBER, R., *Westafrikas Letzes Rätsel* (Salzburg, 1936).
ELLIS, A. B., *The Land of Fetish* (London, 1883).
FENTON, J. S., 'Report on a Visit to Nigeria, and on the application of the Principles of Native Administration in Sierra Leone', *Sierra Leone Sessional Paper*, 1926.
    An Outline of Native Law (1949).
FYFE, CHRISTOPHER, *A History of Sierra Leone* (Oxford, 1962).
    Sierra Leone Inheritance (London, 1964).
GAMBLE, DAVID, 'Family Organization in New Towns in Sierra Leone' in *Urbanization in African Social Change*, Centre of African Studies, Edinburgh University, 1963.
GERMANS, P., *Die Volkerstämme in Norden von Liberia* (Leipzig, 1933).
GORVIE, MAX, *Old and New in Sierra Leone* (Africa's Own Library), 1945.
    Our People of the Sierra Leone Protectorate (Africa's Own Library), 1946.

BIBLIOGRAPHY

HARGREAVES, J. D., 'The Establishment of the Sierra Leone Protectorate', *Cambridge Historical Journal*, No. 1, Vol. 2, 1956.

HARLEY, G. W., 'Notes on the Poro in Liberia', *Peabody Museum Papers*, Vol. 19, No. 2, 1941.

'Masks as Agents of Social Control', *Peabody Museum Papers*, No. 2, 1950.

HARRIS, W. T., 'Ceremonies and Stories connected with Trees, Rivers and Hills in the Protectorate of Sierra Leone', *Sierra Leone Studies, New Series*, No. 2, 1954.

HORNELL, J., 'The indigenous fishing methods of Sierra Leone', *Sierra Leone Studies*, Vol. XIII, 1928.

KILSON, MARTIN, 'The Pragmatic-Pluralistic Pattern: Sierra Leone', in *Political Parties and National Integration in Tropical Africa* (eds.) Coleman, James, S. and Rosberg, Carl G. (Berkeley and Los Angeles, 1964).

LITTLE, KENNETH, 'Conflict and Social Pressures in Sierra Leone', *Crown Colonist*, January, 1947.

LITTLE, KENNETH, 'Social Change and Social Class in the Sierra Leone Protectorate', *American Journal of Sociology*, July, 1948.

LUKE, H. C., *A Bibliography of Sierra Leone* (Oxford University Press, 1925).

MARGAI, M. A. S., 'Welfare Work in a Secret Society', *African Affairs*, March, 1948.

MARTIN, F. J., *A Preliminary Study of the Vegetation of Sierra Leone* (Government Printer, Freetown, 1948).

MATTHEWS, LT. JOHN, *A Voyage to the River Sierra Leone*, (London, 1788).

MIGEOD, F. W. H., *A View of Sierra Leone* (London, 1926).

MITCHELL, P. K., 'Trade Routes of the Early Sierra Leone Protectorate', *Sierra Leone Studies, New Series*, No. 16, 1962.

NEWLAND, H. O., *Sierra Leone, its People, Products, and Societies* (London, 1916).

Parliamentary Papers, 1899, LX, Pts. I and II.

QUILLIAM, A., 'A chapter in the history of Sierra Leone', *Journal of the African Society*, No. 9, 1903.

RANKIN, F. H., *The White Man's Grave* (London, 1836), Vols. I and II.

SAWYERR, HARRY, 'Ancestor Worship—The Mechanics', *Sierra Leone Bulletin of Religion*, Vol. 6, No. 2, 1964.

'Do Africans Believe in God?', *Sierra Leone Studies, New Series*, No. 15, 1961.

SCHWAB, G., 'Tribes of the Liberian Hinterland', *Peabody Museum Papers*, 1947.

Sierra Leone Censuses, 1931 and 1949.

Sierra Leone Sessional Paper, No. 5 of 1926, 'Despatches relating to Domestic Slavery in Sierra Leone'.

Sierra Leone Sessional Paper, No. 7 of 1945, 'Administrative Reorganization of the Protectorate'.

'The Sierra Leone Protectorate Expedition', *Journal of the Royal United Service Institution*, Vol. XLIII, 1898.

THOMAS, N. W., Anthropological Report on Sierra Leone, Parts I, II, and III (1916).

Thompson in Africa. An Account of the Missionary Labours, etc., of George Thompson in Western Africa at the Mendi Mission (1852).

UTTING, F. A. J., *The Story of Sierra Leone* (1931).

VERGETTE, E. D., *Certain Marriage Customs of some of the Tribes in the Protectorate of Sierra Leone* (Government Printer, Freetown, 1917).

BIBLIOGRAPHY

VIVIAN, WILLIAM, 'The Missionary in West Africa', *Journal of the African Society*, Vol. 3, 1896.
VOLZ, W., *Reise durch das Hinterland von Liberia* (Bern, 1911).
WALLIS, C. B., *The Advance of our West African Empire* (1903).
  'A Tour in the Liberian Hinterland', *Journal of the Royal Geographical Society*, March, 1910.
WARREN, H. C., 'Secret Societies', *Sierra Leone Studies*, 1926.
WILSON, L. W., 'The Kasila', *Sierra Leone Studies*, Vol. XV, 1929.
WRIGHT, E. J., 'Psychotherapy and Witchcraft', *Sierra Leone Studies*, No. 21, 1939.

With Specific Reference to the Mende

ADDISON, W., 'Steatite Figures from Moyamba', *Man*, XXIII, 1923.
BOKHARI, A., 'Notes on the Mendi People, *Sierra Leone Studies*, 1918 and 1919.
BOCKHARI, J., 'The Derivation of Mende Names for the Months of the Year', *Sierra Leone Studies*, New Series, No. 4, 1955.
BROWN, STANLEY, 'The *Nomoli* of Mende Country', *Africa*, January, 1948.
CLARKE, W. R. E., 'The Foundation of the Luawa Chiefdom', *Sierra Leone Studies*, New Series, No. 8, 1957.
CROSBY, K. H., 'Polygamy in Mende Country', *Africa*, Vol. X, 1937.
CROSBY, K. H. and WARD, I. C., *An Introduction to the Study of Mende*.
FENTON, J. S., 'Characters in Mende Stories', *Sierra Leone Studies*, 1929.
FITZJOHN, WILLIAM H., 'A Village in Sierra Leone', *Sierra Leone Studies*, New Series, No. 7, 1956.
HARRIS, W. T., 'The Idea of God among the Mende', *African Ideas of God* (ed. Edwin Smith, London, 1950).
  'How the Mende People First Started to Pray to ŋgewɔ', *Sierra Leone Bulletin of Religion*, Vol. 5, No. 2, 1963.
  'ŋgewɔ and Leve', *Sierra Leone Bulletin of Religion*, Vol. 5, Nos. 1 and 2, 1963.
HOFSTRA, S., 'Ancestral Spirits of the Mendi', *Internationales Archiv für Ethnographie*, Band XXXIV, Heft 1-4 (Leiden, 1937).
  'Personality and Differentiation in the Political Life of the Mendi', *Africa*, Vol. X, 1937.
  'The Belief among the Mendi in non-ancestral Spirits', *Internationales Archiv für Ethnographie*, Band XL, 5-6 (Leiden, 1937).
  'The Social Significance of the Oil Palm in the Life of the Mendi', *Internationales Archiv für Ethnographie*, Band XXXIV, 5-6 (1937).
HOLLINS, N. C., 'Mende Law', *Sierra Leone Studies*, 1929.
  'Notes on Mende Law', *Sierra Leone Studies*, 1938.
INNES, GORDON, 'Some Features of Theme and Style in Mende Folktales', *Sierra Leone Language Review*, No. 3, 1964.
  'The Function of the Song in Mende Folktales', *Sierra Leone Language Review*, No. 4, 1965.
KILSON, MARION DE B., 'Social Relationships in Mɛnde Dɔmɛisia', *Sierra Leone Studies*, New Series, No. 15, 1961.
KUP, A. P., *A History of Sierra Leone 1400-1787* (Cambridge, 1961).
LITTLE, KENNETH, 'A Mende Musician sings of his Adventures', *Man*, 1948, 26.
  'A Moslem "Missionary" in Mendeland', *Man*, August, 1947.

BIBLIOGRAPHY

'Land and Labour among the Mende', *African Affairs*, March, 1948.
'Mende Political Institutions in Transition', *Africa*, January, 1947.
'The Changing Position of Women in the Sierra Leone Protectorate', *Africa*, January, 1948.
'The Function of Medicine in Mende Society', *Man*, November, 1948.
'The Mende Farming Household', *Sociological Review*, Vol. XL, Sect. 4, 1948.
'The Poro Society as an Arbiter of Culture', *African Studies*, March, 1948.
'The Secret Society in Cultural Specialization', *American Anthropologist*, Vol. 51, No. 2, 1949.
'The Mende Rice Farm and its Cost', *Zaire* (Louvain), March and April, 1951
'Structural Change in the Sierra Leone Protectorate', *Africa*, XXV, No. 3, 1955.
'The Political Function of the Poro', *Africa*, XXXV, No. 4, 1965 and XXXVI, No. 1, 1966.

MALCOLM, J. M., 'Mende Warfare', *Sierra Leone Studies*, 1939.
MENZIES, A., 'Exploratory Expedition to the Mende Country', *Church Missionary Intelligencer*, 1868.
MICHEL, H., 'Some Notes on Mende Language and Customs', *Sierra Leone Studies*, No. 3, 1920.
MIGEOD, F. W. H., 'A Mende Dance', *Man* XVII, 1917.
  'Mende Drum Signals,' *Man*, March, 1920.
  'Mende Songs', *Man*, Vol. XVI, 1916.
  'The Building of the Poro House', *Man*, XVI, 1916.
NDANEWA, ISAAC, 'The Rationale of Mende "Swears"', *Sierra Leone Bulletin of Religion*, Vol. 6, No. 2, 1964.
RANSON, HARRY, 'The Growth of Moyamba', *The Bulletin (Journal of the Sierra Leone Geographical Association)*, No. 9, 1965.
STAUB, J., 'Beiträge zur Kenntnis der materiellen Kultur der Mendi in der Sierra Leone', *Jahrbuch der Bernischen Historischen Museums in Bern* (1936).
SUMNER, A. T. and HUNTER, R. F., 'Names of diseases in Mendi', *Sierra Leone Studies*, 1922.
VIVIAN, WILLIAM, 'A Visit to Mendeland', *Journal of the Manchester Geographical Society* (1896).
WALLIS, C. B., 'In the Courts of the Native Chiefs of Mendeland', *Journal of the African Society*, Vol. 4, No. 4, 1905.
  'The Poro of the Mende', *Journal of the African Society*, Vol. 4, No. 14, 1905.
  'Tribal laws of the Mende', *Journal of Comparative Legislation*, Vol. 3, 1921.

INDEX

adari, fish, 283; prices for, 285, 288
Administrative methods, *see* British administration, Native administration
Adultery, flogging for, 166
Adult life, social implications of, 130–1
'African Club', 268–9
Ahmaddiyyah, a sect, 274*n*.
Alldridge, T. J.: cited, 24 and *n*., 33*n*., 37*n*., 54 and *n*., 129 and *n*., 255 and *n*., 295*n*., 261*n*.; treaties of friendship with the Mende, 45; quoted, 54–6
Allotments, payments of, 166
Almania, a society, 270, 276
'A-wa-o' ('All come!'), sign of victory, 35

Background, material, of the Mende, 66–71
Bagru river, raided by the Mende, 44
Bai Burch, a Timne sub-chief, conflict with, 47, 48
Bai Comber, Hon., Paramount Chief: cited, 32*n*.; quoted, 178–9
Baiima, Treaty No. 119 signed at, 179
Banbury, G. A. Lethbury: quoted, 51 and *n*.
Bandajuma, police station attacked at, 48
Banton, M.: cited, 15 and *n*.
'Bar', an indefinite quantity, 37
Barracuda, fish, 283
Barrenness, not sufficient ground for dissolution of marriage, 160
barri, the, 67, 102, 125, 128, 131, 148, 154, 190, 259
Barter, 37
Bassir, Mr. O.: cited, 281*n*.
Baw-baw Tamba of Jolu, Sub-chief, asked to be recognized as Paramount Chief, 178

Beatty, K. J.: cited, 233*n*.
bembɛ, hired farm workers, 81
Berry, R. G.: cited, 233*n*.
Biyi, Esu: cited, 250*n*.
Blacksmithing, *see* Occupations
bla lome, a gown, 155
Bo, the 'capital' town of Mendeland, 11, 63, 65, 285, 286; population not all Mende in origin, 63; district census (1948), 65; the *Ramadan* fast ceremonies at, 275–6; account of burial of a Moslem woman at, 276–9; expenses of fish trader from, 286
Bo African Club, *see* Women
Bockhari, J.: cited, 11 and *n*.
Bɔfima, an anti-social medicine, 233, 234 and *n*.
Boi, first girl named, 113
bolemui, 245
Bonduwolo, murder of chief of, 32
bonga, dried fish, 69 and *n*., 281, 283, 284, 285, 286–7, 288; prices for, 284, 286, 288
bonga-trader, the, 281–8
Bongɔi, section of the Humui, 250
Bonthe, a fishing port, 281; fish trade at, 283, 284–8; value of fish per week leaving, 286
Bourne, H. R. Fox; quoted, 52 and *n*.; cited, 57 and *n*.
boya hani, 158
Bridewealth: slavery and, 37; may be advanced for a wife, 100; foregoing of, 115; securing of, 140 and *n*., 154–5; no reclaiming of, 157; refund of, 160; reclaim of, 161–2; the law and, 172 and *n*., 186–9, 213
British, the: political contacts with Mendeland, 43–6; territorial expansion of, 44; authority and influence of, 58; domination by (1898), 90

296

INDEX

British administration: expansion and influence, 44–5; production, 46; military, 52–3, 255; misapplication of methods, 56–9; officials and technicians of, 71; intervention and domination, 90; political confusion resulting from protection, 176–7; the native court and, 186, 197; elections and, 199; and chiefs, 202; and 'municipalization', 206; and cannibalistic murder, 233

Brown, G. W.: cited, 184n.
'Brushing-time', 100
Buckle, V. E. J.: cited, 264n.
Buildings, official, 67
bulei (farm), 132
buleisia (small plots of ground), 100
Bum Kittam creek, 61
Bumpe, 23, 29, 65, 286; treaty at, 45; stormed and taken, 52
'Bundu' (see Sande secret society)
Bunduka of Leuma, 178
Burial ceremony of warrior, 72n.
Butt-Thompson, F. W.: cited, 27 and n., 241 and nn.
buvemui, a bugler, 246

'Cannibalism': outbreaks of, 233 and n.
Cardew, Governor, 24; cited, 38n.; quoted, 57n. and peace treaties, 45–6; his tours, 57; and Protectorate Ordinance, 58
Cassada, substitute for rice, 77 and n.
Catfish, 283
Caulker of Shenge, loyal during revolt, 59
Ceremonies: judicial procedure, 40–2; initiation, 119–20, 122–30, 164n.; funeral, 137–9, 184–5, 192–4, 273, 277–9; and spirits, 219–25, 245, 246–7; and secret societies, 248–51; and *Ramadan*, 275–6
Chalmers, Sir David, Royal Commissioner: his report on Mende Rising cited, 52, 59; same quoted, 54; and Government action, 59
Characteristics of the Mende, 24–5, 74
Chief, the, and his chiefdom: powers of chiefs, 29, 30; basis of political authority, 175–6; Kakua chiefdom and Momo Gbotɔ, 176; political confusion following British protection, 176–7; partition of the Mando chiefdom, 177–9; succession to chieftainship, 179–81; political hierarchy, 179; lineage of Ruling House Mando Chiefdom, 180; present Ruling House of Simbaru chiefdom, 181n.; chief's duties and perquisites, 182; councils, 183; rôle of Poro society, 183–5, 185n.; court and court procedure, 185–9; bridewealth cases in chief's court, 187–8; social insignia of chieftainship, 189–95; ceremonial observance at chief's death, 192–4; women as chiefs, 195–6; chiefdom Speaker, or *Lavalie*, 196–7; sub-chiefs, 197–8; Town Chiefs and Village Headmen, 198; elections of chiefs, a British innovation, 199–201; special staff for chief, 201 and n.; some 200 chiefdoms in Protectorate, 206; the Chiefdom Clerk, 210 and n.; chief's average salary, 211n.

Chiefdoms: 29–31, 45, 53, 85, 90, 92, 179–81, 182, 196–201 and n., 206; Dia, 30, 178; Guma, 30; Mando, 30, 177–9, 180; Malema, 30; Luawa, 63 and n.; Jawei, 65; Upper Bambara, 65; Yawei, 65; Jaluahun, 66; Kakua, 176; Simbaru, 181n.; chiefdom labour, 182; councils, 183–5 and n.; women and, 195–6; Maje, 196; estimates, 203, 209 and n.; tax, 204 and n.; Kpaa Mende, 206n.; clerks, 210 and n.; Poro, 213 and n.

Childhood, 114–15
Christianity: how regarded during Mende Rising, 57n.; the Moslems and, 274–5
'Civilized', non-literate people's ideas of meaning of, 262–3
Clarke, Robert, senior assistant surgeon: cited, 72 and n.
Clarke, W. R. E.: cited, 34n., 35n., 36n.
Cleaning, *see* Occupations
Clearing the bush, *see* Occupations
Cockborough riot, 44
Cooking, *see* Occupations

INDEX

Councils: the *kuwuisia* and chiefs' and chiefdom, 183–5 and *n.*, 197, 203, 207–8, 215, 224
'Country Cloth', cost of a, 289–91; uses of, 289
Creole, origin of term, 24*n.*
'*Creole nyaposia*' (Creole girls), 117
Croeles, the: dress of, 71, 73; Creole speech a lingua franca in certain towns, 106; imitating ways of, 117 and *n.*; Creole habits deplored, 214 and *n.*; the Creole as cultural medium, 262–4
'Creolization', 264
Crosby, K. H., census in Upper Mende country by, 65 and *n.*
'Crowning houses', 84 and *n.*, 92
Cunningham, Col., expedition commanded by, 48–9, 51–2

Dagbadaii, a Poro spirit, 246, 247
dagba gulai ('nursing dress'), 155
Dances: and execution of captives, 36; at harvest, 79; and rice-treading, 80; and initiation, 128; Sande dance, 251–3; at weddings and christenings, 268; at *Ramadan* fast, 275–6; at funeral, 278–9
Danquah, J. B.: cited, 197*n.*
Davis, Lt. R. P. M.: quoted, 49–50 and *n.*, 53*n.*
Dawson, John: cited, 13 and *n.*
Demographic data in Sierra Leone Protectorate, 61–6
Dia, chiefdom, *see* Chiefdoms
Diet, 77, 281
Dress and deportment of the Mende, 71
Duawu Niemy, the Treaty chief of Malema, 179
Dyeing, *see* Occupations
dyinyanga ('genii'), 218, 221–5

Easmon, Dr. M. C. F.: cited, 15, 290*n.*
Education: western, 115; Mission schools, 117, 170; learning crafts, 121; Sande schools, 126–7, 128, 130; Protectorate schools, 170–1; percentages of children at school, 208; improved, 209, 212, 267; 'Creole' class and, 267
Egbo of Nigeria, society, 241
Elephants, significance of, 26*n.*
e longa koe hui ('dying in the battle'), 133 and *n.*

Engineering, *see* Occupations
Etiquette, 23; local, 55; varieties of, 130–1; wives' number of visits to husband, 133; girls' refusal of initial approaches to marriage, 156; and native language, 254–5; Creole social, 267–8
Europeans, attitude to, 73

Fabunde, Chief, of Luawa, 32
Fairtlough, Major, of British Frontier Police, 32
fale gbua nyahanga ('mushroom wives'), 153, 156, 158; procedure over, 153–4
famalui ('greeting present'), 91, 92, 131, 154
Family: land by inheritance and, 85–6, 88–9; kinds of household and, 96–103; Mende family law, 105; interpretations in terminology of, 108–9; duties and obligations, 109–11; polygyny and, 142; and male line descendants of chief, 181; and matter of bridewealth in court, 187–8; ancestral spirits and, 219
Fande, the ('thread'), 34 and *n.*, 35
fandewai, type of cotton, 289
farinha (graded cassada), 285
Farley of Mando-Potolu, 178
Farming: kinds of, 69; average expenditure on making a farm, 169 and *n.*; and tribal system, 258–9; *see also* Occupations
Fatmatta, head of a *kuwui* in Bo, account of burial, 277–9 and *nn.*
Fenton, J. S., C.M.G.: cited, 172*n.*, 196*n.*, 213*n.*
Fishing, *see* Occupations
Fishing grounds, map of coastal, 282
Fitzjohn, William H.: cited, 14*n.*
Fleming, Governor, and peace treaties, 45
Fobaywulo of Gbandi, 31
'Fony-Lady of Mano Bagru', signatory in Treaty No. 68 (of 1861), 196
foo-foo, a Creole dish, 264, 268
Foreka, Chief, of Bomaru, war between Mbawulomeh and, 31, 178
Freeborn, duties and position of, 39–40

298

INDEX

Freetown, 24; transporting of fish to, 285n.
French, inroads made by, 45
'frupper', fish, prices for, 283, 285
Fulani, Fula, the, 25, 73; dress and deportment of, 70
Fyfe, Christopher: cited, 12 and n.

Gallinas, the, 44, 73; conflict in country of, 45
Gamble, David: cited, 16n, 15n.
Garra-dyeing, 171, 290
garra pot, 290
Garrett, Mr., and burning of towns and villages, 45
Gaye, Betsy, a woman chief, 195n.
Gbagba and Dowi of Bomaru, 178
gba'le, cloth, 290, 291
gbamai (ordinary men), 35
gbama nyahanga, women without a husband, 143
Gbandi, weavers, 290
gbatui, medicine which involves the use of hypnosis, 238 and n.
Gbeima (most senior), 244
Gbengben nyɛkɛ ndoli nya ngotua kpu kɔwoma! (The enticing waists of the women have sent me crazy!); Poro song, 121n.
Gbeni, the principal sacred spirit of the Poro, 184, 246, 247; and chief's death, 193
gboa, an initiated girl, 127
Gbonu, 243
gbonu (last initiated boy in Poro initiation), 119
Genie, 221–5, 230
Gevao of Malema, Kabba Sei gives himself up to, 32
Gibas ('let this one be saved'), 114n.
Giehun Tomago, 31
Gilo ('let this one be saved'), 114n.
Gohun, 32
Goldsmithing and gold-working, *see* Occupations
golohg boie (shed, or guard-house), 33
Goodman, Mr., Methodist missionary, spared by the chief of Tikonko, 48
Gorn, section of Mobai town, 67
Gorvie, Rev. Max, cited, 15
Government, modern methods of, 199–215; methods of appointing chief, 199–202; native authority system, 202–6; *Native Treasuries*, 203; *Chiefdom Estimates*, 203; 209 and n; *Revenues* and *Expenditure*, 203–4; Chiefdom Tax, 204 and n.; *Re-Current Development* and *Extraordinary Development*, 204; complaints, 205–6; 212n.; later developments in administrative organization, 206–8; District Councils, 207 and n., 208, 215; anomalies of administrative situation, 208–13; present political trend, 213–15; attraction of western ideas and ways, 214; dissatisfaction and unrest, 215
Guma, chiefdom, *see* Chiefdoms
Gumihun, 129n.

'Hair-straightening', 117 and n.
Hakahoumoi, the (holder of the ladder), 34
hale, *see* Medicine
halemui (medicine man), 228, 229
hale nyamubla, persons owning 'bad' medicine, 230
'hang heads', i.e. consult together, 155
Hargreaves, J. D.: cited, 12n.
Harley, G. W.: cited, 244n.
Harmattan wind, 61
Harris, W. T.: cited, 12 and n.
Harrowing, *see* Occupations
Havelock, Governor, seeks ways to prevent trouble, 45
Hay, Governor, and peace treaties, 45
Headman, the, 183, 198
Hearing Fees, at chief's court, 186
heilopui, infant boy known as, 114
hɛma (praying place), 219
hɛmɔi ('praying man'), 136, 219
henjo mbie ('cooking for the initiate'), 154
hinda wanda, small presents, 157
Hofstra, Dr. S.: cited, 11, 15, 137n., 138 and n., 201n., 218n., 222n., 225 and n., 248n.
honamui, a 'witch person', or 'witch host', 230–1
honei, a witch-spirit, 230–1
'hooyo', 113 and n.
Hotagua, Paramount Chief of the Kakua chiefdom, signed treaty with British (in the 1880's), 181n.
Hotala, section of Mobai town, 67

INDEX

Household: statistics regarding number of persons in, 66; farming, 81; family and kinds of, 96–103; manhood, womanhood, status, and, 132–4; additions to chief's, 141; characteristics of chief's house and, 189–90
Houses, construction of, 66–7
hɔwei ('laying of the plant'), 220; ceremony of the, 221 and *n.*
hubonei, a witch, 230
Hughes, Mr., J. D. W.: cited, 64 and *n.*, 65 and *n.*, 66 and *n.*
Human Leopards, an illegal society, 186
Humonya, Madame, of Nongowa chiefdom, 195
Humui, the, a secret society: their rules determine restrictions of intercourse, marriage, and sexual conduct, 145, 147–9, 164, 240, 249; a rule of, 148*n.*
Hunter's Society, the, 270
Hunters and hunting, *see* Occupations
Hut Tax, collecting of, 58, 85*n.*

Impotency, considered shameful, 160
Infancy, 113–14
Infidelity, detection of, 151–2 and *n.*, 153, 160
Initiation, 113; preparation of the Poro camp, 118; entry into school, 118–19; marking ceremony, 119–20; kinds of training, 120–2; the rites, 122–5; completion of Poro school, 125–6; initiation in the Sande, 126–30; adult life, 130–2; improvement in status, 132–5; widowhood, 135–6; widower ceremony, 136*n.*; old age and ancestorhood, 136–9
Innes, Gordon; cited, 13–14 and *n.*
Islam (Moslems), 150, 155*n.*, 169, 170, 171, 173, 185, 187, 264, 269, 270, 273*n.*; reasons for adopting Moslem traits and professing Islam, 273–5; ceremonies and, 275–80; in Mende life, the part of, 273–80

Jaluahun chiefdom, census of, 66
Jawei chiefdom, census of, 65
Jobai, a Poro spirit, 246
Joloff rice, a dish, 268
Jong, river, 60

Kabba Sei, warrior chief, account and activities of, 30–2, 78–9; gives himself up to Gevao of Malema, 32, 178, 179; signed Treaty No. 119, 179
kafalowoi (fork of the kafa-tree), a kind of shield, 35
Kaikonjo, a spirit, 223
Kailahun, 'capital' town, 63, 65; district census, 65
Kai Lundo of Luawa, chief, 31, 72, 179; feud between Mbawulomeh and, 32
Kai Woni of Pendembu, warfare of, 31
Kakua, chiefdom, *see* Chiefdoms
kamai (to meet around), 243
Kambia, burned down (1858), 43
Kambui Hills, 60
kameihun (the sacred part of the Poro bush), 123, 125, 243, 247
'*kanta*-ing', 250
Kanye, the ('wax'), 34, 35
Kaswela, a water spirit from Bonthe, 223
keje lui ('ginger kola'), 133
kɔli nyahanga (women 'found'), 153
Kema, the first girl initiated in the Sande known as, 117, 127
kema-bla, the, witch-finders, 231
Kenema, 63; outbreak of 'cannibalism' at, 233*n.*
kenyaisia (maternal uncles), 110 and *n.*, 154
Kilson, Marion de B.: cited, 14 and *n.*
Kilson, Martin: cited, 15
Kinship, terminology, 108–9; duties and obligations, 109–12
Kissi, the, dress and deportment of, 70, 73, 147
Koelle: cited, 71
kokondeiyai-bla, bearers of sticks, 246
kokoyagbla (drivers from the fence), 35
kɔli nyahanga (women' found'), 156
Koma, Madame Hawa, in charge of compound at Mobai, 103*n.*
Ko-mahei, war chief, 35
kondo-bla, the, 'antidote-people', 231
kondo-gbandei, counter-medicine to witchcraft, 231
kondo-moi, i.e. the leader of the *kondo-bla*, 231
Kono, the, dress of, 70 and *n.*, 147, 201
ko-sokilisia ('war-sparrows'), 35

INDEX

Kossa, the Mende referred to as, 72
kotu ('good-bye present'), 131, 159
Kotulei-mui (officer, one who passes the stone), 33
kpaa-gotui, large stones known as, 251
Kpaa Mende, the, 76; splitting up of Kpaa Mende chiefdoms (1919), 206n.
kpaa wa ('family farm'), 100, 132
Kpa-bla, or Kpa people, 251
kpakpa, the, 236
kpandoinga (*kpandohu*—void), 243
kpangbahoumoi, road-sweeper in front of Poro spirit, 246
kpao hindui, ex-husband, 135
kpao nyahanga ('husbandless women'), 153
Kpa society, function of, 251
Kpékalay ('the heart of the razor'), ceremonial use of, 249
Kpia, ceremony completing initiation, 122
kpoi hale, a medicine for natural purposes, 235
kpomba nyahanga, women given in discharge of a debt, 157
Kpombali in Luawa, raided, 32
Kpombue (mortgaging and pledging of land), 94
Kpove War (1880), 30, 75
Kpowa-mbei, ceremony completing initiation, 122
Krio, the Creole speech, 264, 265 and n., 271
'krocoss', fish, 283
Kru women, dress and appearance of, 70
Kugbangaa (ordinary warriors), 34
kugbe ('war strength'), 81–2
kuhaa-bla (people from afar), 73
kula-henie ('male cloth'), 290
kulie (a 'fence'), 156; *kulie* method of catching fish, 284
kuloko ('in whose hand the compound is'), role of the, 102–3, 105
Kup, A. P.: cited, 11 and n.
Kussoh, the Mende referred to as, 72
Kutubu, Chief of Upper Bambard: chance to become Paramount Chief, 178
kuwui ('compound'), 101 et seq., 134, 200n.
kuwuisia, the, and chief's and chiefdom councils, 183
Kwellu, police station attacked at, 48

Laborde, Mr., his attempt to promote peace, 45
'Lady, A, of Sherbro Island', signatory in Treaty No. 66 (1861), 196
Lagula, river, 224–5
Land tenure: basis of, 82–3; 'ownership' and 'holding' of land, 83–4; land legal case, 83n.; rights and inheritance in land, 84–6; religious implications of land ownership, 86–8; head of the kin group in relation to land, 88–9; position of chief and land, 89–91; settlement as method of obtaining land, 92–3; pledging of, 94; leasing of, 94–5
lappas, waist cloths, 70 and n., 71, 114, 132, 277
lasi-moi (in Creole, *sebe*), a talisman, 236
Lavalie, chiefdom Speaker, *see* Chief
lavalie, second initiated boy in Poro initiation, 119
'Leaf person', leader of the Humui, 250 and n.
Lebanese, the: dress of, 71, 73
Legal procedure, 40–2
Lema, 284
letay nyahanga ('walk-about women') prostitutes, 131
Leve, *see Ngewɔ*
Limba, dress of, 71
Limeiyama, burned, 32
Literacy: and initiations, 117; difficulties of literate men and women, 170–4; court cases and, 188; political position and, 214–15; a social factor, 256, 258; meaning of 'civilized' and, 262; distinction between non-literates and literates, 265–7; aspects of 'Literate' class, 269–71, 272; percentage of children at school, 208; significance of, 255, 256 and n.
Little, K. L., 'Structural Change in the Sierra Leone Protectorate', cited, 7n.; 'The Political Function of the Poro', cited, 15n.; 'The Mende Farming Household', cited, 82n.; 'A Moslem Missionary in Mendeland', cited, 211n., 229n.
Lokko country, sovereignty taken over, 44
Lokkos, the, 73

INDEX

Luawa, chiefdom, *see* Chiefdoms
Lugbu, treaty at, 45, 53, 54

Mabɔlɛ, the (woman official of the Poro): invocation of, 124, 164, 243, 245–6, 247
Macavoreh, Chief of Tikonko: relations between Ndawa and, 75
Mackerel, fish, 283, 287
Mafwie, town, ruined, 51
'Magao, the, Queen of Lubu', signatory in Treaty (1869), 195
Magic: the supernatural, 216; and genii and other spirits, 222–31; and medicines, 235–6; those professing Islam and, 273
maha, 'chief', 190
mahei mahun gbei bla, a chief's 'eyes and ears', 194
Maje, chiefdom, *see* Chiefdoms
Majo, principal Sande official woman, 126, 127, 129, 154, 164
Makeni, town, 61
Makoto, Madame Lucia, in charge of compound at Mobai, 103*n*.
Malcolm, J. M.: cited, 34*n*., 36*n*.
Malema, chiefdom, *see* Chiefdoms
Mali, kingdom, 25
Mandingo, the: some Mende of Mandingo origin, 28, 38*n*., 73, 169; dress and deportment of, 70; status of, 274; weavers of, 290
Mando, chiefdom: and Upper Bambard amalgamation, 178; lineage of Ruling House, *see* Chief, *see also* Chiefdoms
Manduwo, section of Mobai town, 67
Manina, town in Upper Mende: the genie and the overflowing of the river Lagula into the town, 224–5
manja, rice farms, 182
Mano, 63; fish obtained at, 286
Manyeh, Paramount Chief of Dia, 178
marda, 'grandfather', addressed to a chief, 190
Margai, M. A. S.: cited, 130*n*.
Marriage and 'Friendship', 140–62; social and economic features, 140–4; securing of bridewealth, 140*n*., 172*n*.; advantages of polygyny, 141–3, 165; women's status, 143–4; prerequisites, 144–5; prohibited relationships, 145–7; legal conditions of marriage, 149–50; implications of 'woman damage', 150–3; ways of making a marriage, 153–8; marital obligations, 159; dissolution of marriage, 159–61; re-claim of bridewealth, 161–2

Martin, F. J.: cited, 60 and *n*.
Masimra, 287
Matthews, John: cited, 241*n*.
Matto, Madame, wife of chief Faba of Dodo, 195
Mattru, derivation of the place name, 26*n*., 285, 286
Mattu, part of a claim in respect of a woman called, 161–2
mawɛ, farming household, 81, 132, 134, 96*n*., 141; as a social unit, 96–8; word originates from *mu pelei*, 96*n*.; patriarchal system of the, 97–8, 100; types of houses of the, 98–9, 99*n*.; domestic organization, 99; agricultural arrangements, 99–101; local group, 101–2; rice and palm oil production, 182
mawesia, family houses, 200*n*.
mbaa, female mates, 32
mbagboli ('red rice'), 220
Mba ndoe la hwei lo? ('Will you cross the summons?'), legal question, 41
Mbawulomeh ('rice—little eat'): warfare of, 31, 32; feud between Kai Lundo and, 32
mbele gbia hani, initiation fee for looking after a girl, 129*n*.
mbili-yeisia, drummers, 246
mboleisia, a broom-holder, 246
mboma hitie ('put down the chief's hammock'), 182
mbondaesia, 108, 110
mbondawa-ji-hu ('a community of kindreds'), 104
mboya, final amount as bridewealth, 154–5, 156, 158, 161, 189
Medicine: swearing of plaintiff and defendant on chiefdom, 186–7; the nature of *hale* or medicine, 227–8, 235; its association with the personality of its owner and user, 228*n*.; practitioners in *hale*, 228–30; 'bad' medicine men and witchcraft, 230–3; the *Bɔfima*, 233, 234 and *n*.; medical paraphernalia and practical uses of, 234–9; the Sande medicine, 238

INDEX

Medicine man, 228, 229, 230, 235, 238*n*.
Mema, 284
'Mende', use of the word, 71
Mende characteristics, *see* Characteristics
Mendeland: culture and racial types, 23, 26–7; original settlement, 25; pre-Protectorate, 40; the British and, 43, 44–5, 47–9, 50–6; the Spaniards in, 44 and *n*.; extent of, 60, 61, 63, 70, 71, 72–6, 106, 178–9, 216–17, 256; dress of tribes in, 70; earlier pioneers of, 175
Mendigla of Gowra, 31
Migeod, F. W. H.: cited, 28 and *n*., 71*n*., 241 and *n*.
Miji, the (the 'needle', or 'jumper down'), 34 and *n*., 35
Military technique, 33–6
Missions and Missionaries: service of missionaries, 10; the Mende Missions, 23, 170, 172, 262, 269; Creole missionaries, 53 and *n*.; European missionaries in Mendeland, 71
Mitchell, P. K.: cited, 12*n*.
Moa, river, 60
Mobai, town: census of, 66; divided into sections, 67; plan of, 68; founding of, 103*n*.
'mollet', fish, 287
Momboya, 284
Momo, a Moslem saint, 273*n*.
Momo Babaho, the Treaty chief of Upper Bambara, 179
Momo Gbotɔ, great warrior of the Bo area, 176; acted as Regent for Hotagua, 181*n*.
Money: taxation system, 57, 58; payment of Hut Tax, 58; court fees and fines, 182, 188–9; chiefdom Revenue and Expenditure, 204, 208; illegal perquisites, 213; introduction of money, 255; average annual household expenditures, 257–8, 260; fish prices, 284, 285, 286, 288; fish-trader's expenses, 286; fishermen's rent, 287; prices of country cloths, 289–91*n*.
Mongheri, 29
moo mie, forms of abortion, 133 and *n*.
mori-man, a chief's 'Moslem' adviser, 194, 229 and *n*., 236, 273

Moslems, the, *see* Islam
Moyamba, 63, 285, 286; district census (1948) of, 65; plan of, 107
Nadel, S. F.: cited, 104*n*.
National consciousness, 71–6
Native administration: and misapplied methods, 56–7; an occupation of the Mende, 70; portion of land rent for Treasury of the local, 95; chiefdom administrative rights, 176, 179–81, 182–4, 198; native authority system, 202–6; anomalies of administrative situation, 208–11; enlargement of, 255; the Provincial Administration, 262
Native ambitions, incentives: social incentives of rice farming, 80–2; factors promoting social change, 254–5, 257, 264, 266; sources of social ambition, 258–62
Native courts, 40–2, 46, 185–9, 203, 237
Ndahitie ('quite fit'), ceremony completing initiation, 122, 129*n*.
Ndanewa, Isaac: cited 12–13 and *n*.
Ndawa ('mouth-big'), Chief of Wende, 31, 36, 72; account of, 75–6
Ndegbe lewe, or *Kpowa gowo wuilei* ('the gathering of the herbs'), 129*n*.
Nde gbembi ('My line of blood relatives'), 108
ndehun ('brothership'), 108, 109
ndehun-bla ('family people'), 101, 102, 108–9
Ndema island, 288
nde vu lui ('life kola'), 156
nde yui ('show life'), 150
ndiama lui ('friends'), 154
ndile, witch cum boa-constrictor, 231
ndilei medicine, its use and effects, 231
ndimomoi, the Poro sign, 118
ndɔ-bla (aborigines), 84, 179
ndɔgboé ('land' or 'bush'), 86
Ndɔgbɔjusui (spirit), 132–3, 223 and *n*.
Ndoi (the Earth), 218
ndoinje, first initiated boy in Poro initiation, 119
n dɔ-mahun gbei mui, 85
ndoma nyaha ('love wife'), 144; *ndoma nyahanga* ('love wives'), 153, 156
ndɔmtui ('land man' or 'owner of land'), 89
ndɔ-yenge, chiefdom labour, 182

303

INDEX

nduli, type of cotton, 289
nduwumoi, the dead, 220
Needlework, *see* Occupations
nene jia-mui (a spy), 34*n*.
nessi, the, 236
ngafa (spirit), 111, 218
nga fa bla, a chief's 'gossipers', 194
Ngafa gohu lewe lei ('hitting the spirit's belly'), 123
Ngafagoti, a Poro spirit, 193, 246
ngafa nyamu (evil spirit), 218
ngafa welei, Poro town house, 118–19; the building of, 122
ngafei, the (the 'spirit'), 154, 243
ngegba (*ngi gba*—I am different), boy attendant on barren woman at her initiation into Poro, 245
Ngelegba, the, thunder medicine, 235
Ngewɔ, or *Leve* (Supreme God), 124, 138*n*., 217–18, 227; world creation by, 217–18, 227
Ngewɔ lama ('God willing'), 218
ngeya lo tokomee ('tying a rope on her wrist'), 154
'*ngiye wai*' ('big hill'), 225
ngo-mbuhubla (men in the midst of the battle), 35
ngo yela, 'one word' or 'unity', 184
ngua-moi ('washing man'), 230
nguangua (a small-tailed fish), 283
ngolɛ nje (singing mother), 252
Njayei, secret society, 164, 240; and breaches of rules of, 249–50
Njaloi, the, a spirit, 223
njoe ('family marriage'), 146
nomoli, steatite, regarded as the genii's handiwork, 223
Non-literary: women and, 171–2; in cases in native courts, 188–9; and Native Administration system, 209; and literacy, 256, 258; and meaning of 'civilized', 262; distinction between literates and non-literates, 265–7, 269–71, 274
'*Numo*', 119, 125
numu bao hale, a medicine for protective purposes, 235
Nursing and dispensing, *see* Occupations
Nya baimbaisia ('My lineage people'), 108
Nyagua, Chief, of Panguma, supports Kai Woni, 31, 179
Nyahanga, a goo wu hinga wɛ!, 274
nyalui, infant girl known as, 114

'Nyarroh, Queen of Barri Country', signatory in Treaty No. 113 (1890), 195
Nyawoe, Madame, worked medicine on behalf of besieged in Bo, 82*n*.

Occupations: 69–70; hunting, 26, 27, 69, 82, 281; rice-growing, 37, 78, 80–1; dyeing, 39, 69, 136, 142, 171, 289, 290; spinning, 39, 69, 136, 142, 291; weaving, 39, 69, 289, 290, 291; farming, 69, 77–80, 142, 258–9; fishing, 69, 142, 283–4; gold-working, 69; pottery, 69; blacksmithing, 69, 79; rice-cooking and cultivation, 77, 78 and *n*., 79–82; goldsmithing, 79; tree planting, 86 and *n*.; cleaning, 141; clearing the bush, 141; cooking, 141; harrowing, 141; threshing, 141; engineering, 259; telegraphy, 259; nursing and dispensing, 259; needlework, 268
Offerings: pepper, sheep, goats, 224*n*.
Ogugu, a society, 270
Oh, gbengiwaa leinga-oh! ('The large pot is cooking-oh!'), Poro song, 121*n*.
Ordinance, Protectorate, provisions of, 56, 57, 58
Origins, Mende, 25 and *n*.

palie (deep places), 223
palihun (the deepest part of the bush), 124, 247 and *n*.
Palm kernels and palm oil, *see* Trading
Palm oil 'chop', a dish, 270
Panguma, 29; relieved in the Rising, 52
Paramount Chief's compound, plan of, 191
Parliamentary Papers, 1899, LX, Pts. I and II: cited, 47*n*., 53*n*., 58*n*., 59*n*.
petuja, third initiated boy in Poro initiation, 119
pewa (women's house), 132
pewaisia ('women's houses'), 97 and *n*.
Plantain Island, 287
pla nyahe ('run away woman'), 135
Poe, 'no end', Mende word for 'Poro', 241*n*.
Polyani, Karl: cited, 272*n*.

INDEX

Polygyny: advantages of, 141–3, 165; represents form of capital investment, 142, 172
po nyaha, a widow, 135, 143
poo hini, a widower, 135
Poo logboi (inherited bush), 84
Poro, secret society: 12, 14, 29–30, 40, 48, 90 and *n*.; initiation into, 118–26; and chief's and chiefdom councils, 183–5, 185*n*.; and intervention in commercial matters, 185 and *n*.; Poro spirits and chief's death, 192–3; Poro chiefdom sessions, 213 and *n*.; spirit associated with the Poro, 226; cultural rôle of the, 240–53; traditional explanation of the, 241–3; conjectures about the advent of the, 241; structure of the, 243–5; distinction between the Poro as a society and as an institution, 244*n*.; the Poro organized through medium of 'lodges', 244; women as Poro members, 245–6; Poro spirits, 246–7; sacred bush of the, 247; secret society operation of medical and other services, 248–51; entertainment and recreation, 251–3; 'Literate' class and, 270
Poro Ordinance: forbade placing Poro sign on palm trees, etc. (1897), 202*n*.
Port Lokko, town, 61
Potolu, rebuilding of, 30
Pottery, *see* Occupations
Prostitution, 167–8 and *n*.
Protectorate, British, provisions of proclamation, 46
Puberty, 115–18
pu-bla (white men), 73
Public Works Department, occupations provided by, 69–70
pu-mui (white man), 115 and *n*.
'purrah', 241
Purrus Campus, 'poro bush', 241

quandɛ, type of cotton, 289
Quiah country, annexations in, 44
Qur'ān, the, 275, 276, 277

Ramadan, a religious fast, 100, 275
Rankin, F. H.: cited, 37*n*.
Ranson, Harry: cited, 14*n*.
'Regbafri, principal lady of Manho'. signatory in Treaty No. 78 (1872), 195–6
Religion: 216–27; the Supreme God, 217–18; ancestral spirits, 218–21; the *dyinyinga*, or genii, 221–5; 'nameless' and mischievous spirits, 225–6; spirits of the secret societies, 226–7
Ribbi, river, 44
Rice, *see* Occupations
Rice-farming: cultural significance of, 79–80; social incentives and methods of, 80–2; *see also* Occupations
Rising, Mende, or 'House Tax War': its importance, 43*n*.; origin of, 47 and *n*. 48; the campaign, 48; Poro society and, 183; suppression of the (1898), 262
Rotifunk: massacre at, 48, 283*n*., 286, 287, 288; about £600 worth of fish sold weekly in, 288
Rowe, Governor, in command of 1st West India Regiments, 44

saa hani, form of 'sacrifice', 236
'Sacrifice', forms of, 236
Salaries: of Sande women, 128–9, 154; of Mende women, 149, 166–7, 168; fees in court cases, 182, 213; fees of Headmen, etc., 198; chief's average income, 208, 211 and *n*.; salary of Chiefdom Clerk, 210; of second grade Government clerk, 214; of farm workers, 257–8; of Government factors, 259; of 'Creole' class, 267, 269; of non-Government clerks, 270; of weavers, 291
Sami, and the Poro society, 245
Sande, secret society: initiations into, 115–18, 126, 154; spirit associated with the, 226; medicine of, 238, 240; the Sande dance, 251–3
Sande nya, 117
sangbei (drum), 252
Sangoi of Guma-Vahun, 178
sawri, a purifying medicine, 226
saweisia, medicines compounded of herbs mixed with other natural ingredients, 234–5
Sawyerr, Harry: cited, 12 and *n*.
Scarcies, north-west area of present-day Protectorate, punitive expeditions in, 43 and *n*.

305

INDEX

Schools, Protectorate, 170–1 and *n*.
Secrecy and secret societies, 12–13, 14
Section: 'Sections' of Mobai, 67; Section of chiefdom, 89, 104, 108, 175, 197—8, 213; 'Sections' of Moyamba, 106; Tribal Authority and Sections, 200; section of society, 209; Bongɔi section of the Humui, 250; literate sections of Sierra Leone, 271
Seduction, penalties for, 170
segbullei, a calabash, 80
segbura (calabash rattles), 252
Segbwema, outbreak of, 'cannibalism' at (1938), 233*n*.
Sei Comber, Paramount Chief: cited, 32*n*.
seigbua lo ('thanking present'), 91
Sembehun, 285, 288
Senehun, treaty signed at, 44
Serabu, founder of, 26*n*.; census of, 63, 66; plan of, end of book
Servants, 268 and *n*.
Sessional Paper, No. 5 of 1926, Sierra Leone Govt.: quoted, 38*n*., 39*n*.
Settlement: original settlement of Mendeland, 25, 44, 82; methods of, 26–8, 104, 176; Sierra Leone, 43; primary and secondary, 84; lands split up with increased, 88; method of obtaining land by, 92–3; native methods of, 94
Sewa Mende, the, 76
Sewa, river, 60
Sexes: segregation at Christian services, 130*n*.; and widowhood, 135; and old age, 136; and marriage, 144, 157–8, 160–1; and prohibited relationships, 145–7; sexual behaviour, 147–9; and 'woman damage', 150–3; separation, 164, 170; tension between, 165–7; disharmonies, 173; status of, 244; mixing of, 268; Moslem code of sex morality, 274
Sham Point, 284
Shenge, a fishing port: treaty signed at, 44, 281, 286; fish trade at, 286–8; the Shenge peninsula, 287
Shenke (play with the head), 287
Sherbro, 23, 73; river, 44; annexations in, 44; outbreak of 'cannibalism' in, 233*n*.
shimbeks, small fishing villages, 287

Siaffa, a Moslem saint, 273*n*.
Sierra Leone Government Census: (1931) cited, 61 and *n*., 76*n*., 264*n*.; (1948) cited, 63 and *n*.
Sierra Leone Protectorate, 7, 26; map of Sierra Leone and Mendeland, 62; psychological and cultural change in, 254–5; former conditions of, and changes in, 260–1
'Sierra Leone Protectorate Expedition': cited, 49*n*., 56*n*.
Sierra Leone Protectorate Ordinance: cited, 46 and *n*., 84*n*.
Sierra Leone Railway, direction of, 61; construction of, 255
Sierra Leone Sessional Paper No. 7 of 1945: cited, 207*n*.
Sierra Leone Studies: cited, 15
Simbaru chiefdom, *see* Chiefdoms
Si'mo, cult of, 241
simongama (i.e. incest), 131, 145, 146, 148, 158, 160, 249
Skate, fish, 283
Slavery and slaves, 37–9; worth of slaves, 37; slaves' settlement and domestic status, 38; ban on slave-dealing, 202; domestic slavery abolished (1926), 260
Social cycle, 113
Social differentiation: the Mende attitudes regarding, 73–4; social units, 96; social subordination of village, 105; and marriage, 140–1; in relation to women's position, 163–5, 166; and Poro organization, 243–4; and the new society, 256, 257; Europeans and Africans, 263; and the Creoles, 265–7; education, social changes, 272
Social Trend, Modern, 254–72; factors promoting social change, 254–5; significance of literacy, 255, 256 and *n*.; some features of the new society, 257–8; sources of social ambition, 258–62; the Creole as a cultural medium, 262–4; effect on group relations, 264–6; structural analysis of the situation, 266–71; 'European' class, 267; 'Creole' class, 267–9; 'Literate native' class, 269–71; 'non-literate' class, 271
Societies, secret, as cultural arbiters, 240–1; and operation of medical and other services, 248–51

INDEX

So hinga ('Those who are entitled to procreate'), 245
sokolo, a small piece of tobacco, 127
'Sokoti', a Poro cry, 119, 122, 125
sondu wa hale, a medicine for 'swearing', 235
Songhay, kingdom, 25
Soothsayer: and woman's pregnancy, 132, 133; and infraction of the Humui rules, 148–9; as dream-interpreter, 224; and ceremony in connection with river genie, 224–5; and practitioners in medicine, 228, 229; and *hale* 'sacrificing', 236; and diseased patient, 248
Sowa (head official), 121, 244, 247; and Poro initiation ceremony, 124–5
Sowoisia, senior Sande official women, 126
sowolui (special present to betrothed girl's mother), 154
Sowo vewui ('rice for the head official'), 129n.
Spaniards, the, in Mendeland, 44 and n.
'Spanish', fish, 283
Spinning, *see* Occupations
Spirits: family, 111; pregnancy and evil, 132; Cheif's death and Poro, 193; ancestral, 218–21; the genii, 221–4 and n.; 'nameless' and mischievous, 225–6; secret society, 226–7; old men changed into a spirit, 243; Poro, 246–7
Standard of living: very low, 24–5; social subordination of the village and modern development of towns, 105–6; status of women, 168–9; desire for higher standard of living, 254
'stranger' ('tenant'), 92 and n., 93 and n.
Sumbuya, town, 61, 285
Summoning, at chief's court, 186
Sumner, A. T., cited, 263
'*Sundu frloi folɔŋ hinda nyamu gbi a gbiwie*', 'May this swear be removed and no harm come to you', 237n.
surie, bush plant, 289
Susu, the: men's dress of, 70, 169; status of, 274
Swear, kinds of, 237 and n.

taewui (buffalo), 26n.
Taia, river, 286
Talliah, war-fences at, 49–50, 51
Tangei mbei ma baunga ('the cassada saved the rice'), 77n.
Tarancis, a society, 270, 276
te gu kpe yei ('climbing on the stump'), 150
Tei-la-lei-mui (a warrior), 27n.
Teindia-mei ('crossing the water'), a ceremony, 137, 273
Telegraphy, *see* Occupations
Temne, the, arrival of, 27 and n., 241; British treaty with, 44; Mende attacked by, 45; dress and deportment of, 70, 73, 147; fishing carried on by, 287
tewe yenge ('by turn labour'), 81
Thompson, George, American missionary, 23 and n.
Threshing, *see* Occupations
Tikonko, 23, 29, 286; treaty at, 45, 54; census of, 64, 66
Tilei, the, a medicine, 235
tingoi, a mineral substance, 231
Tingowei, the, a female spirit, 222–3
Tolobu, section of Mobai town, 67
tolo la ('lays hold'), a nominal amount of money, 156
tombui, caves and woods occupied by the *tombuisia*, 225
tombuisia (dwarfs), believed to have once inhabited the Mende country, 225
tɔtogbemui (soothsayer), 149
Town and Country: 'old' and 'new' towns, 67–9; interrelationship of, 103, 104 and n., 105; situations of villages from towns, 106; growth of railway towns, 106 and n.
Trading: and market in Freetown, 24; forms of, 37; modern, 67–9; palm kernels and palm oil, 37, 69; promotes new cultural experiences, 260; fish, 281–3, 284–8
Treaty No. 119, 179
Tree planting, *see* Occupations
Tribal Authorities, 54; and claiming rights in land, 85; chief's interest in bush restricted to rights of jurisdiction and arbitration share with, 90; and election of new Poro chief, 185; women as members of, 195; and appointment of chief, 200; matters connected

INDEX

Tribal Authorities (*cont.*) with, 203–5; non-literacy and, 208; and Chiefdom Clerk, 210; and powerful rivals, 212; some educated people are, 214
Trotter, Lt.-Col. J. K.: quoted, 25 and *n*.
Tucker, Nancy, woman chief of Bagru, loyal during revolt, 59, 195*n*.
Tukpay ('push forward') society, 30–1
tunga ('colonies'), 104*n*.
Turners Peninsula, 44
Types, racial, of the Mende, 28

Upper Bambara chiefdom, census of, 65
Utting, F. A. J.: cited, 27*n*.

Vahun (Guma), part of Kabba Sei's dominion, 32; ceded to Liberia, 178
Vai people, the, 241
Vandi, used as watchword, 34
Villagers and villages, aspects of, 105–8
Virginity, Moslem 'test' of, 155*n*.
Vivian, Rev. William, missionary: quoted, 24 and *n*.; cited, 57*n*.

wa-bi-nyahi goi ('to find the woman'), 155
Wallis, C. B.: cited, 47*n*., 49 and *n*., 52*n*.
Warfare of the Mende, 28
warri, a game, 75
wata nyahanga, 158
Waterloo, 44
Western culture, 23; influence of (1890's), 25; western standards of value, 210–11; attraction of western ideas, 214; no use for, 255–6; practice of European ways, 262–3; European and Creole cultures, 264
Winton, Sir F. de: and driving back the Timne, 45
Witchcraft: witchcraft cases under jurisdiction of District Commissioners, 46; 'bad' medicine men and, 230–1; the witch spirit, 230–1; witch cum boa-constrictor, 231–2
'Woman damage': judicial procedure and, 40, 157; court cases of claims for, 186, 213, 259; implications of, 150–3
Women: status of, 163–74; their position a paradox, 163–5; the woman remains in the background, 163, 164 and *n*.; tensions between sexes, 165–7; 'husbandless women', 167–70; subjection of 'literate' or 'educated' woman, 170–4; and membership of Bo African Club, 173*n*.
Woodgate, Col., expedition commanded by, 48
Wujei, a Poro spirit, 193, 246
Wunde, secret society, 240

Yaku, Chief of Dia, 30–1, 178
Yams, substitute for rice, 77
Yavei, a Poro spirit, 246
Yawei chiefdom, *see* Chiefdoms
Yawri Bay, 287
Yewa, Madame, of Blama chiefdom, 195
Yoko, Madame, of Moyamba, 45, 195; co-operated with British, 48; loyal during revolt, 59; her success mostly due to support from Frontier Police, 177*n*.
Yonni, 284

Plan of Serabu

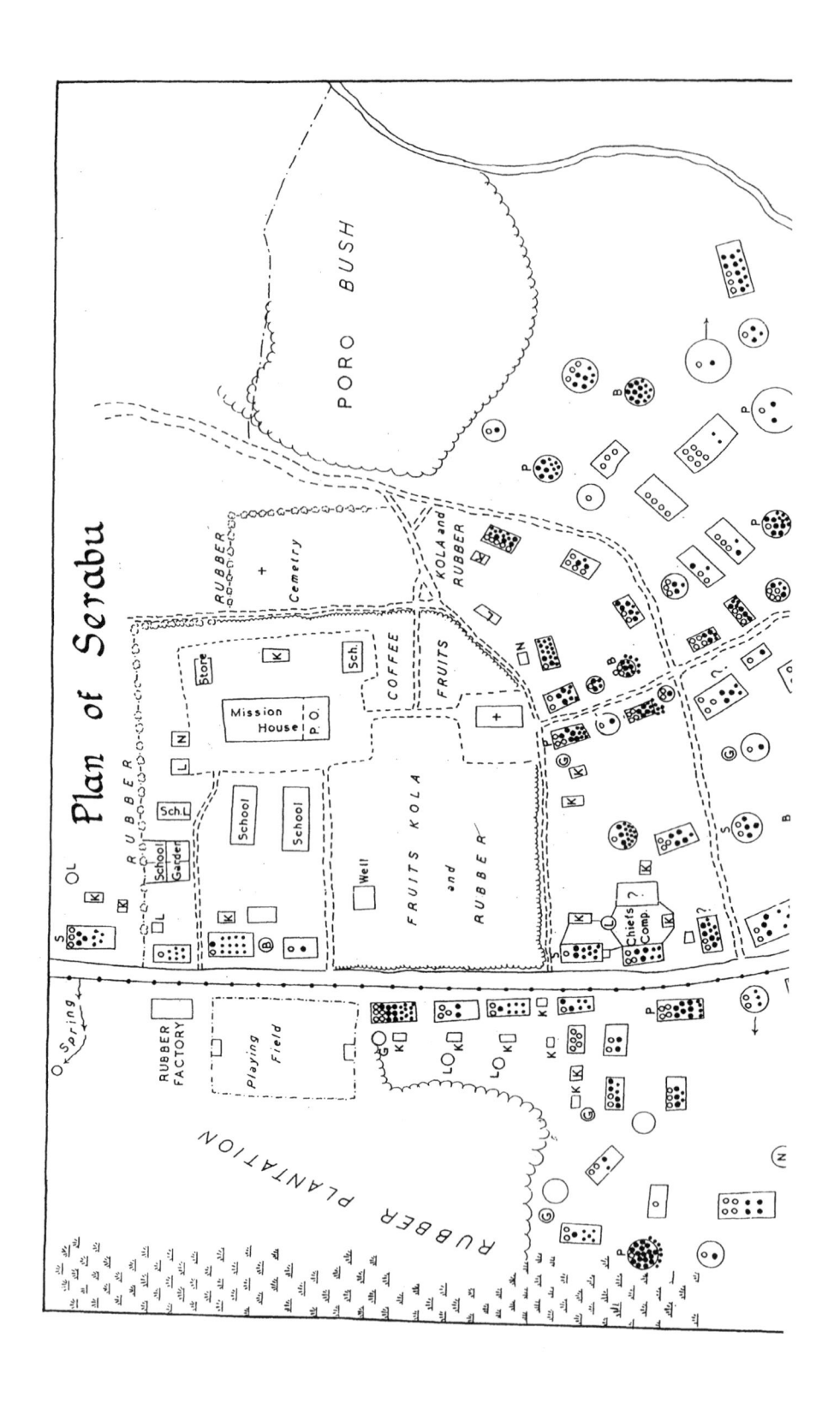

Legend

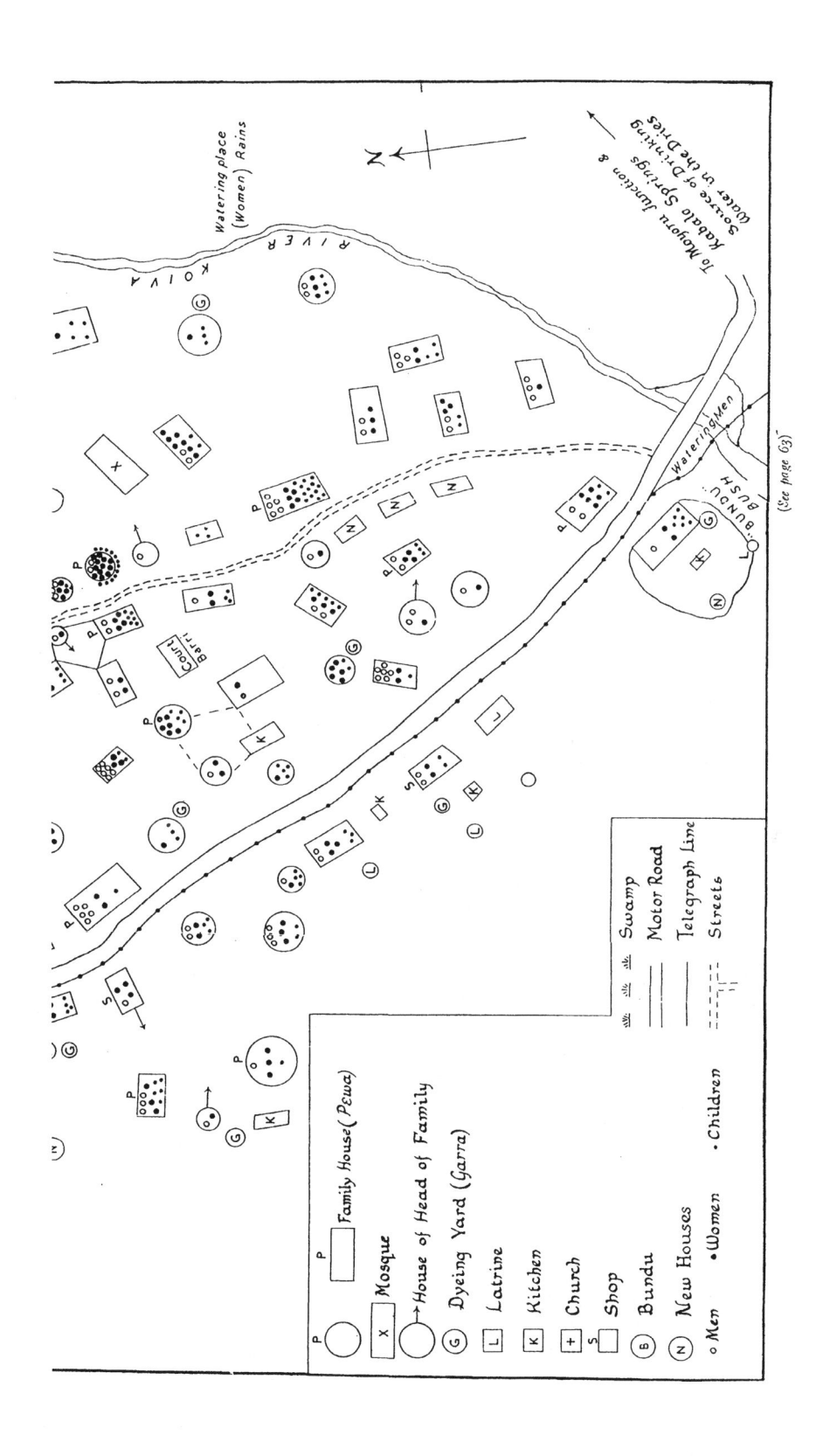

P (circle)	Family House (Pewa)
P (rectangle)	Mosque
X	House of Head of Family
G	Dyeing Yard (Garra)
L	Latrine
K	Kitchen
+	Church
S	Shop
B	Bundu
N	New Houses
○ Men	• Women	· Children

⋇⋇⋇	Swamp
═══	Motor Road
———	Telegraph Line
- - -	Streets

RIVER KOIVA

Watering place (Women) Rains

Watering Men

To Mojoru Junction & Kabala Springs
Source of Drinking Water in the Dries

BUNDU BUSH

Court Barri

(See page 63)

N ↑

Printed in Great Britain
by Amazon.co.uk, Ltd.,
Marston Gate.